THE ARTS

THE ARTS

A GUIDE TO PAINTING, SCULPTURE,
ARCHITECTURE, MUSIC, AND THEATER

BY MICHAEL RHETA MARTIN

Illustrated, with more than 600 drawings,
by LEO R. SUMMERS

THE BOBBS-MERRILL COMPANY, INC.   A SUBSIDIARY OF HOWARD W. SAMS & CO., INC. .

Publishers · Indianapolis · New York · Kansas City

To my son,

GERALD CHRISTOPHER MARTIN

PREFACE

Some years ago my friend Lloyd Bell asked: "When Mozart was composing in Austria, who was painting in France, and who was the leading architect in England? Did they share a common style? Was there any interrelationship among the arts of that period?"

This book is my rather lengthy answer to his questions.

Those of us interested in the arts (or in almost any subject, for that matter) tend to think "in isolation." We haven't been taught to think "across-the-board." The purpose of *The Arts* is, therefore, not only to attempt to fill the need for a one-volume reference work covering all of the arts, but also to point up the important cross-links as well as the creative growth—horizontal and vertical—of the arts of the world.

A word on how to use the book: Suppose, for example, you want to learn the identity of Shakespeare's contemporaries. You are interested in getting a clearer picture, an overview, of the painting, sculpture, architecture, music, and theater of the world of his time. You need only consult the Index at the back of the book and turn to the pages listed next to Shakespeare's name. You will not only discover that Lope de Vega was his counterpart in Spain; that Titian in Italy, El Greco in Spain, and Kōetsu of Japan were the great masters of painting; that Palestrina and Monteverdi were composing in Italy; and that Sinān was building the famed mosque of Suleiman the Magnificent in Turkey; but also that hundreds of others, some very familiar and many less so, were producing enduring works of art.

In the case of an artist whose works spanned two periods, you will find references to him either in both periods or in the one in which he produced his most important work. It should also be noted that, although most artists are listed under the country of their birth, there were instances when it was found necessary to put them under the country in which they worked. Picasso, for example, although a Spaniard, is to be found under France.

Needless to say, space is limited in a book of this kind and an author is forced to make decisions as to the artists who can be included and those who, unfortunately, must be omitted. These decisions, based purely on subjective evaluation, inevitably will meet with criticism. My only defense is to echo the March Hare and the Hatter in *Alice* and protest "No room. No room."

It was also decided that detailed explanations of possibly unfamiliar terms or allusions would have to be eliminated from the text. These can easily be found in the Glossary at the back of the book.

I wish to express my deep appreciation to my friend Jan Williams for her invaluable assistance; to Francis J. S. Hughes for the section on Furniture; to Henry Edwards for the material on Film and the Dance; to Leo R. Summers for the illustrations; to Victor D'Amico, Education Director of the Museum of Modern Art, for his unfailing enthusiasm for the project; and to all of the people at Bobbs-Merrill who designed, edited, and made the publication of this book possible.

Without the patient cooperation and encouragement of my husband (who helped with the Index), children, parents, and friends, I would never have completed *The Arts*.

M. M.

Scarsdale, New York
April 1965

CONTENTS

ILLUSTRATIONS

THE ARTS

PREHISTORY

From the beginning man has attempted to express his hopes and fears, his ambitions and accomplishments, his religious beliefs and concepts of individual worth in artistic terms. From the time he sought to reproduce graphically and plastically the things he saw around him, art became an imitation and interpretation of nature. Man began to experience the delight in mastering technical skill and the pleasure of producing perfection of form.

When we look at what we call prehistoric art, we must remember that it is more than likely that it began as something purely functional. The men who painted or incised animal figures on the cave walls and rock faces during the Paleolithic period were not painting pretty pictures of what they saw around them solely to decorate their caves. Neither were the men and women who produced crude human figures from clay or stone, or the clay pots in which they stored their food, seeking to embellish niches and ledges in their caves. There was purpose behind everything they produced, for the basic need was for survival.

LURISTAN BRONZES,   VENUS OF WILLENDORF,   MAMMOTH, ROUFFIGNAC,
TEHERAN   UPPER PALEOLITHIC   FRANCE

Life for primitive man was a constant search for animal food and skins for clothing, for safety from attack and destruction, and there can be no doubt that the beginnings of prehistoric art were bound up with religious beliefs, with a fear of failure to propitiate the many spirits with which primitive man invested all forms of life, and with fertility cults, when the women of the tribe had been carried off by marauders or were killed.

Perhaps the earliest form of cave art, even predating the animal figures, was the hand silhouette. The left hand was usually depicted, for the right hand would be used to splatter the coloring matter around it. Hand silhouettes could have played a part in the ritual of hunting magic in which the hunters and youths initiated into the activities and responsibilities of manhood recorded their handprints, or they could have been a permanent record of all the members of the tribe who laid claim to occupation of the cave or rock shelter.

HAND PAINTING

Cave painting was essentially an animal art, with the animals presented realistically and in customary attitudes, showing anatomical knowledge and keen observation. It was rarely stylized and no attempt was made to indicate background or scenery, beyond the occasional use of a rock ledge or natural surface to denote horizon or ground line. Aurignacian art represented animals in simple outline, hard and rigid in style, and with no interior modeling. The Magdalenian artists, on the other hand, knew all the fundamental techniques and attained a level of skill that is nothing short of superb. They defined contour in no uncertain fashion by grading from light to dark, although they lacked a knowledge of composition and the ability to arrange figures in relationship to each other. The animals represented were the game that was the staple food of the region. Some were pierced with weapons and had lines radiating from the mouth and nostrils to indicate blood, giving rise to the theory that primitive man was either "making" animals for the hunt during periods of scarcity, or using animal images in magic rituals by ceremoniously going through the actions of killing them by flinging spears at the images, thereby ensuring success in the hunt. It is also possible that these activities were part of the initiating and instructing of the youths old enough to take part in the hunt.

Some of the work is in line and flat wash or is etched into the rock in both shallow and deep engravings. There is also some attempt at low relief, and in the engraved figures of human females there is excessive distortion.

POTTERY, SUSA AND PERSEPOLIS, *ca.* 5000 B.C.

Man took the clay earth to shape bowls and other food containers, the human figure and those of the animals around him. He began to decorate the purely functional objects such as clay bowls, first by incising the clay before it was sun-dried, and later by adding lumps of clay to it to depict bird and animal features. Possibly at the time the cave painters discovered that pigments for painting the body could be used to make their paintings more realistic, man also learned how to decorate pottery by adding color before drying.

The most popular primitive pottery designs were the rectilinear or technomorphic, which implied the broken, disconnected aspects of life, the curvilinear or phyllomorphic style which represented continuity, and the animal or zoomorphic designs.

The first crude human and animal forms were modeled in clay and, with the rock paintings and drawings, belong to the Aurignacian stage of the upper Paleolithic period. Some small, free-standing human figures in the round and a few larger stone reliefs have been found, and were most certainly used in fertility rituals as goddesses or motherhood idols. Female figures invariably have the face eliminated, the hands and feet subordinated to the breasts, buttocks, and thighs, which are greatly exaggerated, and the abdomen grotesquely rounded. There is no attempt at realistic portrayal or individual traits. These characteristics are common in primitive, though more recent, cultures, especially the deliberate elimination of the face. This might have strong religious significance as the depiction of the face of a goddess or fertility spirit was taboo.

3

CAVE AND ROCK PAINTING

EUROPE · *France and Spain*

The most important European rock paintings are found in three separate areas of France and Spain: (1) around the valley of Vézère (Gironde, Dordogne); (2) the Pyrenees and Cantabrian Mountains, and (3) in the Gard, Ardèche, Hérault and Aude river valleys.

Altamira in Spain shows Magdalenian art at its best. Emphasis is placed on spatial relationships rather than line. The red galloping horses and bison are naturalistic, anatomically correct, and full of movement. There is a 40-ft. ceiling painted with 25 animals, mainly bison. Although most of them are shown in a standing position, there is a decided feeling of action. The interior body color is red, while the outlines and interior modeling are black.

Lascaux in the Dordogne, which rivals Altamira, with animal figures 18 ft. long, is known for monumentality of style (although it lacks the fineness of detail seen in the Altamira caves).

BLACK BULL, LASCAUX, FRANCE

GALLOPING HORSE, ALTAMIRA

VENUS OF TURSAC, LASCAUX, FRANCE

WILD BOAR, ALTAMIRA, SPAIN

Although there is a frieze showing ponies, stags, ibexes, and bovids, the horse is the most frequently painted animal in Lascaux.

At **Font de Gaume** in the Dordogne,

4

there are groups of bison that belong to the later Magdalenian period, as attempts have also been made here at depicting a group of reindeer. There are horses at **Le Cap Blanc** and groups of black animals at **Niaux.**

BUFFALO, FONT-DE-GAUME, FRANCE

One of the few groups of human figures is in the **Galeria del Roble** near Morella la Vella, Spain. This is a fighting group in which the figures are reduced to a few skilfully drawn lines, with the concentration on essentials, and showing tremendous movement and animation.

On the walls of open rock shelters in eastern Spain is a different style of painting that belongs to the Neolithic period and is known as the **Eastern Spanish** style. Human figures with the limbs drawn in thin lines and edge-shaped torsos are abstract and schematic.

In the **Cueva Saltadora** in Valtorta Gorge there are three walking figures of archers. The forward movement of their bodies is spontaneous, fresh, and full of vitality. They are obviously narrative pictures of the hunt and unrelated to magic. In a cave at **Gargas** in the French Pyrenees there are more than 150 hand silhouettes.

Scandinavia

Engravings of fish, reindeer, human figures, and weapons are naturalistically drawn on rock faces at **Bardal,** Norway.

America

There are masterly animal figures engraved on rocks in **Nanaimo,** British Columbia, Canada.

Oceania

Hands, feet, and arm silhouettes, similar to those in Australia, are found on rocks on the north coast of Dutch New Guinea. Engravings that are almost reliefs can be found in Sarawak.

AFRICA

Paintings on the rock walls (above ground) in the Atlas region and parts of the Sahara have survived in North Africa. Among the chipped rock engravings near Taghit in the Atlas region is the **Lion of Djattou** (6 ft. long and 4 ft. high). A polychrome wall painting of high artistic quality in the Central Sahara Ahaggar region shows two graceful, animated human figures.

COUPLE EMBRACING, CAVE OF AIN SAKHRI, JUDAH

It is possible to trace the development of Egyptian art from the primitive wall paintings in this region.

Bushmen cave paintings have been found all over South Africa; near Lake Tanganyika and in the cave at In-Guezzam in the Sahara region. Monochrome and polychrome naturalistic

BUSHMAN CAVE PAINTING, AFRICA

paintings of ostriches, elephants, and elands, have been found showing a high degree of technical skill and, in some cases, a knowledge of perspective. Some of the human figures are simple and lively, and the polychrome painting of small yellow bushmen fighting tall black Bantus displays a keen observation of nature. A painting near Orange Spring depicts a mask dance that is lively and full of movement.

ASIA · *India*

The most important polychrome rock paintings are near **Singhanpur**; men, a pig, birds, geometric designs, clothing, and implements are the subjects. The painting of a rhino attacked by six men was found near **Mirzapur**. Many works have been superimposed on older paintings or pecked drawings.

Siberia

Rock pictures are common and consist mainly of engravings and pecked drawings. One near **Abansk** in the Minusinsk district, is of hunters with bows and arrows. Hunting scenes have been found in **Uzbekistan,** and a two-mile stretch along the rock faces of cliffs above the Lena River in **Yatusk**

DANCER, TWO VIEWS, MOHENJO—DARO

is a veritable museum of primitive art. In this area a wild horse in red paint resembles the work of the same period in Western Europe.

AUSTRALIA

Throughout Australia there are rock engravings of animals and weapons that are realistically drawn. Human figures frequently appear with un-accented faces and exaggerated genitals. Most figures are only traced in outline with a few lines scratched within the outline to indicate essential features. Painting styles vary from simple monochrome silhouettes to

WONDJINA HEADS

polychrome figures. In the **Kimberley** region are several oversize and rigidly conventional skeleton-like figures that predate the later wondjina figures. Hand silhouettes are common on open rock faces.

SCULPTURE

EUROPE

One of the best-known small female figures is the *Venus of Willendorf* (Austria) in which the sexual characteristics are abnormally exaggerated and the face eliminated. Similarly out of proportion and abstract is the low-relief female figure with a drinking horn of **Laussel.** The figure of **Mentone,** even more abstract, has the long curves of the body flowing into each other. There were also small female figures found in the **Grimaldi** caves near Mentone and Brassempouy, and

a headless figure was discovered at **Kostienki,** South Russia. The only known male figure came to light near **Brno,** Czechoslovakia.

The art of animal sculpture developed at a much later date and was more naturalistic. An outstanding example of the later Magdalenian period is the high relief of a lion, showing remarkable animation, found in the **Caverne de Montespan,** Haute-Garonne, France.

Female figurines of the middle Neolithic period in **Crete** are the small, squatting figures with abnormally developed thighs and buttocks, some relatively naturalistic, although again, little attention is paid to the heads.

ASIA · *Japan*

Pottery figurines of Japan are cruder than the Paleolithic statuettes of Europe, and resemble the clay idols of the New Stone Age in the eastern Mediterranean and southeastern Europe. Vases and urns are similar to those of China.

India

At **Mohenjo-Daro** and **Harappa** the plastic figures in clay, copper, and steatite are executed in a highly-developed naturalistic style. Stone and bronze bulls of the period are also realistic. Seal amulets carved in steatite show reliefs of animals, human figures, and the still undeciphered Indus script.

MIDDLE EAST

The **Tell Brak** stone carvings of

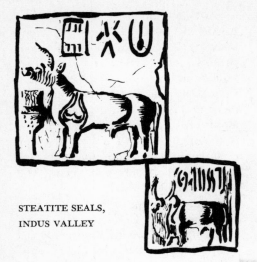

STEATITE SEALS,
INDUS VALLEY

Asiatic and Oceanic ethnic features show little aesthetic development. The pottery was made with coarse clay and the shapes are reminiscent of Chinese Neolithic culture. Basalt and other volcanic rock stone pillars (dolmens) were excavated at **San Augustín** in the upper reaches of the Magdalena River, Colombia. They are carved with a great variety of human figures. Many, with canine teeth, suggest demons. Others are carved with naturalistic figures of animals, birds, and snakes.

POTTERY

EUROPE

Highly-ornamented vessels painted in brilliant colors, under the influence of the Near East, were produced in southeastern Europe. Monochrome vessels, decorated with scratched and incised bands, were found in **Moravia** and **Bohemia**. Gracefully curved bell-beakers with deeply incised designs were native to **Spain**. By the end of the Neolithic period, this style had spread to **England** and as far east as **Hungary**, the decorations developing into a regional geometric style. A coarse earthenware with comb-stamped ornamentation was produced in northeastern Europe. Corded ware was common throughout Europe toward the end of the Neolithic period. The ornament on slender beakers or amphorae, strongly emphasizing the shape of the body, was made by placing twisted cords around the parts to be decorated into the wet clay before firing. At a later period this form of

animals and long-necked alabaster heads are naïvely but naturally conceived. The Subaraean culture at **Tell Halaf** produced an abundance of stone shrines, reliefs, and large deity figures, which are primitive and unattractive, painted clay figurines that are even more crude than the larger works, and beautifully shaped painted bowls of the same period that contrast oddly with the crudity of the figures.

On the other hand, the characteristic style of **Luristan**, a province of western Persia (Iran), indicates an extension of the Scythian culture. Bowls, jars, swords, and horse bits made of bronze are decorated with stylized animal forms and openwork of rigid symmetry. A crude, naturalistic figure surrounded by stylized animals is a recurring subject in various forms of Luristan bronzes.

AMERICAS

Archaic figurines with prehistoric

PAINTED POTS, JEMDET NASR PERIOD,
TELL ASMAR

is firmly rooted in tradition (rigidly stylized or naturalistic) and very expressive.

WOODEN PILLOW,
BALUBA (CONGO)
19TH-20TH CENTURY

decoration was copied by pricking or incising the design into the wet clay.

CHINA

There was an abundance of graceful, beautiful pottery in the Neolithic period. It was decorated with brown or black slip in geometric designs. It was particularly popular in the **Kansu Province** of northwest China. In the **Honan Province** there was a three-legged pot and an urn of the "black pottery" style. Cord or mat-marked pottery was common, including shapes such as the "li" tripod (a fat, three-legged cooking or storage pot), bowls, and plates (some with handles or lugs).

PRIMITIVE ART

AFRICA

The leading art form of Africa is wood sculpture. Made in one piece, it

Classical examples of pole sculpture, often decorated and painted, are the roughly carved ancestor figures of the Bari and Azande of the **Eastern Sudan**.

KNEELING WOMAN,
BALUBA (CONGO)
19TH-20TH CENTURY

FANG SCULPTURE,
GABON

9

In **French West Africa** rigidly stylized sculpture predominates. In the Bakota area of Gabon, **Equatorial Africa,** the guardian figures of ancestral skulls, made of wood and brass, are remarkable examples of geometrical abstractions, developed from endless repetition of the basic outlines of traditional design. On the other hand, the realistic ancestor figures of the **Cameroons,** some of which are larger than life, are remarkably animated.

HORNBLOWER,
BENIN, NIGERIA,
16TH-18TH CENTURY

MASK, CAMEROONS, 19TH-20TH CENTURY

Yoruba art, in stone, bronze, and terra cotta, is of a high standard. Stone carvings reveal unusually correct proportion, fine technique, and fidelity to nature. The works produced at **Ife** and **Benin** represent African sculpture at its highest level. The portrait heads of ancient Ife, in bronze and terra cotta, are the most impressive. These fine examples of realistic portrait sculpture, with racial characteristics spendidly portrayed, resemble the work of ancient Greece or Egypt rather than that of the rest of Africa. The bronze technique of *cire-perdue* originated in Ife and was handed on to the kingdom of Benin, only disappearing in the

AFRICAN MASKS; LEFT, BAPENDE;
RIGHT, BAKUBA (CONGO)

early part of the 18th century. Benin portrait sculpture was exceptionally realistic, but the life-size figures of humans and animals and reliefs of complete scenes reveal a close kinship to tribal wood sculpture with emphasis on the heads and a geometric simplification of the rest of the body.

AMERICA · *Eskimos*

The decoration of weapons and tools, engraved with thin incised lines, is a survival of the Old Bering Sea culture. Realistic scenes of hunting and of men traveling with dogs and sleds engraved on walrus ivory and bone are extraordinarily animated. The present upsurge of soapstone carvings depicting humans and animals differs little from similar pieces of the **Ipiutak** culture of *ca.* 1000 B.C. Elaborately carved and incised wood masks in monochrome or polychrome, in which the displacement of the features is a common characteristic, are produced. Women often illustrate the telling of a story by scratching rough drawings on the ground with a knife.

Northwest America

Painting as an independent art is practiced by the **Nootka Indians** who decorate the smooth walls of their wooden houses with formal and ab-

LIGHTNING SNAKE, WOLF, AND THUNDER BIRD, NOOTKA

stract scenes depicting tribal legends in which birds and animals play an important part. Pole sculpture (totem poles) is characterized by rigid symmetry with figures (usually characters with animal heads, in clan legends) seated one above the other. A variety of masks are carved of wood and decorated with characteristic paintings.

Iroquois and Algonquins. Common to both these tribes was the highly skilled art of embroidering hides with porcupine quills. These were later replaced by beads or dried grasses, using a few colors in a mosaic like design.

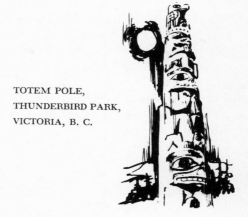

TOTEM POLE, THUNDERBIRD PARK, VICTORIA, B. C.

The Iroquois made grotesquely carved wooden masks, some of which had holes for inserting real hair (this was also done by the Indians in the Northwest and by artists in China and Japan).

Plains and Pueblo Indians. Painted pottery is the best known art of the Pueblos (originating in the 4th century A.D.). Designs run all the way from simple to complicated coils and frets to birds and animals, mainly on bowls and jars. The women of the tribe are the potters and the men the woodcarvers. Primitive, grotesque wooden masks are brilliantly painted, and bird masks are prevalent. The men also carve "kachina" dolls, which are small models of mask dancers, as children's toys.

Navajo. Sand painting (pouring colored powdered rock or earth onto

SAND PAINTING, SYMBOLIC RITUAL

a prepared flat area of sand) is not strictly painting, but a special technique not unlike mosaic. Its main purpose is for healing ceremonies, and the designs, depicting plants, animals, the wind, and rainbow gods are abstract and rigidly traditional.

AUSTRALIA

Primitive art in Australia is predominantly graphic. Outline drawings of humans, kangaroos, birds, and fishes in naturalistic style are found on rock faces and tree bark. The best work is in the Sydney district and, although **Bushmen** art is superior, the technique is similar. X-ray-like drawings of kangaroos, particularly, show a keen

SPIRIT MAN SPEARING KANGAROOS, ABORIGINAL

BOOMERANG, SPEAR, AND SPEARTHROWER, AUSTRALIA

observation of detail in the representation of the spinal column and organs. The rock shelters of **Northern Kimberley** are known for the wondjina figures, derived from the human figure but not naturalistic. Painted in red and black, the limbs are rudimentary and the faces, although conventional, lack mouths. Fighting shields are carved in wood with an intricate diamond pattern. The **Djaro** tribe models extremely primitive animal figures reminiscent of early Mediterranean art. There is some pole sculpture in the round with polychrome paintings for decoration.

ASIA · *Assam*

In the hills of Assam (upper Burma)

CLAY HORSEMAN, LACHISH, ISRAEL

wood carving in the round and in relief is of a remarkably high standard, the principal subjects being human heads and the heads of mithan, a large breed of cattle. Life-size, naturalistic figures are erected over tombs.

India

Peasant art throughout India derives from primitive art absorbed into Hinduism and reflects a charmingly simple naturalism. In **Orissa** and **West Behar** pole sculpture is primitive, depicting heads in the round and arms in relief. In the Nilgiri Hills of **Mysore** a cattle cult is reflected in a truly primitive plastic art form. The marriage toys, carts, riders, animals, village deities, and human figures in wood and brass, made by the hill tribe of **Kutiya Kondhs,** are charming.

Indonesia

The art of Indonesia, a melting pot, reflects the artistic achievement and history of the Javanese, Malays, and Negritos of Micronesia. The curved lines, scrolls, and concentric circles that form the decorative work on tools, vessels, containers, and weapons are developed from metal work and influenced by the Bronze Age art of Southeast Asia. The grotesque masks of **Bali,** the Hindu statues, the medieval Buddhist sculpture of **Java,** contrast strongly with the plastic arts of the other islands. **Sumatra** wood and horn carving is similar to the totem poles of northwestern America.

OCEANIA · *Melanesia*

A prominent feature of Melanesian art is sculpture. In **New Britain** human

MALE STATUETTE, PHILIPPINE ISLANDS

and animal figures are carved from a soft, gray rock in rough outline. The material, being brittle, is worked in simple planes with little attention to detail. In the southern islands the sculptured canoes and prow ornaments are blackened and inlaid with mother-of-pearl. The northern islands tend toward decorated, conventional polychrome human figures.

New Guinea

The most advanced forms of sculp-

JAPANESE BURIAL FIGURES (HANIWA)

MOCHICA (MOCHE)
POTTERY,
PERU

Polynesia

The huge stone heads carved of volcanic rock at **Easter Island** are ancestor figures connected with the sea-bird cult. The masterpiece of these sculptures is the statue *Hoa-Haka-Nana-la* (now in the British Museum). The back of the head has several carved figures in relief, including that of the bird man.

The grotesque, though naturalistic, idols of **Hawaii** are crude in comparison with Polynesian art generally. **Tahitian** carving is symmetrical and inclined to be stiff. Scrolls and spirals in an openwork pattern, and carvings of the *manaia*, a bird-headed animal or demon, attached to both sides of door lintels are representative of **Maori** decorative art. The ornamental ancestor figure called a *tiki* is common throughout Polynesia. Carved in whalebone or nephrite, it is worn as a neck pendant.

ture in the round are found in **Papua**. Beautiful bowls and implements, decorated in carved relief and brilliant colors, are produced. Some bowls are supported by human and animal figures. Figure stools, carved from one solid piece of wood, having flat seats supported by ancestor figures or animals, or with an ancestor figure leaning against the seat, are popular.

PRIMITIVE SOUTH AMERICAN SCULPTURE

WOODEN CUP, BRAZIL,
AFRO-AMERICAN ART

SEATED FEMALE FIGURE, COLUMBIAN,
11TH-14TH CENTURY

KNEELING FIGURE,
TIAHUANACO, BOLIVIA

15

4000-2000 B.C.

The monumental grandeur of the great pyramids of Egypt, burial places of the pharaohs who were gods as well as supreme rulers, are not only spectacular examples of the architecture of early civilizations, but represent the dedication of the people to their religious beliefs and their concern with life after death.

Egyptian history is divided into dynasties of rulers. The predynastic period covered the transition from prehistory to the First Dynasty. The first major division, the Third Dynasty of the Old Kingdom, known as the Golden Age of Egypt, ended with the overthrow of the Sixth Dynasty.

Egyptian art had a distinctly individual character resulting not only from the unique climatic and geographic conditions of the area, but from the secure political and financial power of the ruling monarchs.

Early Mesopotamian art, from the civilizations inhabiting the valley of the Tigris and Euphrates rivers, includes the work of the Sumerians and the Akkadians. The Sumerian artist, in contrast with the Egyptian, was concerned with life on earth and showed a preoccupation with fertility and procreation. As there was no unifying dynastic power in early Mesopotamia, there were less restrictions imposed upon the artist by either the state or religious concerns. With the rule of Sargon of Akkad and his successors, however, art was devoted primarily to the glorification of the ruling kings.

ARCHITECTURE

SUMER

Palaces and temples were built of sun-dried or kiln-baked mud bricks (used in Persia before 4000 B.C.), bundles of reeds covered with mud; important introduction of the corbeled vault (*ca.* 3500).

Unlike the Egyptians, the Sumerians were not preoccupied with death or afterlife; the characteristic architectural momument in Mesopotamia was the ziggurat, or step temple, which had a terraced tower with ramps or stairs, possibly of glazed brick, and a shrine (*shakhuru*) at the summit that was used in temple ritual and was sacred but had no artistic merit.

The mud-brick temples of the Al 'Ubaid period saw the use of recessed outer walls, set upon high brick platforms, decorated with terra-cotta cones (tens of thousands, about 4 in. long) with their ends dipped in color and formed into mosaic patterns. Plaques covered with circular reed impressions usually picturing rows of animals were also common.

The "White Temple," ziggurat to the sky-god Anu, is extant at Urak (Warka). This period (3800-3200) also saw the beginnings of the first real cities.

WHITE TEMPLE ON ZIGGURAT, *ca.* 3500-3000

EGYPT

Earliest houses made of wood, thatch, and materials made from plants; use of splayed-out cavetto (hollow) and khekher (tied bunched reeds) cornices. When stone construction was perfected they retained the traditional foliate shapes in the use of palm fronds, lotus, and papyrus (bud and bell) on column shafts and capitals.

Third Dynasty (2670-2600), known as the Old Kingdom; a golden age for Egypt; Imhotep (Im-hetep), vizier of Zoser (Djoser), second Pharaoh of the dynasty, is credited with the invention of stone masonry and with the building of the Step Pyramid at Saqqara, the oldest monumental stone structure in the world; enlarged from a stone

THE GLORIES OF EGYPTIAN ART

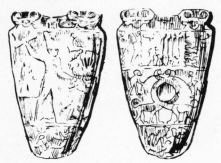

PALETTE OF KING NARMER,
FROM HIERAKONOPOLIS

COLONNADE,
KING ZOSER'S HALL OF PILLARS

STEP PYRAMID OF KING ZOSER, SAQQARA

THE GREAT SPHINX, GIZA, *ca.* 2600

WOODEN PANEL FROM
TOMB OF HESY-RA,
SAQQARA, *ca.* 2700

PYRAMIDS OF MENKURE, KHAFRE, AND KHUFU

mastaba (see Glossary), it was built of a series of six truncated pyramidal mastaba forms (small stone blocks) superimposed one upon the other; around the pyramid there were other buildings, courtyards, etc.

Fourth Dynasty, often referred to as the Pyramid Age. The great pyramids were extraordinary engineering feats with remarkable accuracy of proportion; the great tombs built at Gizeh (Giza) for Pharaohs Cheops (Khufu), Khafre (Chephren), and Menkaure (Mycerinus) were made possible by a strong monarchical system and vast resources of stone and labor.

The Great Pyramid was built for Pharaoh Cheops (*ca.* 2575); it had 2,000,000 stone blocks averaging two-and-a-half tons; it was nearly 500 ft. high and over 750 ft. along each base line; it was obvious development of early mastaba both in shape and function.

INDUS VALLEY

Archaeological findings at Harappa and Mohenjo-Daro (ancient India, now West Pakistan) indicate a high aesthetic level of art appreciation;

architecture was fundamental but unimpressive; it was necessary to import stone (as did Sumer); only sculptured piece found was bust of bearded man; civilization believed overthrown by Aryan invaders (*ca.* 1500).

SCULPTURE

MESOPOTAMIA

Relief sculpture became pictorial (figures and animals) about 2500 B.C.; the **Uruk** people are credited with the development of writing (first primitive pictographs from which cuneiform evolved); steles (commemorative stones) were worked within fixed conventions, but the making of seals became a distinctive art form showing great imagination and ingenuity; the small cylinders were engraved on the outside, and when rolled over the clay of a tablet (or sealing material for a package) impressed a distinctive design; at first geometric in design, later animal and human figures became popular, and a single or double file of oxen or goats was commonly

WELL TOWER, INDUS VALLEY

CARVED COMMEMORATIVE RELIEFS, SUMER

LIMESTONE MONSTER, SUMER

SUMERIAN STATUETTES,
ABU TEMPLE,
TELL ASMAR,
ca. 2700-2500

used; then stars, crosses, fish, and other designs were added; a "brocade style" developed.

There was expert carving in low relief and this same skill was seen in the metalwork, particularly the gold jewelry and figures of the period; small animal figurines were cast with superb detail, exceptional realism; vases made of green steatite were covered with a closely-drawn network of figures in flat relief; in the second phase of the Early Dynastic period (3000-2340) they added colored inlays using exotic secular subjects.

WORSHIPER, SUMER

Sumer

The marble statues from the Abu Temple, Tell Asmar near Bagdad (*ca.* 2700-2500) represent the geometric (conic-cylindrical), expressively simple style of the period; the tallest figure, representing Abu, the god of vegetation, is about 30 in. high;

all have very large eyes, colored by blue lapis lazuli or black limestone, and hair painted black; animal figures

20

SUMERIAN ART

HARP OF QUEEN SHUBAD, UR, SUMER

GUDEA,
GOVERNOR OF LAGASH,
DIORITE, NEO-SUMERIAN,
ca. 2125-2025

GOLD DAGGER AND VASE,
UR, SUMER

BULL'S HEAD,
GILT AND INLAID WOOD,
SUMER, *ca.* 2800

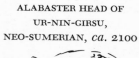

ALABASTER HEAD OF
UR-NIN-GIRSU,
NEO-SUMERIAN, *ca.* 2100

HEAD OF GUDEA,
RULER OF LAGASH,
NEO-SUMERIAN

21

(found in tombs at Ur), more realistic, modeled from softer materials.

Akkad

Lugalzaggisi, king of Uruk, succeeded in extending the rule of the Sumerians from the Persian Gulf to the shores of the Mediterranean only to be overthrown by the first great Semitic

IM-DUGUD, LION-HEADED EAGLE, COPPER RELIEF, SUMER

ruler of Mesopotamia, Sargon, who founded his capital at Agade (2371-2316). The empire of the Akkadians lasted about a century and a half. Mesopotamia was then overrun by the Guti, barbarous wild mountaineers from Iran, and only Lagash, with its famous governor, Gudea, remained.

Akkadian intaglio engraved stone

cylinders represent a departure. These seal figures are more isolated, more detailed, but less varied in subject matter, although some friezes depict narrative events, battles, etc.

Third Dynasty of Ur (2113-2006). A final century of greatness in Sumer and Akkad saw Urnammu, first king of the dynasty (2113-2096), gain control. He built the Great Ziggurat of the Moon God.

PAINTING

Egypt

Religion was the dominant influence in art. Although the art we know comes primarily from tombs or temples, contemporary life was reflected in the painting, pottery, stoneware, furniture, jewelry, glass, and sculpture of the period.

In the tombs of the wealthy Egyptian, walls were painted (or carved in low relief) with the things needed for

AKKADIAN KING, NINEVEH, *ca.* 2300

VICTORY STELE OF NARAM-SIN, AKKADIAN

EGYPTIAN TOMB FIGURES

PRINCE RAHOTEP AND WIFE NOFRET,
LIMESTONE, *ca.* 2650

MENKURE AND HIS QUEEN,
GIZA, *ca.* 2575

KHAFRE, GIZA, *ca.* 2600

STATUE OF KING ZOSER,
THIRD DYNASTY

2ND CENTURY—EGYPT
AND SAQQARA

NEGRO GIRL CARRYING JAR,
BOXWOOD, EGYPTIAN, *ca.* 2000

SEATED SCRIBE, SAQQARA,
ca. 2500

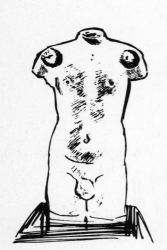

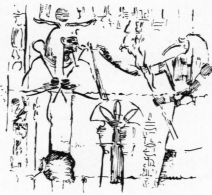

SETHOS I AS OSIRIS
WITH GOD TOTH, ABYDOS

MALE NUDE,
HARAPPA,
3RD-2ND CENTURY

STATUETTE
OF KING PEPY I,
GREEN SLATE,
SAQQARA

24

the next life. Paintings of food (along with the implements needed to eat or drink), hunting scenes, and the raising of cattle took care of the basic need (sustenance), while scenes of singing and dancing and great feasts assured pleasure. Paintings of the gods (human figures with animal heads or masks—Sobek, crocodile's head, Hathor, human head with cow's horns, Horus, falcon, Thoth, ibis, etc.) were most often included; the soul (*ba*) was represented by a bird with a human head; kings and important people were also painted on the walls.

MUSIC

Sumer

Seals and steles of *ca.* 3000 show a Lagash temple with choirmaster, instrumentalists, male and female singers; a document dating from this period provides evidence that it was customary for two choirs of women's voices to sing antiphonally; liturgical music developed; chromatic scale used; instruments included woodwinds, the aulos (double-reed), cithara, and harp.

SISTRUM, HITTITE, ANATOLIA

Egypt

Music played an important part in the life of the early Egyptians, and was heard in war as well as in the everyday life of the marketplace and the temple; the diatonic scale (that influenced later music) was used; instruments were played to accompany singers; the double clarinet originated in Egypt (*ca.* 2160); stringed instruments, pipes, rattles, and drums were also popular; large choruses and groups of musicians were heard at festivals, feasts, and entertainments.

ASIA · *China*

Probably the oldest musical system in the world, it is believed that the court musician to the Yellow Emperor of China, Huang-ti (*ca.* 2700) established the acoustic formula for the pentatonic scale; Ling Lun is credited by the historian Ssŭ-ma Chien with having written the "Song of the Cloudy Gate," popular for centuries, and with establishing the chromatic scale of twelve *lüs* or pitch pipes that corresponded to the circle of perfect fifths compressed into an octave. The basic note was fixed by a standard tube (yellow bell) that was also the basis of weights and measures. Each tone of the series represented a month and hour of the day and was used as the keynote of ceremonial chants. The melodic scales were based on a five-tone series (used to this day) equivalent to do-re-mi-sol-la (black keys of the piano).

Chinese musical instruments have traditionally been classified by the materials of which they are made: silk, metal, stone, bamboo, gourd, skin, wood, and earth. The most important silk-stringed instruments are the *ch'in* (or *k'in*—seven-string psaltery believed invented by the Emperor Fu Hsi, 2852), and *sên* (52-string psaltery) known from earliest times; metal instruments include a variety of bells and gongs (chung-frame of 16 chimes tuned in chromatic scale); stone chimes or *ch'ing* (substitute for or duplicate sound of chung in Confucian ceremonies); bamboo instruments include panpipes and flutes of various kinds; bamboo reeds are used with a gourd base for the *shêng* (mouth organ of 17 reeds) and *yü* (47 reeds); the drums and tambourines are made with skin, wood is used in the *chu* (box and mallet) and in various kinds of percussion blocks, while earth is found in the ancient *hsun*, a kind of ocarina.

India

The *Vedas* have been chanted for at least 3,000 years and suggest music of an even earlier period. India has contributed the *raga*, a form for the improvisation of melody in a given mood and scale.

Hindu octaves are divided into 22 shrutis or microtonal divisions approximately equal to quarter-tones. Hindu scales stress a series of intervals rather than a series of fixed tones.

The tambura, or four-stringed unfretted lute, and hand drums are the instruments most often used to accompany the singers.

Ceylon

The ravanástron, with two strings and played with a round bow, believed to be the oldest instrument known, was discovered on Ceylon; thought to have been invented about 7,000 years ago by a legendary king of the island, Ravana, it is the forerunner of all our stringed instruments.

2000-800 B.C.

The Middle Kingdom in Egypt saw more freedom of expression in the wall paintings of the rock-cut tombs along the Nile. During the period known as the New Kingdom, the great temples of Amon at Karnak and Luxor near Thebes and of Horus at Edfu reflected the immense power of the priests. A new, expressive, more personal style developed during the so-called Amarna period under Akhenaten.

Mesopotamian art flourished under Hammurabi and the Babylonians and under the Assyrians who, influenced by the art of both the ancient Orient and the West, are often referred to as the "Romans of Mesopotamia." Their sculpture and wall reliefs, in powerful simplicity, show a preoccupation with war, heroes, and the hunt. In contrast, a secular gaiety is seen in the art of Crete.

ARCHITECTURE

EGYPT

Middle Kingdom (2133-1786). Tombs of kings and queens carved into hills facing Nile; important nobles built cliff tombs; Sesostris I (*ca.* 1980-1935) erected red granite obelisks in Faiyum

region and other buildings that have not survived; excellent examples of monumental sculpture extant; portraits of Amenemhet III and Senusret III show rare naturalism, individual characterization; relief sculpture bold; servant figures in tombs; painting, which showed increasing freedom from prescribed traditional form, color, and subject matter, was used exten-

EGYPTIAN OBELISK

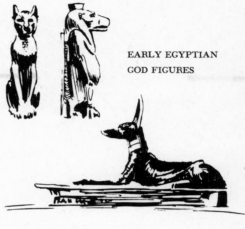

EARLY EGYPTIAN
GOD FIGURES

AMENY, BLOCK-FIGURE SCULPTURE,
MIDDLE KINGDOM

SENUSRET-SENEBEF-NI,
BLOCK-FIGURE,
MIDDLE KINGDOM

LIMESTONE RELIEF FROM TOMB
OF RAMOSE, *ca.* 1360

sively in tombs; magnificent gilded portrait-masks and carved and painted wooden coffins were replacing stone sarcophagi.

New Kingdom (Empire Period, 1580-1100). Temples became the most important buildings of this period reflecting the increased power of the priests; temples of Amon at Karnak, Luxor and Horus at Edfu are examples of Empire style; plan consisted of sacred way flanked by sphinxes; pylons (entrance gates) flanked by massive, forbidding, battered towerlike walls at the entrances; courtyards, which were the only attempt made toward a concept of enclosed space; colonnades of the forecourt; huge Hypostyle (tall, narrow columns) Hall, and sanctuary; windows used to fill space between the two levels on early, fully developed clerestory.

Temple of Hatshepsut (1501-1480). At Deir el-Bahri, the architect **Sen-Mut** built a magnificent mortuary temple for Queen Hatshepsut; it is one of the rock-cut (soft limestone) cliff tombs in the Valley of the Kings, overlooking ancient Thebes; unique in many ways; severely simple, complete harmony of design and background; three beautiful, rising colonnaded terraces out-

"GREAT HALL OF PILLARS,"
TEMPLE OF AMON

QUEEN HATSHEPSUT

29

standing in dramatic effect; the walls are decorated with low reliefs; the surrounding tomb-chapels of court officials are decorated with *gouache* paintings on a wall-coating of plaster.

GILT-WOOD
STATUETTE FROM TOMB
OF TUTANKHAMEN

QUEEN HATSHEPSUT'S MOTHER,
RELIEF FROM MORTUARY TOMB

Akhenaten (Ikhnaton, Amenhotep IV), r. 1367-1350. Great king who attempted to introduce monotheism into Egyptian religion with the worship of the god Aton; court at el-Amarna; imported artisans for work on building program and included housing project for homes for themselves; new naturalistic, expressive style seen in wall paintings, reliefs, and sculpture; famed portraits of the king, his beautiful wife Nefertiti, and others.

Tutankhamen. r. 1347-1339. Probably the most famous tomb of all because of the treasure found when it was discovered (1922); some of the most exquisite objects of gold, including the coffin enclosing the young king's body, wood panels overlaid with gold, silver, and other gems; as this was the tomb of a very unimportant king, one can

GOLD INNER COFFIN OF TUTANKHAMEN

imagine what must have been stolen from the tombs of the great pharaohs.

Others. Great Temple of Ramesses II (r. *ca.* 1290-1224) at Abu Simbel, where four statues of kings, more than 40 ft. high, guard the entrance to a complex of halls and chambers that make up the funerary temple carved into

COURT AND PYLON OF RAMESSES II,
ca. 1290, AND COLONNADE AND COURT OF
AMENHOTEP III, *ca.* 1390

FAÇADE OF MOLDED BRICKS,
KASSITE TEMPLE, WARKA

solid rock; the important funerary temple of Sethos (Sethi) I (1308-1291) at Abydos.

MESOPOTAMIA · *Babylon*

First great king was Hammurabi (r. 1792-1750), who united the land and gave the world his famous law code; stela and possible portrait remain, but works of art follow earlier Mesopotamian works.

Assyrian Empire

With the death of Hammurabi, the Babylonians lost power; they were overwhelmed by the Hittites and then by the Assyrians; Assyria became the Rome of the ancient East.

First of two periods of art was the **Middle Assyrian** (*ca.* 1350-1000). Though most of the art was imitative of other areas, their monumental animals and magnificent wall reliefs and free standing sculptures are a great contribution to world art.

CRETE · *Minoan*

(*fl. ca.* 1700-*ca.* 1400). Secular, both in treatment and choice of subject, which in large measure accounted for spirit of gaiety; absence of temples, death cult, tombs, although outdoor shrines dedicated to the mother goddess were popular; bulls were sacrificed to this goddess and slain with a symbolic double axe (*labyrs*); no restrictions placed by dominant priest class; great freedom of expression, individuality, and naturalism possible in a society unrestrained by a hieratical tradition; marine and floral motifs commonly used.

Palace of Minos at Knossos (Cnossus, *ca.* 1500). Spacious, like the Mesopotamian palaces, built around a great central court, three stories high, rectangular and square rooms (essentially apartments surrounding court) with frescoes and raised reliefs on the walls; use of columns, tapered from capital to foot with no base, intended to give light and air.

Palaces also built at Phaestas and Malia (not extant).

31

AN EXPRESSIVE,

COLOSSAL STATUES
OF RAMESSES II
(ABU SIMBEL)

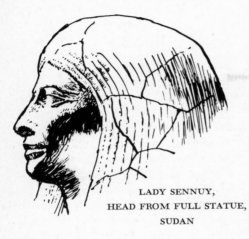

LADY SENNUY,
HEAD FROM FULL STATUE,
SUDAN

PAINTING FROM TOMB
OF USER-HET, THEBES

HORSE AND GROOM, WOODEN STATUETTE

PERSONAL STYLE EMERGES

QUEEN NEFRETITI FROM
TELL-EL-AMARNA, *ca.* 1360

UNFINISHED HEAD
OF NEFRETITI

SHAMASH GIVING LAWS TO THE KING,
HAMMURABI STELE, *ca.* 1760

THE ART OF ASSYRIA AND CRETE

A KING FROM MALATYA,
ASSYRIAN STYLE

ASSYRIAN KING,
AMBER AND
GOLD FIGURE

WINGED GRIFFIN IN IVORY,
NORTH PALESTINE, *ca.* 1500

SNAKE GODDESS,
ca. 1600 (CRETE)

PALACE OF MINOS,
KNOSSOS, CRETE,
ca. 1500

Famed **Boxer and Harvester Vases** show freedom from convention and a rigorous style; other pottery expertly made, utilitarian, decorated with originality and variety of glazes, patterns, and forms; sculpture of period of stone and metal; silver, gold, bronze, and ivory works of great delicacy, using relief, inlay, and engraving.

Mycenaean

(*fl. ca.* 1580-1100). Believed influenced by the Egyptians and their

LION GATE, MYCENAE, *ca.* 1250

LION (LIFE-SIZE), TEMPLE GATE AT HARMAL, *ca.* 2800

INTERIOR, TREASURY OF ATREUS, MYCENAE, *ca.* 1300-1250

funerary building, the Mycenaeans constructed the so-called "Treasury of Atreus," near the Lion Gate, and the "Tomb of Clytemnestra" (*ca.* 1300-1250); cyclopean blocks were used for the walls and gates in the great palaces (hill fortresses) at Pylos, Tiryns, and Iolkos, which were burned (end of 12th century) and never rebuilt; the center of the palace was the royal audience hall (megaron) that was approached through a deep porch with two columns and an antechamber; the great ruler, Agamemnon

VAPHIO CUPS, *ca.* 1500, ATHENS

35

(r. 13th century), was the leader of this domain of warriors and hunters.

Tholos (Beehive) Tombs. Royal mausoleums were built, during the lifetime of a king, into the side of a hill; a great circular shaft was sunk, and within this a corbeled vault was built that resembled a beehive; the vault was surrounded by earth and a raised mound showed above ground; a long vaulted runway or approach (dromos) ended in a rotunda and rectangular tomb chamber.

ASIA · *China*

Little is known of early architecture because the traditional use of wood for building accounts for the disappearance of ancient structures; believed to have been single-story, slanted-roofed houses with a framework of columns and rafters built on a stone base; the size of the building was determined by its function (religious, secular, public, or private).

Bronzes and Jades. Magnificent examples of Shang (*ca.* 1558-*ca.* 1028) and Chou (*ca.* 1027-*ca.* 221) extant; expressed spirit of the ritual for which the sacred vessels were used; carvings

TIGER, CHOU DYNASTY, *ca.* 1027-256

of jade charms, vessels, and jewelry showed exquisite technical skill and great delicacy of design; outstanding achievement.

India

Mukteshvara Temple at Bhuvaneswar (Lord of the Universe, *ca.* 1000); exceptional example of numerous magnificent temples in one of the oldest religious centers in India.

MUSIC

MESOPOTAMIA · *Babylon*

From early Dynastic period music was a part of royal and popular festivals; instruments of percussion, wind, and string types shown in art; a clay whistle of the ocarina type has been found; *balag*, a drum of the shape of a sandglass, was used in the temple by the kalu-priest; the *lilissu*, a sacred kettledrum, was in the temple courtyard and beaten at the eclipse of the moon.

The *naru* (chanter, both male and female) sang laments to the gods; music was performed at the funeral and entombment ceremonies.

Sumer

Sumerian hymn (*ca.* 800), one of

TWO GOVERNORS OF MARI,
19TH CENTURY, SUMERIAN

the earliest pieces of music extant written in musical notation.

HEBREWS

Early music was strongly influenced by exile in Egypt; most music was religious in nature and after 1000 the highest point in musical development was found in the temple music of the time; characterized by power and simplicity rather than sweetness of sound; solo, choral, antiphonal singing and dance music; responsive singing of Old Testament verse; David (1000-960), biblical minstrel as well as king, played *kinnor* (Hebrew form of lyre); wide range of instruments included *shofar* (ram's horn trumpet), *sackbut* (trombone), *dulcimer* (type of organ), drums, and various kinds of noisemakers.

HARVESTER VASE, DETAIL,
HAGIA TRIADA, *ca.* 1550-1500

an important part in all the great religious festivals and rites, especially Bacchanalian, Orphic; Pythian Games (begun *ca.* 1000) devoted to a contest between festival hymn-writers using stringed or wind accompaniment; the lyre (or cithara) was the instrument of the Apollonian cult while the *aulos* (double reed) was used by the followers of Dionysus.

Thaletas. *fl. ca.* 825. Lyric poet, musician; praised by Plutarch and Plato; many compositions and inventions (new measures in verse) ascribed to him.

PHRYGIAN PAINTED VESSELS

GREECE

Music, a term derived from Greek muses, signified for the Greeks all aesthetic and intellectual values; very few examples of early monodic music extant; music, poetry, dance closely linked to divinity myths; music played

CHINA

After the 12th century, two tones were added to the pentatonic series (fa sharp or fi and ti); these served as leading tones to the dominant and tonic. This seven-tone scale (equivalent to Lydian mode) was used until A.D. 1200 when Mongols introduced the scale that is the same as "major" in Western music.

EGYPT

Early dramatic form evolved from religious rites and processions and was the simple enactment of natural or legendary events.

The *Abydos Passion Play* of about 2000 B.C. celebrated the death of the god Osiris, whose limbs having been torn apart were put together again by his sister-wife, Isis. Knowledge of this is from a record by Ikhernofret, who rewrote an earlier version of the story and presented it before Sesostris III (1887-1849).

GIRL MUSICIANS, EGYPTIAN, *ca.* 1415

BLIND MUSICIAN
PLAYING THE HARP

MUSICIAN PLAYING HARP,
PAINTED ON WOOD, 10TH CENTURY

800-400 B.C.

This period of great rulers saw the building of the Palace at Persepolis by the Persians, the palace at Khorsabad for the Assyrian king, Sargon II, the rebuilding of Nineveh by Nebuchadnezzar II in Babylon, and of the Acropolis by Pericles of Greece.

The art of the Classic Age or the Age of Pericles became a monument to the Greek spirit of humanism, idealism, and independence. The Transitional Period, following the Persian Wars, saw the emergence of the individual sculptor in Greece. Important works were produced by Myron, Phidias, and Polyclitus. The great period of the tragic drama in the Greek theater began with the works of Aeschylus.

The Persians combined the art of Asia and Greece, while the contemporary Hebrews, although exceptionally gifted poets and writers, were restricted by Mosaic law from making "graven images" and were therefore unable to develop any individual artistic expression.

39

ARCHITECTURE

GREECE

In the 8th century the Dorian Greeks built a temple (amphiprostyle) to Hera, wife of Zeus, at Olympia; constructed of dried brick and wooden planks, very few fragments remain; it is believed that some parts of the building were painted, certainly the columns.

CORINTHIAN CAPITAL, FROM THOLOS AT EPIDAURUS

Archaic (ca. 650-510)

Harsh and primitive without the gaiety of the Cretan; Doric and Ionic styles in architecture; during the 6th and 5th centuries wooden buildings imitated in stone; unique in that structures were built for human beings by human beings rather than the monumental and colossal structures of the god-kings of the past. Three temples dedicated to Poseidon at Paestum in southern Italy were constructed; ruins of a temple (ca. 460) and so-called basilica (ca. 550) are extant.

Temple of Artemis at Corfu (ca. 600-580). Figures in high relief on pediments in attempt to detach them from architectural setting; possible Mycenaean influence.

Cnidian Treasury (550). First structure to use device of caryatid.

Treasury of Siphnians in Sanctuary of Apollo at Delphi (530-525). First example of the use of two types of relief sculpture, one in low lateral relief, the other in three-dimensional mass.

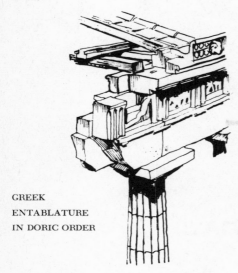

GREEK ENTABLATURE IN DORIC ORDER

COMPONENT PARTS OF THE IONIC ORDER:

CORNICE
FRIEZE
ARCHITRAVE
ABACUS
CAPITAL
SHAFT
BASE
STYLOBATE

Age of Pericles (461-429)

The leader of Athens, at the height of power, built the great buildings of the **Acropolis**: *Parthenon* (447-438), *Propylaea* (437-432), *Temple of Athena Nike* (427-424), and the *Erechtheum* (421-406/5).

Parthenon. Probably the most famous example of Greek Doric architecture; erected in honor of the goddess

THE GREAT TEMPLES

TEMPLE OF APHAEA, AEGINA, *ca.* 490

TEMPLE OF HERA, OLYMPIA, *ca.* 700

TEMPLE OF POSEIDON,
PAESTUM, ITALY, *ca.* 460

GORGON, WEST PEDIMENT, TEMPLE OF
ARTEMIS, CORFU, *ca.* 600-580

THE GREAT TEMPLES

THE ERECHTHEUM, ACROPOLIS

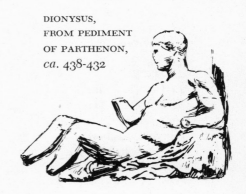

"OLIVE TREE PEDIMENT," 6TH CENTURY,
ARCHAIC GREEK, ACROPOLIS

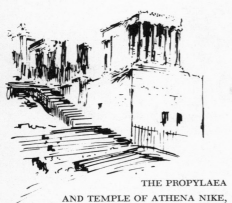

THE PROPYLAEA
AND TEMPLE OF ATHENA NIKE,
ACROPOLIS

DIONYSUS,
FROM PEDIMENT
OF PARTHENON,
ca. 438-432

PORCH OF THE MAIDENS,
ERECHTHEUM (ACROPOLIS)

Athena; architects were Ictinus (Iktinos) and Callicrates (Kallikratos); used white (Pentelic) marble; two-room cella (for cult statue and treasury) enclosed by colonnade (rows of Doric columns); magnificent example of harmony, beauty, and symmetry.

Erechtheum. Probably designed by Mnesicles (who also built the Propylaea), this Ionic temple is a remarkable example of originality; constructed of Pentelic marble with friezes of black Eleusinian limestone on three different levels; asymmetrical; overall harmony of concept, design, and ornamentation; *Porch of Maidens* striking for use of six imposing female figures (caryatids) as columns; folds of gowns resemble column fluting.

Temple of Nike Apeteros (Wingless Victory), a gem of miniature proportions and delicate details; has amphiprostyle Ionic columns; on southwestern slope of Acropolis.

Temple of Apollo at Bassae, designed by Ictinus, is an early example of the use of the Corinthian capital, a variation of the Ionic using an acanthus leaf motif.

Others. Doric Temple of Herakles, Akragas (510); **Temple of Zeus,** Olympia (*ca.* 460); large Doric temple designed by Libon of Elis; on west pediment is statue of Apollo; **Temple of Hephaistos,** Theseum, overlooking the Agora, best-preserved Attic building; **Temple of Poseidon,** Sounion (449-440); **Temple of Nemesis** at Rhamnous (436-432).

Hippodamus of Miletus (mid-5th century). Architect; credited with the introduction of town planning; broad main streets intersecting at right angles with parallel side streets (Piraeus

THEATER OF DIONYSUS, ATHENS

near Athens and Thurii in southern Italy).

ASIA MINOR

City of Gordion. Phrygian capital during Archaic period in Greece, Gordions played important part in transmission of culture westward from ancient culture of Tigris-Euphrates Valley; recent excavations suggest Gordion link between preclassical Greece and the East; palaces of King Midas (8th century) had mosaic floors in irregular, geometric patterns of red, black, and white; city gate, faced with massive blocks of hewn stone.

Temple of Artemis at Ephesus (6th century). Enormous building in Ionic style; built on coast of Asia Minor; reconstructed several times; believed designed by Chersiphron.

MESOPOTAMIA · *Assyria*

The second period of art, known as the Late Assyrian (1000-612), saw the development of the two great cities, Nineveh (fell 612) and Nimrud (Caleh); the greatest king of Assyria

43

was Ashurbanipal (668-626) who collected the greatest cuneiform library ever assembled.

Sargon II (721-705) built a magnificent and beautifully decorated palace at Khorsabad.

Babylon

Nebuchadnezzar II (605-562) rebuilt Nineveh; from his long reign we have the famed Ishtar Gate, with the thousands of brilliant polychromed glazed bricks highlighted by bulls and dragons in sharp relief, and the Hanging Gardens, considered by the Greeks a Wonder of the World.

PERSIA

Great Palace at Persepolis, built by the Achaemenid family: Darius I (r. 521-485), Xerxes (r. *ca.* 485-465), Artaxerxes I (r. *ca.* 465-*ca.* 425); magnificent in space and scale; *Audience Hall of Darius* was 250 ft. square, wooden ceiling supported by 36 (40 ft.) columns; colossal statues of winged bulls, relief carvings (unlike the Assyrians, the Persians emphasized

RELIEF FROM HALL OF A HUNDRED COLUMNS, *ca.* 500

WINGED IBEX, ACHAEMENID PERIOD, PERSIAN, 6TH CENTURY

STAIRWAY TO THE "TRIPYLON," PERSEPOLIS, PERSIA

DARIUS AND XERXES GIVING AUDIENCE, PERSIA, *ca.* 490

the exterior approaches to the palace rather than the interior); columns more slender and closely fluted than Greek and lighter than Egyptians; influence of Greeks apparent; no temples.

Throne Hall (Hall of a Hundred Columns) started by Xerxes.

SCULPTURE

GREECE

Although much of the Greek sculpture that has come down to us is of marble, most of the work of the period was done in hollow bronzes, unfortunately easily carried off by thieves; early sculptured pieces were painted (mostly wood) until superseded by the introduction of marble.

Archaic

7th and 6th centuries, although

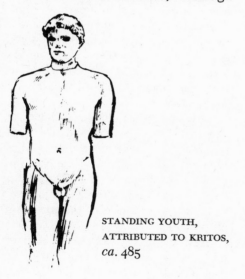

STANDING YOUTH, ATTRIBUTED TO KRITOS, *ca.* 485

experimental, saw an advance over primitive work; the standing male figure (*kouros*) is called "Apollo" in Greek art (Apollo of Tenea, Delian Apollo); standing female figure (*kore*) is always draped (Hera of Samos); to add animation to faces they adopted what became known as the "Archaic smile" (not very successful).

APOLLO, ACROTERIUM FROM TEMPLE AT VEII, ROME, *ca.* 510

Transitional Period (510-480)

This brief period saw the emergence of individual sculptors to prominence; Roman copies in marble exist and must be distinguished from the originals that were in bronze.

Myron of Eleuthera. *fl.* 475-450. Outstanding sculptor of this period; famous for *Discobolus* (*Diskobolos,* Discus Thrower); expressed individualism balanced by classic impersonality and abstract beauty; feeling of relief results from composition in one plane; *Marsyas* from Acropolis and *Goddess Athena* also ascribed to him.

45

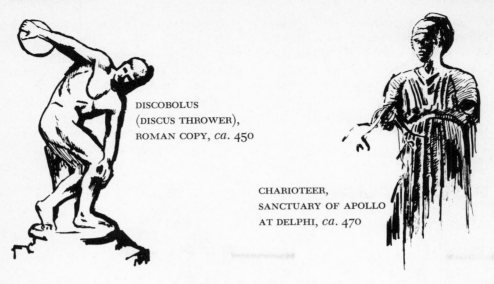

DISCOBOLUS
(DISCUS THROWER),
ROMAN COPY, *ca.* 450

CHARIOTEER,
SANCTUARY OF APOLLO
AT DELPHI, *ca.* 470

DYING NIOBID,
ROMAN COPY,
ca. 450-440

Classic (*ca.* 450–400)

With the battle of Platea (479) the Persian Wars came to an end and art became more refined, developing through the Transitional Period until it reached the perfection of the works of ideal or classic beauty produced during the Golden Age of Athens.

Phidias. *ca.* 490-432. Great Attic master; designed figures for the Parthenon, remarkable in composition, each suited to assigned space; sculpture consisted of 92 *metopes* (high-relief panels) in the Doric frieze; 50 freestanding figures in two pediments; continuous frieze (520 ft., Ionic) on four outer cella walls (part of Elgin Marbles now in Great Britain); famed *Athena Parthenos* (completed 438), great chryselephantine (ivory, gold) statue; colossal statue of Zeus at Olympia, one of the Seven Wonders of the Ancient World.

Polyclitus. *fl. ca.* 460-420. Master of Argive school; established rules of proportion and balance in treatment of human body; "captured motion" in poise of masterpiece, the *Doryphorus* (Spear Bearer, *ca.* 440); *Diadoumenos* (*ca.* 425); *Wounded Amazon*, and other works.

Cresilas. *fl. ca.* 450-420. Credited with statue of *Pericles* (*ca.* 430), earliest Greek portrait statue that has

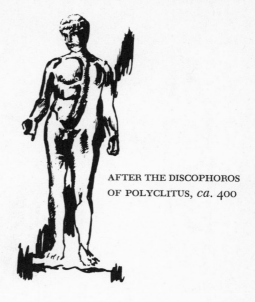

DORYPHORUS
(SPEAR BEARER),
ROMAN COPY,
ca. 450-440

AFTER THE DISCOPHOROS
OF POLYCLITUS, *ca.* 400

siotes, Onatus, Paeonius, Pythagoras
of Rhegium, and Scyllis.

DIADOUMENUS,
AFTER POLYCLITUS,
ca. 430

been identified; statue of an *Amazon*
for Temple of Artemis at Ephesus.

Others. Agoracritus, Alcamenes, Antenor, Bathycles, Calamis, Callimachus, Canachus, Cheramyes, Critos,
Daedalus, Dipoenus, Leochares, Ne-

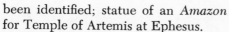

LADY OF AUXERRE,
ca. 650

STANDING YOUTH,
ca. 600, CRETE

47

DYING WARRIOR, FROM TEMPLE AT AEGINA, *ca.* 490

HEKATEION, ALCAMERES,
ca. 448, GREEK

KROISOS
(KOUROS FROM ANAVYSOS),
ca. 525, ATHENS

VOTIVE STATUE FROM SANCTUARY
OF HERA, SAMOS, *ca.* 570-560

KORE 679, ACROPOLIS, *ca.* 530

TORSO, 5TH CENTURY

FLUTIST
FROM SAMOS,
6TH CENTURY

48

GREECE

DEMETER, *ca.* 420, ELEUSIS

KORE 681,
PROBABLY BY ANTENOR,
ca. 530, ACROPOLIS

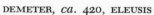

STELE OF ARISTION, GRAVESTONE,
ca. 510, ATHENS

STELE, ALXENOR OF NAXOS,
BOEOTIA, 5TH CENTURY

MOSCHOPHOROS
(CALF-BEARER),
ca. 570, ACROPOLIS

49

ASIA · *India*

Outstanding work of period seen in reliefs on rails and intricately carved gateways of stupas; illustrated legends of Buddha's life; many freestanding statues; all work shows strong Western influence, but with unique Indian quality of expression; rock-cut sanctuaries (*chaityas*) popular under Aśoka.

GRIFFEN GLAZED-BRICK RELIEF, SUSA

WARRIOR, GLAZED BRICK, SUSA

China

Tomb sculpture; fresh, often humorous, rich imagery in animals; excellent lacquer ware.

ETRUSCANS

Famed sailors who traded over a wide area; dynasty of the Tarquins ruled Rome (616-510); fought with Carthage against Greeks (540); finally became part of the Roman Empire.

CHIMERA, ETRUSCAN MONSTER, *ca.* 500

The only known Etruscan sculptor was Vulca of Veii (6th century) who worked in Rome; the Etruscans preferred work in terra cotta and bronze to stone and marble for sculpture and architectural decoration; excellent metalworkers; exquisite jewelry.

SARCOPHAGUS, ROME, *ca.* 520

PAINTING

GREECE

Greek wall painting did not become important until after the Persian Wars (*ca.* 475-450); the Archaic period was the great age of vase painting.

CORINTHIAN VASE, SATYR HOLDING A CRATER, 6TH CENTURY

The Dorians brought a rectilinear geometric style in the decoration of vases (see *Dipylon Vases*); the magnificent crater called the *François*

FRANÇOIS VASE, *ca.* 560

Vase (see illustration) is an excellent example of the next step in development; this was followed by the mature archaic style seen in the work of **Exekias** in his Attic black-figured kylix

DETAIL OF LEKYTHOS, BY THE ACHILLES PAINTER, *ca.* 440-430

(*ca.* 540) that achieves a two-dimensional, decorative effect; **Psiax** in an amphora showing *Herakles Strangling the Nemean Lion* (*ca.* 525), exhibits an Oriental influence and a powerful three-dimensional quality; the technique of leaving the figures red and filling in the background (usually black) developed *ca.* 500; one of the late masterpieces showing excellent draftsmanship is the Attic red-figured kylix of Eos and Memnon by **Douris** (*fl. ca.* 490-480), who is also known for a chalice showing Athena pouring wine for Herakles.

Apollodorus, called the Shadow Painter (*fl.* 440) and **Polygnotus** of Thasos (*ca.* 480-*ca.* 430) were the outstanding painters of Pergamon and Athens; Polygnotus worked out the principle of perspective, able to create illusion of three-dimensional depth.

ARCHAIC PERIOD PAINTING

LEFT: NECK-AMPHORA
BY THE PIG PAINTER,
ca. 490; RIGHT: AMPHORA
BY THE MATSCH PAINTER,
ca. 480

YOUNG CITHAROEDUS SINGING,
BY THE BERLIN PAINTER

LEFT: WARRIORS FIGHTING, AMPHORA,
ca. 530-520; RIGHT: KALPIDE, *ca.* 510

MYTH OF PHAON,
ATTRIBUTED TO MEIDIAS PAINTER,
5TH CENTURY

HORSEMAN, PAINTING ON TERRA-COTTA,
ARCHAIC ART

THEATER

The tragic drama succeeded the ancient dithyramb, which was a choral song or chant sung in honor of Dionysus. It is believed that the dithyramb was improvised at the time of the festival, probably stemming from the fervor generated by the occasion, and was most often the excited telling of the tales of the gods. Between the 7th and 6th centuries B.C., by the time of **Arion** of Methymna, individual poets were composing lines and an *exarchos* (leader) was selected to lead or direct the choral group. By the simple expedient of changing masks (and possibly voices) the performers were able to represent several characters.

Thespis, who is believed to have given (as actor, producer, director) performances of his works in his native Icaria and then in Athens after *ca.* 560, is credited with having introduced the protagonist (*hypokrites* or "answerer") as distinguished from the choral leader, into the presentation.

Pisistratus succeeded in winning the prize for one of his tragedies when he established the first dramatic festival in Athens, the center of public performances in 534.

The Dionysian drama contests were sponsored by the state and prizes were awarded to the winners. Three dramatists were given an opportunity to submit a tetrology (three tragedies and a satyr play) for an all-day performance.

MUSE OF TRAGEDY WITH MASK

Although the chorus (at first 50 members) was the responsibility of a wealthy man of the community, the state chose the *choragus* (director or producer) and paid the actors (all male), who wore masks, high-soled boots (to give them height and dignity), and played more than one role in each drama.

Aeschylus. 525-456. Great dramatic poet; first of the three great tragic poets of Greece; born at Eleusis of noble birth; fought as a soldier of Athens against the Persians (490-479); competed in yearly drama contests (499-458) and won first prize 13 times (484-468) when he was finally defeated by Sophocles; seven of his approximately 90 plays are extant; *The Suppliants*, important as the first surviving play in the history of the theater; Aeschylus changed the standard

53

AESCHYLUS

credited with using an actor in addition to chorus and female characters (women's masks).

Chorilos. *fl.* 534-521. About 160 plays are attributed to him, but only the title of one, *Alope,* is known; said to have improved on the masks introduced by Thespis.

Pratinas. *fl.* 500-497. Best-known as the writer of satyr-plays and is thought to have competed with Aeschylus and Chorilos in the 70th Olympiad.

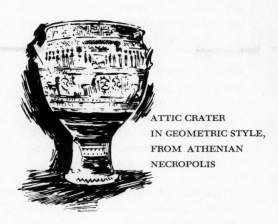

ATTIC CRATER IN GEOMETRIC STYLE, FROM ATHENIAN NECROPOLIS

chorus, originally the single central focus of the tragic drama, and used four choral groups of 12 members each (later changed to 15); introduced a second actor and increased the importance of the dialogue; originated the trilogy on a single theme; *The Persians* (produced 472) example of grandeur of characterization; fragment is left of *Prometheus Bound* (*ca.* 470); *Oresteia* (458), complete trilogy, has survived and is considered his most brilliant work (includes *Agamemnon, The Choephori,* and *The Eumenides*); *The Seven Against Thebes* (467), final part of trilogy, expressed profound religious emotion, powerful dramatic effects; unusual skill in creating conflict between strong, vital characters.

Phrynichus. *fl. ca.* 500. Attic poet; considered one of the founders of Greek tragedy; may have won the 67th Olympiad (512-509); none of his works extant, but believed to have written many plays, including *Egyptians, Alcestis, The Danaides, The Women of Pleuron, The Phoenician Women,* and *The Capture of Miletus;*

MUSIC

GREECE

Music played an important part in the competition at the Olympic Games (begun 776) held every four years; the Pythian Games in honor of the Delphian Apollo (from 586) included the Isthmean and Nemean competitions in music and poetry (the hymn-writers used stringed or wind accompaniment); the Panthenian Festivals also had musical competition; ability to play musical instruments, sing, or dance were regarded as exceptional accomplishments, and one-third of a youth's education was devoted to this end. Greek music is based on the tetrachord (four strings forming the half scale) and modes (eight-tone scales descending in half- and quarter-tone intervals) named Dorian, Phrygian, Lydian, and Aeolian for groups of cities in Asia Minor.

Terpander. *fl. ca.* 700-650. Outstanding leader of Spartan school; noted for vocal and instrumental solos; increased the strings of the lyre to seven or eight; introduced accompaniment, invented a musical notation, and enlarged the scale by combining the Aeolian and Dorian tetrachords; considered the "father of Greek music."

Pythagoras. *ca.* 585-*ca.* 479. Greek mathematician; important for application of theory of numbers to relationship of tones, inventing the science of acoustics; defined intervals of Greek mode (scale used in West until modified in diatonic scale of 18th century); increased the strings of the lyre to 15.

Archilochus. *fl. ca.* 660. Lyric poet, believed to have invented dramatic melody (iambic and trochaic meters); first to alternate longer and shorter verses in form called *epode*, which gave freedom to hymns sung at festivals.

Tyrtaeus. *fl.* 7th century. Athenian lyric poet, musician, and general; wrote martial songs and airs, many commissioned by the Spartan army.

Alcman (Alkman, Alcmaeon). *fl. ca.* 670-631. Founder of Doric school; poet, musician of Sardis; considered by some the originator of lyric poetry; excellent performer on the cithara; wrote hymns, processionals, paeans, *partheniads*, and poetry for choral performances.

Thaletas of Sparta. *fl.* 675. Lyric poet and musician; probably introduced lyrics sung at festivals by chorus accompanied by dancers.

Sappho of Lesbos. *fl. ca.* 600. Leading woman poet; famous for *monodies*, poems to be sung to music of harp, lyre, or cithara; much of work lost.

Arion. *fl.* 600. Poet, musician of Corinth; credited with first use of dithyramb; known as choral lyricist.

400 B.C.-A.D. 1

The Hellenistic period in Greek art refers primarily to the works produced during the spread of Greek civilization throughout the vast area conquered by Alexander the Great. Although Oriental and barbaric styles were, at the same time, assimilated and adapted into Greek artistic expression, the work of the Hellenistic artist remained highly individualistic.

Pergamon (Pergamum) became the center of Western art until the Roman conquest of Greece (146 B.C.). In India, the Mauryan emperors built great stupas and *chaitya* halls and a unique quality of expression was manifested in intricately carved sculpture.

56

SCULPTURE

GREECE · *4th Century*

Praxiteles. *fl. ca.* 360-*ca.* 330. Great master; reflected preference of time for slender graceful form; outstanding portrayal of feminine form; concerned with individualism, realism; known for *Apollo Sauroktonos* (Lizard Slayer), *Aphrodite of Cnidus*, *Hermes with the Infant Dionysus* (only copy exists to-

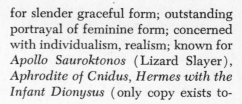

APOLLO SAUROKTONOS
(LIZARD SLAYER),
AFTER PRAXITELES

HERMES AND
THE INFANT
DIONYSUS,
BY PRAXITELES

GIRL, *ca.* 400

day), *Eros of Thespiae, Eros of Paros, Apollo Lykeios*; sons, Kephsodotos and Timarchos, also sculptors.

Scopas. *fl.* 4th century. Great Ionian sculptor, probably born in Asia Minor; believed to have studied under followers of Polyclitus; works are excellent

BATTLE OF GREEKS AND AMAZONS,
PROBABLY BY SCOPAS

57

examples of dramatic realism; two monumental statues of the *Fates*, Athens; *Portrait of Mausolus*, Mausoleum, Halicarnassus (359-351), marble figure over 9 ft.; many other powerful works including that at Temple of Artemis at Ephesus.

Lysippus. *fl. ca.* 370-300. Strong realism; best-known for Roman marble copy of his bronze *Apoxyomenos* (Scraper, *ca.* 330); believed to have been official portrait artist and carved many likenesses of Alexander the Great; also credited with a *Heracles Epitrapezios*, *a Lion Hunt* for King Craterus, Delphi.

Timotheus. *fl.* 4th century. Worked with Scopas and others on Mausoleum of Halicarnassus.

DYING GAUL, ROMAN COPY AFTER WORK AT PERGAMUM

Hellenistic

Agesander of Rhodes. *fl.* 1st century. With Polydorus and Athenodorus, responsible for the *Laocoön* group; influenced sculpture during Renaissance and Baroque periods.

ACROTERIUM (AURA) BY TIMOTHEUS, FROM TEMPLE AT EPIDAURUS

LAOCOÖN GROUP, LATE 2ND CENTURY, (VATICAN)

Pasiteles. *fl.* 4th century. Classic style; important teacher and author of book on sculpture.

Chares of Lindos in Rhodes. *fl. ca.* 280. Believed to have carved the famous *Colossus of Rhodes* (120 ft.

high), one of the Seven Wonders of the Ancient World.

NIKE OF SAMOTHRACE

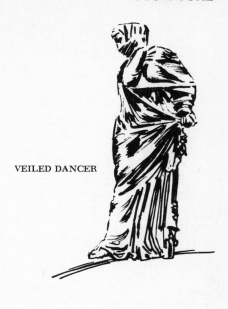

VEILED DANCER

Others. Bryaxis, Cephisdotus, Eutchides, Timotheus, Antigonus of Carystus, Pythocritus, Boethus, Apollonius of Tralles, Apollonius of Athens, Glycon, Tauriscus of Tralles, Sosibus.

BRONZE BOXER,
APOLLONIUS
OF ATHENS

ROMAN EMPIRE

Greco-Roman Period (146-B.C. A.D. 1). The so-called Neo-Attic style of the Greeks was copied by the Romans of this period; an example of archaism is seen in the *Artemis* taken from a house in Pompeii (25); *The Old Market Woman* (2nd century) from Miletus represents the realism of the Late Attic school; the superb *Nymph* found in Tiber (*ca.* 50, School of Arcesilaus), suggests a new sophistication of style.

First portrait sculpture really recognizable as distinctly Roman came under dictatorship of Sulla (82-79); during the reign of Emperor Augustus (27 B.C.-A.D. 14), a new style of heroic portraiture appeared, as seen in the portrait of the emperor himself; narrative reliefs on monumental altars proclaimed the accomplishments of the ruler; high point of relief sculpture reached with great altar erected by Augustus on the Campus Martius; on

THE OLD MARKET WOMAN

AUGUSTUS
OF PRIMAPORTA

APHRODITE
OF THE CNIDIANS

APHRODITE,
GRECO-ROMAN STYLE

ARA PACIS

LIVIA, WIFE OF AUGUSTUS

APHRODITE OF MELOS

BULL CAPITAL,
RĀMPURVA

a wall enclosing the altar is the monumental work called the *Ara Pacis* (Altar of Peace, 13-9).

ASIA · *India*

Under Aśoka Maurya (*ca.* 268-*ca.* 233) who, as a convert to Buddhism,

CATS AND JERBOA MICE, EGYPT

GREAT LION CAPITAL,
SARNATH, ERECTED
BY KING AŚOKA

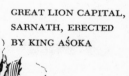

GOLD RHYTON, ACHAEMENID

erected monuments in honor of the Buddha; *lats* (pillars) set up along Buddha's legendary route, highways; edicts inscribed on base (Western style); pillars (40 to 50 ft. high); single shafts of beautifully polished stone, carved ornamentation, showing Persian and Greek influence.

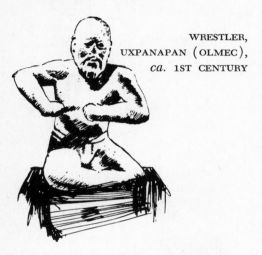

WRESTLER,
UXPANAPAN (OLMEC),
ca. 1ST CENTURY

INCENSE BURNER,
FROM TIKAL,
EARLY MAYAN

ARCHITECTURE

GREECE · *Hellenistic*

Pergamon, one of the great and most beautiful cities of Asia Minor (*ca.* 323-146), was the center of the art of this period.

Acropolis had a theater seating 10,000 and a library of 200,000 volumes (ranked next to the library at Alexandria with half-a-million books as greatest in the world); **Great Altar of Zeus** (*ca.* 180) actually dedicated to Athena Polias, patroness of Pergamon; arch and vault construction used; hexastyle temple generally traditional, though more ornate, taller, thinner, more delicate Doric columns (six at each end and ten on the sides); above the columns ran a triglyph frieze with blank metopes and two sculptured pediments.

The **theater,** constructed during the reign of Eumenes II (*ca.* 170), had a flat circular section (orchestra) with a small altar dedicated to Dionysus in

THEATER OF EPIDAURUS, POLYCLITUS

the center; the auditorium rose 122 ft. (up the hill) in a series of 78 semicircular curved tiers of stone seats.

Two great temples (very large) of 4th century were the **Second Temple of Artemis** at Ephesus (begun 356) and the **Temple of Apollo Didymaeus** at Miletus (335-20).

Dinocrates. *fl.* late 4th century. Architect who designed the new city of Alexandria for Alexander the Great; built funeral pyre of Hephaestion.

Sostratus. *fl.* 3rd century. Designer of the *Pharos* (lighthouse) at Alexandria for Ptolemy Philadelphius that became the model for such buildings.

ROMAN EMPIRE

As the only early civilization to develop monumental secular architecture, the Romans built great buildings. These were the result of feats of engineering skill, including the use of the arch, vault, and dome, and the intro-

duction of concrete as a new material, rather than outstanding artistic imagination.

From this period are the **Temple of Fortuna Virilis**, Rome, late 2nd century, **Temple of the Sibyl**, and **Sanctuary of Fortuna Primigenia**, Tivoli, early 1st century.

Vitruvius Pollio. *fl.* 1st century. Architect and military engineer under Emperor Augustus; author of *De Architectura* (10 vols.), accepted as the final authority in the field for centuries.

TEMPLE OF THE SIBYL, TIVOLI, EARLY FIRST CENTURY

TEMPLE OF FORTUNA VIRILIS, ROME, LATE SECOND CENTURY

63

ASIA · *India*

Empire of Chandragupta reached peak during 3d century; under Aśoka Rājā, his grandson (272-232), artistic endeavor reached new heights with the building of the great towers of Pātaliputra, capital of the Maurya emperors of India, near modern Patna above the Ganges; use of stone for building (and sculpture) began with

GREAT STUPA, SANCHI, INDIA

AŚOKAN COLUMN,
VAISALI, INDIA,
MAURYA PERIOD

STONE TOWERS, INDIA

the Mauryan dynasty; earliest *chaitya* halls (basilica-type cathedrals) hewn from rock at Bhajja (2nd to 1st century), nave separated from the aisles by rows of pillars (plain octagonal shafts), ending in semicircular apse (with rock-cut stupa); use of wood; striking wooden "rose window"; largest, most magnificent cave-temple at Karli, near Bombay (begun 1st century).

Asoka Maurya (*ca.* 268-*ca.* 233) built thousands of stupas; only core remains of *Great Stupa* at Sānchi.

YAKSHĪ, EAST GATE, SANCHI, INDIA, EARLY FIRST CENTURY

MAHA MUNI PAGODA, MANDALAY, BURMA, 1ST CENTURY

SANCTUARY OF FORTUNA PRIMIGENIA, PALESTRINA, EARLY 1ST CENTURY

GREAT WALL OF CHINA (PART) NEAR NANKOW, HOPEI

PAINTING

ROMAN EMPIRE

Probably the most important paintings of the period were the fresco wall decorations discovered in the homes (buried by the eruption of Mount Vesuvius, A.D. 79) of the wealthy Romans of Pompeii and Herculaneum.

Developing through four styles, the first of which showed definite Hellenistic influence, the Pompeian frescoes saw the introduction of perspective (first through line, then through color) that produced an interest in architectural subjects for wall (sometimes marble) panels.

The most decorative style, the fourth (called Pompeian or "intricate"), that placed emphasis on figures, influenced later artists. Excellent examples of some of the works of this

ROMAN WALL PAINTING, POMPEII

drama contest (468); won 24 contests in all; his introduction of a third actor was an important innovation; also introduced painted scenery, increased the size of the chorus, and departed from the use of the trilogy by making

SOPHOCLES

period include the *Aldobrandini Marriage* (Vatican); *Architectural View* from the Villa of Fannius Sinistor (280-230) at Boscoreale, near Pompeii (Met. Mus.); the mosaic (copy of painting) of *Alexander and Darius at the Battle of Issus*, House of the Faun, Pompeii (1st century), works from the Villa of Mysteries, Pompeii (*ca*. 50); the Villa of Livia at Primaporta and Villa Albani, Rome (*ca*. 20).

Magnificent encaustic (wax process) portrait studies were found in mummy-cases of 2nd-century Alexandria.

THEATER

GREECE

Sophocles. *ca*. 496/5-406. Considered by many the greatest of the Greek tragedians; well-born in Colonus; highly-educated, wealthy, handsome; of his approximately 123 dramas, seven have survived intact; gained first great triumph by defeating Aeschylus in

each play a separate entity; first of the seven tragedies extant, *Antigone* (441) has had great appeal for modern audiences with its superb characterization, excellent handling of suspense, and desperate, tragic tone; *Oedipus the King* (*Oedipus Tyrannus*, 431), probably best-known tragedy, expresses the irony of man's fate as seen in the inevitability of Oedipus' doom; *Ajax* (441) is the story of tragic error; *Electra* (*ca*. 420), popular tragedy based on the Agamemnon story, places the emphasis on human beings rather than metaphysical powers; *Philoctetes* (409), written when the playwright was 86 years of age, reminds one of Shakespeare's *Tempest* in its summing up of his profound faith in the inherent worth of man, and is considered the finest example in all Greek tragedy of the interaction between characters and events.

THREE COMIC ACTORS, TERRA-COTTA, GREEK

Euripides. *ca.* 485/80-406. Third and most renowned of the great Athenian dramatic poets; although he gained less recognition in his own time than his famous contemporaries, he has probably been the most popular in recent centuries; won first contest (441); went to court of Archelaus, King of Macedonia (*ca.* 408); wrote 75 plays, 18 extant, the earliest of which, *Alcestis* (438), displays contemporary cynical attitude; *Medea* (431), a sensational tragedy based on the unusual theme of miscegenation, presents the disastrous results of uncontrolled passions of anger and jealousy; *Hippolytus* (428), earliest extant drama based on criminal passion; *Hecuba* (*ca.* 425); *Andromache* (*ca.* 430); *Herakleidae* (*ca.* 430); *The Suppliants* (*ca.* 421); *The Trojan Women*

(415); *Iphigenia in Tauris* (*ca.* 414); *Helen* (412); *Orestes* (408); *Cyclops*, only complete satyr play extant; introduced spirit of humanism and rationalism; attempted to free drama from conventional hero as subject; sympathetic portrayal of women and love; noted for lyric quality of choral passages; influenced later dramatists in what has been called "realism."

MEDEA, EURIPIDES, ADAPTATION BY ROBINSON JEFFERS

Aristophanes. *ca.* 448-*ca.* 380. Great Athenian writer of comedies; frank in criticism of political figures, "progressive" education, and the ideas of the Sophist philosophers; the tragedies of Aeschylus and Euripides are challenged in the gay, yet serious, lyrical, and witty play, *The Frogs* (405), in what is considered one of the best examples of literary criticism in history; *The Acharnians* (425) and *The Knights* (424) are antiwar plays; *The Clouds* (423) satirized Socrates; *The Wasps* (422); *The Peace* (421), on the

Peloponnesian War; *The Birds* (414), an amazing fantasy of escape; *Lysistrata* (411), ribald, amusingly simple, popular; and *The Thesmophoriazusae* (411), an extremely witty, humorous play about women; last plays are *The Ecclesiazusae* (392) and *The Plutus* (388), a form of morality drama.

Menander. 342-*ca.* 291. Successful dramatist of New Comedy; established the style imitated by later Latin writers and the comedies of manners that developed much later in northern

MENANDER WITH HIS MASKS, ROME

Europe; wrote more than 100 plays, titles of about 80 of these tales of love listed; best-known works, brilliant *Epitrepontes* (The Arbitration) and *Perikeiromene* (She is Shorn of Her Locks, or The Girl with Shorn Hair), a tale of separated twins; exposed double standard of morality; very influential.

Philemon. *ca.* 360-*ca.* 262. Poet of New Attic comedy; defeated Menander in several contests and was more popular in his time; wrote the plays on which Plautus based his *Mercator* and *Trinummus*; only fragments of works survive.

Diphilus. *fl. ca.* 300. One of the leading Athenian poets of the New Comedy; although only fragments of his plays are extant, he is believed to have written at least a hundred of them.

Apollodorus of Carystus. *fl.* 300-260. Poet of New Attic comedy; winner of five prizes; author of at least 47 plays; Terence based his *Hecyra* and *Phormio* on Apollodorus' plays.

Many Greek **playhouses** built; orchestra still held central position but in some theaters (Assos and Priene) it took semicircular shape; scenic design changed as more emphasis was placed on characters; chorus and actors separated and given more freedom of action; use of panel backdrops, painted doors and walls gave depth and perspective to buildings in scenery. Costumes more in keeping with period, and acting more realistic.

ROME

Mime (*mimus*). Adaptation of Doric form; very popular, immoral, outspoken, and satirical short sketches of life; **Theocritus** polished the style in the third century; numerous actors were used; grotesque masks and bright costumes enhanced the performances that were particularly popular during the 1st century.

Plautus (Titus Maccius Plautus). *ca.* 254-184. Comic poet; comedies influenced by Menander; used rough, racy, vernacular Latin; sharp characterization of high society; narrow range of plot, but imaginative variety of treatment; use of stock characters and situation comedy; 21 comedies extant, including *Amphitryon* (adapted by later dramatists), *Aulularia* (Pot of

Gold, or The Comedy of the Little Pot), *Miles Gloriosus* (The Bragging Soldier), *Menaechmuses* (*Comedy of Errors* by Shakespeare based on it), *Asinaria* (The Comedy of the Asses), *Rudens* (The Rope), considered one of the most interesting, *Mercator* (The Merchant), and *Mostellaria* (The Ghost).

Terence (Publius Terentius Afer). *ca.* 195-159. Dramatist of Carthage; influenced by Menander and Apollodorus of Carystus; six plays extant; *Andria* (Girl of Andros, 166), *Hecyra* (The Stepmother, 165), *Heautontimorumenos* (The Self-Tormentor, 163), *Eunuchus* (The Eunuch, 161), amusing, technically superior, skilful handling of double plot, although condemned as immoral, most successful and popular play, *Phormio* (161), a delightful farce, and *Adelphi* (The Brothers, 160).

In Rome in 240 **Livius Andronicus**, a Greek captive (later freed by his master) presented comedies translated from the Greek.

SCENE FROM NEW COMEDY, NAPLES

ROMAN THEATER AT ORANGE, SOUTHEASTERN FRANCE

MUSIC

GREECE

Music was an integral part of lyric poetry, tragic and comic drama, choral dancing and song; manuscript fragment of choral *stasimon* (stationary chorus) from Euripides' *Orestes*, rare example of notation; highly skilled singers were required to perform complex tone intervals; in Hellenistic age, text, used by chorus, less essential to movement of drama, but important in conveying mood; relationship of music and drama similar to modern opera.

Two schools of music. *Phrygian*, associated with Dionysus (played the aulos), emotional, with an exciting, stimulating quality that was popular with the people; in sharp contrast was the *Dorian*, music of Apollo (preferred cithara and lyre), simple, restrained melody.

Aristoxenus of Tarentum. *fl.* 4th century. Foremost musical theorist; systematized (with Euclid) scales, transposition; *Elements of Harmony* and

STATUETTES OF TANAGRA TYPE, GREECE

Elements of Rhythm, important works.

Didymus. 62 B.C.-A.D. 10. Grammarian of Alexandria; author of lost treatise on harmony; credited with development of musical scale called "natural scale" to conform to mathematical requirements; recognized the difference between major and minor whole tone, now called "comma of Didymus."

Instruments. *Lyre* (national instrument), *cithara, magadis* (harplike with "trumpetlike" tone), *auloi* (pipes or flute, though more like modern oboe as it used reeds), *syrinx* (pipes of pan), *tympanon* (hand drum), and *krotola* (wood or metal castanets).

ROME

Music and the dance played an important part in the life of the Etruscans; they danced at festivals, religious ceremonies, and at funerals (which were celebrated with games); the double "flute" was the most popular instrument, although they are credited by the Greeks with the invention of the trumpet. Other Roman instruments included the *hydraulus* (water organ, invented 2nd century), *tibis* (pipe or bagpipe), *tuba* (trumpet), *buccina* (trombone), and *tympanum, scabillum, cymbali, systrum, crotola,* all percussion instruments.

CHINA

The Emperor She Huang-ti in 246 ordered all musical instruments and books of music destroyed, as they were, in his opinion, largely responsible for the neglect by the people of more important duties. This order, carried out quite effectively, set music back for centuries in China. Under the Han dynasty (215 B.C.-A.D. 221) it began slowly to regain favor.

A.D. 1-400

The Romans, as great engineers, city planners, and organizers, contributed enormously to the art of the Western world. The Pantheon, built during the reign of Emperor Hadrian, is an example of their remarkable use of interior space. The amphitheater of the Colosseum, the Forum of Trajan, the Baths of Caracalla, the vaulted Basilica of Constantine are other outstanding examples of Roman architecture.

In the 4th century, Christianity had spread throughout the Roman Empire and was recognized as the official religion. St. Peter's in Rome became the prototype for early churches.

This was also the brilliant period of Gandharan art and the Golden Age of Guptan art in India.

ARCHITECTURE

ROMAN EMPIRE · *1st Century*

Pont du Gard, Nîmes (*ca.* 50), famed early aqueduct (880 ft. long); used principle of gravity to bring water to the town through a system of underground and open concrete channels from mountains about 25 miles away; lower arch supported bridge (155 ft. above water), upper series supported water channel.

PONT DU GARD, NÎMES, ROMAN AQUEDUCT

Colosseum. Built toward the end of the first century (believed completed in 80); huge oval amphitheater for public entertainment; gladiatorial contests; vast concrete bowl raised upon tiers of arches; covered about six acres and had a seating capacity of about 50,000; 80 archways served as entrances and exits; imposing ruin.

2nd Century

Considered Rome's greatest architectural period; **Forum of Trajan** (completed 113) built for Emperor Trajan (r. 98-117); **Apollodorus,** Greek architect-engineer from Damascus, in charge; civic project; unique Roman conception; based on unified plan of related structures and courtyards; large paved quadrangle, approached through triple archway, flanked by two arched colonnades; adjacent to square was **Basilica Ulpia,** rectangular hall of polychrome marble; double outside colonnades of red granite, white marble capitals, balcony above, second tier of columns supporting roof beams; semicircular apses at either end of housed courts; two libraries, one for Greek and one for Latin books, separated by a courtyard enclosing Trajan's Column (see Sculpture).

Pantheon: Largest domed structure of period; believed originally built by Agrippa, minister of Augustus (27), as a temple to the gods; reconstructed by Hadrian (120-24); huge cylindrical base; system of relieving arches and abutments embedded in base, supporting massive dome (nearly 130 ft.) of poured concrete; 140 ft. high at summit; source of light, called *oculus* (eye), 29-ft.-round opening in middle of dome; simplicity yet magnificence of round form influenced other buildings.

Baths (Thermae). **Trajan** (110), **Caracalla** (217), and **Diocletian** (302); public buildings providing hot, cold, and tepid swimming pools, dressing rooms, lecture halls, gymnasiums, art galleries with statuary and murals, and libraries; cross vaulting in **Baths of Trajan,** earliest known use of concrete; method permitted spanning of larger spaces, increasing light; influenced later architecture.

Apartment Houses. Rome had almost 50,000 multiple dwellings by the 4th century; the **House of Diana,** for example, was a five-story dwelling; stairways led from shops on the ground

TRAJAN'S COLUMN,
ROME, 106-113

INSULA OF THE HOUSE OF DIANA, OSTIA

stantine's Church of the Resurrection, Jerusalem (327-35).

Basilicas. Shape from main hall of public baths: Basilica of Constantine, Rome (*ca.* 310-20); Basilica of Leptis Magna, Libya (early 3rd century).

BASILICA OF CONSTANTINE, ROME

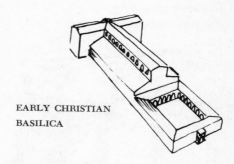

EARLY CHRISTIAN
BASILICA

floor to the living quarters above; there were balconies for the third-floor apartments. Trajan built a port at Ostia and, as the city became an important commercial center, public and private buildings were added.

Others. Mausoleum in Diocletian's Palace at Spalato (early 4th century); Mausoleum of Constantine's daughter, Santa Costanza, Rome (324-26); Con-

Early Christian

The simplicity of design in Roman architecture was continued by the early Christians, who were also interested in the interior of the edifice; the basilica was adopted as ideal because it was not only simple but flexible,

73

allowing for additions and changes; the entrance gateway (*propylaeum*) was at the end of the rectangular plan; the *atrium*, a square colonnaded court with a fountain (*kantharos*) in the center; the *narthex*, which was often in two parts (outer porch and inner hall), was the entrance into the church; the *nave* was the central aisle of the interior (with one or two narrow aisles on each side, forming either three- or five-aisled basilicas); source of light was the *clerestory* (clearstory); semicircular recess (presbytery) at head of aisle was the *apse*, with raised platform (*bema* or transept) for altar; columns often of varicolored marble, floors and walls (*triforium*) decorated with mosaics; the roof was either trussed (simple opening) or coffered (flat, decorated) wood construction (it is interesting to note that none was vaulted like the Romans); under the altar was a subterranean area known as the crypt (*confessio*) where holy personages were buried; **St. Peter's**, Rome (begun 326 by Constantine) was the prototype of early churches; it had

CATACOMB OF DOMITILLA (CUBICULUM OF THE SIX SAINTS)

CONSTANTINE THE GREAT, ROME, 4TH CENTURY

ARCH OF CONSTANTINE, ROME

five aisles, the colonnades on either side of the nave (155 ft. long, 55 ft. wide) were surmounted by architraves; the most important church in Western Christendom (scene of papal coronations) was **St. John Lateran**, Rome (built by Constantine before 311); the largest and most impressive

TRAJAN, *ca.* 100

EQUESTRIAN STATUE
OF MARCUS
AURELIUS,
ROME

basilica (having arcades that replaced architraves) was **St. Paul** (*San Paolo fuori le mura*), built by Theodosius (386), destroyed by fire (1823), and rebuilt.

France

Maison Carrée, Roman temple, built at Nîmes (1st century) by Princes Caius and Nicius; elegant design influenced later architects.

Syria

Temple of Jupiter Heliopolitanus (Great Temple of the Sun), Baalbec (1st-2nd century); partly constructed in megalithic style; entrance portico, great quadrangle, as large as the Forum of Trajan.

SERIGÜZEL SARCOPHAGUS, BYZANTINE

CHRIST BETWEEN PETER AND PAUL,
SARCOPHAGUS OF JUNIUS BASSUS

SCENES OF THE PASSION OF CHRIST

PALACE OF SHAPUR I, NEAR BABYLON

TEMPLE OF THE CROSS, PALENQUE (MAYAN)

ASIA · *India*

Golden Age of Guptan Art. *ca.* 320-*ca.* 490. Rock-cut *chaitya* hall still accepted architectural style; decoration more elaborate (shafts fluted); Hindu and Buddhist architects developed cella-type temple plan, with columned portico.

China

Period of pagoda building in honor of Buddha at Chin capital of Loyang in the 4th century.

AMERICAS · *Maya*

Temples built on pyramidal base of concrete, faced with stone; two narrow compartments, flatroofed; naturalistic, conventionalized, geometric carving adorned walls, columns, lintels; brilliantly painted.

SCULPTURE

ROMAN EMPIRE

Outstanding achievements of period were the magnificent narrative reliefs on monumental triumphal arches and columns; exceptional examples include the great **Arch of Titus,** Rome (71-81); realistic pictorial sequence of military scenes; campaigns in Judea; the **Column of Trajan** (106-113, 140 ft. high), spiral band of reliefs representing the Dacian campaigns; the **Antonine Column of Marcus Aurelius,** and the **Arch of Septimus Severus** in the Roman Forum; one of the largest and most elaborate commemorative arches of the period is the **Arch of Constantine,** Rome (312-15).

GLADIATOR'S HELMET WITH RELIEF,
FROM POMPEII

Following imitation of Greek works, Roman artists developed individual styles; outstanding portraiture, both small busts and monumental equestrian statues (Marcus Aurelius, 161-180) are extant.

Portland Vase. Combined techniques of glassworkers and cameo cutters; typified Roman skill in minor arts.

Early Christian

Sarcophagi Sculpture. Term sarcophagus indicated type of limestone used in construction of coffin; variety of decoration, some secular, classical frieze or landscape motifs; earliest known Christian sarcophagus, Junius Bassius (359).

ASIA · India

Gandharan Art. School flourished northwestern India; strongly Buddhist; reached height under Kanishka (*ca.* 144); early Buddhas reflected Greco-Roman influence with heads of Greek Apollo, dressed in togas and carved in Augustan style; standing Buddha at Hoti Mardan, near Peshawar (late 2nd century); in time faces became more masklike, more Oriental; narrative reliefs reflected Roman influence and workmanship.

Mathuran Art. Completely Indian; representation of Buddha seen in life-size standing Buddha, Sarnath (2nd century); certain fixed canons of proportion developed; system similar to Egyptian and early Greek, but Western influence slight except in reliefs through Gandhara.

Deccan or Andhra Style. Outstanding in central India (late 2nd and 3rd centuries); **Great Stupa**, Amaravati, excellent example of sculpture and reliefs; although Gandharan influence is apparent, Andhran art is more abstract in concept, with ivorylike delicacy and precision.

Golden Age of Guptan Art. First representation of both Buddhist and

FASTING BUDDHA, GANDHARA

77

Brahman subjects; first four-armed Sivas, Buddhas with large decorated nimbuses; **Buddha of Mathura,** brilliant example of majestic serenity, seldom surpassed; Sarnath, center of Buddhist sculpture, produced high-relief statue of Buddha preaching first sermon, masterpiece; use of metal, copper rather than bronze seen in excellent Buddha from Sultanganj; monolithic lion pillars; colossal relief of the **Boaravatar of Vishnu** at Udayagiri in Bhopal, among great monumental carvings of Gupta period.

China

Wei Dynasty. Gained new impetus with introduction of established tradition of Buddhism; work in northern grottos or rock temples followed Gandharan and Mathuran models.

Tai Kuei. d. *ca*. 395. Sculptor, painter; credited with invention of lacquer statuary.

AMERICAS · *Maya*

Sculpture used mainly for architectural decoration; skilled stone mosaic work and outstanding stucco reliefs; impressive sculpture on stela and altars reminiscent of Buddhist style; feathered serpent one of most common symbolic motifs; magnificent heads.

PRIESTESS OF BACCHUS, LEAF OF IVORY DIPTYCH

PAINTING

ASIA · *China*

Confucian tradition flourished at the courts of the southern dynasties during the early centuries.

Wang Hsih-chih. 321–79. Great Chinese calligrapher; introduced "one-brush" technique; varied intensity and breadth of continuous stroke; influenced painting of following periods.

Ku K'ai-chih. *ca*. 345-405. Considered the greatest of the ancient

FALL OF MANDHATA, DETAIL, FROM NAGARJUNAKONDA

masters; mostly copies of works extant; court painter (Chin dynasty) at Nanking; great horizontal scroll *Admonitions of the Instructress to the Court Ladies* (*Nu-shih-chien*), a moral treatise now in British Museum; illustrated poem by Ts'ao Chih, *The Nymph of the River Lo* (*Lo-shen-fu*); skilful portraiture, simple delicate line, subtle shading; worked on silk and paper.

ROMAN EMPIRE

The "ornate" and "intricate" styles of wall decoration continued in Pompeii (until 79) as seen in the paintings in the House of Mesor (30 B.C.-A.D. 60); a strong realistic style appears in the wall painting of *Hercules and Thelephos,* Herculaneum (*ca.* 50, now in Naples); figures were also important in the frescoes of the 2nd century at Dura, Syria.

MUSIC

ROME

Popular music was created and performed for festivals, contests, and colossal public spectacles; because of the huge arenas, the music had to be loud and the instruments very large (including the use of hydraulic and pneumatic organs that required several people to operate); only large choruses and several groups of musicians could be heard in the tremendous amphitheaters; smaller ensembles, in a more intimate situation, attempted a poor imitation of the Greek classical style.

Christian Music

In the fourth century schools of singing were established by the Greek churches at Alexandria and Antioch.

St. Ignatius. 49-107. Bishop of Antioch; introduced antiphonal singing based on Hebrew psalm singing, Greek chorus, and Roman chitaroedic chants.

St. Basil (Basilius) **the Great.** *ca.* 330-79. Father of Greek Church; active in Nicaia and Palestine; revised liturgy; created one of main types of Mass.

St. John Chrysostom. *ca.* 347-407. Greatest of Greek fathers; developed second main type of Mass; Oriental influence strong; psalms sung antiphonally and responsorially.

St. Ambrose. 340-97. Bishop of Milan; considered the founder of hymnody and Ambrosian chant; interested in reforming ceremony and music of the Church; attempted to eliminate secular and pagan elements; wrote excellent hymns; used four authentic modes comparable to Greek primary modes; no meter.

Prudentius. 348-*ca.* 405. Early Spanish Latin Church poet; composed hymns regarded as more brilliant than those of Ambrose, but intended for private rather than public worship (as Ambrose's were).

Syria

Bardaisan (Heresiarch Bardesanes). 154-222. Scholar, poet, astrologer, and Christian theologian; used music as means of spreading his doctrines; wrote mystic hymns of Gnostic type used by Syrian Christians for more than two centuries; founder of Syriac poetry; fitted texts, divided into regular stanzas, to well-known tunes that could be used for all the verses of the hymn.

St. Ephraim (Ephraim Syrus). *ca.* 308-*ca.* 73. Theologian, poet; deacon at Edesse in eastern Syria; adapted psalms to popular melodies that he taught to choruses of women singers; composed simple chants that became standard; works published, Rome (1732-43).

Hilary of Poitiers. d. 366. Introduced Syrian hymnody by translating Oriental hymns into Latin; not readily accepted.

THEATER

ASIA · *India*

The drama in India was the outgrowth of the performance of legends at religious festivals. There was no public theater as such, but private performances were held in the homes of the wealthy, and public productions were held in temple courts. There was no scenery, and very few stage properties were used. A highly developed gesture language, derived from the dance, was adapted by the actors, and all these movements, as well as the costumes worn by the performers, were carefully regulated by convention or custom.

Bhasa. *fl. ca.* 350. Noted early dramatist; *The Vision of Vasavadatta* and *Yaudandharayana's Vows* are among his works.

Bharata. *fl. ca.* 250. Author of important treatise, *Natyasastra,* a compilation of dramatic theory and form; his classification of the ten major types of plays and the accepted description of each prevailed for centuries.

Asvaghosa. *fl. ca.* 2nd century. Author of earliest known Sanskrit dramas to have survived.

ROME

Seneca, Lucius Annaeus (the Younger). *ca.* 4 B.C.-A.D. 65. Famous Stoic philosopher; native of Córdoba, Spain; many prose works and the tragedies *Hercules Furens, Troades, Phoenissae* or *Thebais, Medea, Phaedra* or *Hippolytus, Oedipus, Agamemnon, Thyestes, Hercules Oetaeus;* very melodramatic approach; extremely influential.

Laberius, Decimus. *ca.* 105-43. Poet, knight, author of popular mimes (farces) and comic and satirical poems; little survives of his work.

The **pantomime** developed during the reign of Augustus; a serious form of dance, it was probably performed by a single dancer with changes of character indicated by a change of mask and costume; dancer wore clapper to maintain rhythm and was accompanied by wind, brass, and string instruments; tragic materials, derived from drama or mythology, were used, and occasionally pornographic subject matter.

400-1000

Byzantine art, a fusion of elements from the Hellenistic world, Rome, and the East, and tempered by the strong influence of Christianity, reached its height under Justinian, one of the greatest patrons in the history of art, who directed the building of the Hagia Sophia at Constantinople and San Vitale at Ravenna, center of Byzantine rule in Italy. An important contribution of the Byzantine architect-artist was a new concentration on interior decoration. The brilliant mosaics served not only to beautify the building, but also to present a graphic illustration of the ritual for the illiterate.

In Russia, which continued independent, the Byzantine style survived until the late 17th century when Peter the Great introduced the art of Western Europe.

This was the period of the rapid expansion of Islam that reached from Spain in the West to the Indus Valley in the East and had a profound influence on the future of Asia, Africa, and Europe. Western Europe, although isolated and semi-barbaric, produced brilliant illuminated manuscripts during the Carolingian period,

81

and Gregorian music became the universal language of the Roman Catholic Church.

Glorious Buddhist frescoes by Wu Tao-tse decorated the palaces and temples of Ch'ang-an during the T'ang dynasty in China. Indian art celebrated the revival of Hinduism with the building of magnificent temples and the creation of graceful sculpture.

The Mayan civilization in America produced not only a remarkably accurate calendar and discovered the principle of position in the writing of numbers centuries before these ideas, fundamental to higher mathematics, were known in the Western world, but it also erected impressive pyramid temples and created massive architectural sculptures.

ARCHITECTURE

EASTERN EUROPE · *Byzantine*

Great achievement of the Justinian period (r. 527-65) was the building of the cathedral of Hagia or Sancta Sophia (name from Greek meaning "Holy Wisdom") in Constantinople (532-37); the original church rebuilt by Theodosius II (r. 408-50) had been again destroyed by fire; Justinian I commissioned the mathematician Anthemius of Tralles, and the architect and engineer Isidorus of Miletus, to build the Hagia Sophia; largely experimental and bold in conception, it was a combination basilican and central-plan structure; Greek cross, four arms of equal length on a square, crowned with a magnificent dome (220 by 107 ft.); architectural sculpture seen in carved capitals; columns of dark-green variegated marble used in nave arcade; in the niches the columns were of Egyptian porphyry; nonrepresentational glass mosaics on gold grounds for brilliant interior decoration; great treasury of art until city was sacked by Crusaders (1204); minarets of the faith of Islam added in 15th and 16th centuries.

WESTERN EUROPE · *Italy*

Ravenna replaced Rome as the capital of Western Christianity; attempt was made to retain Roman architecture with added Eastern influences.

Sant' Apollinare Nuovo (*ca.* 493-526), oblong basilica, simple exterior, magnificently decorated interior.

Sant' Apollinare in Classe (533-49),

HAGIA SOPHIA, ISTANBUL

MAUSOLEUM OF GALLA PLACIDIA,
RAVENNA

three-aisled arcaded basilica; the altar, used by the bishops, screened off from the congregation, was moved down into the nave.

S. APOLLINARE IN CLASSE, RAVENNA

San Vitale, built by Justinian (526-47), contemporary structure to Hagia Sophia, centralized church, aisles produce octagonal-shaped, two side chambers typical of Eastern style.

Circular tomb built (*ca.* 520) for **Theodoric** (Ostrogoth king); ten-sided crypt, upper part a circular chapel;

S. VITALE, RAVENNA

built of blocks of hewn stone; topped by shallow dome (107 ft.) Istrian marble.

Arian Baptistery (now called Santa Maria in Cosmedin) and **Baptistery of the Orthodox** were domed octagon 6th-century buildings, noted for their fine mosaics.

Mausoleum of Galla Placidia the Empress (440-50); built in form of Greek cross; dome rests on pendentives; brilliant mosaics.

Spain

Church of San Juán de Baños, Castile (661), used wood and stone; arcades with horseshoe arches; exterior colonnades are of Late Antique-Oriental origin (taken over by Arabs).

At the town of Naranco, near Oviedo, once the capital of the Visigothic kings, an ancient church (later dedicated to Santa Maria) is extant (built 848-50); only 12 ft. wide, it has a unique ribbed tunnel vault; so arranged that you entered from the side and climbing stairs arrived at the king's seat (later the altar).

83

Germany

Used wood construction adopted from the Franks; gradually used stone.

S. JULIAN DE LOS PRADOS, SPAIN (CAROLINGIAN)

ORATORY, SHOWING APSE, FRANCE (CAROLINGIAN)

SAN SALVADOR DE VAL DE DIOS, SPAIN (CAROLINGIAN)

CAROLINGIAN PERIOD

Charlemagne (r. 768-814) extended his Frankish empire, aided the papacy against the Lombards in Italy, and was crowned Roman Emperor (800) by Pope Leo III; most important building of period was the **Palatine** or Palace Chapel at Aachen (Aix-la-Chapelle, built 796-804) by Odo of Metz; influenced by San Vitale, Ravenna, it was vaulted octagon, surrounded by ambulatory with galleries above; two lateral buildings in form of three-aisled chapels with apses; definite forerunner of Romanesque style.

Gate House (The Basilican Gate) at Lorsch, near Worms (767-74), was built by Chorodogung, Bishop of Metz; arches and columns of lower story are of Roman arch type; front is faced with red and white slabs of stone; there is also a system of attached columns below with arches between (like Colosseum, Rome) and of small fluted pilasters above.

Germigny-des-Prés near Orléans (built for Theodulf, 806) is the only surviving Carolingian church in France; has Byzantine Greek cross plan with tall, raised central dome, four lower corner vaults and tunnel-vaulted arms; apses are of horseshoe plan.

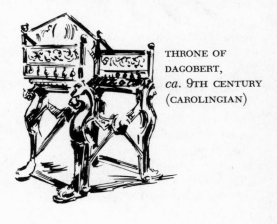

THRONE OF DAGOBERT, *ca.* 9TH CENTURY (CAROLINGIAN)

ISLAM

First Muslim building was the mosque in Medina (623) erected by order of the prophet himself; his house was attached to the mosque and he is buried there; has served as a model.

Jerusalem

Dome of the Rock built (691) by Caliph 'Abd al-Malik (r. 685-705); first major construction of Islamic civilization; large cupola above, and two ambulatories around a rock outcropping; brilliant glass mosaics cover the interior walls; vegetal motifs; use of jewelry designs made of mother-of-pearl and semiprecious stones; decorations combine Byzantine and Iranian motifs (Byzantine style, in manner of Sassanian stuccoes).

Syria

Great Mosque of Damascus built by Umayyad Caliph al-Walîd (706-15), the son of 'Abd al-Malik; often destroyed by fire, last repaired (1893); al-Walîd also built mosques in Medina and Jerusalem.

Spain

Great Mosque at Córdoba (Cordova) built (begun 785) by the first caliph (kalif) in Spain, Abd-al-Rahmân (r. 756-88) and enlarged by Hishâm I (r. 793-96); one tower, 100 cupolas, 1,106 marble pillars, supporting double arches of red brick and white stone; again extended (961-65).

Samarra

Great Mosque and the **Mosque of Abu Dulaf,** typical of Abbasside architecture of the 9th century; large palace, the Jawsaq al Khāqānī, was built (*ca.* 838) by al-Mutasim, son of Hârûn al-Rashîd; the Bulkuwāra palace is believed to have been built by the caliph al-Mutawakkil (849-61), and the caliph al-Mutamid (873-82) probably built the Qasr al Ashiq (Lover's Castle); these palaces are rich in decorative paintings in flat, brilliant colors.

Egypt

Al-Azhar Mosque built by J'afar, the first Fatimite Sultan of Egypt, at Cairo (978); additions were constructed by Kait Beg (1468-96).

ASIA · China

Pagoda, essentially an imitation of the Indian stupa, popular during Budhist ascendancy; early square or octagonal multistoried tower seen in rock-cut pagodas and Yün-kang cave shrines; Sui and T'ang Dynasties regarded as imperial age of architecture; and leading state architects were Yan Su, Yü-wen K'ai, Ho T'iao, and Yen Pi; **Ta-yen-t'a** (Great Gander Pagoda), built under Hsüan-tsang (652), most

PRANCING HORSE, T'ANG DYNASTY, CHINA

SPANISH AND ASIAN ART

CAPILLA DE VILLAVICIOSA,
MOSQUE, CORDOVA

YÜN-KANG, ANTEROOM OF CAVE IX,
SHANSI, CHINA

SHUKONGŌ-JIN,
POLYCHROME CLAY FIGURE,
NARA, JAPAN

MUSICIAN AND DANCER,
DETAIL OF FRIEZE, T'ANG DYNASTY

famous of all Ch'ang-an (618-906) remains; masonry construction, single-story brick buildings and hipped-roof pavilions appeared; **Small Gander Pagoda** (707-10) and tomb pagoda of Hsüan-tsang (669) also important examples of the architecture of the period.

Japan

Importation of Chinese and Korean artisans aided in building of famed Buddhist temples; essentially Chinese in feeling, but more ornamental and delicately carved; Golden Hall (Kondo) of Todaiji Temples and five-storied wood pagoda of Hōryūji, Nara (607-16, rebuilt 708), outstanding surviving examples of magnificent architecture of Asuka and Nara periods.

India

Hindu temple an object of worship rather than a place of prayer; Buddhist influence had waned and Hindu and Jain revived; northern Indo-Aryan style dominated the period; use of corbeled arch, *gopurams* (gateways), *choultries* (ceremonial halls) with

SANCTUARY OF KHADIMAIN, BAGDAD (ABBASSIDE)

ornately carved (thousand) columns; shrines known for *sikhara* (towers) that were rounded at the top and decorated with sculptured reliefs; truncated pyramid buildings were representative of the Dravidian or southern style; magnificent Brahman **Temple of Kailasha** at Ellora, free-standing, hewn and carved from a single mass of rock is brilliant example of this style; **Shore Temple** of Mamalla-puram has carved *rathas* (pagodas) of unusual beauty.

Cambodia

Period 800-1000 marked emergence of early Classic period of Khmer (people from northern Indo-China) style based on both Chinese and Indian works; first capital, founded by Yaśovarman I (889-910), at Angkor; true temple-mountain, pyramidal structure, stairways on four sides, lion-guarded; city called Yaśodkharapura, built around temple of Phnom Bakheng between Angkor Wat and Angkor Thom, remained capital until founding of new capital at Angkor Thom (see next period).

AMERICAS · Maya

Classic Period. The Maya built their great ceremonial centers roughly between 300-900; towering pyramid-temples (some more than 200 ft. high); plazas, courts and stela; ruins at Palenque (Chiapas, Mexico), Tikal, Yaxchilan, Quirigua, Copan, and Piedras Negras, Guatemala.

Peru

Pre-Inca Indian civilizations include early Chimu culture at Trujillo; Nazca farther south; Tiahuanaco cul-

MAYAN AND AZTEC FIGURES

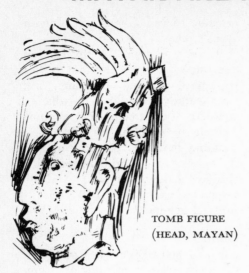

TOMB FIGURE
(HEAD, MAYAN)

ture reached peak (600-1000) at Lake Titicaca in Andes; built great ziggurats, round and square buildings with corbeled vaulted construction; used copper clamps for joining carefully squared stones; city planning included irrigation projects.

MEXICO · *Aztec*

Teotihuacan (Seat of the Gods). Ancient temple city of Mexico; center of flourishing civilization (200-800); most famous buildings: **Pyramid of the Sun** (200 ft. high, uppermost platform over 130 ft. square), and **Pyramid of the Moon,** the two largest temples, and **Temple of Quetzalcoatl,** which is lavishly decorated with butterfly sculptures, heads of plumed serpents, and snake reliefs.

Zapotecs, ancient Mexican culture (*ca.* 300-1000), built pyramid temples, palaces, and catacombs in religious centers of Monte Alban and Mitla.

TERRA-COTTA
FIGURES (MAYAN)

STELA
WITH FIGURES
IN RELIEF,
COPAN
(MAYAN)

FEATHERED SERPENT, PYRAMID TO
QUETZALCOATL (AZTEC)

SCULPTURE

ASIA · *China*

Cave Temples. Important for their sculpture, rather than as works of architecture; **Yün-Kang,** near Shansi (*ca.* 490), considered a "Wonder of the Eastern World," is the work of thousands of sculptors and stonemasons; 20 large and 20 smaller caves included there; **Mai Chi Shan** (Mountain of the Hay Stack), has 200 chambers; **Gallery of Buddhas** (258 figures arranged in rows along the face of the mountain) carved during Wei dynasty (4th to 6th Century); **Tun-huang,** oldest and largest complex of caves extant in China, known as Ch'ien-fo-tung (Cave of the Thousand Buddhas) or Mo-kao-k'u; 20 miles southwest of Tun-huang, on north bank of the Tang River is **Hsi Ch'ien-fo-tung** (Western Cave of the Thousand Buddhas); others include Yü-lin-k'u, T'ien-t'i-shan, Yung-ching, Mai-chi-shan, Lo-han-tung

COLOSSAL BUDDHA AND ATTENDANT, YÜN-KANG, CAVE XX, NORTHERN WEI PERIOD

(Cave of the Lohans Kansu), Wang-chia-k'ou, Wan-fo-tung, T'ien-lung-shan, Wu-t'ai-shan (Mount Wutai).

Tang Period (618-907). Two types of early funerary sculpture: unglazed and decorated with motifs in cold painting and use of well-known three-color (green, yellow, brown) glaze of T'ang ceramics; showed highly developed technique, powerful realism; common to place 12 standing figures in grave with heads of animals of Zodiac; superb horses and camels, usually in pairs; six horses of Emperor T'ai Tsung (649) outstanding examples of this type of sculpture. Buddhist figures of the 7th century were modeled in the round, worldly, vigorous, with little spirituality; Bodhisattva, Kwan Yin, assumed a feminine form in this period and became the popular Goddess of Mercy; beautiful rounded form and free-flowing drapery; exquisite jade and lacquer work.

India

Descent of the Ganges, supreme achievement; rock sculpture (80 ft. long, 30 ft. high); freestanding sculpture included eight-armed Sivas, Tri-murti (three-headed) Sivas, the Kail-asha Temple, Elephanta Rock Temple on an island near Bombay, and the *Stone Deer* at Mamallapuram; all are examples of the exceptionally fine Hindu sculpture of this period.

Japan

Tori. *fl.* 7th century. Great Busshi (master sculptor) from Korea, imported by Asuka rulers (552-673) to cast the principal bronzes for the Kondo (Golden Hall) at Hōryūji, Nara; responsible for the *Shaka Trinity*

(623) and possibly the *Yakushi* figure (607); established Buddhist style popular in Northern Wei dynasty of China; Tori's technique one of many popular styles, but he was most influential.

Yamaguchi-no-Oguchi-no-Atai. *fl.* mid-7th century. Sculptor referred to in the *Nihon Shoki* and credited with one or more of the *Four Guardians* of the Hōryūji; believed to have been ordered (by Emperor Kotoku) to carve 1,000 images of Buddha.

Great Buddhas erected; enormous *Todaiji* or *Daibutsu* at Nara (752); sculptors worked with clay, bronze, wood, dry lacquer; *kanshitsu* (lacquer and cloth) technique introduced (*ca.* 665); sculpture of 9th century mostly of wood; soft, sensuous figures of solemn dignity.

Java

Durga of Candi Singasari, huge Brahman sculptures; Java has some of the finest examples of Buddhist and Hindu sculpture and architecture.

AMERICAS · Maya

Early Mayan lintel (*ca.* 400) at Piedras Negras, Guatemala, considered one of the finest mural sculptures in ancient American art; amazing foreshortening of figures; apparent knowledge of anatomy; realism in composition.

Peru

Gateway of the Sun, 10-ft. monolith decorated in symbolic and highly stylized relief found in ruins of Tiahuanaco in the Andes.

PAINTING

ASIA · China

Important wall paintings in caves of Tun-huang; oldest painted during Wei period (520-24); tempera medium used (no frescoes); glorified Buddha, provided magnificent record of Chinese art from 6th to early 8th centuries; little other contemporary painting has survived; scroll-like compositions dominate period; decorative, high level of achievement in art of illustration.

Wu Tao-tse (Tao-tzŭ or Tao-hsüan). 700-770. Greatest T'ang artist; unsurpassed in Buddhist historical and portrait painting; most important work more than 300 paintings on walls of temples and palaces of Ch'ang-an, Loyang; changed whole conception of landscape painting with use of free bold strokes; monochromes.

Yen Li-pên. *ca.* 600-73. Celebrated early T'ang artist; credited with painting famous horizontal silk scroll *Portraits of the Emperors.*

Li Ssu-hsun. 651-716. Noted landscape artist; regarded finest colorist of period; precise, careful handling; realism, use of brilliant greens and blues; son, Li Chao-tao (*ca.* 675-730), also first-rate artist.

Wang Wei. 699-759. Founder of Southern School of landscape painting; first artist to vary from tradition; expressionist; superior monochrome landscape painting in "broken ink" (p'o-mo) technique.

Huang Ch'üan. *fl.* 10th century. Leader of Szechuan group; flower and bird painters; originated "boneless method" of painting, use of color without outlining beforehand; influenced Sung painters.

Chang Seng-yu. fl. first half 6th century. Worked at Nanking; *The Five Planets and Twenty-four Constellations* attributed to him.

Tung Yüan. *fl.* late 10th century. Artist of Five Dynasty period; celebrated for ability to create atmosphere and limitless space; *Clear Weather in the Valley*, well-known work.

Li Ch'eng d. 967. Perfected Southern school of landscape; bold, free style; first to emphasize old, gnarled, grotesque pine trees in foreground; *Angling from Skiff amid Snowy Trees.*

Chü-jan. *fl.* late 10th century. Monk painter; distinctive landscape style of Southern school; strong contrasts; rich, vigorous effects; excellent, precise technique; known also for official murals.

Han Kan. *ca.* 720-80. Famous painter of horses.

Chang Hsüan. *fl.* 713-42. Court painter; famed for *Silk Beaters* or *Women Preparing Silk*; skilful grouping of figures; grandeur of style.

Hsieh Ho. *fl. ca.* 500. Painter; formulated *Six Principles*; important criticism.

Japan

Very few works extant; paintings of mystic sects pictured deities; grim, powerful figures of Five Great Myo-o; during Heian period, elegant court life inspired invention of *Yamato-e;* secular style of exquisite dignity and grace; almost purely native in technique; usually mounted as *emakimono* (picture scrolls).

EUROPE

Religious, particularly biblical, subjects were the basis of medieval art. There were also illustrations of the lives of saints. Illuminated manuscripts

GOSPELS OF
ST. GAUZELIN,
COVER
(CAROLINGIAN)

—Bibles, psalters (Book of Psalms), and missals—were of greatest importance (only a small number of panel pictures survive); flat, pure color and gold were most popular; a heavy black line was drawn around the figure to separate it from the gold background (usually laid on around the areas to be painted); tempera was the medium used for panel paintings (possibly mixed with oil) and applied to a smooth plaster ground (sometimes a gold ground was used).

British Isles

Irish monasteries, in order to spread the Gospel, developed the Hiberno-Saxon style, that combined Celtic and Germanic elements; the *Gospel Book of Durrow* (Dublin) is considered the earliest example of Hiberno-Saxon illumination and is generally dated about the second half of the 7th century: the famed Northumbrian

ARDAGH GOLD CHALICE WITH BRONZE,
GILT AND ENAMEL, DUBLIN

(near Durham) manuscript, the *Lindisfarne Gospels* (written by Eadfrith, 698-721) shows an advanced, imaginative, complex, decorative style; illuminated copies of the *Ecclesiastical History of the English Nation* (731) by the monk, Venerable Bede, were probably done at Canterbury in the late 8th century; certainly the best-known manuscript of the period is the Irish *Book of Kells* (760-820).

France

The Court of Charlemagne (Carolingian Period). One of the earliest manuscripts of this group was the *Godescalc Gospels* (781-83); the *Gospel Book of Charlemagne* (*ca.* 800-10), and probably the most influential single work of the period, the *Utrecht Psalter* (*ca.* 820-32), produced at Rheims; pen-and-ink drawings were used instead of painted illustrations; the *Gospels of St. Médard* of Soissons; the small *Psalter of Dagulf* presented by Charlemagne to Pope Adrian I are others of this group.

Under the brilliant patronage of Charles the Bald (West Frankish King, 843-77), book illumination (*Psalter, Book of Hours* and *Codex Aureus*), ivory carving and metalwork flourished

in northwestern France toward the middle of the 9th century; famous reliquaries; golden altar of Milan; covers of great manuscripts and decorative secular pieces were outstanding.

The most important work done in the territory of the East Franks (now southern Germany) was by the **Ada Group** (named for the half-sister of Charlemagne who commissioned an important manuscript), and at the scriptoriums of the monasteries of Fulda and St. Gall.

Others: Gospel Book of Archbishop of Rheims, the *Ebbo Gospels* (816-35); *Bible of Moutier-Grandval* (*ca.* 840); *Vivian Bible* (846) at Tours; *Gospels of Francis II* made by Franco-Saxon school (possibly at St. Amand near Tournai); *Paris Psalter* (*ca.* 900), leading example of the work of the so-called Second Golden Age, used late classical motifs.

THE NATIVITY
(DETAIL), MOSAIC,
ROME

Spain

Beatus of Leibana. *fl.* 786. Monk; famous for *Commentary on the Apocalypse;* flat illustrations; angular, rigid figures, more ornamental than realistic.

BYZANTINE

Lavish use of gold; brilliant color; mosaic quality; *Rabula Gospel,* northern Mesopotamia; *Etchmiadzin Gospel,* northern Armenia (6th century); *Sinope Gospel; Vienna Genesis* (9th century); *Joshua Roll* (Vatican); *Codex Purpureus* (6th century).

ISLAM · *Mosaics*

Great Mosque, Damascus, Syria (705-11). Important introduction of architectural theme; no human figures or animals show; buildings appear either in small groups or within landscape settings; large panoramic scene on west wall of portico presents a river landscape showing Hippodrome and village; palace pavilion, private home, and gateway are subjects on inside of west portico of the courtyard.

Khirbat al Mafjar, Jordan (724-43). Geometric designs in Roman-Byzantine tradition, although richer and more varied, dominate mosaics; decorating the raised apse of the audience chamber of a large bathhouse was one figural mosaic; on floors were found *Tree with Animal Scenes* executed by Syrian masters.

Frescoes

Qusayr 'Amra, Jordan (*ca.* 724-43); an Umayyad bath and mansion were discovered (1898) with frescoes that show an unusual variety of subjects: hunting scenes, athletes, wrestling matches, many nude women and family groups; Greek mythological personifications of Speculation, History, and Poetry were surprising find; animals better drawn than humans.

Qasr al-Hayr al-Gharbî, Syria (*ca.* 730). Two large frescoes, *Gaea and Marine Centaurs* and *Musicians and Hunting Cavalier* show new interest in, and influence of, the East.

SWIMMERS (DETAIL) CAVE OF THE NAVIGATOR, KIZIL, TURKEY

Jawsaq Palace, Samarra (838-83). In city founded by the son of Hârûn al-Rashîd, paintings were found in the palace, especially in the harem; one, an elaborate acanthus scroll, with animals and human figures, is late version of favorite Roman theme; most show East Hellenistic style, dominantly Sassanian Iran; lack of expression and individual features, concentration on bodily volume and form; many hunting scenes.

Manuscript

Treatise on the Fixed Stars (Kitâb Suwar al-Kawâkib ath-Thâbita) written by the Persian, 'Abd-ar-Rahmân as-Sûfî, on constellations (*ca.* 965); illustrations very Oriental in quality; fine line drawings and calligraphy.

93

MUSIC

EUROPE

Monasteries, founded by Pope Sixtus (432-40) and Leo the Great (440-61), trained singers (and choirs); as the liturgy became more complicated and elaborate, and the repertory increased, congregational singing declined, the training of adequate singers became more difficult; as there was as yet no printed music, melodies were taught aurally and had to be memorized.

Gregorian chant introduced into England, Spain, France (Franks), and Germany; *Antiphonarius canto,* great collection of ancient ecclesiastical music, 600 compositions; by the 11th century, Gregorian music became the universal language of the Roman Catholic Church.

St. Gregory, the Great. 540-604. (Pope of Rome, 590-604). Credited with the reform of liturgical music and the compilation and editing of plain-songs or chants; placed the *scola cantorum* on a permanent basis in Rome; sent teachers and singers all over Europe; the Benedictine, St. Augustine, was sent (597) with 40 monks to the British Isles; converted Druids to Christian faith, sang hymns; Gregory, however, condemned the worldly or secular arts.

Odo (Hoger of Werden), Abbot of Cluny. 927-42. Important teacher and composer; devised earliest effective system of notation; assigned letters to tones arranged in orderly progression; fostered choral music; author of *Dialogus de musica* (notation enabled music to be recorded and eliminated necessity of learning chants by rote)

and *Musica enchiriadis* (*Handbook of Music*) that established the *organum* and *diaphonia* (see Glossary).

Alcuin, Abbot of Tours (796-804). English prelate; leader of foremost school of Carolingian period; arranged the scales into the Ecclesiastical or Church Modes; extremely influential as head of Charlemagne's palace school.

Rhabanus Maurus, a German monk, thought to be the composer of *Veni Creator Spiritus,* famous hymn of the 9th century.

BYZANTINE

Music predominantly vocal; neumatic musical notation system; use of *neumes* (signs); indicated rise and fall of singing voices in chants; did not indicate exact pitch; foundation of music of Eastern Christendom; parallel to Gregorian music.

St. John of Damascus, *ca.* 700-54. Master of *canones;* great composer of hymns; organized liturgical song; reformed musical notation.

St. Andreas, Archbishop of Crete. *ca.* 620-700. Credited with the invention of *canones.*

ASIA · *China*

Shen Yüeh. 441-513. Poet; first to classify the tones of Chinese speech and use them, apart from words, as the basis of music as a separate art form.

General. A dual system of notation used (*neumes of p'ing tse* system); in primary tonal patterns, a balance between yang (masculine) and yin (feminine) elements was maintained;

various types of melodic movement were contained within four principal *neumes*.

During T'ang dynasty (618-906) the festival orchestra was used for large state celebrations; thousands of musicians played 300 different instruments; **Pear Garden School** established for musicians, actors, dancers; music an integral part of the plays; used to accompany rhythmic gestures and dances; occasionally themes expressed mood, as in Western opera.

ISLAM

Earliest treatises on music written in the 8th century; ban on instrumental music lifted by caliphs from middle of 7th century; reached high point under Hârûn al-Rashîd (786-809); music schools established in Spain by Moors that rivaled those of Baghdad; **al-Farâbi** (870-950) wrote important musical treatises; melody of Arabic-Persian song based on *maqam* or mode similar to Hindu *raga*; music sad, plaintive; adoption of Persian instruments.

THEATER

ASIA · *India*

Kalidasa. *ca.* 400-455. Great Sanskrit poet and dramatist; famous for *The Recognition of Sakuntala*, outstanding for its excellent characterization, superior plot construction; contained both prose and verse and a commonly used prologue; also wrote *Urvasi, Malavika,* and *Agnimitra*.

Shudraka, King. *fl.* 5th century. Recognized as the author of *Mrichchakatika* (*Little Clay Cart*), sometimes called *Vasantasena;* light touch, subtle humor and somewhat melodramatic; appreciated by Westerners and often considered the most dramatic of Indian plays; written in ten acts, it is characteristically long.

Harsa (Harsadeva), King. Ruled Kansuj (606-47). Wrote plays on religious and secular subjects including *Nagananda, Mahaviracharita,* and *Uttararamacharita,* based on the deeds of Rama; the love story, *Malatimadhava;* unusual ability to portray heroic dignity and create an atmosphere of solitude and sorrow.

Visakhadatta, Prince. *fl.* 8th century. Political theme used in *Minister's Signet Ring,* only surviving play.

China

The T'ang dynasty was the classical period in Chinese theater; production of many historical plays, based on concepts of ancestor worship; *History of the Three Kingdoms, Strategy of an Unguarded City,* popular examples of the genre.

This period saw the use of sumptuous costumes, elaborately embroidered backdrops or curtains, the use of few stage properties, colorful make-up that had symbolic meaning and the establishment of a form of elegant drama that remained unchanged for centuries.

EUROPE · *Liturgical Drama*

Continuation of (or addition to) religious rites (as in Greece); readings of the Gospels in dialogue, interspersed with hymns and responses by the choir,

95

created dramatic effect of the Mass; stories of the Advent and the Resurrection enacted by the priests on altar steps; additional spoken parts were added at feast days; Latin, language of the Church, also used in drama.

Medieval theater developed from above; used a series of platforms or small structures, that indicated various localities mentioned in the play, and the space between was the acting area; the audience and the actors mingled during the performance.

Germany

Hrostwitha (Roswitha). *ca.* 935-1000. Benedictine nun; convent of Gandersheim; six short plays modeled on Terence; mixture of tragedy and comedy; *Dulcitus,* story of martyrdom of Christian maidens, typical example; also wrote *Abraham, Callimachus, Fides et Spes Gallicanus,* and *Phaphnutius;* wrote poetical chronicles of Otto I; unusual in that she produced comic scenes at a time when only liturgical dramas were performed.

1000-1300

Romanesque art, that centered in the church and the monasteries, developed under feudalism. Monastic life made for a centralized system of artistic activity in which architects, artists, sculptors, builders, and craftsmen worked together. It was an age of anonymity and group effort.

Romanesque was the first truly European style, having evolved slowly through contact with Byzantium and the Orient. The Crusades had fostered the flowering of art through trade, and artists were influenced by the sacred images of the Eastern Church.

Romanesque painting, with its abstract and rigid formalism approaching the stiffness of Egyptian reliefs, was centered in the churches where it adorned the walls and illuminated manuscripts.

In the second half of the 12th century Romanesque art gave way to the Gothic. The gradual disappearance of wall surfaces, as the Gothic style of church building developed, saw the rise of the art of stained glass. The figures were two-dimensional and formal and, with the abstract patterns of their borders, blended perfectly into their architectural setting.

PAINTING

EUROPE

Bayeux Tapestry. 1073-83. Under the direction of Bishop Odo of Bayeux, it is generally believed to have been

BATTLE OF HASTINGS (DETAIL)
BAYEUX TAPESTRY

STAINED GLASS WINDOW, GERMAN

embroidered (wool thread on linen strip 230 ft. long by 20 in. wide) in an English workshop in Canterbury; an eloquent pictorial document, on a rare secular subject, it depicts the Norman Conquest of England by William the Conqueror (Battle of Hastings, 1066); for centuries it was shown at the Feast of Relics at the Bayeux Cathedral (Normandy).

Stained Glass Windows. Achieved radiant effects by prismatic transformation and combination of light and color; introduction of new secular themes in

ST. MATTHEW, HABAKKUK, STAINED GLASS
WINDOW, BOURGES

illuminated manuscripts enhanced the technique that developed as an art by the second half of the 12th century; allied to the art of mosaics, it replaced mural and ceiling painting; abstract two-dimensional design; 175 panels at Chartres; rose windows of Chartres, Rheims, and Notre Dame, Paris are exceptional examples.

Illuminated Manuscripts. Outstanding work done by monastic orders; Cluniac copyists and illuminators leaders in the art.

England

Decided change in the style of the illuminated manuscript in the first half of the 12th century, showing a definite tendency toward the monumentality of the Romanesque; first appear in a manuscript known as the *Albani Psalter* (1119-46) at the Abbey of St. Albans; beautifully illustrated calendar pictures, a fine *Beatus* initial and others introducing important psalms; 46 pages of life of Christ and lives of the saints; it is thought that three different artists worked on this psalter.

Dover Bible (12th century). This Canterbury manuscript was in two volumes; painted (miniature technique), not colored outlines; the figures are large with a feeling of powerful movement.

Bible of Cathedral Library, Winchester; most important manuscript of period; six distinct masters worked on this masterpiece.

Ramsey Abbey Psalter, Huntingdonshire (*ca.* 1285-1300); excellent illustration of Thomas à Becket story.

Other Manuscripts. *Gospel of Otto III*, Reichenau School, Germany; *Exultet Rolls* produced in Benedictine monastery of Monte Cassino in southern Italy; *Psalter of Saint Louis* (1256), France.

Frescoes. Best example from Santa Maria de Mur, Spain (now in Boston Museum); painted *al secco*; Christ in majesty within *mandorla*; disciples painted life-sized; influence of Byzantine style apparent; brilliant use of red, ocher, black, and cobalt blue.

Italy

Cimabue, Giovanni (Cenni di Pepo). 1240-*ca.* 1302. Florentine master; painter, mosaicist; work transition from formalized Byzantine style to freer expression of Giotto (his pupil) and followers; introduced natural treatment of heads and faces; influenced Duccio; work shows power of mystical conception; *Virgin Enthroned, Madonna with Angels* (Assisi), and *Crucifixion*.

Berlinghieri, Bonaventura. 1228-74. Tuscan artist; famous for studies of St. Francis, church at Pescia (1235); scenes of *St. Francis Receiving the Stigmata* and *Preaching to the Birds*;

CRUCIFIX, PAINTED WOOD, CIMABUE, FLORENCE

unusual power and expressiveness of figures; bounded by lines, located in space, more illusion than reality; powerful color and line evidence of Byzantine influence.

ASIA · *China*

Founding of the *wen-jen* (literary-scholar) movement, late 11th century; creative imagination of the painter emphasized; period of the great calligraphers and "painting for pleasure" by cultivated persons; importance of spontaneous expression, the use of free-flowing strokes, and the creation of the "playing-with-ink" technique; subjects called "Four Gentlemen"—bamboo, plum blossom, orchid, and chrysanthemum.

Li Lung-mien (Li Kung-lin). 1040-1106. Last of great T'ang figure painters; excelled in use of monochrome and "floating cloud" techniques; *Gathering of Scholars in Western Garden*,

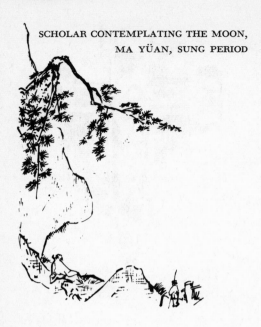

SCHOLAR CONTEMPLATING THE MOON, MA YÜAN, SUNG PERIOD

landscape painter; dramatic use of space; powerful line; scroll, *The Four Greybeards*, distinctive, intricate brushwork; influenced Japanese.

Chao Mêng-fu. 1254-1322. Academic court painter to Kublai Khan; calligrapher, painter of horses, landscapes, monochrome scrolls.

HORSES CROSSING A RIVER, CHAO MÊNG-FU

Ceylon

Most important collection of 12th-century painting is preserved in shrines at Polonnaruwa, second capital of the country.

AMERICAS · *Maya*

Three Mayan codices (illuminated manuscripts) exist: the *Dresden*, which is the best, the *Peresianus*, and the *Tro-Cortesianus*; frescoes of Chichen Itza a rare attempt to portray either a crowd of people or everyday activities; little knowledge of perspective, stiff handling of clothing or drapery; emphasis on serpent, two-headed dragon, long-nosed god, jaguar, Quetzal bird in design.

Japan

Takanobu, Fujiwara-no. 1142-1205. Portrait artist, Kamakura period; portrait of *Minamoto-no-Yoritomo*, masterpiece of early historical paintings; dignity, realism.

best-known work; most famous name in the art of Northern Sung, as the perfect representation of Chinese culture.

Su Tung-p'o (Su Shih). 1063-1101. Considered foremost Sung calligrapher, poet; led *wen-jen* group in stressing *li* (inner spirit) of subject; known as "The Gay Genius" (biography by Lin Yutang).

Mi Fei (Mi Fu). 1052-1107. Leader of *wen-jen* group; outstanding painter, calligrapher of Southern school; highly individualistic, brilliant, imaginative; impressionistic style creating "pointillist" effect with splashes of ink, later known as Mi dot.

Hsia Kuei. *fl.* 1190-1225. Distinguished landscape painter; restrained, delicate brush strokes; academician; *Clear View over Rivers and Mountains, Landscape in a Rainstorm* among many works.

Ma Yüan. *fl. ca.* 1190-1225. Sung

DETAIL FROM CHOJU GIGA SCROLL,
ATTRIBUTED TO TOBA SOJO

Toba Sojo (Kakuyu). 1053-1140. Priest-painter; founder of caricature art in Japan; credited with famed *Choju Giga* (Scroll of Animals), set of four scrolls of frolicking monkeys, hares, and other animals behaving like human beings.

Mitsunaga, Tokiwa. *fl.* second half of 12th century. Master court painter; *Tomo-no-Dainagon*, three scrolls, his masterpiece.

Fujiwara Takayoshi. *fl. ca.* 1120. Illustrated Lady Murasaki's *Tale of Genji* and *Nikki* (Diary).

India

Illuminated manuscripts: Buddhist, and a few Hindu, at Bengal, Bihar, and Nepal; Jain of Western India; and at Orissa, followers of Krishna; many palm-leaf, birch-bark, and paper manuscripts in great library collections; earliest illuminations (1100), decorative panels; later manuscripts have figures; drawing in black outlines, colors are strong; use of yellow, green, crimson, some blue, and black; red, most popular background color; figure drawing resembles that in Jain caves at Ellora and sculpture of period.

At Tanjore the Chola worshipers of Shiva decorated the temple built by the great Rajaraja I; paintings exe-

cuted on very fine lime plaster applied to stone walls; gum tempera technique.

ISLAM · *Arab-Muslim*

al-Wâsitî, Yahya ibn Mahmûd. *fl.* 1237. Famed artist from Wâsit in southern Iraq; illustrated the *Maqâmât* (Assemblies); known as the "Schefer Harîrî" manuscript.

Badr ad-Dîn ibn 'Abd Allâh. *fl. ca.* 1218-19. One of the artists who illustrated *Book of Songs* (Kitâb al-Aghânî) probably in northern Iraq; magnificent treatment of *Enthroned Ruler with Attendants.*

Manuscripts: *Maqâmât* (Assemblies) of **al-Harîrî** (1054-1122) illustrated by Syrian artist (1222); popular work; art shows so-called Hellenistic influence; main character Abu Zayd, sage made to appear like Byzantine Christ; architectural backgrounds; use of gold.

The Choicest Maxims and Best Sayings (Mukhtâr al-Hikam wa-Mahâsin al-Kalim) of **al-Mubashshir** (11th century), probably illustrated first half 13th century by Syrian artist; sages shown in Arab-Muslim dress; figures skilfully placed within geometric framework, unusual concern for plastic quality of figures and movement showing similarity to Romanesque missals; rarely has Arab-Muslim artist shown such vitality and spiritual quality.

Book of Antidotes (Kitâb ad-Kiryâq), written in 1199, probably illustrated by Northern Iraqi artist (13th century); new realism apparent; scenes based on accurate observation; interest in medicine, agriculture.

Kalîla and Dumna (1200-20), famous animal book of fables; Arabic version of much older Indian collection, translated by **Ibn al-Muqaffa** (d. 759); illustrated (probably by Syrian) with miniatures arranged in simple, balanced compositions, usually with an animal on either side of an axis, usually a tree, in definite heraldic fashion; main characters are two jackals.

Dioscorides' *De Materia Medica* (1229), in the Topkapu Sarayi Müzesi in Istanbul; artist from Northern Iraq or Syria; figures on gold within arched frame; most figures of teachers (either Greek or Muslim) and students; important plant drawings; another edition, written (1083) and illustrated (1224) in Baghdad, Iraq (now in Met. Mus. and Freer, Washington); human figures are added to show use of medicinal herbs; unique in its decorative charm and genre paintings.

CHRIST, DETAIL OF THE DEESIS, MOSAIC, HAGIA SOPHIA

iental influence evident in well-balanced, powerfully moving figures.

SCULPTURE

EUROPE

Romanesque

Superb sculptural capitals, relief compositions, including the *tympanum* over the central portal of the Abbey Church of Ste. Madeleine at Vézelay, France; vitality shown in *trumeau* (central post) between the wide double doors.

The high point of Romanesque sculpture was reached in the magnificent figures on the west portal of Chartres Cathedral (completed 1145); the central portal contains a *Majestas Domini* (Christ seated in a *mandorla*); combination Celtic, Classical, and Or-

JAMB STATUES, CHARTRES CATHEDRAL

Germany

Outstanding examples of Romanesque sculpture are the bronze doors (1007-15) and candlestick (1022-38)

cast for Bishop Bernward of Hildes-
heim, Lower Saxony; doors cast solidly
rather than in separate panels later
attached to wood; biblical subjects; influenced by the *Psalter of Utrecht* and
miniatures of the School of Echter-
nach; interweave of figures seen in
later Gothic figures.

France

By the end of the 11th century, a
monumental sculpture was introduced
by the school of Languedoc (West
Frankish territory); leading examples
can be seen on the portals of St. Pierre
of Moissac and the figure of *Isaiah* at
the Church of Notre Dame, at Souillac
(12th century).

Poland

One of the best examples of Eastern
European metalwork is the huge
bronze door of the Gniezno Cathedral
(*ca.* 1129); the two wings contain 18
reliefs in fine detail, representing the
life of St. Adalbert, patron saint of
Poland; bas-reliefs are framed by floral
designs intertwined with animal and
human forms.

Gothic
France

Iconographic carving in depth; 2,000
figures on exterior of Chartres; vigorous naturalism seen in *trumeau* at
Amiens; *Annunciation* and *Visitation*
on west portals, Rheims Cathedral (*ca.*
1225-45).

Italy

Pisano, Nicola (Niccolò). *ca.* 1205-
78. Considered first great Italian sculptor to combine Gothic and classic
forms; famed architect; marble pulpit
for baptistery in Pisa, first great work;
designed Perugian fountain.

Pisano, Giovanni. *ca.* 1245-*ca.* 1320.
Worked with father, Nicola (above);
masterpiece, the pulpit for Saint Andrea, Pistoia (1298-1301); architect,
Pisa (*ca.* 1278) and Siena (1284-89).

Antelami, Benedetto. *ca.* 1150-*ca.*
1230. Considered greatest Italian Romanesque sculptor; earliest-known relief, *Deposition* for the Cathedral of
Parma (1178); strong movement,
originality, and strength of conception;
influenced by French provençal sculpture; exceptional work for the Baptistery of Parma (which he also designed,
1196); not as competent as an architect.

Arnolfo Di Cambio. *ca.* 1245-before
1310. Sculptor, architect; student of
Nicola Pisano; statue of *Charles of An-
jou* as Roman senator; monument of
Cardinal de Braye in Orvieto; *Boniface
VIII*; façade of Cathedral of Florence.

Germany

Nicholas of Verdun. *fl.* 12 century.
Goldsmith from Lorraine; responsible
for base of altar of Kloster Neuberg;
worked on Anno shrine in parish
church of Sieburg (1183), Albinus
shrine, St. Pantaleon, Cologne (1186).
Magnificent sculpture on portals of
Strasbourg Cathedral (*ca.* 1220).

Others. Master Bartolomé (Spanish), Rogerus von Hemarshausen,
Master of Naumberg (German), William Toreel (England).

ASIA · *Japan*

Jōchō. *fl.* 1015-57. Leading sculptor;

CATHEDRAL FIGURES
WESTERN EUROPE

DEATH OF THE VIRGIN,
FAÇADE OF CATHEDRAL OF FLORENCE
ARNOLFO DI CAMBIO

CATHEDRAL FAÇADE,
ANTELAMI, FIDENZA, ITALY

PRESENTATION IN THE TEMPLE,
BAPTISTERY, PARMA, ANTELAMI

MADONNA AND CHILD,
PISANO,
PRATO CATHEDRAL

ABRAHAM AND MELCHIZEDEK,
REIMS CATHEDRAL, AFTER 1251

MARBLE PULPIT, PISANO, BAPTISTERY, PISA

ANGEL DRAWING A CURTAIN, DETAIL OF TOMB, ORVIETO

wood sculpture of 13th century; employed as court sculptor to Fujiwara no Michinaga; in early days worked on figures for Hōjōji; son, Kakujo, worked in Kyoto.

Unkei. 1180-1220. Great master of sculpture in polychrome wood; leader of Shichijo Bussho (Seventh Street Workshop); perfected multiple-block technique, adding theatrical effects; important influence on other sculptors.

MUCHAKU BOSATSU (HEAD) ATTRIBUTED TO UNKEI

KUYA SHŌNIN PREACHING, KAMAKURA PERIOD, KYOTO

known for Byodoin's *Amida* for Phoenix Hall, a unique balance of Chinese and Japanese styles; credited with improvement of multiple-block technique, responsible for development of

105

Kōkei. *fl.* 1175. *Daibusshi* (master sculptor); father of Unkei; famed work at temple of Enjōji, northeast of city of Nara; most famous statue, *Dainichi* (with son).

Tankei. d. 1256. Sculptor; oldest son of Unkei; member of Shichijo Bussho.

Kato Shirozaemon (also called Toshiro). 12th century. Studied in China; with others credited with invention of *Cha-No-Yu* (tea ceremony); known for beautiful ceramics.

Meien. Leader of Sanjo Bussho (Third Street Workshop) in Kyoto; traditionalist.

Raijo. Leader of Shichijo Bussho in early part of 12th century.

PRIEST MYO-E,
13TH CENTURY, JAPAN

China

Sculpture, having reached its zenith during the T'ang period, went into decline as seen, for example, in the *Great Buddha* of the K'ai-yuan-ssŭ (1036) near Li ch'eng; a period of magnificent ceramics; great pottery factory was established at Ching-Te-Chen by Emperor Chen Tsung (1000).

Cambodia

At Angkor Wat is the statue of the *Muchalinda Buddha;* the Great Naga or serpent was the supreme deity; Muchalinda was the Serpent King and when Buddha sat beneath the Tree of Muchalinda, the serpent (*naga*) coiled around the Buddha and the union became the Muchalinda Buddha (in Hindu legend the naga is called Vasuki and the god Vishnu); on the cloister (gallery), around the entire lower story of the great temple tomb, are reliefs in a continuous stone frieze (6 ft. high).

MAHĪSAMARDINI, FROM
TRIPURANTAKAM, INDIA

AMERICAS · *Maya*

Produced a type of decorated stele, erected at fixed intervals; complicated calendric symbols and religious figures carved on reliefs.

ARCHITECTURE

WESTERN EUROPE

Romanesque

Developed from Roman basilica; used principally in abbey churches of Italy and France; ornamentation added; wheel or rose windows illuminated the nave; importance of stone construction; introduction of Latin-cross plan; choir section enlarged.

Italy

Most brilliantly decorated church of the so-called Second Golden Age of Byzantine Art surviving today is *St. Mark's*, Venice (begun 1063); with the *Cathedral of Pisa* (1053-1100), with its red and white marble paneled fa-

LEANING TOWER OF PISA

SAN AMBROGIO, MILAN

CIBORIUM, S. MARIA IN COSMEDIN, COSMATI, ROME

çade, Baptistery, and famed Campanile (bell tower), known as the Leaning Tower of Pisa (1174-1272), we are introduced to the Tuscan Romanesque style; the advanced Lombard style is represented by *San Ambrogio*, Milan

(11th century); brick structure, major innovation use of ribbed groin vaults, higher in the center than at the transverse arches; impressive with its austere exterior design, massive piers, atrium, low squat nave and wide, domed cross-vaults; *San Michele*, Pavia (Tuscany) use of marble, single, very broad gable across top; *Modena Cathedral*, Lombard (Tuscany, 1099-1106); *San Zeno*, Verona, elegantly combines marble and reddish sandstone and rests the columns of its Lombard porch (in front of the portal) on the backs of lions; the *Palatine Chapel*, Palermo (1132-43), famous example of Norman architecture; columns and lavish wall mosaics purely Byzantine in style.

France

The Third Abbey Church at Cluny, rebuilt in the 11th century (High Altar consecrated, 1095) and early 12th century (destroyed during the French Revolution) was the most important Monastic Romanesque building of the period in Burgundy; five-aisled, many-windowed clerestory; highest contemporary barrel vaulting; first external flying buttresses; altar columns of unusual beauty; double-transept (influenced English), each with an octagonal tower over the crossing, and two eastern apses to each arm; 15 absidioles opening off transepts and ambulatory; other Burgundian churches were the Abbey Church (*La Madeleine*) at Vézelay (1120-32) and *St. Lazare Cathedral* at Autun; *Abbaye-aux-Hommes*, St.-Étienne, Caen, built by William the Conqueror, used half-barrel vaults over the aisle and represented the future development

CATHEDRAL OF NOTRE DAME, PARIS

ABBEY OF MONT-ST-MICHEL, FRANCE

by Normans of ribbed vault principle; *Abbaye-aux-Dames* (*La Trinité, ca.* 1065-80), Caen, neighboring church, used concealed flying buttress, foreshadowing pointed-arch principle; Corinthian capitals and barrel vaults are typical of the Provençe style as seen at *St. Trophême*, Arles, and *St. Gilles*, Gard, which are also noted for their magnificent western portals; the five-aisled, barrel-vaulted church of *St.-Sernin*, Toulouse (*ca.* 1080-1120) has superb exterior design; *Notre Dame-la-Grande*, Poitiers; *Cathedral at Angoulême*; in Ile de France, small Romanesque churches, such as *St.-Etienne*, Beauvais, had advanced vaulting that foreshadowed the Gothic.

England

Norman style adopted; *Winchester Cathedral* (*ca.* 1093), *Tower of London* (1078-1128), *Norwich* (1096-1140) and *Durham* (1093-1128) cathedrals; *Westminster Abbey* (Church of Peter the Apostle, 1056), *Iffley Parish Church*, Oxford (1160), *Peterborough Cathedral* (*ca.* 1140), all excellent examples of Romanesque English architecture.

SALISBURY CATHEDRAL

Germany

The imperial cathedral on the Rhine at Speier had the earliest large-scale groin vaults in medieval Europe; these vaults were an addition to a cathedral built (*ca.* 1030-60) with a flat timber ceiling; the abbey church of *Maria Laach* is the best-preserved of the German Romanesque churches including those at Mainz, Worms; the double church, Schwarzrheindorf (1149-51), with a transept 53 ft. long, closely approximates the height of the Viking

mast-church and is one of the earliest instances of the great central tower later used in English Gothic; there were also churches in Cologne, but they were destroyed during World War II.

Sweden

Cathedral of Lund (12th century) built of local sandstone in Rhenish style and the Church (formerly Cathedral) of *Gamla Uppsala* (13th century), were typical of German Romanesque stone structures with the added austerity of Northern expression.

Norway

Stave Church, Borgund, built (*ca.* 1150) entirely of timber; roofs and gables covered with cut shingles; nave and sanctuary, each with pinnacle, rise

STAVE CHURCH, NORWAY

above arcaded exterior porch, breaking into gables, finials, and spirelets; classic example of style.

Gothic

Gothic architecture saw the merging of interior and exterior design creating harmony and unity; important substitution of a pointed for a rounded arch helped achieve the quality of ver-

FLYING BUTTRESS, AMIENS CATHEDRAL

tical motion; crowns of individual vaults could be raised to equal heights; pointing and narrowing of arches allowed for changes in shapes; additional support, needed where the vault rested on the wall, was supplied by the use of the long, thin flying buttress (stone support) that bolstered the exterior of the building at various points; Gothic building broader with side chapels added; the spire is the highest expression of a sweep heavenward, which is representative of the Gothic mind and religious attitude.

France

Cathedrals: Notre Dame, Chartres (begun 1194), Rheims (rebuilt 1210), Amiens (1220-88), Notre-Dame, Paris (1163-1235), Rouen (begun 1200), Cologne (1248-1322), Dijon (13th century), St. Denis (1140-44), Sens (1140-64), Senlis (1153-91), Laon (begun 1160), Noyon (choir, 1157, nave, 1170), Beauvais (1247-72), upper church, Sainte Chapelle, Paris (1243-48), St.-Urbain, Troyes (1261-75), and Le Mans (end of 13th century).

England

Cathedrals: Wells (begun before 1191), Lincoln (1192-1233), Ely (1198), Bristol (begun 1298), Salisbury (1220-70), parts of York, Wells, and the choir and transept of Westminster Abbey (1245-70).

Spain

Cathedrals: León (begun 1199), Burgos (begun 1220), Toledo (started 1227).

Italy

St. Francis of Assisi (1228), Santa Croce, Florence (started 1294); secular building, the Palazzo Vecchio, Florence (1219-1301).

Germany

St. Elizabeth's, Marburg (started 1235).

MISTRA, ST. THEODORE, MARBURG, GERMANY

EASTERN EUROPE · *Russia*

Novgorod: Many churches had been constructed of wood, which was plentiful, and the builders were called by the Kievans "carpenters"; Vladimir, son of Yaroslav the Wise, rebuilt (1045-62); the Cathedral of Sancta Sophia (originally built in 988 of oak, it was burned in great fire, 1045); decorated by Greek artists with frescoes (rather than mosaics as Sancta Sophia, Kiev, 1015-37); in the 12th century, 41 churches erected and new materials were used; Church of St. Nicolas the Wonder-Worker (1113) built by Mstislav I in the courtyard of his palace; St. George (1119-30) in Yirev Monastery credited to "Master Peter" believed to be the first native architect; because of the problem of snow accumulation on the roofs of these northern churches, a new solution was found in a roof consisting of four equal gables surmounted by the central drum and dome; oldest church in Novgorod with gabled roof is the Church of the Annunciation on Lake Myachin. Other churches of the period worth noting included: Church of SS. Boris and Gleb, Kideksha (1152), Church of the Intercession of the Virgin on the Nerl, near Vladimir (1166), Prince Andrei Bogoliubski's Palace, Bogoliubovo (*ca.* 1160), Cathedral of the Dormition, Vladimir (1158-61, rebuilt 1185-89), Church of St. George, Yuriev-Polski (1229-34).

Kiev: Vladimir Monomakh built (989) the Cathedral of the Dormition of the Virgin known as the Desyatinnaya; Vladimir's son, Yaroslav the Wise (1017-57) commissioned the building of what is considered one of the greatest monumental religious structures in Russia, the Sancta Sophia (1015-37); departed from completely Byzantine prototype with its arrangement of 13 cupolas with low domes placed on high and narrow drums; interior higher and narrower, and the many piers, more massive than in Greece, appeared to break the interior space into many small compartments and to emphasize the vertical proportions.

Chernigov: The Church of the Transfiguration (founded 1017) was richly decorated with frescoes.

Greece

Two important churches built at the Monastery of Hosios Loukas, near Delphi (1000-1025).

ASIA · *Cambodia*

The Khmers built the great temple city of Angkor Thom at the end of the 12th century; the great temple of **Angkor Wat** was built by King Sūryavarman II (1113-50) as a monument to the Devaraja and its founder; an almost indescribable temple, it is an enormous stepped pyramid with terraced levels connected by galleries and staircases, magnificent sculptural ornamentation; during the reign of Jayavarman VII (founded new capital of Angkor Thom, 1181-1201), half the Khmer monuments were constructed; a great gem of Khmer architecture is the sanctuary of **Bantéai Srei** (ancient Iśvarapura), known as the "Citadel of Women"; three shrines dedicated to Siva; two temple libraries; voluptuous *Apsaras* ("divine dancers"), surrounded by foliage, form the greater part of the rococo decoration; the last Khmer building of any size built at Angkor was the **Bayon** (early 13th century), which was more a work of sculpture than architecture.

AMERICAS · *Toltec*

Capital at Tollan (site of modern Tula, north of Mexico City) had pyramids and temples; *Temple of the Morning Star* had caryatids and snake pillars; excellent street drainage system and many secular palaces; served as model for later Mayan and Aztec civilizations.

Maya

Yucatán cities of new Kingdom (after 1000) were at Chichén-Itzá, Uxmal, and Mayapán; palaces and other secular buildings predominated; *Temple of the Warriors* (El Castillo) at Chichén-Itzá had pillars shaped like plumed serpents; *Caracol* (observatory) at Chichén-Itzá, and nunnery at Uxmal were other important buildings.

MINARET OF JAMI AL-KABĪR (ABBASIDE) IRAQ

POLONNARUVA, KIRI VEHERA, DAGOBA, CEYLON

TEMPLE OF VISHNU, ANGKOR WAT

MUSIC

EUROPE · *Italy*

Guido d'Arezzo (Aretinus). *ca.* 980-1050. Benedictine monk; created foundation of modern system of musical notation; established four-line staff, using both lines and spaces; gave definite position to each scale degree; invented set of syllables to denote individual tones of scale; gave names to the six tones of the hexachord; credited with Guidonian hand, chart devised to make it easier to teach sight-reading; *Micrologus* (*ca.* 1025) principal source of early polyphonic music; extremely important.

Jacopone da Todi. *ca.* 1230-1306. Umbrian monk; known chiefly for lauda, *Stabat Mater Dolorosa*, that became part of the official liturgy of the Church.

France

Perotin (Perotinus, called Magnus Magister). *fl.* 1180-1236. Choirmaster, Notre Dame Cathedral; succeeded Léonin (*ca.* 1183); composer of *clausulae* (forerunner of motet), three *quadrupla* (*clausulae* in four parts), using long notes in tenor; improved notation.

Léonin (Leoninus). 12th century. Organist, choirmaster, Notre Dame, Paris; composer of great book of organum music; one of first to mark time values in music.

Cotton, John (Johannes Cotto). 1050-1130. Monk at Afflighem, near Brussels; author of important treatise on music; first to make use of contrary motion (English origin debated).

Germany

Hermannus Contractus. 1013-54. Musical theorist, composer; monk, trained at St. Gall; two important treatises, one on Greek modes and the other on new notation (intervals on staff); wrote hymns.

Secular Music
France

The great period of the *troubadours* of southern France; lyric poets (usually noblemen who were talented amateurs) combining poetry and music, composed new melodies to accompany

DETAIL FROM ILLUMINATED MANUSCRIPT

their verses of courtly love; the *trouvères* (troubadours of northern France) borrowed their melodies from the rich, informal music of the people; names of 460 troubadours and 200 *trouvères* are known; just to mention a few of the better-known ones: troubadours—William IX, Count of Poitiers, Duke of Aquitaine (1070-1127), Bernard de Ventadour (*fl.* 1150-94), Marcabrun (*fl. ca.* 1150–90), Peire Vidal (d. 1215); *trouvères*—Huon d'Oisy (d. *ca.* 1191) Blondel de Neslé (d. *ca.* 1203), Gace Brulé (d. *ca.* 1210).

Spain

The troubadours of Spain were called *trovadores* and were very popular; Alfonso the Wise, King of Castile and León (1221-84) was a poet and composer and encouraged music and song at his court.

Britain

The early Celtic Bards (priests)

known as *Druids*, played a crude harp known as a *crwth*; ancient contest, the Eisteddfod, revived in Wales.

Germany

Minnesingers. Counterpart of chivalric troubadours; songs of nature, patriotism, and religion more popular than songs of love; used no jongleurs and always sang their own compositions; lacking the freshness, light-heartedness of their French contemporaries, their music and song was heavier, although it often displayed humor; played viols and lutes; Tannhauser (1205-70) took part in a song contest (1260; opera by Wagner based on his life).

Walther von der Vogelwide. *ca.* 1170-1230. Famous minnesinger; versatile lyricist, artistry of utmost simplicity; *Love is Two Hearts' Happiness, The Times Are Out of Joint*, best-known songs.

Others. Jongleurs. Entertainers who accompanied troubadours and other performers; descended from mimus and ioculatores who followed Roman legions; appeared at court festivals as well as at the feasts of peasants and townspeople; took part in religious plays; sang, recited, fiddled, performed acrobatics and magic.

Minstrels. Most important secular musicians; poets of popular verse; spread songs of the troubadours; composed lays.

Goliards. Wandering students and the lesser clerics of England, France, and Germany who composed the Latin verse and songs that became an important source of the troubadours' art; they wrote graceful verse on classical and sacred subjects; they

parodied the Mass and caricatured public officials; their verse was sometimes elegant, occasionally obscene, and usually extremely skilfully written; knowledge, cleverness revealed new freedom of spirit, enjoyment of life; important in notation of secular music.

Chansons de gens (popular songs) was the music of the itinerant musician or minstrel who sang in the market places and private and public halls; as wanderers (travelers) they spread news in song; played a variety of instruments including the violin, gigue, gittern (early guitar), psaltery, regals, rote, organistrum, and the tabor. *Chanson de Roland*, songs about the victories of Charlemagne were very representative of the period.

THEATER

EUROPE · France

Probably the one play that fulfills the present-day conception of dramatic art that was presented in the medieval period was *Adam* (1147–74), based on the biblical character, and written in French by an Anglo-Norman in England.

A series of plays known as *Les miracles de Notre Dame* (The Miracle of Our Lady) were performed; each a separate entity presenting first the sins of the characters, and then in the second part the miracle or repentance; not generally realized is that the greater part of the play deals with secular and often comic matters.

Bodel, Jean. d. 1210. Author of half-religious, half-secular work, *Le jeu de*

Saint Nicolas (The Play of St. Nicholas, *ca.* 1205); mixes crusades and religious elements with scenes at an inn and comedy of everyday life.

Adam de la Halle (Adam de la Hale). *ca.* 1230-*ca.* 1287. Outstanding *trouvère*; wrote earliest comic opera *Le Jeu de Robin et Marion* and *Jeu de la feuillée* (The Play of the Greenwood) which mixes the real and the fantastic in an original, delightful way.

Rutebeuf. *ca.* 1230-*ca.* 1285. Writer of interesting *Le Miracle de Théophile* (The Miracle of Théophilus) which is the story of a man who gives his soul to the devil (early Faust).

Switzerland

First Passion Play in German verse performed at Muri Monastery (1250).

ASIA · *China*

A period of popular theater; the khans enjoying theatrical entertainment, encouraged the performance of plays, the writings of songs, and the development of the techniques of acting. One of the best plays of the period was *The Romance of the West Chamber* (*Hsi-hsiang-ki, ca.* 1260) in 16 scenes by Wang Shih-fu; the *Orphan of Chao* by Chi Chun-shiang (later adapted by Voltaire); *Dream of the Goldpieces* by K'iao Meng Fu; *Autumn in the Han Palace* by Ma Tung Li; *Pavilion on the Stream* by Kuan Han K'ing; *Rain under the Wutung* by Po Jen Fu, and *Joining the Shirt,* a four-act drama by Chang Kuo-pin, leading woman dramatist.

India

Ramakrishna of Gujarat (*fl.* 12th century). Noted author of *Gopalakelicandrika,* a well-known mystery play; performed as a shadow play recited to pantomime.

ISLAM · *Persia*

Shi'ite passion plays, puppet theater, and shadow plays were extremely popular during this period; performances of shadow plays showing scenes of camels marching through the desert, land battles with horsemen and foot soldiers, sailing ships with sailors climbing the masts, and fortresses besieged with machines, came very close to the action shown in the painted miniatures of the period. The shadow figures, sometimes the everyday people performing their usual activities, were made of multicolored hide, and were held against a white screen with a light focused on them from behind. The Turkish shadow figures were called *karagöz.*

CHINESE ACTOR IN COSTUME

1300-1450

Europe in the 14th and early 15th centuries was undergoing a period of great change. The feudal manor system was breaking down, and the rise of towns saw the land-owning aristocracy challenged by the power of the city merchants. The awakening of an interest in science, brought about by the flow of learning from the Orient through the Moslem world into Spain and on into the rest of Europe, saw the development in painting of three-dimensional form, the creation of linear perspective, and the experimentation with pyramidal construction. The growing resistance to papal demands by the rulers of the rising territorial states, and the Great Schism (1378-1417) dividing the Church between Rome and Avignon, seriously weakened the papacy. All this resulted in an increased secular emphasis.

This was also a period of great art patrons, including Philip the Good of Burgundy, sponsor of Jan van Eyck, the Duc de Berry, who commissioned a beautiful, secular illuminated Book of Hours, and the brilliant Medici family of Florence.

PAINTING

EUROPE · *Italy*

Giotto di Bondone. *ca.* 1267-1337. Great Florentine painter, architect, and sculptor. His rejection of the Italo-Byzantine style of his teacher, Cimabue, foreshadowed the Renaissance; introduced naturalism and individuality of interpretation that freed painting from the rigid conceptions of medieval art; the plastic qualities inherent in his work give an "earthbound" concrete feeling as opposed to the "other world" or abstract tone that dominated the works of his

LAMENTATION OVER CHRIST BY GIOTTO, ARENA CHAPEL

contemporaries; rediscovered art of creating illusion of depth on flat surfaces; strong definition of mass, sharp relief, and contours are sculptural in quality; greatest surviving works: fresco cycle in Arena (Scrovegni) Chapel, Padua; frescoes on life of St. Francis, Upper Church of St. Francis, Assisi, and in Bardi and Peruzzi chapels of Santa Croce, Florence.

Uccello, Paolo (real name di Dono, called Uccello which means love of birds). 1396-1475. Famous for superb battle scenes including three paintings of *The Battle of San Romano* (London, Florence, Paris; 1432 stylized version ·hung in Lorenzo de' Medici's bedroom); delightful, colorful *A Hunt* (Oxford); poetic, grandiose treatment of space, perspective; geometric design very modern in feeling.

Castagno, Andrea del. 1390-1437. Famed for over-life-sized portraits of Florentine scholars and warriors, revolutionary in spirit and the first of their kind; influenced the Venetians of the Paduan school, Mantegna and his followers; *Crucifixion*, fresco, Santa Apollonia Museum (Florence); *Young David* (Washington) shows statuesque grace; very personal style.

Lorenzo Monaco (Piero di Giovanni). *ca.* 1370-1425. Monk. Frescoes depicting life of Mary (1420-24); elongated figures in Gothic style with flowing decorative drapery; emphasis on vertical architectural background; *Adoration of the Magi* (1420-22, Uffizi); miniature painting in missal in Laurentian Library (1409); *Coronation of the Virgin*, magnificent altarpiece (London).

Maso di Banco. *fl.* early 14th century. Florentine artist; pupil of Giotto; dramatic, colorful works made him important early Renaissance painter; frescoes, *Miracles of St. Sylvester*, Church of St. Croce (Florence) and *Pietà* (Uffizi), two excellent extant works.

Duccio di Buoninsegna. *ca.* 1255-1319. First leading representative of the Sienese school; style perfection of Italo-Byzantine tradition; greatest work, *Maestà*, 92-panel altarpiece of the Cathedral (Opera del Duomo) of Siena (1308-11); strong, monumental form, abstract rather than realistic character dominates style; genius in lyric charm of interpretation, subdued yet luminous use of color, and careful design of draperies; *Madonna Rucellai* (*ca.* 1285), *The Calling of the Apostles Peter and Andrew*, other works.

Martini, Simone. 1283-1348. Leading artist of Sienese school; worked at papal court at Avignon (1339), greatly admired by friend Petrarch; best-

ROAD TO CALVARY BY SIMONE MARTINI

known work, portrait of *Guidoriccio da Fogliano*, fresco, Palazzo Pubblico, Florence, that commemorates the condottiere's victory over other nobles (1328); poetic quality, figure isolated in irregular architectural landscape; polyptych, *Annunciation* (with Lippo Memmi), *Crucifixion, Descent from the Cross* (Antwerp), *Way to Golgotha* (Louvre), *Pietà* (Berlin); *Madonna in Majesty* (1315) for Palazzo Consiglio, Siena; belongs to decorative

Gothic tradition; style admirably suited to interpret the aristocracy of Siena.

Lorenzetti, Pietro. *ca.* 1280-1348. Dramatic quality of work shows relationship to Giotto rather than others of Sienese school; most important frescoes in transept of lower church of San Francesco, Assisi; tragic poignancy of *Descent from the Cross* makes this work a masterpiece; importance of movement and action in work believed to show influence of sculptor Giovanni Pisano.

Lorenzetti, Ambrogio. *fl.* 1319-48. Known for unusual fresco series, unfortunately badly damaged, decorating the Sala dei Nove (Council of Nine, Palazzo Pubblico), Siena (1337-79), on sociological theme of good government; scenes of everyday life with obvious symbolic, propaganda subject matter; *Presentation in the Temple* (1342, Uffizi), *Annunciation* (1344, Siena); believed to have died (with brother Pietro) in plague of 1348.

Sassetta (Stefano di Giovanni). 1392-1450. Considered most influential of early Sienese painters; continued tradition of pictorial narrative and poetic sensitivity; aware of perspective and anatomy; sophisticated, poetic works; although he did not have the power of Duccio nor the intensity of Martini, his work had great charm and an individuality of atmosphere; intimate, direct style best suited to small works.

Masaccio (Tommaso di S. Giovanni of Valdarno). 1401-28/9. Epoch-making figure of Florentine art; through his monumental realism, use of newly-discovered laws of perspective, knowledge of human form, and naturalistic treatment of figures and landscapes led to critics' assessment that modern painting really began with this artist; *The Tribute Money*, considered masterpiece, and *Expulsion from Eden* (Brancacci Chapel), Church of Santa Maria del Carmine, Florence; *Madonna with St. Anne* (1424/25, Uffizi.)

Fra Angelico (Fra Giovanni da Fiesoli, born Guido di Pietro). *ca.* 1387-1455. Florentine master; although referred to as the "last of the Gothic painters," his style was based rather on the personal and mystical faith of the Renaissance than on the idealized and traditionally mannered religious theme of late Gothic art; color important in giving depth to image (beginning of understanding of three-dimensional form); *Annunciation*, Monastery of

ST. ANTHONY,
FROM POLYPTYCH
OF PERUGIA
BY FRA ANGELICO

San Marco, Florence (*ca.* 1440); *Virgin and Child with Angels* (London); *Coronation of the Virgin* (1434-35, Louvre).

Lippi, Fra Filippo (Lippo Lippi). *ca.* 1406–69. Carmelite painter of early

MADONNA
ENTHRONED
BY FRA FILIPPO LIPPI

Renaissance, Florence; influenced by Fra Angelico and Masaccio; outstanding work, great frescoes of *John the Baptist* and *St. Stephen*, Prato Cathedral, including scene, *Banquet of Herodias* that exemplifies boldness, use of light and color that point up freshness and spontaneity of Lippi's gay, graceful, narrative style that influenced his pupil, Botticelli.

Domenico Veneziano (Domenico di Bartolomeo da Venezia). *ca.* 1400-1461. Florentine; introduced the technique of finishing tempera works with an oil glaze; pioneered in representation of nude figure; most important work is altarpiece, Santa Lucia dei Bardi (Uffizi); light used to create illusion of space, for third-dimensional quality and decorative unity; *St. John in the Desert*, part of Predella of Santa Lucia (Washington); *Madonna with Saints*, frescoes in St. Croce, Florence; *Portrait of a Young Lady* (Met. Mus.).

Gaddi, Taddo. *ca.* 1300-*ca.* 1366. Florentine; assistant to teacher, Giotto; leading painter on death of master; fresco decoration of Baroncelli Chapel in Santa Croce, scenes of life of *Mary,* (1338) show interest in complicated architectural patterns; work more lyrical than Giotto's with more lively movement and use of realistic detail.

Starnina, Gherardo (Gherardo di Jacopo). 1354-1408. Pupil of Antonio Veneziano; fragments of his frescoes in the St. Jerome Chapel of Santa Maria del Carmine (1404) with new and individual characterization and movement of figures show his influence on Masolino and Masaccio.

Gentile da Fabriano. *ca.* 1370-*ca.* 1427. First great representative of the Umbrian school; considered an outstanding primitive; first Italian painter of landscape in modern sense; *Adoration of the King* (1423) showed his concept of his surrounding countryside; first differentiation between night and day; influenced Venetian painters.

Squarcione, Francesco. 1394-1474. Founder of Paduan school; important as teacher of northern Italian artists, including Mantegna.

Boccati, Giovanni. *ca.* 1420-*ca.* 1480. Considered first important artistic personality in Perugia; not founder of school, but early developer of local style; *Madonna Enthroned under a Rose Arbor* (1447) San Domenico, Perugia, chief work; closely akin to Fra Filippo Lippi in style.

Altichiero da Zevio. *ca.* 1320-*ca.* 1385. Venetian Gothic painter, follower of Giotto; founder and leader of school of Verona; fresco, Cavalli Chapel, Verona (1369); masterpiece, large *Cruci-fixion* at Padua; unusual treatment of space; color muted.

Giovanni di Paolo. 1402/3-*ca.* 1482. Sienese painter; highly imaginative, great vivacity; figures elongated; architectural stage set popular with artist who used arches and doorways to create interesting geometrical patterns as seen in *St. John in Prison*, part of polyptych, best-known work.

Andrea (Bonaiuti) **da Firenze.** *fl. ca.* 1343-77. Works strongly Sienese; frescoes in Spanish Chapel of Santa Maria Novella ranked most important work after Giotto's Arena Chapel; frescoes in Campo Santo, Pisa, (1377); late work more elaborate in decorative massing of figures, but weaker than work of contemporaries in Florence.

Pisanello (Antonio Pisano). 1395-1455. Veronese; much-traveled medalist, painter, draftsman; known for powerful animal and nature drawings; worked at court of Ferrara, painted excellent portrait of *Lionello d'Este* (*ca.* 1440); although famous in his own time as a portrait painter, valued more today as a medalist.

Orcagna (Andrea di Cione) *ca.* 1320-*ca.* 1368. Florentine; represents the sharp break with Giotto tradition; established more plastic as well as illusionistic style after middle of century; most important painting for altar of Strozzi Chapel in Santa Maria Novella (1354-57); also sculptor and architect.

Daddi, Bernardo. *fl.* 1327-55. Florentine; among founders of guild of St. Luke (1339); influenced Taddo Gaddi in greater interest in space and use of brighter color; frescoes, Chapel of Santa Croce; influenced by Giotto.

ADAM AND EVE, DETAIL FROM GHENT
ALTARPIECE BY VAN EYCK

Flemish

Eyck, Jan van. *ca.* 1380/90-1440/41.
A founder of the Flemish school; revolutionized craft of painting by the use of slow-drying oils as a medium; largely responsible for the transfer of interest from the medieval world of the illuminated manuscript to the panel picture; court painter to Philip the Good, Duke of Burgundy; served as diplomat; important portrait artist; *Giovanni Arnolfini and his Wife* (1434, London), *Portrait of Man in Red Turban* (1433), *Man with Carnation;* famed 12 panels of Ghent including *The Adoration of the Lamb; Annunciation* (Washington), *Madonna of the Nave* (Berlin); works show serenity and dignity; profound influence.

Eyck, Hubert van. *ca.* 1370-1426. Evidence of man and work in question; believed brother of above; possibility created miniatures in so-called *Turin Book of Hours;* credited with *Crucifixion* (Met. Mus.), *Crucified Christ* (Berlin).

Rogier van der Weyden. *ca.* 1400-1464. Master artist; successor to Jan van Eyck as leader of Flemish school; trained at Tournai, School of Robert Campin (Master of Flémalle, d. 1444); not influenced by visit to Italy; mystic; famed works: *Portrait of Francesco d'Este* (Met. Mus.), *The Annunciation* (*ca.* 1435, Louvre), *Descent from the Cross* (Prado), *Bladelin Altar* (1452,

CHRIST APPEARING TO HIS MOTHER,
ROGIER VAN DER WEYDEN

DESCENT FROM THE CROSS, ROGIER
VAN DER WEYDEN

Berlin); outlined features, achieving individual interpretation and characterization; influential.

Switzerland

Witz, Conrad *ca.* 1400-1447). Exceptional feeling for volume, painting of *Miraculous Draught* (Geneva) first truly realistic landscape; excellent panels extant of altarpiece, Basel (*ca.* 1435); visual realism anticipates Patinir and other Dutch painters.

Germany

Lochner, Stephan. *ca.* 1405-51. Gothic elements, use of gold in background, foreshadows Cranach; in *The Last Judgement,* his portrayal of "the damned" as masterpieces of the grotesque, influenced Bosch; *Presentation of the Christ Child at the Temple; Madonna and Child in Rose Garden* (Cologne) most popular work; highly imaginative artist.

Master Bertram. *ca.* 1345-after 1415. *Grabow Altarpiece* (1379-83, Hamburg), masterpiece; *The Creation of the Animals* (*ca.* 1380).

Master Francke. *fl.* first third of 15th century. *St. Barbara Altarpiece* (Helsinki), *St. Thomas à Becket* (Hamburg), lyrical poetic works; *The Scourging* (*ca.* 1425), tragic, dramatic effects.

Russia

Rublev, Andrei. 1370-1430. Most important icon painter of period; believed to have worked with Theophanes (Greek master) in the Cathedral of the Annunciation (1405, Moscow); considered one of the founders of the School of Moscow; *The Old Testament Trinity* (1419, Troitse Sergieva Monas-

tery, Moscow), best-known work; power yet subtlety of work seen in symbolic line and color.

France

Illuminated Manuscripts: Book illumination remained, in Northern Europe, the most important form of painting; by the 14th century,

BOOK OF HOURS OF JEANNE D'EVREAUX (DETAIL)

the manuscript artist was concerned with secular as well as religious subjects, three-dimensional representation, architectural background, well-rounded figures, and a new kind of iconography; the demand of the universities for books led to the use of lay scribes and illuminators, instead of relying completely on the monks. Some of the more interesting and important examples of the period include the brilliant Book of Hours known as *Les Très Riches Heures du Duc de Berry* (1413-16) by the Limbourg brothers (Pol, Jean, and Hermann) and others; the *Hours of Jeanne d'Evreaux* (1325-28) by Jean Pucelle; *Lancelot,* French prose work on the Arthurian legends (1310-20); *Chronicles of Froissart* (*ca.* 1400), Northern French, possibly illustrated by Guillaume de Bailly of Troyes; *The Gotha Missal* (1375, Cleveland Mus.) from court of Charles V, illuminated by Jean Bondol; and from Italy, the *Decretals of Pope Gregory IX* (late 14th century).

ASIA · *China*

Ni Tsan. 1301-74. Perhaps most brilliant of Yüan dynasty masters; work an expression of "poetry of loneliness"; magnificent vertical scrolls, always on paper; never put figures into his landscapes; use of dry-brush technique; famed for winter and autumn landscapes; delicate yet strong, free-brush technique.

Huang Kuang-wang. 1269-1354. Important master of period; influenced Ming and Ch'ing painters; known for two long horizontal scrolls in palace collection portraying landscapes of Fu-ch'un-shan and its surroundings; formulated fundamental traditions of landscape painting in his discourses on mountains and waters; his *Autumn Mountains* considered one of the finest Chinese pictures ever painted.

Wang Meng. 1308-85. Yüan master; massive compositions; crowded but worked out with mathematical precision; balanced masses; showed greater detail in architectural elements such as pavilions and studios than contemporaries; works have strength and unity of plan.

Wu Chen. 1280-1354. Yüan hermit; master poet-painter, whose poems (calligraphy) are important part of entire composition; best-known for *élan* of bamboo paintings, landscapes have gnarled old trees, bare hills, and rugged rocks; dry-brush technique applying mosslike dots.

Others. Ts'ao Chih-po (1272-*ca.* 1361), Sheng Mou (*ca.* 1310-61), and Tang T'sung (*ca.* 1340-80).

Japan

Mincho. (Also known as Chō Densu or Chōdensu. 1352-1431. Muromachi master; priest-painter of Tofukuji monastery, Kyoto; religious works of Zen Buddhism; thick, water-color technique, broad impressionist style; *Hut in the Valley* (1413), oldest pure-ink landscape known.

Mokuan. *fl.* early 14th century. Master of *suiboku* art; worked in China where he gained fame; Zen Buddhist priest; first important *sumi-e* paintings by Japanese artist.

Takashina Takakane. *fl.* early 14th century. Scrolls on silk; *Kasuga-gongen-reikenki* (1309) depicts miracles of famous Kasuga shrine.

Bompo. 1348-*ca.* 1420. Ink monochrome paintings of orchids; influenced by Chinese *sumi-e* work.

Shubun. early 15th century. Zen priest; great master of *suiboku* art; influential teacher.

Myotaku. 1307-88. Zen priest; known for paintings of Fudo in ink outline technique.

India

Vijayanagar painting. 14th century Jain temple of Tiruparutikundram has elaborately painted walls, brackets, pillars, and ceiling; Jain subjects, life of Krishna and other Hindu gods; strong color, gum tempera on plaster technique.

At **Madanpur,** King Madana Varma

(1130-65) built a temple to Vishnu; ceiling paintings were added (about 1400); large lotus panel predominates; also small panels depicting animal fables.

PERSIA (*Mongol Style*)

Tabriz

The manuscript of Jami, '*al-Ta-warikh* (Universal History), of Rashîd al-Dîn (1314) shows interesting use of silver paint; Chinese influence; very large (17 by 12 in.); *Shah-nama* (Demotte) of Firdawsi (1330-36) is considered one of the outstanding works of 14th-century Persia; court and battle scenes; powerful work in *Kalila wa Dimna* (Album from the Imperial Palace of Yildiz, 1360-74); from the library of the Sultan Ahmad (who attempted to rule during the siege of Tabriz by Timur, 1386)*Aja 'ib al-Makhluqat*, (Book of the Marvels of the World, 1388, Baghdad); the beautiful illustrations for the *Diwan* of Khwaju Kirmani (1396) were signed by **Junayd.**

Shiraz

Shah-nama of the Wazir Qawam al-Din Hasan (1341), exceptional drawings of animals and flowers; the extremely interesting scientific anthology or dictionary, *Mu'nis al-Ahrar*, by **Muhammed b. Badr Jajarmi** (1341); use of gold, red; good draftsmanship; in the *Anthology of Iskandar Sultan* (1410-11) there are four exquisite double-page miniatures (rare in Persian manuscripts); beautiful copy of the *Kalila wa Dimna*, made for Baysunghur (d. 1433) by artists of the

Timurid School (1410-20, now in Gulistan Palace Library, Teheran); **Shams al-Din** produced two subtle, brilliant small books of Sa'di's works (1427) for Baysunghur, Hera.

SCULPTURE

EUROPE · *Italy*

Donatello (Donato di Niccolò di Betto Bardi). *ca.* 1386-1466. Great Florentine sculptor of early Italian Renaissance; strength of realism in early work shown in *Lo Zuccone*

DAVID BY DONATELLO, FLORENCE

(Pumpkin Head, Baldpate, or Prophet, 1423-25), Campanile, Florence; experimented with all styles and techniques; *Singing Gallery*, Florence (1433-40); *Herod's Banquet*, Siena (1427); early low reliefs include *Madonna, Saint Peter Receiving the Keys from Christ* (London); use of classical counter-poise in great equestrian statue, *Gattamelata*, Padua (1445-50); altarpieces, *John the Evangelist, Judith and Holofernes;* famed *David* (*ca.* 1430-32) represents the lyrical, more restrained Donatello; unique characterization and individual interpretation seen in *Repentant Magdalen* (*ca.* 1454-55); influenced Michelangelo.

Ghiberti, Lorenzo. *ca.* 1378-1455. Master Florentine sculptor; famous for

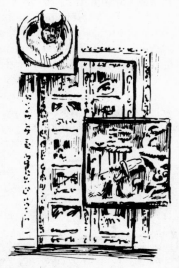

DOORS OF PARADISE, BRONZE, GHIBERTI, BAPTISTERY, FLORENCE

bronze doors of Baptistery; won competition (1401) over Brunelleschi; 20 magnificent scenes from the life of Christ (1403-24); softly modeled figures and groups range from bas relief to high relief; second set of doors (hung in main portal of Baptistery, 1452) stories from Old Testament; *St. John the Baptist* (1404), *St. Matthew* and *St. Stephen* (1428) for Church of San Michele; *Commentaries,* autobiography.

Pisano, Andrea (du Pontedera). *ca.* 1270-1349. Leading sculptor, architect, goldsmith of Pisan school; famous for first set of doors of Baptistery, Florence; 20 reliefs from life of *St. John the Baptist;* succeeded Giotto as chief artist for Cathedral of Florence (1336); chief artist, Cathedral of Orvieto (1347).

Quercia, Jacopo della. 1367-1438. Master of early Renaissance Sienese sculpture; poetic, magnificent tomb of *Ilaria del Carreto,* in Cathedral at Lucca, outstanding example of work; *Fonte Gaia* in public square at Siena, bronze relief, *Zacharias;* tomb of *Antonio Galeazzo Bentivoglio,* San Giacomo Maggiore, Bologna; reliefs (*The Creation of Adam, ca.* 1430), for jambs of main portal San Petronio, Bologna, powerful figures in bold relief.

MADONNA AND CHILD
BY JACOPO
DELLA QUERCIA

Rossellino, Bernardo (Gambarelli). 1409-64. Florentine sculptor, architect; worked for Pope Nicholas V in Rome; noted for marble tomb of humanist *Leonardo Bruni* of Arezzo, Santa

Croce, Florence; first example of arched tomb with sarcophagus placed in semicircular niche (became standard for wall tombs); also tombs of *Beata Villana*, Florence, *Filippo Lazzari*, Pistoia.

Orcagna (Andrea di Cione). *ca.* 1308-68. Gothic architect, sculptor, and painter of Florence; marble tabernacle, Or San Michele; figures in the round; façade of Orvieto Cathedral.

Tino da Camaino. d. *ca.* 1337. Sienese sculptor who is believed to have been the first in Europe to produce monumental figures in the round as a separate work of art, and not as relief subordinate to architectural background; developed Italian style of Gothic sepulcher; tomb of *Maria of Hungary* at Naples; chapel in duomo and baptismal font in Cathedral, Pisa; humanist approach.

Bonino da Campione. d. 1397. Sculptor active in northern Italy; tomb of *Bernardo Visconti*, though not completed, considered masterpiece; tombs of *Cansignorio*, Verona, *Folchino degli Schizzi* (1357), Cremona; reliefs on lintels of San Marco; other famous tombs.

Matteo da Campione. d. 1396. Leading Lombard artist of the period; façade of *Monza Cathedral*; offered directorship of work on Cathedral of Milan.

Maitani, Lorenzo. *ca.* 1275-1330. Sculptor, architect; designed façade of Orvieto Cathedral; reliefs on doorways; influenced Ghiberti.

Nanni di Banco. *ca.* 1375-1421. Florentine sculptor- and architect; studied with Donatello; *Assumption*, portal della Mandorla of the Duomo, St. Philip, Florence Cathedral (*ca.*

1420); *Four Saints* (for niche), Or San Michele, Florence (*ca.* 1410-14); seated figure of *St. Luke.*

Agostino di Giovanni. *fl.* 1310-50. Sienese sculptor and architect; worked on Church of St. Francis, Siena; marble reliefs for high altar of Vescovado, Arezzo; praised by Giotto; bas relief of Church of San Francesco, Bologna; important teacher; collaborated on above with brother **Agnolo di Ventura.**

Filarete (Antonio di Pietro Averlino). *ca.* 1400-1469. Florentine architect and sculptor; bronze door of St. Peter's, Rome; *Porta Giova* of Sforzesco Castle, Milan; primarily an architect (see next period).

Cavallini, Pietro. *ca.* 1250-1330. Mosaicist, sculptor, and painter; influenced Giotto and Cimabue.

CATHEDRAL OF FLORENCE, DOME BY BRUNELLESCHI

France

Beauneveu, André. *ca.* 1330-before 1413. One of the last great wandering artists of the so-called Middle Ages; forerunner of Renaissance masters; praised by Froissart; served court of Charles V as sculptor, architect, artist; tomb figures, St. Denis; *St. Catherine* at Courtrai, Flanders; designs for stained-glass windows of Sainte-Chapelle, Bourges; miniature painter for Jean de France (Duc de Berry); grisaille at beginning of psalter attributed to him.

VIRGIN OF PARIS,
NOTRE-DAME, PARIS

VIRGIN
AND CHILD,
IVORY,
FRENCH

Burgundy

Sluter, Claus. d. *ca.* 1406. Leading Flemish master of Burgundian school; assistant to Jean de Marvilles at Dijon (1385), in service of Philip the Bold; succeeded him (1389); designed magnificent tombs for *Philip* and *John the Fearless; Well of Moses* for portal of the Chartreuse at Abbey of Champmol near Dijon; important in freeing sculpture from architecture; powerful freedom of expression.

MOSES WELL BY SLUTER

Germany

Multscher, Hans. *ca.* 1400-1467. Sculptor and painter; best-known for *Man of Sorrows* in stone on main portal of Ulm Cathedral; later works, influenced by Sluter, more realistic.

127

PIETA, PAINTED STONE, UPPER BAVARIA,
GERMANY

ARCHITECTURE

EUROPE · *Italy*

Brunelleschi, Filippo. 1377-1446. Great Florentine master architect of the early Renaissance whose ideas influenced all Italian building of the 15th century; first to establish sound, scientific theory of perspective; studied jewelry, sculpture, and goldsmith's trade; second to Ghiberti in sculpture competition for doors of Baptistery; visited Rome with Donatello; designed and constructed dome of *Santa Maria del Fiore Cathedral*, Florence, one of the most important projects in terms of size; *Foundling Hospital*, Gothic in feeling, placing dome over crossing; exceptional construction, considered outstanding achievement in civic architecture; *Pitti Palace*, Church of S.

Maria degli Angeli, San Lorenzo, Pazzi Chapel, Santo Spirito (basilica with round-headed arcades and flat roof, Romanesque, bases and capitals of Corinthian columns, classical Roman).

Michelozzo (Michele di Bartolommeo). *ca.* 1396–1472. Florentine architect and sculptor; succeeded Brunelleschi (1446); built *San Marco* and other monasteries for Cosimo de' Medici; *Palazzo Medici-Riccardi*, Florence (begun 1444) became prototype of many palaces; as sculptor, many marble madonnas, terra-cotta figures, friezes, and ornaments for doors; very successful and much admired by contemporaries.

Orcagna (Andrea di Cione). 1308-68. Florentine architect for *Or San Michele* (see Sculpture).

Rossellino, Bernardo. 1409-64. Florentine; built *Palazzo Piccolomini, Pienza Cathedral,* Pienza; employed at Vatican.

Buon or **Buono,** Bartolomeo, d. *ca.* 1464. Venetian architect; *Porta della Carta* of Doge's Palace.

Spain

Alhambra. Built (1348-1354) by Moors in Granada; group of buildings on hill overlooking the city; citadel extant; palace of kings, quarters of nobles and officials; halls, chambers with intricate geometric ornament and honeycomb vaulting that surround a series of open courts with fountains and gardens; largely destroyed with expulsion of Moors (1492), but extensively restored (after 1828).

Cordova. Famous 14th-century synagogue, constructed in mosque form

MEDICI-RICCARDI PALACE, FLORENCE.
MICHELOZZO

rather than the basilican type of Gali-
lean temple common in central Europe.

Germany

Stettheimer, Hans. *ca.* 1350-*ca.* 1432.
Most important Bavarian architect;
late Gothic style, several hall churches;
tapering south tower, known as high
"Steffel" at *St. Stephen's Cathedral,*
Vienna.

Erwin (von Steinbach). *ca.* 1244-
1318. Architect for *Strasbourg Cathedral* (1277-1339).

Ensingen, Ulrich von. *ca.* 1359-after
1417. Directed building of *Ulm Cathedral*; octagonal tower of Strasbourg
Cathedral.

Parler, Peter. 1330-99. Court archi-
tect to Charles IV, Prague; choir of
All Saints Church, Prague Cathedral,
Charles Bridge over the Moldau.

Late Gothic Cathedrals

In **England,** Exeter (completed
1369), nave at Lichfield (completed

1361, begun end of 12th century), nave
and west front Winchester (1371-
1460), choisters and choir, Gloucester
(1332-57), Lady Chapel, Ely (1321-
49); in **Italy,** Cathedral at Milan
(started 1386); in **Germany,** Ulm
Cathedral (started 1337), choir, St.
Sebald, Nuremberg (1361-72).

Byzantine

Church of St. Mary Pammakaristos,
Constantinople (1315).

Japan

Golden Pavilion of Kinkakuji built
at Kyoto (1397).

HALL IN THE NISHI HONGANJI TEMPLE,
KYOTO, JAPAN

Mexico

Aztecs built their capital, Tenochtit-
lan (1325).

MUSIC

EUROPE · Burgundian School

Dufay, Guillaume. *ca.* 1400-1474.
Founder and leading composer of this
group that reconciled the late Gothic of

129

France and the Italian; interest in songs and polyphonic settings of un-changing parts of the Mass; motets still very Gothic; famous for three-part *chansons;* singer in papal chapel

EARLY MUSICAL NOTATION:

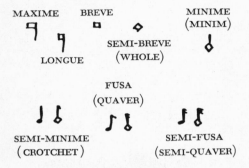

MAXIME   BREVE   MINIME
                            (MINIM)

      LONGUE   SEMI-BREVE
                 (WHOLE)

              FUSA
            (QUAVER)

SEMI-MINIME   SEMI-FUSA
(CROTCHET)   (SEMI-QUAVER)

(1428); canon of Cambrai (1436); introduced the use of secular melodies in place of Gregorian *cantus firmi;* first to use folk song (*L'homme arme*) in a Mass; important influence.

Binchois, Gilles (de Binche of Mons). *ca.* 1400–60. Leading master; chaplain to Philip, Duke of Burgundy

DUFAY AND BINCHOIS, FROM EARLY
MINIATURE

(1430); received first musical training in choir of Cathedral of Cambrai; famous for imaginative, inspired songs using solo voice accompanied by two instrumental parts, carefully con-structed; both church and secular songs.

France

Machaut, Guillaume de 1300-1377. Great master; perfect representative of French *ars nova;* poet, musician, scholar; served Charles V; Canon of Rheims Cathedral (1333); composed only polyphonic Mass entirely con-ceived by a single composer (*Messe Notre-Dame,* for four voices); com-posed 23 motets, 42 *ballades, notées* (that anticipate great Romantic *lied*); influenced by Philippe de Vitry's *Ars Nova;* used syncopation imitation; im-portant influence in Italy.

Vitry, Philippe de. 1291-1361. Famed authority on musical theory; Roman Catholic prelate, poet, musician, in service of French kings; Bishop of Meaux (1351); important treatise, *Ars Nova* (*ca.* 1325); introduction of time signature, use of red notes (to indicate modifications of rhythm), develop-ment of principle of binary rhythm by which he freed music from restriction of six "rhythmic modes" of *ars antiqua* that used triple rhythm only; wrote motets successfully using innovations in sphere of harmony and form; very influential.

Muris, Johannes (Jean). Before 1300-*ca.* 1351. Musical theorist, philos-opher, mathematician; originally cred-ited with *Speculum musicae* of Jacobus of Liége; author of *Ars novae musicae* that supported theories of his friend Philippe de Vitry.

England

Dunstable, John. *ca.* 1390-1453. Leading musician, astronomer (astrologer), mathematician; widely-traveled; served Duke of Bedford (regent of France, 1422-35); contemporaries, Dufay and Binchois, influenced by him; more than 50 works, all but three songs, religious; probably the first to write instrumental accompaniments for church music; used thirds and sixths and often gave an original *cantus firmus* to soprano instead of tenor; very influential.

Power, Lionel (Leonel). d. 1445. Important contemporary of Dunstable (works often confused); by linking the five parts with unchanging *cantus firmus* in the tenor, or by allotting to each part the same initial theme, he unified the Ordinary in the Mass; *Alma redemptoris*, earliest complete Mass on a *cantus firmus*; wrote early treatise on descant; much church music.

Tunsted, Simon. d. 1369. Musicologist; leading Franciscan at Oxford (1360); believed to have written treatise *De quatuor principalibus musicae* (1351, published in Vol. IV of *Scriptores* by Coussemaker) in which musical terms were defined and mensural music discussed.

Benet, John. *fl.* 15th century. Associated with Power and Dunstable; composer of Masses, motets whose name appears in continental manuscripts; important in English church music.

Odington, Walter de (Walter of Eversham). d. *ca.* 1330. Benedictine monk; author of *De speculatione musicae*, important as study of rhythm in 13th century; invented type of rota or round; believed to have written *Six Men's Song* in canon or round.

Italy

Landini (Landino), Francesco. 1325-97. Outstanding blind Florentine organist at San Lorenzo; also virtuoso on flute and lute; 154 secular compositions extant, all but 13 are ballades (*ballata*), 12 madrigals and canzones.

Giovanni da Cascia (Johannes de Florentia). *fl.* early 14th century; composer, court of Verona; secular music including madrigals and canzonettas.

Spain

Don Juan I of Aragon (1350-95) founded the music institute of Barcelona and presented poetic-musical festival plays.

Germany

Wolkenstein, Oswald von. 1377-1445. Last great representative of medieval art of the minnesinger; to Spain, Persia; although aware of many-voiced art music, he remained true to lyric form of earlier centuries.

Frauenlob, Heinrich. d. 1318. Poet, musician; established earliest Meistersinger school at Mayence, early 14th century.

ASIA · Japan

During the Muromachi or Ashikaga period (1333-1615) there was very little musical development; a simple bamboo recorder gained in popularity, and some folk songs were sung; several short pieces (*kouta*) are extant, but traditional court music suffered.

China

Opera developed into an art form during the 14th century and gained in popularity.

India

Music became the province of professionals, usually members of a low caste of society, employed by the upper castes as entertainers.

THEATER

ASIA · *Japan*

Noh Theater. When the dance and music of Kagura were supplemented by spoken dialogue, the Noh drama came into being. At first they were purely religious performances intended to propitiate the chief gods of the Shintō religion, and were acted exclusively at shrines. They were obviously written only for the nobility and the highly-educated of Japan, as they were too sophisticated and difficult for the average person to understand.

The outstanding manager-dramatist

MASKS, JAPANESE NOH THEATER

NOH THEATER

of the period was **Kwanami Kiyotsugu** (1333-84) who managed the Noh theaters at Nara, and was taken into service by the ruling shōgun. He was responsible for 15 of the 235 known complete works in the Yōkyoku Tsuge collection of Noh dramas.

Zeami Motokiyo. 1364-1443. Outstanding Noh manager; son of Kwanami; known to have produced at least 93 famous plays, including *Atsumori* and *Hagoromo* that are still performed; responsible for music, pantomimic dance, and management; may have had a hand in libretti, but they were generally written by Buddhist monks as almost all literary men of the period belonged to this group.

China

Best-known play of the Ming period was *P'i-p'a-ki* (Story of the Lute) written in 24 scenes by someone' named **Kao** and first performed in 1404.

India

Vyasa Srirāmadeva. Famous writer of shadow plays during first half of 15th century; most works based on episodes from the *Mahabharata* and the *Ramayana*.

MIDDLE EAST

Muhammad ibn-Daniyal (al-Khuza'i al-Mawsili) wrote the only extant dramatic poetry of Islam, the important *Tayf al-Khayal fi Ma'rifat Khayal al-Zill* (1310).

EUROPE · *France*

Basoche, Clercs de la. Guild of clerks, Parlement of Paris, formed early in the 14th century. They played a major role in the development of the theater in France, producing farces, morality plays, comedies, and satires. Special groups of amateurs (*confrèries*) most famous, Confrèrie de la Passion, Paris (founded 1402).

The earliest known serious secular miracle play performed in the French language was *The History of Griselda* (1393).

England

Coventry Mysteries. Famous series of 42 religious plays performed regularly at Coventry, England (until 1591). It has been suggested that these mysteries were performed considerably earlier than the earliest records indicate (1416). All over England trade guilds performed **Mystery Cycles.** The actors were members of the Guilds, ordinary citizens, and artisans of the towns and countryside. The success of the Corpus Christi festival (1311) encouraged others to follow suit.

MARTYRDOM OF ST. APOLLONIA, MEDIEVAL MYSTERY PLAY, AFTER FOUQUET

Italy

Mussato, Albertino. *fl.* early 14th century. Wrote *Ecerninis* (1315), a Latin tragedy based on the life of the Paduan tyrant Ezzelino III.

Frulovisi, Tito Livio dei. *fl.* 1430-50. Wrote several romantic and sentimental Latin plays in Plautan style (1432-34).

Switzerland

First drama concerned with birth of Christ performed at St. Gall monastery (1400).

1450-1525

The most important, far-reaching events of the 15th and 16th centuries were the great European voyages of discovery that opened the Oceanic Age of global history, and for the first time, Europe assumed a primary role in world events.

The most significant country in Europe in terms of art was Italy, the heart of the Renaissance. Florentine humanism took on a consciously classical flavor. The Medici Library (among others) made Greek and Latin classics available, and the secular and humane philosophy of Greece and Rome evoked a rebirth of individualism.

Lorenzo de' Medici, a poet as well as a great patron of the most important artists and writers of the period, established the vernacular language as acceptable. With his death (1492) and the final fall of the Medicis (1494), the artists were forced to flee Florence for other ducal courts.

When the foundation for the new St. Peter's was laid (1506), Rome became the intellectual and artistic capital of the Western world. The popes gathered around them the foremost artists of the day and transformed the city into one of the most magnificent the world has seen.

The unbelievably versatile "Renaissance man," best represented by Leonardo da Vinci and Michelangelo, was a painter, architect, sculptor, musician, poet, scientist, engineer, and inventor.

From Italy the spirit of the Renaissance moved north, producing great artists in the other countries of Europe.

This great burst of artistic talent in the West was duplicated in China during this brilliant period by the artists of the Ming Dynasty.

LORENZO DE' MEDICI
OF FLORENCE
BY VERROCCHIO

PAINTING

EUROPE · *Italy*

Florence. **Leonardo da Vinci.** 1452-1519. Great master artist, architect, musician, engineer, scientist; epitomizes the "Renaissance man" in amazing versatility; workshop of Verrocchio (1466); worked at court of Sforza, Milan (1482), famed for notebooks from this period; *Virgin of the Rocks* (*ca.* 1485, Louvre); *Last Supper*, Santa Maria della Grazie (*ca.* 1487-98);

Mona Lisa del Gioconda (*ca.* 1503-06, Louvre); *Adoration of the Magi* panel (1481-82, Uffizi); *St. Anne, Mary and Child* (1500, Louvre); first of high Renaissance painters in Florence; designed, organized popular and elaborate festivals, pageants, including *Il Paradiso* (1487, Milan); wrote *Treatise on Painting* (1491).

Raphael (Raffaello Santi or Sanzio). 1483-1520. Master artist; influenced by Perugino, later by Leonardo, Masaccio, and Michelangelo; famous for Madonnas: *Sistine Madonna* (Dresden), often thought the single most famous

LADY WITH
AN ERMINE,
BY LEONARDO
DA VINCI

POPE JULIUS II (DETAIL)
BY RAPHAEL

altarpiece of period; *Cowper Madonna* (Washington), *Madonna with Goldfinch* (Uffizi); brilliant frescoes (Vatican); 52 religious subjects covering one ceiling known as *Raphael's Bible*; also classical themes, *The Triumph of Galatea* (Villa Farnesina, Rome), *St. George and the Dragon* (Washington); portraits, *Baldassare Castiglione* (Louvre), *Giuliano de' Medici* (Washington).

Botticelli, Sandro (Alessandro di Filipepi). 1444/5-1510. Master artist;

BIRTH OF VENUS
BY BOTTICELLI

painter for the Medicis; great colorist, developed lyric romanticism expressed in movement of figures and linear design; influenced by teachers, Fra Filippo Lippi, Verrocchio, and Pollaiuolo; frescoes for Sistine Chapel (1481-82, Rome); great portraits including *St. Augustine* (Florence); *Birth of Venus* (ca. 1480); *Three Graces* from *Primavera* (1478, Uffizi); *Madonna of the Eucharist* (Boston); *St. Sebastian* (Berlin); *The Adoration*

of the Kings (Uffizi); *Adoration of the Magi* (Washington).

Ghirlandaio, Domenico del (di Tomasso Bigordi). 1449-94. Important fresco painter; influenced by Masaccio; teacher of Michelangelo; great portraits; works for Sistine Chapel (1481), Sassetti Chapel (1485) and choir of Santa Maria Novella (1490); masterpiece, *Old Man with his Grandson* (Louvre).

Pollaiuolo, Antonio. 1433-98. Sculptor, painter, engraver, goldsmith; exceptional draftsman; considered first artist to study anatomy by dissection; vitality, action, concern with human form; important copper engraving of *Ten Fighting Nudes*; frescoes; studies of dancing nudes; *Deeds of Hercules* (1460, Medici Palace); *Martyrdom of St. Sebastian* (Washington).

Sarto, Andrea del (d'Agnolo). 1486-1531. Great colorist; called the "perfect painter" by contemporary Florentines; religious frescoes; monumental compositions; *Madonna of the Harpies* (1517, Uffizi).

Piero di Cosimo (di Lorenzo). 1462-1521. Mythological and religious works with outstanding landscape backgrounds; emphasis on light and color as means of expression; *Coronation of the Virgin with Saints* (Louvre); *The Discovery of Honey* (Worcester).

Bartolommeo, Fra (Bartolommeo di Paolo). 1472-1517. Dramatic quality; most famous work, *Pietà* (1516, Pitti Palace); influenced by Leonardo and Raphael.

Filippino Lippi. ca. 1457-1504. Son of Fra Filippo Lippi; influenced by Botticelli; continued decorative style, lyric romanticism; late work strikingly baroque; *Tobias and the Angel* (Met. Mus.); altarpiece, *Adoration of the Magi* (1496, Uffizi).

Gozzoli, Benozzo (di Lese di Sandro). 1420-98. Florentine, Tuscan artist; worked as sculptor with Ghiberti and with Fra Angelico on frescoes; *Procession of the Magi* (Palazzo Riccardi, Florence), best-known of many series of lives of saints and others; contains portraits of the Medici family; series of frescoes on Old Testament in Campo Santo (Pisa) damaged during World War II.

Credi, Lorenzo di (d'Andrea d'Oderigo). 1459-1537. Worked with Leonardo and Perugino; pedantic naturalism; *Annunciation* (Uffizi) and *Madonna and Child* (Louvre).

Carpi, Ugo da. *ca.* 1455-1523. Wood engraver; important works using chiaroscuro, a term he originated.

Venice. Bellini, Giovanni, *ca.* 1430-1516. Considered the outstanding leader of the 15th-century Venetian school; helped transform painting by

AGONY IN THE GARDEN BY BELLINI

the use of Flemish oil technique; teacher of Giorgione and Titian; style shows the change from carefully drawn, scientifically oriented style of Verrocchio to monumental, emotional power of the High Renaissance; emphasis on light and color, space and movement; *Pietà di Brera* (Milan); *Agony in the Garden, Madonna Enthroned with Saints* (Venice); *St. Francis in Ecstasy* (Frick, N.Y.); interest in mythology reflected in *Orpheus and the Feast of the Gods* (Met. Mus.); excellent *Portrait of Doge Leonardo Lorendanco* (London); *Portrait of a Condottiere* (Met. Mus.).

Giorgione (Giorgio da Castelfranco, called Zorzi). *ca.* 1478-1510. Brilliant paintings on secular subjects, genre, landscapes; emphasis on space; *Adoration of the Shepherds* (1500-15, Met. Mus.); *The Tempest* or *The Storm* (Venice); *Sleeping Venus* (Dresden); *Three Philosophers* (Vienna).

Antonello da Messina (di Giovanni degli Antoni). *ca.* 1430-79. Thought to have introduced Flemish oil technique into Venice; *Saint Jerome in His Study,* meticulous detail, framed in Gothic architecture; *Virgin Annunciate* (Palermo), important use of light, observation of nature.

Bellini, Gentile. 1429-1507. Brother of Giovanni; known for famous portrait of *Sultan Mohammed II* (1480, London); *Caterina Cornaro, Queen of Cyprus* (Budapest); *Corpus Christi Procession on the Piazza di San Marco* (1496, Venice).

Crivelli, Carlo. *ca.* 1430/5-95. Tempera artist; *Annunciation* (London), *Pietà* (Boston), large *Coronation of the Virgin* (Brera).

Carpaccio, Vittore. *ca.* 1450-*ca.* 1526. Historical painter; interested only in rich color and the glory of the city he loved; very personal depth of feeling; chief works are four large decorative series of paintings for various Scuoli of Venice on the *Legend of St. Ursula* (1490-95); *Life of Mary* (1504).

Palma il Vecchio (Jacopo d'Antonio Negretti). 1480-1528. Portrait, religious, and landscape painter; more conservative than contemporary Giorgione; most important work, paintings for altar of Santa Maria Formosa (1509-24, Venice); *Adoration of the Shepherds* (Louvre), *Holy Family* (Phil. Mus.), *Three Sisters* (Dresden).

Sebastino del Piombo. 1485-1547. Friend and associate of Michelangelo (1512); keeper of papal seals, Venice (1531); best-known for portraits and influence on Raphael and Michelangelo; *Portrait of Andrea Doria* (Rome), *Portrait of Roman Lady* (Berlin).

Vivarini, Alvise. *ca.* 1445/6-*ca.* 1503 /4. Pre-Bellini; excellent altarpiece, *Madonna Enthroned with Six Saints* (1485, Berlin); *Virgin and Child* (London), *St. John the Baptist* (Venice).

Pordenone (Giovanni Antonio de Sachis). 1484–1539. Influenced later mannerists with unique distortion of form to achieve dramatic effect; *Glorification of San Giustiniano* (1532, Venice).

Cima da Conegliano, Giovanni Battista. *ca.* 1459–*ca.* 1517. Religious painter; severe, solemn style; *Madonna with Saints* and *Tobias with an Angel* (Venice), *Madonna and Child* (Bologna).

Catena, Vincenzo di Biagio. *ca.* 1470-1531. Portrait artist of ability; *Fugger* (Berlin); *Christ Appearing to St. Christine* (1520), romantic spirit and color.

Milan. **Boltraffio,** Giovanni Antonio, 1466/67–1516. Outstanding pupil of Leonardo; possibly finest work attributed to master, *Madonna* (Louvre); *Madonna of Casio Family* and *Virgin and Child* (Milan), *Portrait of Youth* (Met. Mus.); excellent, *St. Barbara* (Berlin).

Padua. **Mantegna,** Andrea. 1431-1506. Great master of Paduan school; worked in Mantua; outside Venice, most celebrated artist of northern Italy; introduced Gothic devotional fervor into work of northern artists; one of first to make extensive collection of Greek and Roman works, influenced by the classics; great frescoes in church of the Eremetani Padua (destroyed 1944) included *St. James Led to His Execution* (*ca.* 1455, Ovetari Chapel); fresco *Camera degli Sposi* (Mantua) shows Cardinal Francesco Gonzaga's triumphant return from Rome; important late work, decoration of Isabella d' Este's Studiolo in Castello (from 1497); superb draftsman, first engraver to make prints major works of art; powerful sense of volume and form; simplicity and directness not again equaled before Rembrandt.

Campagnola, Giulio. 1482-1516. Paduan miniaturist of surprising modernity; some work attributed to Giorgione believed to be his.

Siena. **Francesco di Giorgio Martini.** 1439-1502. Important Sienese artist; alone attained reputation away from own area in this period; book illumination and altarpieces.

Umbria. **Piero della Francesca.** *ca.*
1416-92. Great Umbrian master; unique
style; monumental, stylized figures,
decorative design, and powerful perspective; importance of architectural
background; atmospheric use of light;
extremely important influence on art of
central Italy; outstanding fresco por-

DUKE OF URBINO BY PIERO DELLA
FRANCESCA

trait of *Sigismondo Malatesta;* fresco
series for choir of San Francesco in
Arezzo, scenes from *Legend of the
Holy Cross,* probably most famous
work; *Nativity* (London); *Crucifixion*
(Met. Mus.); *Resurrection of Christ*
(Borgos); diptych, *Federigo da Montefeltro and Wife* (Uffizi), wrote treatises on perspective and anatomy.

Perugino, Il (Pietro di Cristoforo
Vannucci). 1450-1523. Important Umbrian artist; worked with della Francesca; pupil, with Leonardo, of Verrocchio; teacher of Raphael; fresco,
The Delivery of the Keys (1482, Sistine
Chapel, Vatican, Rome); spent last
period in Perugia; great altarpiece,
The Ascension (1496-98); spacious
landscapes, contributing to serenity of
mood; *Pietà* (1495, Pitti Palace); *Conflict of Love and Chastity* (Louvre),
Crucifixion (Washington), *Virgin and
Child with Saints* (1496, London).

Signorelli, Luca. *ca.* 1441-1523. Umbrian artist; studied with della Francesca; influenced by Pollaiuolo in
powerful treatment of anatomy, as
seen in *Madonna and Child* (Uffizi);
End of the World (1499-1500, Orvieto
Cathedral) anticipates to some extent
Michelangelo's *Last Judgment*; austerity, sadness pervade work; *Triumph
of Chastity* (Washington).

Melozzo da Forlì. 1438-94. Umbrian
artist; spent much time in Rome; influenced by Piero della Francesca;
worked with Joos van Ghent in Urbino
(*ca.* 1473-76); famous group portrait,
Pope Sixtus IV, with four nephews receiving Platina, new Vatican librarian
(1477), future Pope Julius II stands at
center of painting (Vatican); great
fresco of *Ascension,* cupola of St.
Apostoli (1481, Rome).

Parma. **Correggio** (Antonio Allegri).
ca. 1489-1534. Outstanding artist; very
successful and influential in his own
time; considered last of the great per-
sonalities of the High Renaissance;
Holy Night (Dresden), figures lit from
below, influenced the Mannerists;
works had unique quality of decorative
illusion; finest fresco work in Church
of San Giovanni Evangelista (1520-23,
Parma); *Marriage of St. Catherine*
(Louvre); *The Rape of Ganymede,*
one of his boldest compositions;
smaller, more intimate, romantic house
altars closely related to mythological
scenes.

139

Flemish School

Memling, Hans. *ca.* 1433-94. Master portrait and religious artist; German-born, citizen Bruges (1465); follower of Van Eyck and Rogier van der Weyden; strong portrait studies, very personal style; *Man with a Medal* (Antwerp), *Young Man* (Met. Mus.); *Mystical Marriage of St. Catherine* (1479, Hôpital St. Jean, Bruges), central panel, masterpiece; *Annunciation* (Met. Mus.); altarpiece, *Adoration* (Madrid); *Bathsheba* (Stuttgart), *Madonna and Child with Angels* (Washington).

Bosch, Hieronymus (Jeroen Anthoniszoon). *ca.* 1450-1516. Master of diabolical, symbolic language of satire as applied to man and religion; *Garden of Delights* (detail from *Hell*, Madrid); *Last Judgment* (Vienna), *Ecco Homo* (Phil. Mus.), *Christ Crowned with Thorns* (London and Prado); *Ship of Fools* (Louvre); *Paradise and Hell*

ST. JOHN THE BAPTIST IN THE WILDERNESS BY BOSCH

(Venice); *Prodigal Son* (Rotterdam); *Carrying of the Cross* (Ghent); *Death of the Miser* (Washington); best work of last period shows pity and compassion very rare in early work.

David, Gerard. 1460-1523. Successful Dutch painter; severe symmetry, balanced composition, highly opulent decoration; important and influential miniaturist in own time; *Wedding at Cana; Adoration of the Kings; Rest on the Flight into Egypt* (Washington); altarpieces.

Massys, Quentin (Matsys). *ca.* 1466-1530. Leader of Flemish Renaissance painters of early 16th century; influenced by Leonardo; important interest in average man and surroundings rather than preoccupation with religious subjects; excellent portraits.

Christus, Petrus (Pieter Christus or Cristus). d. 1472/3. Master of Painter's Guild, Bruges (1444); more conventional and less imaginative than his teacher, Jan Van Eyck; excellent interiors; ranks with best of portrait artists of period; *Portrait of Young Girl* (Berlin) and *St. Jerome in His Study* (Met. Mus.); *Lamentation* (Brussels), masterpiece.

Goes, Hugo van der. *ca.* 1440-82. Outsanding student of Van Eyck; famous *Portinari Altarpiece*, triptych (1476-78, Uffizi); *Adoration of the Shepherds*, central panel, well-known.

Bouts, Dirk (Dirck, Dierik Thierry). *ca.* 1415/20–75. Influential Flemish painter; lacked brilliance or imagination of a Rogier van der Weyden, but excellent sense of form and line; *God's Judgment* (Brussels), *Entombment* (London), *Madonna and Child* (Met. Mus.), *Last Supper* (Louvain); *Portrait of Young Man* (1462), first time portrait is given landscape background.

Clouet, Jean (possibly Janney Clanet or Jehannet of France). 1485-1540. Court painter to Francis I of France; extremely successful portrait artist; *Equestrian Portrait of Francis I* (Louvre).

Ghent, Joos van (Jooris van Wassenhove). *ca.* 1430–80. Worked in Rome; large altar panel, *Last Supper* (Urbino); associated with Hugo van der Goes.

Mabuse, Jan de (Jan Gossaert). *ca.* 1478-*ca.* 1533. Historical, portrait painter; influenced by David and by Italian masters.

Patinir, Joachim. 1475/80-1524. Landscape artist; first to attempt aerial perspective; epic more than lyric painter; influenced by Bosch; worked with Massys; outstanding small works including *Charon's Boat* (Prado).

Lucas van Leyden (Hughensz van). 1494-1533. Powerful realist; influenced by friend Dürer; *Card-Players* (London) and *St. Jerome* (Berlin); etchings.

Germany

Dürer, Albrecht. 1471-1528. Most important and influential master of the period in Germany; superb draftsman, painter, engraver; oils, water colors with tempera; precise, subtle in color, perceptive use of light, but lacking vibrance, warmth of Italian masters he admired; worked in Italy; *Portrait of His Father* (1498, London), *Self-Portrait* (1500), *Portrait of Hieronymus Holzschuher* (1526, Berlin), and *Jakob Fugger* (1520, Munich) are exceptional realism and character studies; *Adoration of Magi* (Uffizi) and *Adora-*

SELF-PORTRAIT,
DÜRER

ANGEL PLAYING THE LUTE BY DÜRER

tion of Trinity (Vienna); famous drawings include *Hands of an Apostle* (1508, Vienna) and *Mother Barbara* (1514, Berlin); very fine engravings on both wood and metal; *Four Horsemen of the Apocalypse* (1498), *Life of Virgin, Melancholia* (1514, Washington), *Great and Little Passions* (printed 1511).

Schongauer, Martin. 1430-91. Master painter, engraver; leader of most important center of late Gothic art at Colmar; one of earliest to perfect copper engraving; work well-known in

141

Italy and Spain; influenced by Rogier van der Weyden; masterpiece, *Madonna of the Rosehedge or Rose Arbor;* expressive, gracefully curved figures seen in small pictures, usually less than 18 in. high, including *Holy Family* (*ca.* 1485, Vienna); *Birth of Christ* (Munich), *Adoration of the Shepherds* (Berlin); influenced Dürer.

Altdorfer, Albrecht. *ca.* 1480-1538. Master of School of the Danube; pupil of Dürer; probably the first German to paint pure landscape in oils; intense interest in nature; known for paintings of sheltered, secure places in forests; several outstanding battle pictures (Issus, Arbela, Alexander); *Landscape with Footbridge* (Berne), first landscape; *St. Florian,* altarpiece (Uffizi); *Virgin Amidst Angels; St. George and the Dragon* (Munich).

Holbein, Hans, the Elder. *ca.* 1465-1524. Master draftsman, engraver; known for silverpoint portrait drawings; altarpieces of great beauty, *Saint Sebastian* (1516, Munich), masterpiece; stained-glass windows.

Pacher, Michael. *ca.* 1435-98. Leading south German master of the Gothic; altarpiece, *The Fathers of the Church* (Munich), famous example of style; monumentality of isolated figures against Gothic architectural background; dynamic line and brilliance of color anticipates Baroque; excellence as woodcarver exemplified in the winged *St. Wolfgang,* altarpiece (1486-90).

DEAD CHRIST (PANEL), HOLBEIN THE YOUNGER

France

Fouquet, Jean. *ca.* 1415/20-*ca.* 1480. Considered founder of 15th-century school of French painting; combined Flemish and Florentine styles; painted first French landscapes; noted for illuminations for Duc de Berry's Book of Hours (*Les Très Riches Heures du Berry,* Chantilly); panel portraits, *Étienne Chevalier* (kneeling with St. Stephen, Berlin), *Agnes Sorel* (Antwerp), and *Charles VII* (d. 1465); illustrated French translations of Boccaccio; best work in miniatures.

ÉTIENNE CHEVALIER AND ST. STEPHEN, BY FOUQUET

Others. Enguerrand Charonton (*ca.* 1410/15-after 66); Nicolas Froment (*ca.* 1425-*ca.* 84): Master of Moulins (*fl.* 1480-1500); Master of the Villeneuve (famed *Pietà, ca.* 1460, Louvre).

Portugal

Gonçalvès, Nuno. *fl.* mid-15th century. Considered greatest Portuguese artist; superb altarpiece, *St. Vincent Polytych* (1458-64, Lisbon), showing King Alfonso, Henry the Navigator in six large panels (oils); extraordinary psychological analysis of subjects; first to stress loneliness, isolation, solitude of man.

Spain

Bartolomé Bermejo (*fl.* 1470-98), School of Valencia; **Jaume Huguet** (*fl.* 1448-92), Catalonia.

ASIA · *China*

Shen Chou (also known by courtesy name of Shên-Shih-t'ien). 1427-1509. Great master of Ming period; considered founder of Wu school at Soochow; outstanding representative of this 15th-century southern school of landscape artists; recluse; scholar; strong element of realism; color secondary to brush strokes and graduation of ink tones; *Happy Fisherman of River Village* (Freer, Washington); *Gardening*, album leaf, ink, and color on paper (Nelson, Kansas City); *Poet on a Mountain;* very influential.

Wen Cheng-ming (Wên Pi). 1470-1559. Scholar-painter; associated with Shên Chou; individual style; strong landscapes; elegant restraint, clear vibrant color; influence of Yüan masters evident in late works: *Mountain Landscape* (Boston), *Epidendrum and Bamboo* (Peking), *Cypress and Rock* (Kansas City).

T'ang Yin. 1470-1523. Renowned member of Wu school; remarkably versatile; imposing landscapes, greatest contribution; gay genre pictures, studies of beautiful young women, often against somber landscape; flowers and ink bamboo paintings; exaggerated tonal contrasts; *Landscape, Early Spring* (Peking); *Voyage to the South* (1505, Freer, Washington), ink on paper.

Wu Wei. 1458/9-1508. Famed, eccentric artist, highly regarded by Emperor Hsien-tsung; great originality; magnificent landscapes; charming figure paintings; *Scholar Seated under a Tree* (Boston), ink and light color on silk.

Tai Chin. *fl.* 15th century. Founder of Chê school; invited to court, appointed to Academy during Hsüan-tê era, but preferred to return to Chekiang; influenced by Ma-Hsia style; great influence because of powerful, original, dynamic yet refined style.

Chang Lu. *ca.* 1464-1538. Master of Chê school; lively, strong brush stroke; *The Fisherman* (Gokokuji, Kyoto), masterpiece; *Lao-tzu Riding on a Water-buffalo* (Peking).

Li Tsai. *fl.* 15th century. Master of Ming period; outstanding landscape painter; attached to Academy during Hsüan-tê era; highly praised by Japanese master Sesshū who visited China (1468).

Chou Ch'en. *fl.* 1500-35. Renowned landscape artist; teacher of T'ang Yin (see above).

Lü Chi. *fl.* 1488-1505. Most famous bird and flower painter of Ming period; elegant, decorative large paintings; bold ink painting with brilliant color in realistic portrayal of birds; fond of "one corner" or asymmetrical composition; *Geese Beside a Snowy Bank* (Peking).

Japan

Sesshū. 1420-1506. A leading painter of the Muromachi period; worked in China and returned with new techniques to Japan; magnificent compositions; powerful brush stroke; very influential.

Tosa Mitsunobu. 1434-1525. Leader of Tosa school; highly thought of in China; known for illustrated history and battle scenes; simple composition, subtle use of color.

Persia

Bihzād, Kāmal al-Dīn. *ca.* 1455-1535/36. Lived in Herat; studied with painter Mirak Naqqas; employed on staff of royal library; contributed miniatures to illustrate a copy of Sa'di's *Bustan* (1488/89); believed to have accompanied Shah Ismail Safavi to capital of Tabriz (1510); credited with miniatures for two manuscripts of the *Khamsa* of Nizami for Shah Tahmasp (1493-94); brilliant teacher; tremendous influence; considered one of the greatest Persian painters; numerous works.

Khamsa, of Mir Ali Shir Nawa'i, attributed to **Shah Muzaffar,** Herat (1485).

SCULPTURE

EUROPE · *Italy*

Michelangelo Buonarroti. 1475-1564. Greatest sculptor of the High Renaissance; influenced by Della Quercia, Donatello; overwhelming power and monumentality; important works include *Pietà* (1513-16, St. Peter's, Rome); *David* (1501-04); *Bound Slave,* for unfinished tomb of Pope Julius II (1513-16); *Moses* (*ca.* 1513-

ISKANDAR AND THE SEVEN SAGES, FROM KHAMSA MANUSCRIPT, BIHZAD

DAWN, FROM MEDICI TOMB, MICHELANGELO

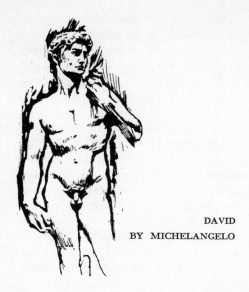

DAVID
BY MICHELANGELO

15); figures for the tombs of the Medici (1524-34); *Youth Crouching* (Leningrad); *Cupid Kneeling;* figure of *Victory*; *Christ Risen* (London); and the moving work of his old age, the *Rondanini Pietà* (*ca.* 1555-64); incomparable influence.

Verrocchio, Andrea del (di Cione). 1435-88. Great Florentine master sculptor, painter, woodcarver, gold-

EQUESTRIAN FIGURE
OF COLLEONI
BY VERROCCHIO

smith, musician, and mathematician; important teacher of Leonardo and others; studied with Donatello; bronze statue of *David* (Bergallo, Florence); works for the Medici tombs; famous equestrian statue of *Bartolommeo Colleoni* (Venice); *Boy with a Dolphin,* fountain figure; superb portrait of *Lorenzo de' Medici* in terra cotta (Washington); numerous small works.

Sansovino, Andrea (Contucci). 1460-1529. Tuscan sculptor and architect; studied in Florence with Pollaiuolo; worked for King John of Portugal; *Baptism of Christ* over the east door of the baptistery, Florence; *Madonna and Child;* bas reliefs on exterior of marble temple, Santa Casa; emotionalism and exaggerated movement often "mannerist" in style.

Pollaiuolo, Antonio. 1429-98. Sculptor, goldsmith, engraver, painter; leading Florentine sculptor in bronze (after Verrocchio); tombs of *Sixtus IV* and *Innocent VIII;* bronze group, *Hercules Strangling Cacus;* terra-cotta bust, *The Young Warrior.*

Agostino (d'Antonio) **di Duccio.** 1418-after 1481. Florentine, noted for excellent low reliefs, sculptural decorations; best-known for façade of Oratory of San Bernardino, Perugia, in colored marble and glazed terra cotta; superb example of polychrome architectural sculpture; *Pietà*, altar of the cathedral, Perugia; marble of colossal figure for Cathedral, Florence, later used by Michelangelo for his statue of *David.*

Della Robbia, Luca (di Simone di Marco). 1399-82. Founder of the Robbia atelier of sculpture and ceramics; early works in gold, bronze, and marble; perfected process for making clay reliefs and figures permanent by

145

glazing them with a compound that included tin, antimony, and other substances; ten marble panels in high relief, *Cantoria* or *Singing Gallery* (*ca.* 1435, Florence); bas reliefs set into side of Giotto's *Campanile;* architectural reliefs with madonnas, prophets, saints, etc. for many churches; family carried on tradition; known for "Della Robbia Blue."

Della Robbia, Andrea. 1435/7-1525. Nephew of above; small figures in marble for chapel of S. Maria delle Grazie, near Arezzo; 14 medallions of nude *bambini* (babies) in swaddling clothes placed between arches on the

THE ANNUNCIATION, GLAZED TERRACOTTA BY DELLA ROBBIA

loggia of the hospital of the Innocents (Foundling Hospital, Florence); *Madonna,* Santa Maria Maggiore; *Assumption of the Virgin* (Met. Mus.).

Desiderio da Settignano. 1428-64. Florentine; pupil of Donatello; known for charming, delicate studies of young women and children; portrait bust of *Marietta degli Strozzi* (Berlin); excellent tomb decorations; tabernacle, Church of San Lorenzo, Florence.

Mino da Fiesole (di Giovanni). 1431-84. Florentine; pupil of Desiderio da Settignano; worked in Rome; marble altar, S. Maria Maggiore; tomb of *Pope Paul II;* excellent portraits; tombs of *Bernardo de'Giugni, Count Hugh of Magdebourg,* latter considered best work.

Torrigiano, Pietro. 1472-1522. Florentine; worked for Lorenzo de' Medici; notorious for violent temper, believed to have broken Michelangelo's nose; fled to Rome and worked for Pope Alexander VI on Borgia tower; tomb of *Henry VII and Queen* in Westminster Abbey (1518); polychrome, terracotta busts, including *Sir Henry Guilford, St. John Fisher,* Bishop of Rochester, in England; worked in Spain.

Benedetto da Maiano (di Leonardo). 1442-97. Florentine; outstanding portraits in marble and marquetry: *Giotto, Dante, Petrarch, Filippo Strozzi, Galeotto Malatesta;* pulpit of Santa Croce; tomb of *Filippo Strozzi,* Church of Santa Maria Novella; brother Giuliano (1432-90); also sculptor.

Finiguerra, Maso (or Tommaso). 1426-64. Florentine goldsmith and engraver; Cellini considered him first master of his time in *niello* engraving; pax of the Crucifixion for the Baptistery, Florence.

Rossellino, Antonio. 1427-ca. 1479. Brother of Bernardo; famous for tomb of *Cardinal James* of Portugal in San Miniato al Monte, Florence; *Nativity Group* (Met. Mus.); sarcophagus of *St. Marcolinus* (Forlì Mus.); *Madonna* (Berlin); Portrait of *Giovanni da San Miniato* (London).

Lombardi, Alfonso. 1497-1537. Sculptor of Ferrara; portrait medallions; decorated door of S. Petronio, Bologna for coronation of Charles V; tomb of *Ramazzotto Scaricalasiao*, Bosco; *Death of Our Lady*, Hospital of La Vita, Bologna; portrait busts includes one of *Charles V*.

Solari, Christoforo. *fl.* 1480-1521. (Known as Il Gobbo, the Hunchback); gained recognition in Lombardy; large statues of *Adam* and *Eve* on eastern façade of the duomo of Milan considered best work.

Vecchietto, Il (Lorenzo di Piero). *ca.* 1412-80. Sienese; goldsmith, architect, painter as well as sculptor; influence of Donatello (finished some of his works); life-sized studies of *St. Peter* and *St. Paul; Risen Christ* for the bronze tabernacle in the Cathedral of Siena; *Christ Carrying the Cross* (Hospital of the Scala, Siena).

Others. Andrea Riccio (*ca.* 1470-1532), Giovanni Della Robbia (1469-1529), Girolamo Della Robbia (1488-1566), Guido Mazzoni (1450-1518), Pietro Lombardi (1435-1515), Francesco Laurana (*ca.* 1420/25-1502), Andrea Ferrucci (1465-1526), Andrea Bregno (1421-1506), Giorgio Andreoli (*ca.* 1465-1555), Antonio Amadeo (*ca.* 1447-1522).

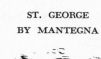

ST. GEORGE
BY MANTEGNA

THE LAMENTATION (DETAIL)
BY NICCOLO DELL'ARCA

ST. SEBASTIAN
BY MANTEGNA

Germany

Stoss, Veit (Stosz). 1447-1542. Master woodcarver, sculptor, painter, engraver; influenced by Nicolaus Gerhaert and the *High Altar* of the Master of the Nordlingen; great carved altar (Marienkirche), his masterpiece; tomb of *Casimir IV,* (1477-89, Cracow, Poland); *Crucifixion* in St. Sebald's, *High Altar* (Bamberg Cathedral), *Annunciation* (St. Lawrence's, Nurem-

FLYING ANGEL,
DETAIL FROM ANNUNCIATION
BY STOSS

VIRGIN AND CHILD,
BOXWOOD
BY STOSS

berg); tombstone of *Archbishop Olesnicki* (Gniezno Cathedral).

Krafft, Adam. 1450-1508/9. Outstanding master of Nuremberg; style bridged late Gothic and early Renaissance; individuality of portrait characterization; self-portrait seen in figure crouching in front of the tabernacle, Church of St. Lawrence (Nuremberg); tombs and reliefs for *Seven Stations of the Cross* (St. Sebald's).

Gerhaert, Nicolaus (Nicholas of Leyden) *ca.* 1420/30-87. Early leader of late Gothic sculpture in Germany; interested in accuracy of anatomical form, concern for use of space; best-known work tomb of *Archbishop Jacob von Sierk* in Trier; crucified *Christ,* Baden-Baden; portrait busts.

Vischer, Peter, the Elder. *ca.* 1455/60-1529. Leader of a family of sculptors and metalworkers; foundry, Nuremberg; bronze tomb of *St. Sebald,* Nuremberg; imposing bronze tomb of *Emperor Maximillian,* with larger-than-life-sized bronze statues of *King Arthur* and *Theodoric* in armor; tomb of *Archbishop Ernest of Saxony* (Magdeburg Cathedral).

Riemenschneider, Tilman. *ca.* 1460-1530/31. Leading Bavarian sculptor, woodcarver; clean, restrained composition, expressive figures; *Ascension of the Virgin,* altar, Church of Our Lord (Creglingen); tomb of *Bishop Scherenburg,* figures of *Adam* and *Eve* for Chapel of the Virgin (Würzburg Cathedral); *Saint Burchard* (Washington); important influence.

Leinberger, Hans. *ca.* 1480/85-1531/5. Bavarian master; work shows influence of late Gothic, but anticipates baroque; *Virgin and Child* (Landsnut), *Resting Christ* (Berlin), *James the Elder* (Munich).

Notke, Bernt. *ca.* 1440-1507. Sculptor of Lübeck; monumental group (over 9 ft. high), *St. George and the Dragon* for Nicolai Church (1489, Stockholm); used gilt armor set with green and red stones, rich sculptural trappings on the horse.

Others. Michael Wohlgemuth (1434-1519), Hans Backoffen (1470-1519), Gregor Erhard (*ca.* 1468-1540), Erasmus Grasser (1450-1518), Adolf Daucher (*ca.* 1460/65-1523), Hans Brueggemann (*ca.* 1480-1540), Jörg Syrlin (*ca.* 1425/30-91).

Spain

Siloé, Gil de. *ca.* 1475-1505. One of last Gothic artists in Spain; son Diego (d. 1563) influenced by Italian Renaissance.

Fancelli, Domenico Alessandro. 1469-1518. Italian working in Spain; influenced by Mino da Fiesole; monuments: *Cardinal Diego Hurtado de Mendoza* (Seville Cathedral); *Catholic Kings* for the Royal Chapel at Granada.

France

Colombe, Michel. 1430-after 1512. Early Renaissance artist; known for royal tombs in Cathedral, Nantes.

Netherlands

Meit, Conrad. *ca.* 1480-*ca.* 1550. Court sculptor to Margarethe, Stattholder of Netherlands in Malines, Antwerp; family monuments; also known for alabaster figures; *Judith* (Munich).

Portugal

Chanterene, Nicholas. d. 1551.

French sculptor of Portuguese court, Coimbra (1518-28); *King Manuel, Queen Maria,* entrance statues of Jeronimos basilica; Sintra altar; façade figures of Santa Cruz; alabaster tomb, *Bishop Alonso;* monument of *Alvaro da Costa.*

ARCHITECTURE

EUROPE · *Italy*

Alberti, Leone Battista. 1404-72. Considered by many the founder of the High Renaissance; versatile Florentine genius; architect, writer, painter, organist, and sculptor; designed Churches of *San Sebastiano* and *San Andrea,* Mantua; *San Francesco,* known

FAÇADE AND LEFT SIDE, SAN SEBASTIANO, ALBERTI, MANTUA

as the Temple of the Malatesta, Rimini; first adaptation of Roman triumphal arch to church architecture; *Palazzo Rucellai* (1446-51) and the façade of *Santa Maria Novella,* Florence; *Palazzo Strozzi;* ten-volume work on architecture, *De re aedificatoria* (1485), extremely important influence.

Bramante, Donato (di Pascuccio d'Antonio). 1444-1514. Great Renaissance architect, painter, probably only artist in Italy in his day with knowledge of principles of mathematics and statics as applied to the construction of vaults; first developed round arch, column, cornice, frieze, and capital by adapting scientific knowledge to classical forms; designed and decorated study of Duke of Montefeltro, Urbino, first important example of illusionistic space; worked in Bergamo; employed by Duke Lodovico Sforza, Milan; S. Maria presso, S. Satiro; S. Maria delle Grazie; cloisters of S. Maria della Pace; *Tempietto* in the courtyard of S. Pietro, Montorio (1502); employed by Popes Alexander VI and Julius II; drew plans (later used as basis of Michelangelo's plan), car-

THE VATICAN, ROME

ried out only in part, for the reconstruction of *St. Peter's,* Rome; long gallery at the Vatican connecting the old palace with the Belvedere; court of the loggia finished by Raphael (containing his frescoes).

Sangallo, Giuliano da (Giamberti). 1445-1516. Florentine architect, sculp-

tor, military engineer; assisted Raphael in designing and building *St. Peter's,* Rome; built octagonal sacristy of *Santo Spirito,* Florence; cloister of Cestello, Pazzi; *St. Maria delle Carceri,* Prato (1485); *Palazzo Gondi,* Florence; *Villa Reale,* Poggio a Caiano, charming country house.

Giorgio, Francesco di Martini. 1439-1502. Master Sienese architect, engineer, sculptor, painter; gained recognition and employed by lords of other cities; served Duke Federigo da Montefeltro of Urbino; design for dome of *Milan Cathedral;* architect, *Cathedral of Siena;* important military inventions.

Filarete (Antonio di Pietro Averlino). 1400-69/70. Architect, sculptor, author of *Trattato architetture,* written in form of a romance (25 vols.), includes first design for wholly symmetrical (central) town plan; worked for Francesco Sforza (1451-65); designed hospital (*Ospedale Maggiore*), Milan; began cathedral at Bergamo.

Pollaiuolo, Simone. (Il Cronaca). 1457-1508. Florentine architect; known for great cornice of Strozzi Palace; *Church of San Bartolommeo,* San Miniato, considered his masterpiece; great hall of *Palazzo Vecchio.*

Bramantino (Bartolommeo Suardi). *ca.* 1460-*ca.* 1536. Milanese master; painter, architect; when in 1499 Bramante and Leonardo had left Milan, Bramantino became the leading artist of the city; designed original Trivulzio burial chapel; court painter and architect to Duke Francesco Maria Sforza (1525).

Laurana, Luciano da. *fl.* 1468-82. Sienese architect known especially for ducal palaces of Urbino and Gubbio built for Federigo da Montefeltro, Duke of Urbino.

Agnolo, Baccio d'. 1460/62-1543. Florentine architect and woodcarver; decorations for church of Santa Maria Novella; designed the *Villa Borghese, Bartolini Palace,* house of Taddeo Taddei; campanile of *Santo Spirito,* Florence (unfinished); campanile of *San Miniato di Monte;* in charge of principal monasteries and convents of Florence.

Giocondo, Fra Giovanni. *ca.* 1433-1515. Veronese architect; known for design of marble, *Loggia del Consiglio* (1476-93, Verona; for King Louis XII, he designed the *Pont Notre Dame,* Paris; architect at *St. Peter's,* Rome (1514).

Raphael (Raffaello Santi). 1483-1520. Famous artist of Renaissance; few architectural works documented; *Palazzo Vidoni Caffarelli,* Rome, attributed to him; succeeded Bramante as chief architect of *St. Peter's* (1514); mature style influenced by Michelangelo.

Austria

Pilgram, Anton. *ca.* 1450/60-1515. Noted architect and sculptor; works bridge late Gothic and early Renaissance; known for *St. Stephen's Cathedral,* Vienna.

Spain

Guas, Juan. d. 1496. Outstanding Breton architect trained in Brussels; settled in Toledo with workshop of Flemish assistants; known for church and cloister, *San Juan de los Reyes,* (1479-80, Toledo); large townhouse, *Infantado Palace,* Guadalajara (1480-

83); chapel of *San Gregori,* Valladolid (1488).

Vasquez, Lorenzo. *fl.* 15th century. Leading architect of Valladolid; born, Segovia; believed to have been trained in Bologna; sometimes called the Spanish Brunelleschi; *Colegio de Santa Cruz,* (1486, Valladolid), Gothic in style; *Medinaceli Palace,* (1492-95, Cogolludo), Renaissance style reminiscent of Filarete's *Banco Mediceo,* Milan; *San Antonio de Mondejar* (before 1508); *Calahorra Castle,* Granada.

Egas, Enrique. d. 1534. Noted designer of the *Hospital Real* in Santiago de Compostela (1501-11); *Hospital de Santa Cruz* (1504-14, Toledo).

Gumiel, Pedro de. d. 1514-17. Chief proponent of "Cisneros style" of *mudéjar* decoration; architect to Cardinal Ximénez, Alcala; credited with design of academic theater of the University of Alcala (1518-19).

Russia

Tsar Ivan III, the Great, (1462-1505) undertook a vast building program greatly influenced by Western European architecture; many architects, sculptors were imported to work at the Kremlin, Moscow; building of the new cathedral of the *Dormition* was entrusted to two Russians (**Miskin** and **Krivtsov**) and the work began (1471), but the building started to collapse, and the job went to Aristotele **Fioravante** of Bologna, Italy (1475-79); Alevisio **Novi** was commissioned to rebuild the old *Cathedral of St. Michael the Archangel* (1505); *Church of the Annunciation* in the Kremlin was built (1484-89).

AMERICAS · *Inca*

1438-1527 was Golden Age of Inca Empire; great stone structures of Cuzco, Cajamarca, Sacsahuamán, and Machu Picchu in the highlands of Peru, and Pachacamac on the coast date from this period. Walls of skilfully-cut stones joined without mortar or metal clamps; smooth or rough-hewn surfaces are without ornamentation and rely for effect upon the arrangement of small trapeze like openings for doors and windows.

MACHU PICCHU, PERU (INCA)

ISLAM · *Istanbul*

Chinili Kiosk, known as the porcelain pavilion, in Tapkapu Serai (old Seraglio), was built for Sultan Muhammad II, the conqueror of Constantinople, by the architect **Kammal-al-Din** (1466-70); restored during the reign of Murad III (1590).

Cairo

Many important additions to the *al-Azhar Mosque*, originally built by the first Fatimite Sultan of Egypt (978), were made by Kait Beg (1468-96).

P'AI-LOU (GATEWAY), NEAR PEIPING, MING DYNASTY

MUSIC

EUROPE · *Franco-Flemish School*

Josquin Després (Des Préz). *ca.* 1450-1521. Considered one of the great musicians of all time and the first modern composer; singer in Milan Cathedral (1459-72); in service of Duke of

JOSQUIN DESPRÉS

Milan (1474-79); member Papal Chapel (until 1494); choirmaster, Cambrai (1495-99); in Paris for Louis XII (*ca.* 1500); Duke of Ferrara (1503); great ability more apparent in his church than secular music; 29 Masses, 119 motets, approached *a capella* ideal; 86 secular compositions included *ballades, bergerettes,* and *chansons* (nearly all with French words); use of imitation, division of choir, and freedom of expression mark works as Renaissance (showing independence of spirit) rather than Gothic.

Ockeghem (Okeghem), Jan (Johannes) van. 1425/30-95. Great master; considered founder of Second Netherland (Flemish) School; chorister, Antwerp Cathedral (1443-44); chapel, Duke of Bourbon (1446-48); chapel, King of France (1452, Paris); *maître de chapelle* (1465); imaginative, inventive; first to use imitation systematically enough to develop its potentialities; under his guidance vocal polyphony gained in sophistication; master of counterpoint; dominated second half of 15th century; 16 Masses, motets, and *chansons*; as great teacher, his influence was tremendous.

Agricola (Ackermann), Alexander. *ca.* 1446-1506. Leading Flemish composer; educated in the Netherlands; pupil of Ockeghem; served Charles VIII of France, Lorenzo de' Medici, Duke of Mantua, Philip I of Castile (1505), and the Duke of Austria; wrote motets, four-part songs, volume of five Masses.

Obrecht, Jacob. 1450-1505. Leading Dutch composer; important teacher at Cambrai, Bruges, and in Florence, where he introduced the work of the Flemish contrapuntists to the Italians; chapel master, Antwerp Cathedral; composer of many Masses, motets, and secular works; remarkable technique; considered only real representative of the Netherlands in this period.

Busnois, Antoine de (Busne). d.

SINGING ANGELS FROM CANTORIA, FLORENCE, DELLA ROBBIA

1492. Burgundian court composer; pupil of Ockeghem; surpassed master in writing of songs, 77 of which are preserved and show careful workmanship and witty, tender mood; enjoyed a vogue for more than half a century.

Compère, Loyset. d. 1518. Leading writer of *chansons*; pupil of Ockeghem; canon and chancellor of St. Quentin Cathedral; composed Masses and motets.

Mouton, Jean (de Hollinque). *ca.* 1470-1522. French composer; link between his teacher, Josquin, and his pupil, Willaert; Canon of Thérouann, and later Saint-Quentin; court musician to Louis XII and Francis I of France; distinguished contrapuntist; exceptional writer of songs that are subtle, moving; works include Masses, motets, psalms, and a few French *chansons.*

Rue, Pierre de la (Petrus Platensis). *ca.* 1460-1518. Known as Pierchon; composer, disciple of Ockeghem;

served Maximilian (from 1492), Philip of Burgundy in Brussels (1496-1506), Margaret of Austria, Regent of the Netherlands, thereafter; canon at Courtrai (1516); 30 Masses; six separate Kyries or Credos, many *chansons* and motets.

Latins, Arnold de. *fl.* late 15th century. Composer; singer Papal Chapel (1431); 13 sacred works, including a complete Mass; 14 surviving three-part *chansons*.

England

Aston, Hugh. *ca.* 1480-after 1549. Leading Tudor composer; master of choristers, St. Mary Newarke Hospital and College, Leicester (*ca.* 1525-48); *Hornpipe* for virginals, early instrumental work, anticipates methods (variation form with drone bass) of Elizabethan and Jacobean composers; canon, St. Stephen's, Westminster; composed church music.

Fayrfax, Robert. d. 1521. Celebrated Tudor composer; Doctor of Music, Cambridge (1501-02), Oxford (1512); organist, St. Albans Abbey; Gentleman of Chapel Royal; mostly church music.

Cornyshe, William. *ca.* 1468-1523. Composer, playwright; Gentleman of Chapel Royal (1496); favorite of Henry VIII; presented pageants, interludes at court; wrote secular part songs.

Italy

Squarcialupi, Antonio. 1416-80. Famous Florentine organist and lute player; lived in Siena (1450); organist of Santa Maria, Florence (1467) for Lorenzo de' Medici; known for manuscript (called Squarcialupi manuscript) in Laurentian Library; largest

surviving collection of 14th-century music, including 145 pieces by Landini, and the music of 11 other composers; wrote *sacra rappresentazione* for Lorenzo.

Germany

Isaac, Heinrich (Isaak, Hendryk). *ca.* 1450-1517. Leading composer; thought to be a Netherlander from Brabant, but the Italians called him "Arrigo Tedesco" (Harry the German); extremely versatile; worked for Lorenzo de' Medici in Florence (1480-92); served Emperor Maximilian (1497); considered first of German contrapuntal masters because of greatest work, *Choralis Constantinus* (published Nuremberg, 1550-55); music for religious drama, *San Giovanni de San Paolo,* by Lorenzo (1488), for whom he also set carnival songs; organist, choirmaster, composer of *canzona* ("gingerbread venders", popular), madrigals, and church music.

Walther, Johann. 1496-1570. Protestant church singer, musician, and com-

MUSICIANS
(AFTER DÜRER)
PLAYING PIPE
AND TABOR

poser; choirmaster; served Elector of Saxony (1525); director, chapel, Dresden (1548-54); adviser, friend of Martin Luther, with whom he worked on framing of *German Mass* (music of Reformed Church, 1524-26); published *Geystlich Gersangk-Buchleyn* for four voices, first Protestant songbook (1524); composed religious songs, church music, and instrumental pieces.

Luther, Martin. 1483-1546. Famed Protestant reformer, musician; created church hymnody in which congregation and choir sang in German; reformed liturgy in his Latin Mass (*Formula Missae,* 1523); *German Mass* (1524-26); wrote words for at least 36 chorales; motets; treatise on music (1538); "A Mighty Fortress is Our God," typical Luther hymn.

Hofhaimer, Paul. 1459-1537. Leading organist of day; founder of important school of players and composers for the organ; served at Innsbruck (1479), Augsburg (1507), Salzburg (1519); composer at court of Emperor Maximilian I; enobled by emperor, and made Knight of Golden Spur by king of Hungary; wrote three- and four-part songs.

Finck, Heinrich. 1445-1527. Austrian composer, educated in Poland; served at Polish court; Kapellmeister at Stuttgart and Salzburg; compositions include Masses, motets, and secular part songs.

Behaim, Michel. 1416-74. Meistersinger; soldier and court singer in Hungary, Norway, the Palatinate, and elsewhere; author of *Buch von den Wienern,* dealing with siege of the Imperial Palace of Vienna (1462), and other works.

Paumann, Conrad. *ca.* 1410-73.

Famed blind organist of Nuremberg (1446); church organist, Munich (1467); *Fundamentum organisandi* (1452), noted early work and keyboard tablature; leading figure in development of instrumental music.

Fulde, Adam von. b. *ca.* 1450. Foremost German musical scholar; important *Tract on Music* (1490).

MUSIC-MAKING ANGELS: INSTRUMENTS INCLUDE PSALTERY, "TROMPETTE MARINE," LUTE, TENOR TRUMPET, PIPE

THEATER

EUROPE · *Italy*

Ariosto, Ludovico. 1474-1533. Outstanding poet, author of *Orlando Furioso;* began to write comedies (*ca.* 1495); first extant play, *The Casket* (1508); *I suppositi* (The Pretenders, performed *ca.* 1512); *The Charlatan* (1520); *Lena* (1529); excellent portrayal of contemporary manners.

Politan (Angelo Poliziano, originally Ambrogini). 1454-94. Poet, humanist; teacher under the Medicis in Florence; wrote *Sacra rappresentazione* with Lorenzo de' Medici; *Orfeo* (1471), earliest Italian play of any real quality, considered one of the better lyric works of the period; delicacy of expression; unity of dramatic effect.

Machiavelli, Niccolò. 1469-1527. Brilliant statesman and author of *The Prince;* wrote clever satiric comedies including *La Clizia* (1506), and better-known *La Mandragola* (The Mandrake, performed Florence, 1520); exposed contemporary stupidity and corruption.

MACHIAVELLI

Trissino, Gian Giorgio. 1478-1550. Poet; first Italian poetic drama written according to classical rules; his *Sophonisba* (1515) imitated Euripides, and *The Identical Twins* (1548, Venice) imitated Plautus; used blank verse, that influenced other dramatists and writers of madrigals.

Commelli, Antonio. *fl.* late 15th century. At court of Ferrara; produced *Filostrato e Panfila* (1499), first tragedy written in Italian that combined elements of mystery plays with Roman playwrights; plot had been used by Boccaccio in his tale of *Gismonda*.

Bibbiena, Cardinal Bernardo Dovizi

da. 1470-1519. Dramatist; wrote *La Calandria* (The Comedy of Calandro, performed in Urbino, 1513); based on Plautus' *Casina*; *Menaechmi*, portrayed life in the 16th century.

Boiardo, Matteo Maria (Count of Scandiano). *ca.* 1440-94. Poet; wrote comedy *Timone*.

Rucellai, Giovanni. 1475-1526. Author of one of the first tragedies, *Rosmunda* (1515), based on a play by Seneca.

Sacra rappresentazione, performed in celebration of St. John, the patron saint of Florence, under the guidance of Lorenzo de' Medici (performed 1453-92), were very important in the development of opera and theater in Italy; Lorenzo, with Politan, took months to prepare these elaborate performances; based on Greek legend, they combined biblical pageantry, masquelike musical interludes, and brilliant, elaborate sets designed and painted by Raphael, Brunelleschi, Leonardo, and others.

Portugal

Vicente, Gil. *ca.* 1470-*ca.* 1537/9. Outstanding dramatist, poet; believed to have written 44 plays, many in Castilian; considerable influence in shaping Spanish and Portuguese theater; leading figure of Iberian Renaissance; religious trilogy, *Barca do Inferno* (The Boat of Hell, 1517), *Barca do Purgatorio* (1518), and *Barco do Gloria* (1519).

France

Under Louis XI, "Brothers of the Passion" established a theater (*ca.* 1467) that presented both religious and secular works.

Spain

Encina, Juan del. *ca.* 1469-1533/4. Leading dramatist, poet, musician; worked in Italy and for the Duke of Alba; often referred to as the founder of Spanish drama; precursor of Lope de Vega; first play *Triunfo de la fama* (1492) written to commemorate the Fall of Granada; *Cancionero* (published 1496) contained musical and lyrical compositions; *Placida y Victoriano* (performed in Rome, 1513).

England

Medwall, Henry. Chaplain to Cardinal Morton; author of earliest English secular drama, *Fulgens and Lucres,* interlude in two parts (1497, printed 1513-19).

GERMAN ARMOR, AUGSBURG, *ca.* 1480

ITALIAN ARMOR, 1460.

1525-1600

The early Baroque period in Italy produced the Great Venetian masters, Titian, Tintoretto, and Veronese, whose monumental mural compositions, with their dynamic concept of space and obvious emphasis on grandeur, contrast sharply with the decorative, brilliant, yet shallow technique of the "Mannerist" painters, who concentrated on personal self-expression and a completely self-conscious style of individuality.

El Greco, the greatest artist of the Counter Reformation, expressed spiritual intensity through powerful motion, elongated figures, and brilliant color. In sharp contrast, Pieter Brueghel the Elder introduced the powerful realism of the Flemish school.

PAINTING

EUROPE · Italy

Michelangelo di Ludovico Buonarroti. 1475-1564. Great master painter, sculptor, architect, and poet of Florence and Rome; independent, accepting only those challenging commissions he decided worthy of his genius; powerful figures, dynamic expression very close to being sculpturesque in quality; had profound influence on other artists; most famous masterpiece, ceiling of Sistine Chapel (Vatican, Rome), including *The Deluge, The Creation of Adam,* and the *Last Judgment* (1508-12); frescoes for Pauline

CREATION OF ADAM, DETAIL OF SISTINE CEILING BY MICHELANGELO

Chapel that included *Conversion of St. Paul* and *Crucifixion;* only easel painting extant, tempera, *Holy Family* (*ca.* 1506, Uffizi); *Madonna and Child with St. John and Angels* (*ca.* 1494, London).

Titian (Tiziano Vecellio). *ca.* 1477-1576 (debated). Extraordinary Venetian genius; dramatic monumentality characterized his work; sumptuous, sensual color; vitality and sharp perception evident in his great portraits including *Charles V* (Prado), *Pope Paul III and Grandsons* (Naples),

VENUS OF URBINO BY TITIAN

Alfonso d' Este, Duke of Ferrara (Met. Mus.), *Philip II* (Prado), *Man with the Glove* (Louvre), *Pietro Aretino,* and others; pupil of Bellini, friend of Giorgione; *Assumption of the Virgin* (1516) introduced baroque style; *Christ Crowned with Thorns* (Munich) painted in broad, wild brush strokes directly onto canvas; other great works include *Bacchanal* (Prado), *Venus of Urbino* (Uffizi), *Pietà* (Venice), *Entombment* (Madrid), *Ecce Homo* (Leningrad), *Venus and the Lute Player* (Met. Mus.), *Rape of Europa* (Boston), *Venus with a Mirror* (Washington), *Madonna with Members of the Pesaro Family* (Church of the Frari, Venice); reached greatest freedom of expression in *Nymph and Shepherd* (Vienna).

Tintoretto (Jacopo Robusti). 1518-94. Great Venetian Renaissance master inspired and influenced by Michelangelo and Titian, but developed completely individual style; first important work, *Crucifixion* (1565), part of great cycle painted for Sculoa di San Rocco (1564-87); won most commissions in open competition; *Venus and Vulcan* (Munich), *Leda* (Florence), *Susanna and the Elders* (Vienna); melodramatic use of light influenced El Greco (see *Christ Walking on the Sea of Galilee, ca.*

159

SUSANNA AND THE ELDERS (DETAIL) BY
TINTORETTO

1562, Washington); outstanding portraits include *Cornaro* (Pitti), *Sansovina* (Uffizi), *Morosini* (London), *Old Man* (Berlin), and *Venetian Senator* (Frick, N.Y.); last work, *The Last Supper* (1592-94, Venice).

Caravaggio, Michelangelo Merisi da. 1573-1610. Master of extreme chiaroscuro; founder of naturalistic school in Rome; influenced Rembrandt, Ribera, and Spanish artists; use of peasant or humble people an innova-

CALLING OF SAINT MATTHEW (DETAIL)
BY CARAVAGGIO

tion; *Cardplayers* (Louvre), *Christ at Emmaus* (London), *Bacchus* (Uffizi), *The Fortune Teller* (Louvre), *Conversion of St. Paul* (Rome), *Madonna of the Rosaries* (Vienna), *The Death of the Virgin* (Louvre), *The Entombment* (Vatican), *Calling of St. Matthew* (Rome), among most moving of all religious paintings in art; considered by some first of the baroque artists.

Veronese, Paolo (Caliari, called Il Veronese from birthplace, Verona). 1528-88. Venetian master; renowned painter of sumptuous religious feast scenes; great decorative opulence; mythological, secular splendor; *Marriage* or *Wedding at Cana* (Louvre) shows Veronese playing cello, Bassano, a flute, and Titian, a bass viol; *Allegory of Venice* decorates the Great Council Hall of the Doge's Palace; *Finding of Moses* (Madrid), *Rape of Europa* (Venice), *Vision of the Cross* (London), *Christ in the House of Levi* and *Battle of Lepanto* (Venice); masterpieces of *trompe l'oeil* painting decorate door and windows of Barbaro villa, designed by Palladio, 40 miles from Venice.

Bronzino, Agnolo (di Cosimo Allori). 1503-72. Florentine court painter, excellent portraits product of mannerist stylistic movement; emphasis on surroundings and personal interests of sitter; *Eleanora di Toledo and Son, Giovanni de' Medici,* and *Don Garzia* (Uffizi), *Young Woman and her Little Boy* (Washington), *Portrait of a Young Man* (Met. Mus.).

Bassano (Jacopo da Ponte). *ca.* 1510-92. Venetian artist who was probably the first Italian to paint genre scenes; pictures of country life best work; influenced by Tintoretto in use of highlights; *Banquet of Rich Man* (Cleveland), *Adoration of the Shepherds* (Bassano), *Execution of John the Baptist* (Copenhagen).

Parmigianino (Francesco Mazzola). 1503-40. Important Mannerist painter and graphic artist; use of abstract form; delicacy of style; famous for *Madonna with the Long Neck* (*ca.* 1535, Uffizi), elegant, elongated figure, complex, diagonal design; *Vision of St. Jerome* (Washington); *Madonna with the Rose* (Dresden), most popular work; considered first important Italian etcher; drawing of warriors in classical costume, frieze (Met. Mus.).

Giulio Romano (Pippi de Gianuzzi). 1499-1546. Leading figure in school of Mantua (from 1524); studied and worked with Raphael; excellent portraits and frescoes executed for patron Duke Federigo Gonzaga, Mantua; late works unique, used highlights of blazing red against black shadows.

Moroni, Giovanni Battista. *ca.* 1525-78. North Italian artist (Bergamo); excellent portrait artist; touch of melancholy; unusual clarity and sharpness of technique; numerous altarpieces.

Lotto, Lorenzo. *ca.* 1480-1556. Venetian painter; frescoes, altarpieces; excellent portraits; influenced by Bellini and Titian; altarpiece of St. Lucia at Jesi, one of best works.

Clovio, Giorgio (called Macedo). 1498-1578. Regarded as one of the greatest Italian miniaturists and illuminators; master colorist and technician; brilliant illuminations for *Book of the Hours of the Blessed Virgin*.

Carracci, Lodovico. 1555-1619. Founder of Bolognese eclectic school; noted teacher of Reni, Albani, and Domenichino.

Carracci, Annibale. 1560-1609. Outstanding of three members of family (brother Agostino, cousin Lodovico), to work in Bologna; mythological, biblical subjects; exceptionally fine *Bacchante* (Uffizi); *Virgin Mourning over Christ* (Rome) and *Christ and the Woman of Samaria at the Well* (Vienna); ceiling fresco for Palazzo Farnese (1597-1601, Rome); restrained elegant movement contrasted with Mannerists.

Campi, Giulio. *ca.* 1500-72. Founder of school at Cremona; painter, architect; frescoes, Church of Santa Margherita; *Virgin and Child with Saints Celsus and Nazarus*, Church of Sant'Abbordio (Cremona).

Ferrari, Gaudenzio. *ca.* 1470-1546. Leader of Lombard school; frescoes of 21 scenes from the life of Christ in Santa Maria della Grazia (Varallo); magnificent cupola of church at Saronno (1535), showing all musical instruments in use at that time; tendency toward the baroque; *Annunciation* (Berlin).

Agostino Veneziano (or Agostino di Musi). *ca.* 1490-*ca.* 1540. Engraver; studied with Raimondi, executed plates after Raphael, Dürer, Michelangelo, and others.

Abbate, Niccolò dell'. *ca.* 1509-71. Worked at Fontainbleau, France; very imaginative landscapes; graceful, sinuous line; elongated figures, subtle use of sfumato; remarkable landscape, *Men Threshing Wheat* (*ca.* 1555-60, Fontainbleau); *The Death of Eurydice* (London).

Sodoma (Giovanni Antonio Bazzi). 1477-1549. Sienese painter; frescoes in Vatican; most important work, frescoes in Agostino Chugi's bedroom, Villa Farnesina (Rome); *St. George and the Dragon* (Washington).

Zucchero (Zuccaro or Zuccari), Federigo. 1543-1609. Founded Academy of St. Luke, Rome (1574), modeled after Royal Academy of England; worked in England, Spain, and Venice; famous for two portraits of *Mary Queen of Scots* (Chatsworth), *Lady in Fancy Dress* (Queen Elizabeth, Hampton Court); gained recognition as writer.

Primaticcio, Francesco. 1504-70. Mantuan artist; important in founding School of Fontainebleau; style synthesis of Giulio Romano's linear technique and Corregio's softness or delicacy; to Paris (1532); court painter to Francis I (see Sculpture).

Cambiaso, Luca (also Cambiasi, known as Lucchetto da Genova and Luchino). 1527-85. Genoese painter and sculptor; graceful design, excellent colorist; to Spain (1583) to paint frescoes at Escorial Palace for Philip II; outstanding work there *Assemblage of the Blessed* (on choir); *Madonna in Candlelight,* Palazzo Bianco (Genoa), mysterious dark mood, anticipates Georges de la Tour by a century.

Others. Domenico Beccafumi (*ca.* 1486-1551); Jacopo Pontormo (Carrucci, 1494-1556/7); Rosso Fiorentino (Giovanni Battista di Jacopo, 1494-1540); Michelangelo Anselmi (1491-1554); Alessandro Allori (1535-1607).

France

Clouet, François. *ca.* 1510-72. Most important French portrait painter of his time; court painter to Francis I, Henry II, Francis II, and Charles IX; excellent

FRANCIS I BY CLOUET

use of space and placement of figures in compositions; considered to have had more grace and refinement than Anthonis Mor; elaborate costume; *Diane de Poitiers Bathing* (Washington), *Henry II* (Uffizi); *Elizabeth of Austria* (Louvre) attributed to him; full-length portrait of *Charles IX* (*ca.* 1569, Vienna); excellent draftsman.

Limousin, Léonard. 1505-74. Famous for enamel plaques produced at Limoges; excellent portraitist; worked at Fontainbleau (1535), influenced by Clouet; received title "Enameller to the King" (1548); famed portrait of *Francis I.*

England

Hilliard, Nicholas. 1547-1619. Elizabethan miniature portrait painter and goldsmith; paintings on parchment encased and worn as jewelry; *A Young Man Among Roses* (ca. 1588, London), best-known work.

YOUNG MAN AMONG ROSES
BY HILLIARD

ASSUMPTION OF THE VIRGIN
BY EL GRECO

HOLY TRINITY BY EL GRECO

Spain

Greco, El (Domenico Theotoco-puli), *ca.* 1537-1614. One of the world's great masters; born in Crete; believed to have studied with Titian and worked with Tintoretto in Venice (*ca.* 1566-70); from Tintoretto he learned expressionism that became so important in his work; to Rome (*ca.* 1570), influenced by Michelangelo; to Toledo, Spain (*ca.* 1572); developed unique style immediately recognizable through elongated figures, dramatic landscapes, intensity of expressed emotion through motion, brilliant color, and the use of light; famous works include *View of Toledo* (Met. Mus.), *Burial of Count Orgaz* (*ca.* 1586, Toledo), *Agony in the Garden* (London), *Grand Inquisitor, Cardinal Don Fernando Nino de Guevara* (*ca.* 1600, Met. Mus.), *Portrait of a Nobleman* (Madrid), *Christ Driving the Money Changers from the Temple* (Minneapolis), *St. Francis in Ecstasy* (*ca.* 1585, Detroit), *Holy Trinity* (Prado),

Saint Maurice and the Theban Legend (*ca.* 1580, Escorial), *Fray Felix Hortensio Paravicino* (*ca.* 1605, Boston), *Saint Louis, King of France* (Louvre), *Virgin with Saint Inés and Saint Tecla* (Washington), *Saint Martin and the Beggar* (after 1600, Washington); *Baptism of Christ* (1614, Hospital, Toledo), last picture.

Ribalta, Francisco de. *ca.* 1555-1628. Valencian artist; known for individual "light and dark" chiaroscuro style; thought to have visited Italy and been influenced by Raphael and Carracci; first Spanish painter to have followed Caravaggio; essentially Spanish in subject matter, gloomy atmosphere, and intensity of feeling; primarily religious artist.

Navarrete, Fernandez Juan (called *El Mudo* because he was deaf and dumb). 1526-79. Court painter to Philip II (1568); pupil of Titian; the Italian High Renaissance reached Spain through Navarrete; eight fine altarpieces; excellent historical painter; *Nativity, Christ on the Cross, Assumption, Martyrdom of St. James* (Escorial); *Holy Family, St. John the Evangelist* for Sacristy of the College of the Nativity; *Abraham;* used his beautiful mother as model for the Virgin in many of his works.

Coella Sanchez, Alfonso. 1515-90. Important portrait artist; pupil of Anthonis Mor, whom he followed to Lisbon; court painter to Philip II; best-known portrait of *Philip II* (Berlin); *Sixtus V* and *Cardinal Alexander Farnese;* with Diego d'Urbino (1570), painted triumphal arches raised to celebrate entrance of Anne of Austria to Madrid for her marriage to Philip; decorated altar at Espinar (1574);

best-known works, *St. Paul with St. Anthony, St. Stephen with St. Lawrence, Martyrdom of St. Sebastian* (1582, Escorial); called the "Spanish Titian."

Macip, Vicente Juan (known as Juan de Juanes). *ca.* 1500-79. Religious painter; influenced by Raphael; considered leader of group of Spanish Mannerists.

Carducci, Bartolommeo (Bartolome Carducho). 1560-1608. Italian painter, sculptor, architect; worked for courts of Philip II and Philip III; best-known works, frescoes in library of Escorial Palace and *Descent from the Cross,* Church of San Felipe el Real.

Morales, Luis de. 1509-86. Religious painter; worked on Escorial; *Virgin and Child* (Berlin, London); lack of power; few works remain.

Flemish

Brueghel, Pieter, the Elder (Peasant Bruegel). 1525-69. Outstanding master; first among Northern artists to paint easel pictures for private patrons; visited Italy, but developed completely individual style; scenes portraying the lives of everyday people; often emphasized the sadness, loneliness, or aimlessness of their lives; famous series of the seasons (from 1565); *The Return of the Hunters* (Vienna), *Haymaking* (Raudnitz), *The Harvesters* (Met. Mus.), *Land of Cockaigne* (Munich), *Triumph of Death* (Prado), one of his most remarkable works; *Wedding Dance* (Detroit), *Peasant Wedding* (Vienna), *Massacre of the Innocents* (Vienna), *Adoration of the Magi* (London), *Parable of the Blind* (Naples), fantastic *Dulle Griet* (Mad Meg), *Proverbs* (Berlin).

IMAGINARY LAND OF COCAGNE BY
BRUEGHEL

Mor, Anthonis van Dashorst (Il
Moro in Spain and Anthony More in
England). 1519-76/7. Excellent portrait artist; court painter to Charles V,
Philip II, and Mary Tudor; most works
life-sized; painted kings, queens, and
many men of learning.

Aertsen, Pieter (called Lange Pier).
1508-75. Born Antwerp; to Amsterdam
(1566); religious, genre, and important
still-life painter; influenced Italians,
although style typically Dutch; triptych, *Crucifixion* (1546, Royal Mus.,
Antwerp); *The Egg Dance* (Amsterdam); *The Cook* (Brussels).

Germany

Grünewald, Matthias (Mathis Got-
hart-Neehardt). 1455/60-1528. Religious painter; considered the last and
greatest representative of German
Gothic art; worked at Mainz; dramatic
intensity and emotional quality unique
in German art; outstanding colorist;
noted for paintings of the Passion of
Christ; expressionist fervor shown in
famous *Isenheim Altarpiece* (*ca.* 1510-
15, Colmar, Alsace), *Virgin Adored*

by Angels, Nativity, and *Crucifixion,*
often reproduced; *Mockery of Christ*
(Munich); *Crucifixion* (Basel); inspired Van Gogh.

Holbein, Hans, the Younger. 1497-
1543. Outstanding portrait painter;
born in Augsburg, but lived much of
life in England, and ten years in
Basel; series of 41 drawings of *Dance
of Death,* engraved on metal and wood
by others; *Artist's family* (Basel); portraits of court of *Henry VIII* (including famous study of the King, 1540,
Rome); *George Gisze* (Berlin); *The
Ambassadors* (London); *Joseph Hubert Morett* (Dresden), formerly attributed to Leonardo, considered by
some his greatest portrait.

ERASMUS OF ROTTERDAM
BY HOLBEIN

Cranach, Lucas, the Elder. 1472-
1553. Court painter, engraver; influenced by visit to Flanders in painting of the nude figure; first naked
Venus in history of Northern European
painting (Leningrad); *Breslau Madonna* (1504-25) outstanding; *Holy
Family* (Vienna); *Expulsion of the
Money-Changers* (Dresden); *Portrait
of Luther* (1529, Uffizi); *Portrait of
a Saxon Lady* (Stuttgart); *Judgment*

DETAIL FROM PAINTING BY CRANACH
THE ELDER

of Paris (Met. Mus.); *Rest on the Flight into Egypt* and *David and Bathsheba* (Berlin).

Cranach, Lucas, the Younger. 1515-86. Well-known as portrait artist; melancholy strength in interpretation of sitters; *Squire Jorg* (Leipzig); *Luther's Daughter* (Paris); *Leonhard Badehorn* and *Mayor of Weissenfels* (Berlin); *Venus and Cupid* (Munich).

Baldung, Hans (called Grien). 1484/5-1545. Primarily religious painter; pupil of Dürer; fame rests on altarpieces; major work at Freiburg-im-Breisgau; of all German painters, nearest to spirit of Renaissance; sense of humor (rare in German art); exceptional draftsman; excellent portraits with realistic delineation of character; *Margrave Christoph von Baden; Count Palatine Philip* (Munich); *Rest on the Flight* (Nuremberg); *Venus* (Hague); *Adoration of the Magi* (Berlin).

Tom Ring, Ludger (or Ludwig) the Younger of Münster. 1530-84.

Known for uniquely Germanic character of "fantastic" works and as a painter of flowers; portrait of wife *Anna Rorup* (Cologne); device of scattering flowers around base of vase of flower paintings became popular technique.

Aldegrever, Heinrich. 1502-after 1555. Painter and engraver; called one of the greatest of the German "Little Masters."

AMERICAS · *Mexico*

Mexican School of Painting. Probably founded in 16th century by Simon Pereyns and his pupils Francisco Morales, Francisco de Zumaya, Andres de la Concha, and Juan de Arrue. Earliest works religious; show Flemish influence felt in Spain; (Van Eyck had been in Aragon); works of **Martin de Vos** (1536-93) imported into Mexico.

ASIA · *Japan*

Kano Motonobu. 1476-1559. Leading painter of Ashikaga shōgunate; son of Masanobu; combined elements of traditional Japanese style with *Kanga* (Chinese style of Muromachi *sui-boku-ga* paintings; new technique established Kano school; influential in emphasizing design instead of color.

Sesson. *ca.* 1504-89. Great master of the late Muromachi period; self-taught; worked in northeastern Japan; vigorous brushwork, dramatic motion.

Kano Eitoku. 1543-90. Master of Kano school; grandson of Motonobu; introduced gold, brilliant colors into painted screens featuring landscapes and figures; unusual originality; strength, subtlety of design; lavish splendor.

Hasegawa Tōhaku. 1539-1610. Leading master; unusual style created Hasegawa school; influenced by Mu Ch'i, Chinese painter of Sung dynasty, whose work gained more recognition in Japan than in his native country; carried Muromachi *suiboku-ga* style into Momoyama period.

Kaiho Yusho. 1533-1615. Founder Kaiho school; used strong, slashing brushwork and bright color.

China

Ch'in Ying. *fl.* first half of 16th century. Regarded as last of "four great masters of Ming period"; pupil of Chou Ch'en; *kung-pi* method and so-called "blue and green" landscape style returned to popularity through his work; delicate landscapes, very colorful and decorative figure paintings; very successful in his own period.

Hsu Wei (Wen Ch'ing). 1521-93. Unusual artist, calligrapher, writer; curiously resembles the 19th-century Dutch artist, Van Gogh, in violence, tragedy, and brilliance of life and work; individuality, originality, and powerful brush strokes provoke strong emotional response.

India

The 16th century was the formative epoch of Islamic painting in India; influence of Vijayanagar painting on the Deccan schools immense; defeat and destruction of Vijayanagar by an Islamic confederacy in 1565 drove Hindu artists to serve the courts of the victors; in a series of illuminations of the *Nujum-al-Ulum* (*ca.* 1570) for Ali-Adilshah of Bijapur, the major figures are Hindu, only the format, back-grounds, and secondary figures are Persian.

The first great Moghul emperor Babar (r. 1526-30) did not interest himself in art, but his son Humayun (d. 1556), who could not hold the empire together and fled to the court of Shah Tahmasp of Persia, developed an appreciation of Safavid illuminators (pupils and followers of the great Bihzād, including **Aqa Mirak** and **Mir Musavvir**) there; when he returned to Kabul he brought with him **Mir Sayyid Ali**, young artist well-known for his work on Nizami's *Khamsa* (1539-42) for the Shah. With his assistants, he illustrated *Hamzah Nama*, legend of Prince Hamzah (1555-70). In later pictures of the *Hamzah* series and other Moghul works (*ca.* 1570), European influences become apparent in a plastic roundness of forms stressed by the use of fine shading lines and folds that deny the supremacy of the silhouette and cross and encircle the forms.

'Abd-al-Samad ('Abdu 's-Samad or Hvaga 'Abdu 's-Samad). *fl.* 16th century. Calligrapher and painter from Shiraz; one of the founders of Moghul painting in India; in employ of emperor Humayun (1540); emperor and young son (Akbar) took lessons in drawing and painting from him that accounted for interest in painting that flourished during Akbar's reign; went to Kabul; known to be in Tabriz with Akbar (1542-1605); earliest picture ascribed to him by Western scholars is the royal picnic scene in the Moghul Album known as the *Moraqqa 'Gulsan* in the Imperial Library (Teheran); last painting is in folio 82 in manuscript of Nizami's *Khamsa*

THE ARREST OF SĀH ABU' L-MA' BY TULAQ
HAN QOCHĪ, 'ABD-AL-SAMAD

(1593) in collection of Dyson Perrins
(England); other miniatures attributed to him.

Basawan. Most important Hindu
painter of 16th-century India; member of school founded by second
Moghul emperor, Humayun (1530-
56), continued by Akbar (1556-1605);
illustrated numerous important manuscripts (name appears under more
than 100 pictures) including *Bahāris-
tān* of Persian poet Jami (1414-92),
Dārāb-nāma and *Akbar-nāma* (London), and *Rasm-nāma* (Jaipur).

ISLAM

Muhammadi of Herat. Outstanding
artist of 16th century; individual style;
figures slim and elegant; exceptional
draftsman; line drawings with touches
of color; work led to the popularity of
separate paintings instead of illustrated manuscripts popular with
wealthy nobility.

Aqa Riza. Leading artist at court of

Ibrahim Mirza, Meshhed (1556-77);
known for single figure paintings and
the development of calligraphic line
for emphasis without shading; beautiful illustrations for *Qisas al-Anbiya*
(History of the Prophets) of Nishapuri
(*ca.* 1590-1600) for Shah Abbas I.

*The Order of the World and her
Wonders* of Shaykh Ahmad Misri, illuminated cosmographic work of
Syrian or Egyptian (1563, Istanbul);
rather crude, direct decorative style;
flat, rather modern-folk-art effect.

SCULPTURE

EUROPE · *Italy*

Sansovino, Jacopo (Tatti). 1486-
1570. Famed Venetian sculptor, architect; pupil of Andrea Sansovino
(whose name he assumed); sculptural
works for buildings he designed in-

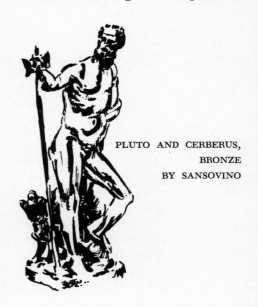

PLUTO AND CERBERUS,
BRONZE
BY SANSOVINO

clude figures of evangelists in St. Mark's, Venice; statues for campanile: *Apollo, Athene, Mercury,* and *Peace;* large statues of *Mars* and *Neptune* on steps of Doge's Palace.

Cellini, Benvenuto. 1500-71. Renowned goldsmith; most skilful worker in metals of his day; studied with Michelangelo Bandinelli; completed medals, jewel settings, vases, caskets, candlesticks, metal plates, and other ornaments for Pope Clement VII;

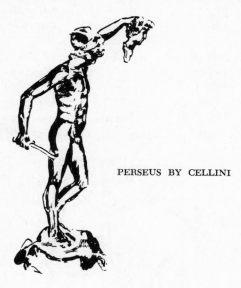

PERSEUS BY CELLINI

GOLD CUP
BY CELLINI

exquisite detail; most famous work, the gold *Salt Cellar of Francis I* of France; bronze statue of *Perseus with the Head of Medusa* in Loggia dei Lanzi (Florence) for Grand Duke Cosimo I de' Medici; popular autobiography.

Primaticcio, Francesco. 1504-70. Cellini's rival at court of Francis I; worked with Giulio Romano on decoration of Palazzo del Tè (Mantua); to Fontainbleau (1532-45); commissioned by the king to work on buildings there; excellent stucco decoration; court architect to Catherine de' Medici.

Bologne, Jean (known as Giovanni da Bologna and Giambologna). 1529-1608. Flemish sculptor attached to court of the Medicis, Florence; leading master of Mannerist school; *Neptune Fountain,* Bologna; masterpiece, *Rape of the Sabines* (completed 1583, Loggia dei Lanzi, Florence); equestrian statue of *Cosimo I;* important free-standing works; influential teacher.

Udine, Giovanni da. 1487-1564. Pupil and assistant to Raphael, bas reliefs in stucco; ornaments for Loggia of Vatican, Pitti Palace, and Palazzo Vecchio.

Giulio Romano (Pippi de Giannuzzi). 1499-1546. Better-known as painter, architect; worked with Udine on Raphael's plasterwork ornamentation for Loggia (Vatican); opened school for plasterers in Mantua; influential.

Bandinelli, Bartolommeo (Baccio). *ca.* 1493-1560. Large statue of *Hercules and Cacus,* commissioned by Leo X and Clement VII (Palazzo Vecchio); *Adam and Eve,* Boboli Gardens; bas reliefs in choir of cathedral (Florence).

Tribolo, Il (Niccolò Pericoli). 1485-1550. Architect, sculptor in employ of Grand Duke Cosimo I of Tuscany; marble statues of *Sibyls, Assumption of the Virgin* (Bologna); tomb of *Adrian VI* (with Michelangelo, Pisa).

Guglielmo della Porta, Fra. *ca.* 1510-77. Famous for tomb of *Pope Paul III* in choir of St. Peter's, Rome.

Campagna, Gerolamo. *ca.* 1539-*ca.* 1626. Venetian sculptor; pupil of Cattaneo; tomb of *Doge Leonardo Loredano; St. Justina* over portal of Arsenal; altar of San Giorgio Maggiore (Venice); *Duke Federico Montefeltro* statue (Urbino); works in Verona.

Others. Antonio Begarelli (*ca.* 1498-1565), Bartolommeo Ammanati (1511-92), Domenico del Barbiere (1501-65), Vincenzo Danti (1530-76), Leone Leoni (1509-90), Battista Lorenzi (d. 1594), Domenico Beccafumi (1486-1551).

France

Goujon, Jean. 1520-72. Leading sculptor of French Renaissance; decorations in low relief for buildings and monuments; worked with Pierre Lescot on the oldest wing of the Louvre; château of Diane de Poitiers at Anêt; statue *Diane Chasseresse* (Louvre); famed *Fountain of the Innocents* (Paris); believed to have become a Huguenot and been killed.

Richier, Légier (Ligier). 1500-*ca.* 1572. Studied with Michelangelo in Rome; worked in Lorraine; masterpiece, *The Entombment,* Church of St. Étienne (Saint-Mihiel), dramatic over-life-sized figures grouped at the foot of the cross; mausoleum of *Rene,* Prince of Orange, Church of Saint-Pierre (Bar-le-Duc).

Pilon, Germain. 1535-90. Sculptor at the court of the Valois; bronze portraits of *Henry II, Catherine* de'

GISANTS, TOMB OF HENRY II, BY PILON

Medici; kneeling figure of *Chancellor Rene de Birague* (Louvre) considered best work; marble bust of *Charles IX* (Met. Mus.); medallions.

Franqueville, Pierre de (Pietro Francavilla). 1548-1618. Worked in

RELIEFS FROM
FONTAINE DES INNOCENTS
BY GOUJON

Italy; recalled to France by Henry IV; *Le Temps qui Enlève la Vérité,* now in Garden of Tuileries; court sculptor under Louis XIII; also painter and architect.

Spain

Berruguete, Alonzo. *ca.* 1488-1561. Leading sculptor, architect, painter; worked under Michelangelo in Rome; court artist, Charles V; influenced by Italian Renaissance, but work strongly Spanish; wood altar screens, Church of San Benito el Real (Valladolid); choir stall, Toledo Cathedral; marble tomb, *Cardinal Tavera; Sacrifice of Isaac, St. John,* and *St. Sebastian.*

Germany

Hering, Loy. 1484/5-after 1554. Noted for life-sized crucifixes carved of wood; most important work, seated figure of *St. Willibald* (Eichstatt); many drawings.

Jamnitzer, Wenzel. 1508-84. Goldsmith; family workshop at Nuremberg produced heavily decorated gold goblets, vessels, and tableware for the nobility.

Gerhard, Hubert. 1550-1620. Bavarian artist; influenced by Giovanni da Bologna; bronze group of *St. Michael Triumphing over Lucifer,* St. Michael's (Munich); Augustus fountain (Augsburg).

Low Countries

Floris, Cornelis (de Vriendt). 1514-75. Flemish artist of Antwerp; developed Roman grotesques and framed fantastic figures with scroll and ribbons; influential as architect.

Colins (Colin, Colyns), Alexandre. 1527/9-1612. Flemish sculptor; decora-

tions on castle of Heidelberg; reliefs on tombs of *Maximilian I* and *Hans Fugger* (Innsbruck).

ASIA · *India*

The Tamil craftsman succeeded in producing metalwork of superb grace and simplicity; images of gods and goddesses as well as portrait figures of kings and queens; life-sized figures of *King Krishna Deva Raya* and two of his chief queens, temple of Tirumala, exceptional examples; probably outstanding achievement seen in dancing *Sivas* (from 11th century on).

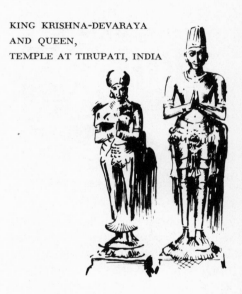

KING KRISHNA-DEVARAYA AND QUEEN, TEMPLE AT TIRUPATI, INDIA

ARCHITECTURE

EUROPE · *Italy*

Palladio, Andrea. 1518-80. Great Venetian architect; highly personal, classic, grandiose style; famous for designs for *palazzi* and *ville,* town and

LA MALCONTENTA, OVERLOOKING BRENTA
CANAL, VENICE, PALLADIO

VILLA ROTONDA, VICENZA, PALLADIO

country houses, that influenced architects of other countries (Inigo Jones imported Palladian style into England); published monumental work, *Four Books on Architecture* (1570, English translation, 1713); *Villa Trissino* at Meledo, almost completely symmetrical; *Villa Rotonda* (del Capra, Vicenza) shows important relationship of architecture to nature in designing the building to fit into surrounding landscape; (this was also done at about the same time by Michelangelo with the *Palazzo Farnese*); de-

signed churches, *San Giorgio Maggiore* (1565) and *Il Redemtore* (1576-92, Venice) in Mannerist style; *Basilica* (1546-50, Venice), two stories of arcades surrounding an older ceremonial hall; *Teatro Olimpico* (begun 1580), new adaptation of classical theater.

Michelangelo Buonarroti. 1475-1564. Florentine genius; most famous as painter and sculptor, he was responsible for the tomb of *Pope Julius II*, for whom he also designed the square, cathedral, and palace of Pienza (*ca.* 1560); designed façade of *San Lorenzo* church, although *Medici Chapel* considered first architectural work; *Laurenziana* (Laurentian) *Library* for the Medici (begun 1524), stairway designed (1558-59), most representative of Mannerist style; plans for great dome of *St. Peter's* (1546-64, Rome); *The Conservators' Palace, Campidoglio* (*ca.* 1545, Rome); *Palazzo Farnese* (see above).

ST. PETER'S, ROME, BY MICHELANGELO

Peruzzi, Baldassare. 1481-1536. Sienese master; worked with Bramante and Raphael in Rome; masterpiece, *Palazzo Massimi,* although lacking the dignity or grandeur of his *Farnese* and *Vidoni Palaces,* has unusual sophisticated elegance.

Vignola, Giacomo Barozzi di. 1507-73. Mannerist architect of Rome; published important treatise on the *Five Orders of Architecture* (1570) that established laws for ornamental arch; worked with Vasari and Ammanati on *Villa Giulia* of Pope Julius II; succeeded Michelangelo as architect for *St. Peter's;* fortified castle, *Caprarola,* north of Rome; Jesuit church of *Gesù,* considered his masterpiece, influenced Baroque churches everywhere.

Sangallo, Antonio da the Younger. 1485-1546. Leading Renaissance architect; designer of monumental *Palazzo Farnese* (1530); also worked on *St. Peter's.*

Fontana, Domenico. 1543-1607. Important in rebuilding of Rome under Pope Sixtus V; built *Sistine Chapel* of Church of Santa Maria Maggiore (*ca.* 1580); *Lateran Palace,* Vatican Library (1587-90); obelisk in front of *St. Peter's;* royal palace at Naples (1600); left designs for the improvement of the harbor at Naples.

Giulio Romano. (Pippi de Gianuzzi). 1499-1546. Student of Raphael; worked for Duke of Mantua; designed own home (*ca.* 1544) which is an excellent example of Mannerist classicism; ducal palace, church of *San Benedetto,* and *Palazzo del Tè* (1525-35), all in Mantua.

Sansovino, Jacopo (Tatti). 1486-1570. Venetian architect; designed the *Library of St. Mark* (1536-53), important Renaissance building; sculptor.

Sanmichele, Michele. 1484-1559. Veronese Mannerist architect; fortified city with town walls, two ornamental gates; built *Porta Nuova, Porta Pallio, Palazzo Bevilacqua, Palazzo Canossa;* round church of *Madonna di Campagna* near Verona; sumptuous palace of the *Cornari.*

Porta, Giacomo della. 1541-1604. Roman architect; pupil of Vignola, completed many of his master's works including façades of churches of *Santa Caterina de'Funari* and *Il Gesù* (*ca.* 1575-84); finished cupola of *St. Peter's* (1588-90) and *Palazzo Farnese* (after plans of Michelangelo's); *Villa Aldobrandini* near Frascáti; *Palazzo Chigi.*

Vasari, Giorgio. 1511-74. Florentine Mannerist architect and painter; designer of *Uffizi Palace* (begun in 1570; author of *The Lives of the Painters, Sculptors and Architects* (1550), not always reliable, but important biographical source; considered a founder of modern art history and criticism.

Serlio, Sebastiano. 1473/5-1554. Bolognese painter, architect, engraver; pupil of Peruzzi; associated with Titian; published *Regole generali d'architectura* (beginning in 1537), important treatise on classical architecture (influenced Spanish and English architects); to Fontainbleau where he worked with Rosso Florentino and Primaticcio; more theoretician and designer than architect.

Tibaldi, Pellegrino. 1527-96. Bolognese architect and painter; worked as head architect at cathedral *Fidele* and *San Sebastiano* (Milan) and *San Gaudenzio* (Novara).

Spain

Herrera, Juan de. *ca.* 1530-97. Famed architect of the magnificent *Escorial Palace* built (1559-84) for Philip II of Spain; worked with Juan de Bautista of Toledo (1563-74) and then was placed in complete charge

THE ESCORIAL PALACE, SPAIN

until the building was completed; also designed the *Valladolid Cathedral* (not completed), *Exchange* at Seville, and the palace at Aranjuez (rebuilt castle, of Simancas); erected Segovia bridge, Madrid.

Siloe, Diego de. *ca.* 1495-1563. Master architect and sculptor; masterpiece, *Granada Cathedral* (begun 1528), one of the most complex in the history of cathedral design; cylindrical rotunda chevet ringed by an ambulatory and radiating chapels; considered best of Plateresque buildings; chevet of *San Jeronimo* (1523/4, Granada); tower of *Santa Maria del Campo* (near Burgos); *Salvador Church* (Ubeda); *San Gabriel* (Loja); *Gaudix Cathedral*; famed staircase descending into northern transept of *Burgos Cathedral* (Es-

calera Dorada), exquisite wrought metalwork; influenced by Italians.

Covarrubias, Alonso de. 1488-1570. Best-known work, *Alcázar* (1537, Toledo), quadrangular plan with projecting corner towers; remodeled *Puerta Bisagra* (Toledo); hall church (1539, Getafe).

Vandelvira, Andres. 1509-75. Pupil of Diego de Siloe; great work, cathedral of *Jaén* (begun 1546); *Santiago Hospital Church* (1562-75, Ubeda).

Ruiz II, Hernan. d. 1556/58. Andalusian; architect for *Hospital de la Sangre,* church in Seville (1560-70), influential design; remodeled minaret of the mosque of *Cordova* (1593).

Portugal

Torralva, Diogo de. 1500-1566. Leading architect of first half of 16th century; masterpiece, main cloister of *Cristo Monastery* (1557-62, Tomar); *Church of the Graça* (1527-37, Évora), rebuilding of the apse at Belem (1540-51); octagon church of Dominican nuns (1543-57, Elvas); chapel of *Santo Amaro* (begun 1549); *Chapel of the Conçeiacāo* (*ca.* 1550/1, Tomar); influenced by Italians.

Terzi, Filippo. 1520-97. Leading Italian architect working in Portgual (began in 1576); military engineer; Master of Royal Works under Philip II; influenced by Herrera and Vignola; Augustinian house of *Saō Vicente de Fora* (begun 1582), great basilica on terrace overlooking Lisbon; church and cloister of *Serra do Pilar;* cloister of Augustinian College (1596, Coimbra).

Alvares, Alfonso, *fl.* 1551-75. Leading Aletejano master; royal *Mestre de confiança* (1571); *Leiria Cathedral*

(1551); *Salvador Church* (Vieiros); *Santa Maria do Castelo* (1559, Estremonz); *Santa Maria* (after 1565, Alcaçovas); with Manuel Pires, designed *Espírito Santo* (Évora).

France

Delorme (de l'Orme), Philibert. *ca.* 1515-70. Leading architect of French Renaissance; studied in Rome; *Palace of the Tuileries* for Catherine de' Medici (from 1563); worked for Henry II; directed work at *Fontainebleau* (1543-59); built châteaux at *Anet, Meudon* (part of Tuileries), *Muette, Saint-Germain, Saint-Maur*; gallery at château of *Chenonceaux*; many works destroyed during Revolution; published influential book, *Architecture* (1568).

Bullant, Jean. *ca.* 1515-78/80. Talented designer of pavilion at Tuileries; studied in Rome; succeeded Primaticcio as head artist at Fontainebleau; author of important *General Rule and Five Orders* (pub. 1564).

Lescot, Pierre. *ca.* 1510-78. Classicist; studied in Rome; collaborated with sculptor Goujon on southwest pavilion, oldest wing of the Louvre; *Hôtel Carnavalet* (1544); *Fontaine des Innocents.*

Low Countries

Floris, Cornelis. 1514-75. Flemish master; famed for *Town Hall,* Antwerp (1561-65); introduced strapwork, popular ornamentation.

Vredeman de Vries, Hans or Jan. 1527-after 1604. Artist of the Netherlands; noted for fantastic architectural ornamentation pattern books (1565-68).

Denmark

Steenwinkel, Hans von, the Elder. *ca.* 1545-1601. Flemish court architect working in Denmark; collaborated in designing of *Kronborg* near Hëlsingør; built several buildings for Tycho Brahe, the astronomer.

Poland

Bernardoni, Jean-Marie. d. 1605. Church of *St. Peter and St. Paul,* (1597, Cracow).

England

Smythson, Robert. 1536-1614. Outstanding architect of period; responsible for the rebuilding of *Longleat* (Wilts) for Sir John Thynne, most important example of Elizabethan architecture; *Manor* for Earl of Shrewsbury (Worksop); *Wardour Castle* for Sir Matthew Arundell; *Hardwick Hall* for famed "Bess of Hardwick" (1590, Derbyshire); *Wollaton Hall* (1588, Nottinghamshire).

ISLAM · Turkey

Sinan (Kodja Mi mār Sinān). 1489-1578. Greatest architect and builder of Ottoman Empire; known especially for magnificent mosque, *Sulaymāniya* (higher than Hagia Sophia), with exquisite tile decorating the mihrab and rear wall, built for the great Suleiman I (1550-56, Constantinople); built *Selimiye* immediately following the death of Selim I (finished 1522, Adrianople); designed the mosque of Selim II (1551-74), *Mosque of Roxilane* (1539), *Prince's Mosque* (1548); many less important mosques, chapels, schools, palaces, etc; credited with 343 buildings in the 75 years he worked; primarily concerned with grandeur of interiors; important teacher; **Yusuf,** his favorite pupil, architect of palaces in Lahore, Delhi, and Agra (built by Emperor Akbar); buried beneath his great *Sulaymāniya* (mosque) when nearly 90.

MUSIC

EUROPE · *Italy*

Palestrina, Giovanni (Pierliugi da). *ca.* 1525-94. Master composer of sacred music embodying the spirit of the Counter Reformation; appointed by Pope Julius III (1551) master of boys in Julian Chapel; first book of Masses appeared (1554); appointed to Sistine Chapel Choir (1555); returned to Vatican (1571); Mannerist style embodying diatonic and modal imitative polyphony, carefully balanced use of dissonance, rhythm, and melody; less literary and more polished than work of contemporaries, although Gabrieli

PALESTRINA

considered by some his equal; works include *Stabat Mater,* motets in four to eight and twelve parts; 93 Masses, Lamentations, Magnificats, Psalms, Litanies, madrigals (sacred and secular); *Missa Papae Marcelli, Song of Solomon, Improperia,* still sung in Sistine Chapel on Good Friday.

Willaert, Adrien (Adriaan). *ca.* 1480-1562. Great Flemish composer in Italy; founder of Venetian school; maestro di cappella, St. Mark's (from 1527, Venice); one of the first to use double chorus with great skill, there being two organs and two choirs at St. Mark's; created new harmonic style; developed the *canzone,* instrumental piece; prolific composer of Masses, motets, and, most important, madrigals.

Gabrieli, Giovanni. 1555-1612. Venetian composer, organist, master of counterpoint; first organist at St. Mark's (1586); composed elaborate motets with orchestral accompaniment, works for organ, orchestral compositions, and church music; teacher of Schütz and Praetorius; called father of "chromatic style"; in *Sacrae symphoniae* (1597), baroque use of contrasts in dynamics represents introduction to modern orchestration.

Gabrieli, Andrea. *ca.* 1520-86. Venetian organist and composer; pupil of Willaert; organist at St. Mark's (from 1585); composed madrigals, motets, Masses, works for organ, and instrumental music.

Vecchi, Orazio. 1550-1605. Master composer of madrigals; dramatist; maestro di cappella, Modena Cathedral, and court musician (1598-1605); published six books of *canzonette,* two books of madrigals, Masses, motets;

L'Amfiparnasso (performed Modena, 1594) important link between madrigal comedy and opera; attempt to give musical setting to *commedia dell'arte;* important influence on literature and drama.

Peri, Jacopo (called Il Zazzerino). 1561-1633. Credited with composing first opera, *Dafne* (1597), to libretto by poet Rinuccini (same as Schütz); *Euridice* (1600), first opera music extant; member *camerata* of Count Giovanni Bardi.

Rore, Cipriano de. 1516-65. Flemish-Venetian composer; pupil of Willaert; maestro di cappella, St. Mark's (*ca.* 1549); considered greatest madrigal writer of period; established five-part madrigal in imitative polyphony as the standard form; motets, Masses, including *St. John's Passion* (1557).

Amati, Andrea. *ca.* 1530-*ca.* 1611. Founder of great Cremonese school of violin makers (from 1564).

Cavalieri, Emilio de. *ca.* 1550-1602. Florentine composer; one of first to use solo voices with instrumental accompaniment and mode of notation called figured bass; most important work, *La rappresentazione di anima e di corpo* (1600), morality play set to music in recitative, considered first oratorio; four music dramas; important influence.

Soriano, Francesco. 1549-1621. Singer, composer; chorister, St. John Lateran (1564, Rome); pupil of Palestrina; court of Mantua (1583-86); maestro di cappella (Rome); composed Masses, motets, psalms, 110 canons, other church music, madrigals, and *villanelle.*

Zarlino, Gioseffo. 1517-90. Venetian theorist, conductor, and composer; pupil of Willaert; successor to de Rore as choirmaster at St. Mark's (1565, Venice); theorist who suggested equal temperament for keyed instruments; explained harmony as based on difference in formation of major and minor triads; established the major and minor chords; explained double counterpoint; mathematical basis of music in *Istitutioni harmoniche* (1558); important influence.

Verdelot, Philippe. d. *ca.* 1540. Flemish composer; singer St. Mark's; choirmaster San Giovanni (1530, Florence); one of the earliest composers of Italian madrigals (100 for four, five, and six voices), Masses, and motets.

Caccini, Giulio. *ca.* 1546-1618. Composer, singer; served Grand Duke of Tuscany (Florence); composed arias for *Dafne* and *Eurdice* by Peri (1597); wrote solo songs with figured bass accompaniment; composed madrigals.

Nanini, Giovanni Maria. *ca.* 1545-1607. Great contrapuntist, composer; studied with Palestrina (Rome); succeeded him at S. Maria Maggiore; maestro di cappella, S. Luigi de' Francesi (1575); singer, Papal Chapel (1604); established first music school (composition) in Rome opened by an Italian (with Palestrina and brother Giovanni Bernardino); wrote motets, three books of madrigals (1579, '81, '86); *canzonets* (1593).

Marenzio, Luca. 1553-99. Outstanding composer of madrigals; in service of Cardinal d'Este (1578-87); at Polish court (1596-98); Papal Chapel; resourceful, expressive technique; strong influence on English madrigal style; published 16 books of madrigals; other volumes of church and secular music.

Gastoldi, Giovanni Giacomo. *ca.* 1556-1622. Composer of *balletti*, madrigals, motets, and church music; chapel master, (1582-1609, Mantua); partsongs with "fa la" refrain; *Balletti for Five Voices* (1591), most popular work; influenced Morley.

Ingegneri, Marc Antonio. *ca.* 1545-92. Cremonese composer, choirmaster; teacher of Monteverdi; church music and madrigals.

Spain

Victoria, Tomás Luis de. *ca.* 1549-1611. Outstanding composer of church music, one of the most remarkable in the history of Spanish music; subtle, expressive polyphony; studied with Palestrina, mutual influence; passionate mysticism essentially Spanish in feeling; last and greatest work, *Officium defunctorum* (1572-1605); motets, Masses, magnificats, hymns, etc.

Morales, Cristóbal. *ca.* 1500-1553. One of the leading masters of polyphonic church music; prolific; singer, Papal Chapel (1535, Rome); published two books of Masses, magnificats, and motets; clarity of form and freedom of expression evident in work.

Cabezón, Antonio de. 1510-66. Blind organist and composer; one of the earliest composers for the keyboard; works for harp and lute published posthumously (1578); organist to Charles V and Philip II; liturgical pieces and variations on secular songs; believed English virginalists learned art of variation from Cabezón and Spanish contemporaries.

Guerrero, Francisco. 1527/28-99. Chorister, composer of outstanding church music; chorister, maestro de capilla (1574), Seville Cathedral; also composed secular madrigals.

Others. Miguel de Fuenllana (*fl.* 16th century), Luis Milan (*ca.* 1500-after 1561), Philip Rogier (1562-96).

France

Jannequin, Clement. *ca.* 1485-*ca.* 1564. Leading composer of secular music; long "pictorial" three- and four-part *chansons* or "tone poems"; considered to have foreshadowed program music by use of imitative descriptions in tone; *Le Chant des Oiseaux, La Guerre, La Chasse,* and *La Bataille.*

Costeley, Guillaume. *ca.* 1531-1606. Leading composer; probably the most original of the French songwriters of period; subtle master of rhythm, use of nuances that characterized work of Couperin and later adopted by Debussy; organist, French Court; wrote keyboard music; more than 100 polyphonic chansons.

Sermisy, Claude de (Claudin). *ca.* 1490-1562. Composer, choral master; at Sainte-Chapelle (1508-14, Paris); singer King's Chapel (1515) later becoming master of choristers; with Francis I visited Bologna, where French choir competed with Papal Choir (1515); sang with choir of Henry VIII at Field of Cloth of Gold (1520); works included Masses, motets, a Passion, and *chansons.*

Arcadelt, Jacob. *ca.* 1514-*ca.* 1560. (Paris.) Leader Venetian school of madrigalists although believed to be of Flemish origin; served papal singers; Duke de Guise, Paris (from 1555); wrote five books of madrigals (1539); church music, French *chansons.*

Goudimel, Claude. *ca.* 1505-72. Huguenot composer; music for psalms;

Psalter, eight books (1566); popular in hymnals for centuries.

Germany

Senfl, Ludwig. 1490-1543. Outstanding composer; studied under Isaac and succeeded him as Kapellmeister, Vienna (1517); director court chapel, Munich (1523); attached to Roman Catholic court, but wrote polyphonic choral settings of Lutheran chorales; prolific, versatile; church music shows severity, grace; Magnificats, motets.

Hassler, Hans Leo. 1564-1612. First important German composer to study in Italy (with Gabrieli, Venice); organist to Fugger, Augsburg (1585-1600); leading master of polyphony and Venetian polychoral style; 24 Italian *canzonette* (1590), madrigals, Masses, compositions for the organ.

England

Byrd, William. 1543-1623. Great master; one of the earliest and most important contributors to music for the keyboard; 120 pieces in Parthenia col-

WILLIAM BYRD

lection (1611); first composer of English madrigals; chamber music established character of instrumental music in England; excelled in church music, especially for the Roman Catholic Church; granted monopoly by Elizabeth I (with Tallis, 1575) for publishing printed music in England.

Bull, John. 1563-1628. Celebrated Elizabethan composer; virtuoso of the harpsichord and organ; Chapel Royal (1591); *Star*, anthem for voices and viols.

Dowland, John. 1563-1626. Leading composer of songs, unsurpassed as lutanist; famous for *Songes or Ayres* (four books, 1597-1603), considered most important English contribution to literature of solo song (art song) with lute accompaniment.

Tye, Christopher. *ca.* 1500-1573. Elizabethan composer of church music and anthems; master of choristers, Ely Cathedral (1542-61); four-part setting of *Acts of Apostles* (1553); Masses, motets.

Morley, Thomas. 1557-1603. Important theorist, composer of madrigals; *Plain and Easy Introduction to Practical Music* (1597), first comprehensive treatise on composition printed in England; organist, St. Paul's Cathedral (1591); noted for madrigals, settings of Shakespeare's songs, anthems, and services.

Tallis, Thomas. *ca.* 1505-85. Called "Father of English Cathedral Music"; teacher of Byrd; gentleman of Chapel Royal (from *ca.* 1545); first publication (with Byrd, see above) *Cantiones Sacrae* (1575) contained 17 motets by each composer.

Others. John Taverner (*ca.* 1495-1545), William Mundy (d. *ca.* 1591).

Flemish

Lasso, Orlando di (Roland de Lassus). 1532-94. Called "Prince of Musicians"; brilliant, prolific master considered bridge between older Flemish school and Monteverdi; versatile composer of some 2,000 works; including Masses, motets, Passions, madrigals, French *chansons*, etc; studied in Italy; choirmaster, St. John Lateran, Rome (1553-54); worked for Duke of Bavaria, Munich (from 1556); most famous work, *Seven Penitential Psalms* (*ca.* 1565); granted Knight of the Golden Spur by the Pope.

ORLANDO DI LASSO

Clemens, Jacobus (Jacques Clement, called Clemens non-Papa). 1510-*ca.* 56. Leading contrapuntist, composer; introduced new use of well-balanced polyphony with expressive, gay melody and clear harmony; Kappellmeister, Emperor Charles V, Vienna; wrote *chansons*, Masses, motets, psalms.

Gombert, Nicolas. *ca.* 1490-1556. Outstanding composer; Josquin's greatest pupil; one of the first to take secular music seriously; wrote pastoral songs; served Charles V (1526-40); ability to set music to meaning of text; wrote over 250 works.

Crecquillon, Thomas. d. *ca.* 1557. Composer of *chansons*, motets, Masses; choirmaster, Imperial Chapel for Charles V; work rather French in flavor.

Monte, Philippe de (Mons). 1521-1603. Composer of 36 books of secular music; 300 Masses and motets; member, chapel of Philip II, Spain (*ca.* 1555); Kapellmeister, Emperor Maximilian II (1568).

THEATER

EUROPE · England

Shakespeare, William. 1564-1616. Greatest dramatist in English literature; complete technical mastery; extraordinary insight, depth of character analysis, and understanding of human motivation; sonnets (1592-96); comedies in this period include *Love's Labour's Lost* (*ca.* 1595), *Taming of the Shrew* (1594), *Midsummer Night's Dream* (*ca.* 1595), *Merry Wives of Windsor* (1600-1601), *Much Ado About Nothing* (1598-99), *As You Like It,* (1601) *Twelfth Night* (1599-1600); histories include *Henry VI* (three parts, 1589-91), *Richard II* (1592-93), *King John* (*ca.* 1593), *Richard II* (1595/96), *Henry IV* (two parts, (1597/98), *Henry V* (1598/99); tragedies include *Romeo and Juliet* (1594-96), *Merchant of Venice* (1596-98), *Julius Caesar* (1599).

WILLIAM SHAKESPEARE

CHRISTOPHER MARLOWE

GLOBE THEATER

Marlowe, Christopher. 1564-93. Great Elizabethan dramatist; more fiery spirit than Shakespeare; established blank verse as appropriate vehicle of expression; *Dr. Faustus* (*ca.* 1588), important innovations in not using royal personage as central figure and in uniting tragic elements with elements of morality play; *Tamburlaine* (*ca.* 1587), *The Jew of Malta* (*ca.* 1589), *Dido, Queen of Carthage* (*ca.* 1593); tragic scenes influenced Shakespeare; exceptional delineation of character.

Kyd, Thomas. *ca.* 1557/78-*ca.* 95. Leading Elizabethan dramatist; best-known exponent of English "tragedy of blood"; *Spanish Tragedy* (*ca.* 1589); skilled handling of play construction; may have been the source of ghost and play-within-a-play of Shakespeare's *Hamlet.*

Lyly, John. 1553/54-1606. Introduced high comedy written in prose to England; *Campaspe* (1584), tragicomedy, forerunner of later comedy of romance; *Sappho and Phao* (1584); *Endimion* (1591); *Midas* (1592); *The Woman in the Moone* (1597); classical dramas a link between Italian Renaissance and Elizabethan dramatists; works limited by use of boy actors.

Sackville, Thomas. 1536-1608. Important in writing of *Gorboduc* (1652, in collaboration with Thomas Norton), a drama in blank verse generally considered the earliest English tragedy; use of dumb show at beginning of acts unique.

Bale, John. 1495-1563. Reformation dramatist; plays transition from medi-

181

eval morality play to historical drama of Renaissance; *Kynge Johan* (before 1548).

Peele, George. *ca.* 1557-96. Dramatist; *Arraignment of Paris* (1584); *Old Wive's Tale* (*ca.* 1591); *Edward I* (printed 1593).

Greene, Robert. *ca.* 1560-92. Poet, playwright; *The Honorable History of Friar Bacon and Friar Bungay* (*ca.* 1589-91); *James the Fourth* (*ca.* 1591).

France

Jodelle, Étienne. 1532-73. Poet of the Pléiade; wrote first French tragedy or "literary" drama; *Cléopâtre captive* (1552), old classical chorus retained; *Eugène* (1552), first French Renaissance comedy, satire with echoes of medieval farce; *Didon se sacrifant* (1553).

Garnier, Robert. 1534-90. Regarded most important tragic poet of his century by his contemporaries; verse tragedies include *Bradamante* (printed 1582) and *Les Juives* (printed 1583).

Larivey, Pierre de (Glunta). *ca.* 1535-*ca.* 1611. Playwright of Italian descent who attempted to introduce transalpine plays to audiences of France; one of the creators of French comedy; *Les esprits* (The Wits), best-known work; true sense of theater; influential.

Grevin, Jacques. 1538-70. Dramatist; his *Jules Cèsar* (1558), one of the earliest French tragedies; *Maubertine: or, The Paymistress* (1558) and *Esbahis* (1560), comedies.

Spain

Lope de Rueda. *ca.* 1510-65. Most important precursor of the Golden Age of Spanish theater; actor, manager; created dramatic genre known as *pasos*, earthy quality, characteristically Spanish, free from restraint, lyrical, half-comic, half-serious; founded popular national theater.

Cervantes Saavedra, Miguel de. 1547-1615. Greatest figure in Spanish literature; famous for novel *Don Quixote*; best-known drama, *Numancia* (*ca.* 1587); *The Great Sultana* (printed 1615).

Cueva, Juan de la. *ca.* 1550-*ca.* 1610. One of the forerunners of Lope de Vega; most famous play, *Los siete infantes de Lara* (1579).

Portugal

Sa de Miranda, Francisco de. *ca.* 1496-1558. Founder of classical theater in Portugal; lived in Italy, influenced by Renaissance; two comedies, *Os Estrangeiros* (*ca.* 1527) and *Vihalpandos* (*ca.* 1537), laid the foundation of classical style.

Ferreira, Antonio. 1528-69. Dramatist, poet; known for *Ines de Castro* (1587), first original and complete tragedy in Portuguese; comedies include *Bristo* and *O Cioso*; works printed after his death.

Italy

Aretino, Pietro (Bacci). 1492-1556. Satirist; *La Cortigiana* (The Courtesan, or The Play of the Court), Venice (1534), attack on papal court, considered best work; *Il marescalco* (The Blacksmith, printed 1533), farce; *L'ipocrito* (The Hypocrite), Venice (1541), satire; referred to as "The Scourge of Princes."

Tasso, Torquato. 1544-95. Poet at court of Ferrara; best-known work,

Aminta (1573), pastoral; *King Torris-mondo* (1587), chivalric romance.

Guarini, Giovanni Battista. 1537-1612. Poet, court of Ferrara (1567-82); *Il pastor fido* (The Faithful Shepherd, 1585), pastoral drama.

Grazzini, Antonfrancesco (Il Lasca) 1503-84. Florentine playwright; *La gelosia* (Jealousy, 1550) influenced Shakespeare's *Much Ado*; *La pinzochera* (The Devotee, printed 1582), amusing comedy.

Cinthio, Giraldi. 1504-73. Playwright; *Orbecche* (1541) and *Arrenopia* (printed 1583), comedies of romance.

Andreini, Isabella (1562-1604) and Francesco (1548-1624). Leaders of Gelosi troupe of strolling players through Italy and France; Francesco wrote several plays that were translated into French.

Bracciolini, Francesco. 1566-1645. Charming pastoral play, *L'amoroso sedgno* (Lovers' Trials, printed 1597).

Germany

Sachs, Hans. 1494-1576. Celebrated meistersinger; wrote 208 playlets including *The Wandering Scholar from Paradise* (1550) and *The Horse Thief* (1553); important in the development of secular theater; prolific; good sense of dramatic contrast; delightful humor.

Netherlands

Gretser, Jakob. 1562-1625. Early Jesuit dramatist; *Timon* (1584).

JAPANESE ARMOR, *hiodoshi* TYPE, 1550

1600-1700

The Baroque period was one of remarkable contrasts in art as well as in religious and scientific thought. The restrained objectivity of Vermeer contrasted sharply with the restless, searching introspection of Rembrandt, whose dramatic use of light differed from the powerful, extreme chiaroscuro of Caravaggio, while the magnificent splendor of Rubens contrasted with the classical poise of Poussin.

France emerged as the leader of the artistic world; the "elegant age" of Louis XIV produced the Palace of Versailles, the Gobelins tapestries, and the gardens of the Tuileries.

The "limited" Baroque architecture of Sir Christopher Wren dominated the Restoration period in England where a compromise was reached between the French and Italian Baroque and English Gothic to produce a completely independent style.

The Dutch landscape artists and genre painters represented the growing interests of the "middle class," as did the great printmakers of Japan.

184

PAINTING

EUROPE · *Low Countries*

Rembrandt von Rijn. 1606-69. Great Dutch master; use of light and shadow for dramatic effect; golden tone of portraits seen in early studies of *Saskia* and *Titus*; amazing ability to evoke form, character, sympathy, and understanding of fellow men with a few brush strokes; works dematerialize reality in manner similar to El Greco's, combining elements of Mannerism and Baroque; famed masterpieces include *The Polish Rider, The Cloth Syndics, The Jewish Bride, Night Watch, The Mill, Supper at Emmaus, Return of the Prodigal Son, Portrait of Jan Six,*

GARDEN OF LOVE (DETAIL) BY RUBENS

RAPE OF THE DAUGHTERS OF LEUCIPPUS BY RUBENS

ARISTOTLE CONTEMPLATING THE BUST OF HOMER, REMBRANDT

many brilliant self-portraits and portraits of others; unsurpassed etchings adapt use of powerful chiaroscuro effects to engravings; extraordinary influence.

Rubens, Peter Paul. 1577-1640. Baroque splendor best represented by this great Flemish master; monumental compositions show Italian influence, but robust early color and models characteristically Flemish; vitality, motion, luminosity of paint characterize his genius; later works brighter, more subtle, with lyrical intensity and

185

warmth; everything turned into a personal expression of the glorification of life; works include *Rape of the Sabines* (London), *Martyrdom of St. Levien* (Brussels), *Rape of the Daughters of Leucippus* (Munich), *A Festival in a Garden* (Prado), *Descent from the Cross* (Antwerp); versatile; diplomat.

Hals, Frans. *ca.* 1580-1666. Dutch master; famed for naturalness, informality, gaiety, vivacity of portraits; bold brush strokes in cool grays, greens, and ocher; penetrating characterization as seen in masterpiece, *Regentessen of Haarlem Almshouse,* and in *Malle Babbe* (or Crazy Barbara, fishseller, known as the Witch of Haarlem, Berlin).

Vermeer van Delft, Jan. 1632-75. Master Dutch genre and landscape artist; great colorist; painting of daylight unequaled; calm serenity of interiors give subtle sense of intimacy; bold geometrical design, jewel quality

THE LETTER, BY VERMEER

of fabrics, exceptional portraits; works include *Young Woman Weighing Gold* and *Girl with a Red Hat* (Washington), *Young Woman with a String of Pearls* (Berlin), *Artist in His Studio* (Vienna), *Portrait of a Young Girl* (Hague), *Young Woman at a Casement* (Met. Mus.), and *The Lace-Maker* (Louvre).

Dyck, Sir Anthony van. 1599-1641. Flemish portrait and religious painter; studied with Rubens; worked in Italy; court painter to Charles I of England where he painted over 350 portraits (1632-41); forerunner of English school of portrait artists including Reynolds, Gainsborough, etc; famed equestrian portraits; restrained color; works include *Queen Henrietta Maria and Her Dwarf, The Betrayal of Christ, St. Martin Dividing His Cloak;* engravings.

Ruisdael, Jacob Isaacsz. van. *ca.* 1628/29-82. Most celebrated of the Dutch landscape artists; considered originator of modern concept of landscape; important handling of sky and clouds, often creating somber mood that influenced later German romantics; magnificent trees, wooded scenes; rare etchings much prized.

Hooch, Pieter de. 1629-83. Outstanding Dutch genre painter; known for interiors; intriguing use of open doors to create depth and allow clever handling of light; fluent brushwork using thin, often translucent, pigment; warmth of domestic scenes; *The Bedroom* (Berlin).

Hobbema, Meindert. 1638-1709. Dutch landscape artist; pupil of Ruisdael; known for studies of wooded dunes of Haarlem region, pink-roofed mills among tall trees, ruins, and views of towns; work in England influenced landscape artists there.

Steen, Jan. 1626-79. Dutch genre painter of scenes of merrymaking, tavern, and home life; superb sense of humor; excellent draftsman; sympathetic studies of middle-class life.

Brueghel, (Bruegel) Jan de Velours. 1568-1625. Known as "Velvet Brueghel;" brilliant narrative technique close to miniaturists; landscapes, genre, animals, flowers, and fruits; painted backgrounds for Rubens and others; wealthy court painter.

Brueghel (Bruegel), Pieter, the Younger. 1564-1637. Called "Hell Brueghel"; painted infernal regions with frightening realism; brother of Jan.

Terbrugghen, Hendrik. 1588-1648. Dutch painter; studied in Italy and introduced Baroque style of Caravaggio to Netherlands; forerunner of Rembrandt; own work influenced more by Vermeer.

Terborch (Terburg), Gerard. 1617-81. One of the great Dutch "little masters" of genre painting; fine portrait artist; worked for Philip IV in Spain; painted the wealthy class of burghers; interiors have atmosphere, quiet light, fine color; *Curiosity* (Met. Mus.), *The Suitor's Visit* (Washington).

Teniers, David, the Younger. 1610-90. Flemish genre painter; protégé of Rubens; court painter; sparkling silvery tone and brilliant technique unsurpassed in genre works of period.

Ostade, Adriaen van. 1610-84. Dutch genre painter of village life; influenced by Rembrandt, Brouwer, and pupil, Hals; brother **Isaac** (1621-49), outstanding winter landscapes.

Brouwer (Brauwer), Adriaen. *ca.* 1605-38. Flemish painter of genre and rustic scenes; pupil of Hals; outstanding observation of life in country inns; helped by Rubens, who admired his work; freedom of brushwork anticipated impressionists of later period.

Goyen, Jan van. *ca.* 1595/96-1656. Important early Dutch landscape and seascape artist; worked at The Hague; interesting treatment of light and filtered color effects created misty seashores and atmosphere of sodden countryside.

Metsu, Gabriel. 1630-67. Outstanding among minor Dutch masters; brilliant color; conversation pieces of small groups of people in richly decorated interiors; works prized today.

Others. Jakob Jordaens (1593-1678), Pieter Saenredam (1597-1665), Hercules Seghers (*ca.* 1589/90-*ca.* 1638), Carel Fabritius (*ca.* 1620/22-54), Frans van Mieris the Elder (1635-81), Aelbert Cuyp (1620-91), Gerard Dou (1613-75), Jan van der Heyden (1637-1712), Gerard van Honthorst (1590-1656), Willem Kalf (1622-93), Frans Snyders (1579-1657), Salomon van Ruisdael (*ca.* 1600-1670), Pieter Claesz (1597-1661), Philips Wouverman (1619-68), Hendrick Avercamp (1585-1634), Anthonie Palamedes (*ca.* 1600/01-73), Jacobus Vrel (*fl.* 1654-62), Abraham van Beyern (*ca.* 1621/-22-90), Emmanuel de Witte (*ca.* 1617-92).

Roelas, Juan de las. *ca.* 1558/60-1625. Religious painter of the school of Seville; influenced by Tintoretto, whose style he introduced into Spain; teacher of Zurbáran.

ROKEBY VENUS BY VELASQUEZ

MAIDS OF HONOR BY VELASQUEZ

Spain

Velásquez, Diego Rodriguez de Silva y. 1599-1660. Great master of the Spanish school; penetrating perception marks magnificent portraits; bold yet subtle use of light and color to gain dramatic effect without destruction of form anticipated impressionism of later period; court painter to Philip IV; exquisite portraits of infantas; *Las Meninas* (Maids of Honor, Prado); sympathetic studies of dwarfs and buffoons; superb use of reds seen in portrait of *Pope Innocent X* (Rome), but famed for unrivaled use of gray; great collection of works in Prado Museum, Madrid, and in other museums.

Murillo, Bartolomé Estéban. 1618-82. Religious and portrait artist; worked with Velásquez; helped found Seville Academy; noted for emotional quality and religious sentimentality of work; through understanding of popular mentality, he became the most successful painter of the period of the Counter Reformation in Spain; various studies of the Immaculate Conception in museums throughout the world, including several in the Prado, Madrid, and one in the Cathedral at Guadalajara, Mexico; St. Anthony and the Infant Christ (Berlin); also painted urchins and peasant life with surprising realism.

Zurbarán, Francisco de. *ca.* 1598/99-1664. Leading representative of the mysticism of Catholic Spain in the 17th century; all work executed for churches or convents; well-known for paintings for Carthusian Monastery and those in Latin America; not influenced by Velásquez as were others of the period; reserved color, simplicity, and lack of sentiment or compassion characterize his work.

Ribera, José (Jusepe) de. 1588-1652. Known as *Lo Spagnoletto;* outstanding Spanish master painting in Italy; although influenced by Caravaggio, follower of *tenebroso* ("cellar illumination") concept; passionate, intense, often violent use of color; combined religious mysticism and realism; sadistic violence of subject matter often extreme, although he also painted women with sentimental sweetness; Pope presented him with the Order of Christ.

Carreño de Miranda, Juan. 1614-85. Court painter, successor and protégé of Velásquez; portraits.

Herrera, Francisco de. 1576-1656. Founder of naturalistic school of Seville; teacher of Velásquez; dramatic, realistic compositions; good draftsman.

Pacheco, Francisco. 1564-1654. Best-known as theoretician; author of *Arte de la Pintura* (1649) and a *History of Painting;* father-in-law of Velásquez; painted series for monastery; influential.

Others. Juan Bautista Martínez del Mayo (*ca.* 1612-67), Claudio Coello (1642-93).

Germany

Elsheimer, Adam. 1578-1610. Known in Italy as Adamo Tedesco; influenced Dutch landscape artists; teacher of Teniers; small landscapes of rare charm and individuality; biblical and mythological subjects with naturalistic landscape backgrounds; interesting use of light in night scenes; excellent etchings.

Willmann, Michael Lukas. 1630-1706. Painter of late Baroque; studied in Netherlands; influenced by Rubens; attempts at overdramatic effects often unsuccessful.

Liss, Johann (Jan Lyss). *ca.* 1597-*ca.* 1629/30. Genre painter; studied in Haarlem; leading painter in Venice (1621); also mythological and religious subjects; rich color.

France

Poussin, Nicolas. 1594-1665. Master classical artist who worked in Italy but remained uniquely French; influenced by Raphael, Venetians, and antiquity; carefully organized mythological, religious, or historical scenes or allegories; after 1645, figures become

CHILDHOOD OF BACCHUS BY POUSSIN

less important in heroic landscapes; works include *Orpheus and Eurydice* (Louvre), *Triumph of Neptune and Amphitrite* (Phil. Mus.), *Rape of the Sabine Women* (Met. Mus.), *Shepherds in Arcadia* (Louvre), *Cephalus and Aurora* (London), *The Gathering of the Ashes of Phocion* (Louvre), and *Saint John on Patinos* (Chicago).

Claude Lorraine (Claude Gellée). 1600-1682. Outstanding landscape artist; largely self-taught; worked in Rome; painted and sketched from nature; painting of sky gave new depth to landscapes; use of light and color influenced Turner, English watercolorists, and later impressionists; exceptional sketches and etchings; successful during lifetime; works include *Landscape with Moses and the Burning Bush; Harbor at Sunset* (Frick, N.Y.), *Embarkment of the Queen of Sheba* (Louvre), *Seaport at Sunset* (London), *A Pastoral* (Yale).

Le Nain, Louis. 1593-1648. Considered the best painter of three brothers (**Antoine,** *ca.* 1588-1648, and **Mathieu,** 1607-77) though they worked closely together; depicted humble, depressed peasants and forgotten masses when allegorical compositions were more popular; large works, subdued color; *Peasant's Family* and *Forge* (Louvre); *Milkmaid's Family* (Leningrad); *Two Young Girls* (Rotterdam).

La Tour, Georges du Mesnil de. 1593-1652. Long-neglected artist now highly respected; unique, highly original style; strange melancholy, mysticism in poetic, simple yet moving abstract and rather medieval style; subtle color in candlelit scenes; *St. Irene with Wounded St. Sebastian* (Berlin); *Nativity with Shepherds* and *Joseph the Carpenter* (Louvre).

ST. JOSEPH THE CARPENTER BY GEORGES DE LA TOUR

Lebrun, Charles. 1619-90. Virtual dictator of art world of France under Louis XIV (1662–83); founded *Académie royal de Peinture et de Sculpture* (1648) that replaced old guild system of apprenticeship; in charge of decoration of Hall of Apollo (Louvre) and Hall of Mirrors, War and Peace, (Versailles); director of Gobelins (1663), responsible for sets of tapestries dealing with *The Seasons, Life of the King,* and *Royal Homes; Chancellor Sequier on Horseback* (Louvre), excellent portrait; important influence.

Callot, Jacques. 1592-1625. Famous engraver; etcher; first to use hard grounds; in Italy (1609-22); figures from Commedia dell'Arte; horrors of war in *Misères de la Guerre;* exceptional draftsman.

Champaigne, Philippe de. 1602-74. Portrait artist from Flanders; best-known for studies of *Richelieu;* somber tones, flat, delicate washes.

Rigaud, Hyacinthe (Rigau y Ros). 1659-1743. Portrait painter to Louis XIV; originally influenced by Van Dyck, developed more intimate and personal style; shrewd observer despite idealized portrayals.

Others. Claude Vignon (1593-1670), Simon Vouet (1590-1649), Eustache Lesueur (*ca.* 1616/17-55), Pierre Mignard (1612-95), Jean-Baptiste Jouvenet (1644-1717), Nicolas de Largillière (1656-1746), Nicolas Tournier (1590-after 1670), Valentin de Boulogne (1594-1632).

England

Streater, Robert. 1624-80. First Englishman to practice mural painting; decoration of ceilings, walls of important buildings.

American Colonies

Foster, John. 1648-81. Wood engraver; first known portrait print in colonies, *Rev. Richard Mather* (1671); book illustrations, maps; essentially an amateur.

Italy

Reni, Guido. 1575-1642. Extremely popular Baroque painter of Bolognese school; pupil of Carracci; rival of Caravaggio in Rome; use of gold and silver tonality in sumptuous, voluptuous frescoes; *Aurora* (1615), ceiling fresco in Palazzo Rospigliosi (Rome), best-known work; softness of color, extreme sentimentality, exceptional feeling for form contributed to success; fine portraits; works also in Genoa, the Vatican, and Ravenna.

Castiglione, Giovanni Benedetto. 1616-70. Known as *Il Grechetto*. Genoese master, considered one of the greatest animal painters; admired Rembrandt; court painter, Mantua; biblical and mythological subjects; *Noah Entering Ark with Animals* (Florence) and *Israelites with Their Herds* (Milan).

Domenichino, Il (Domenico Zampieri). 1581-1641. Bolognese master; worked with Carracci on decorations for Farnese Gallery; *Diana's Hunt*, Borghese Gallery (Rome), outstanding landscape; considered by Rubens important Baroque artist; sensitive style.

Guercino (Giovanni Francesco Barbieri). 1591-1666. Famous for great ceiling decoration at Villa Ludovici (Rome) representing Aurora's chariot crossing the sky above architectural scene; also known for large altarpieces; leading painter of Bologna after Guido Reni's death; drawings.

Cortona, Pietro Berrettini da. 1596-1669. Florentine artist; established model for Baroque ceiling painting with work at Palazzo Barberini (Rome); decorations for Pitti Palace; frescoes influenced Tiepolo.

Rosa, Salvator. 1615-73. Leading artist of Neapolitan school; pupil of Ribera; court painter, Rome; noted for etchings; landscapes rich in contrasts and battle scenes showing ruins in somber atmosphere; fine portraits; *Adoration of the Shepherds* (Vienna).

Strozzi, Bernardo. 1581-1644. Known as *Cappuccino*. Genoese artist; worked in Venice; excellent portraits.

Gentileschi, Orazio. *ca.* 1562/65-1637/38. Influenced by Caravaggio; worked in Rome, Genoa, France; court painter to Charles I (1626); *Finding of Moses* (Prado); *Annunciation* (Turin); *Rest on the Flight* (Louvre).

Maratti, Carlo. 1625-1713. Portrait artist of Rome; also known for monumental altarpieces and frescoes; *Portrait of a Cardinal* (London).

Others. Francesco Albani (1578-1660), Giuseppe Arpino (1560-1640), Evaristo Bachenis (*ca.* 1607-77), Carlo Saraceni (1585-*ca.* 1620/25), Andrea dal Pozzo (1642-1709).

ASIA · *Japan*

Moronobu, Hishikawa. 1618-94. Noted master printmaker; pioneer in designing and executing woodcuts for

LOVERS IN A GARDEN, MORONOBU, JAPAN

book illustration; first work on large single sheets in black and white (1670), later hand-colored; real founder (though not inventor) of popular school of *ukiyo-e* printmakers; *ukiyo-e* prints (called "pictures of the passing scene" or "pictures of the the floating world") were scorned by the wealthy aristocracy but adored by the people and bought by the prosperous merchants and rising middle class; leading painter of Genroku era, Moronobu was an important influence on other artists.

Kōetsu, Honnami. 1558-1637. Famous for calligraphy and for lacquer pieces with designs in gold relief (*takamakiye*); considered by some experts the greatest genius after Sesshū.

Korin, Ogata. 1658-1716. Leading artist of the Edo period; imaginative design, refined and polished style seen in outstanding paintings of nature, particularly birds; revolutionized the art of lacquering; works completely Japanese in feeling, no foreign influence; brother, **Kenzan** (1663-1743), famous ceramist.

Kano Tannyu. 1602-74. Last of the four supreme masters of the Kano School; founded separate school (Edo Kano); very original, vigorous style; magnificent doors of Nagoya Castle; extremely versatile.

Tosa Mitsuoki. 1617-91. Master of Tosa School; elegant decorative style; distinctive purity of line; designs used by lacquer masters of Kyoto in next century.

Matabei, Iwasa. 1568-1650. Gained fame as forerunner of *ukiyo-e* style; portrayed realistic scenes of contemporary life; influenced later printmakers.

Sōtatsu, Nonomura. (Tawaraya).

d. 1643. Achieved originality by combining styles of earlier periods with "wet brush" technique of Mu Ch'i, decorated beautiful poem scroll, with calligraphy by Honnami Kōetsu; very successful.

Kano Sanraku. 1559-1635. Outstanding figure of the Momoyama period; delicate coloring seen in his paintings of peonies on gold foil that covered the sliding doors of the Imperial Hall of the Daigakuki.

Kano Sadanobu. 1597-1623. Noted artist who gained fame for doors of Nagoya Castle.

Miyamoto Niten. 1584-1645. Also known as Miyamoto Mushashi; a samurai whose skill as a swordsman was legendary; remarkably talented *suiboku* artist; brushwork swift and terse, like a swordsman's.

Iccho Hanabusa. 1651-1724. Founder of school of Hanabusa at Yedo (Tokyo); portrayal of charming simplicity of peasants created realistic style that influenced both Hokusai and Hiroshige.

China

Tung Ch'i-Ch'ang. 1555-1636. Highly-gifted landscape artist of the Ming dynasty; unusual self-expression freed other artists from academic restrictions and made him a controversial figure; important influence.

Wang Hui. 1632-1717. Great master of Ch'ing dynasty; great purity and elegance of brushwork; very imaginative.

Li Liu-fang. 1575-1629. Brilliant small album pictures; free spirit revealed in these pure examples of "thought writing" (*hsieh i*).

Wu Li. 1643-1708. Noted Ch'ing

artist; studied Western painting in monastery in Macao; influence of Western art seen only in boldness of his work; great love of nature; depth of spiritual content important element in pictures.

Su Fang. 1622-96. Portrait artist; attempted to emphasize life and grace of subject rather than decorative ornamentation popular at that time.

India

Great period of Moghul painting; usual procedure was for a group (or team) of artists to work on large compositions, one to draw the outlines, another responsible for the landscapes, another for portraits, and a fourth as

SHAIKH HASAN CHISHTI, BICHITRI, MOGHUL

colorist. Under Akbar (d. 1605), who had established his magnificent white city of Fatehpur Sikri as his capital and built a great library there, **Mir Sayyid Ali, 'Abdu 's-Samad,** and **Farruq Beg,** as well as a score of other artists and musicians worked together; **'Abdu 's-Samad's** best known work is in pure Persian style; *Princes of the House of*

Timur (British Mus.) is an example; under Akbar's successor, Jehangir (d. 1627), the vogue for European realism produced a startling portrait like *The Death of Inayat Khan from His Debauches* (*ca.* 1618); under Shah Jehan (r. 1628-58), "night pieces" in imitation of European artists (like Honthorst) were accepted style. Aurangzeb (r. 1658-1707) was a puritan Sunni and abolished court art.

Chitarman. *ca.* 1608-49. Moghul artist; magnificent miniatures in album for Shah Jehan (1628).

Persia

Muhammad Zaman was sent to Italy by Abbas II and returning to Persia (1675) introduced European techniques and styles to Isfahan.

Mu'in Musawwir, influenced by European techniques, though a pupil of Riza-i 'Abbas, illustrated works combining both styles.

SCULPTURE

EUROPE · *Italy*

Bernini, Giovanni Lorenzo (Gianlorenzo). 1598-1680. Master Baroque sculptor, architect; worked for Pope Urban VIII in Rome, and at the court of Louis XIV in France (1665); portrait busts include famous portrait of the king in the Louvre, *Francesco d' Este, Innocent X; Apollo and Daphne* (1620, Villa Borghese); equestrian statue of *Constantine; David* (1623); fountains for the Piazza Barberini (*Triton*), Navona, and Trevi; tomb of *Urban VIII* (St. Peter's); famed

BLESSED LODOVICA ALBERTONI BY BERNINI

FOUNTAIN OF THE FOUR RIVERS (DETAIL)
BY BERNINI

FRANCESCO D'ESTE BY BERNINI

Ecstasy of Santa Theresa (1645-52)
and other religious works; extremely
successful.

Algardi, Alessandro. 1602-54. Noted
for tomb of *Leo XI*, bronze of *Innocent
X*, and dramatic relief (*The Expulsion
of Attila*), at St. Peter's (Rome).
   Others. Francesco Mochi (1580-
1654) and Andrea Bolgi (1605-56).

France

   Coysevox, Antoine. 1640-1720. Leading Baroque sculptor; influenced by
Bernini; produced great part of Versailles sculpture; *Winged Horses* at
entrance to Tuileries gardens; outstanding portrait busts of *Louis XIV,
Richelieu, Mazarin, Duc de Chaulnes,
Charles Lebrun,* and others.

CHARLES LEBRUN BY COYSEVOX

   Girardon, François. 1628-1715. Decorative sculpture in gardens of Versailles
including *Rape of Proserpine, Bain
d'Apollon;* influenced by Lebrun;
Tomb of Richelieu (Sorbonne), considered masterpiece.
   Puget, Pierre. 1622-94. Better-known
as architect; works of sculpture gained
recognition in later periods; *Perseus
and Andromeda; Milo of Crotona*
(1671-83, Louvre), considered best

work; bas reliefs of *Alexander and Diogenes* and the *Gallic Hercules.*

Sarrazin, Jacques. *ca.* 1588-1660. Founder and director of *Acadèmie royale de Peinture et de Sculpture* (1654); works include caryatids on Lemercier's central pavilion (Louvre); tomb of *Henry II* (Chantilly); four statues for the high altar in Church of Saint Nicholas des Champs (Paris).

Anguier, François. 1604-69. Gained fame with mausoleum of *Henry II,* Duc de Montmorency (Moulins).

Anguier, Michel. 1614-86. Brother of François; *Nativity* at the church of Val de Grâce.

Others. Étienne Le Hongre (1628-90), Guillaume Dupré (*ca.* 1574-1647), Pierre Legros (1629-1714), Antoine Lepautre (1621-91), Swiss-French brothers—Jean Jacques Keller (1635-1700) and Jean Balthasar Keller (1638-1702).

Spain

Montañés, Juan Martínez. 1568-1649. Considered by many Spain's greatest sculptor; prolific; Baroque works, mostly in wood (called *Dios de la Madera,* God of Wood Carving by contemporaries); dramatic intensity strong but withdrawn, introverted in contrast to flamboyance of Bernini; first in Spain to show *Christ upon the Cross* with feet parallel (using four nails); famous *Mater Dolorosa,* painted wood with inlaid glass teardrops; robes and draperies often filled in with gesso to achieve realism; many important religious works, all in Seville; *Christ of the Passion, Adoration of the Shepherds, Christ of Clemency, St. Francis Borgia* (University Chapel),

and the *Immaculate Conception.*

Mena, Pedro de. 1628-88. Late Baroque sculptor; pupil of Alonso Cano; famed work, 40 saints for choir stalls of Malaga cathedral; *Madonna and Child with St. Joseph* (Madrid); half-length figures and busts of *Ecce Homo* and *Dolorosa; Virgin of Bethlehem; St. Francis* (Toledo), very moving piece of work.

Mora, José de. 1642-1724. Leading Baroque sculptor of Granada; Andalusian temperament seen in expression of solitude, sorrow in figures; *Soledad; St. Bruno; Christ on the Cross.*

Cano, Alonso. 1601-67. Primarily noted as architect, Cano's sculpture is strongly realistic; *Immaculate Conception* and *Madonna of Bethlehem* (Granada); *Virgin and Child* (Seville); *St. Diego of Alcala,* Palace of Charles V (Granada).

Fernández, Gregorio. 1576-1636. Leading artist of Valladolid; religious naturalism, emphasis on subject rather than form; *Pietà, Baptism, Assumption of the Virgin, St. Bruno* are all baroque in style.

Low Countries

Duquesnoy, François. *ca.* 1594-1644. Flemish sculptor known as *Il Flamingo* and François Flamand; worked in Italy and in France; friend of Poussin; marble statues of *St. Susanna, St. Andrew,* small ivory figurines, tombs, church decorations.

Vries, Adriaen de. *ca.* 1560-1627. Dutch; worked at court of Emperor Rudolph II of Austria and in Prague; influenced by Italians; bronzes include *Hercules, Adonis and Venus, Mercury and Psyche,* and *Triton* (Prague).

Desjardins, Martin (van den Bo-gaert). d. 1694. Dutch; one of the chief decorative sculptors at Versailles.

Czechoslovakia

Bendl, Johann Georg. 1620-80. Noted sculptor and wood carver of Prague; large wood carving, *Flight of Frederick of the Palatinate from Prague,* St. Vitus' Cathedral; statue of *St. Wenceslas,* portal of St. Salvator's Church.

Germany

Schlüter, Andreas. 1664-1714. Lead-ing architect and sculptor; equestrian statue of the *Great Elector of Berlin,* tomb of Frederick I and his consort, *Dying Warriors* (Berlin Arsenal).

ELECTOR FREDERICK WILLIAM,
EQUESTRIAN STATUE,
BY SCHLÜTER

Permoser, Balthasar. 1651-1732. In-troduced Italian Baroque to Germany; court sculptor to Augustus the Strong, Saxony; influenced by Bernini; *St. Augustine, St. Ambrose,* and several large figures in Dresden.

Petel, Georg. *ca.* 1600-1634. Bava-rian; first German to adopt Baroque style; influenced by Rubens; many successful small works; several cruci-fixions.

England

Stone, Nicholas. 1587-1647. Worked with Inigo Jones; tombs of *Bodley* (Ox-ford) and *Donne* (St. Paul's, London).

Gibbons, Grinling. 1648-1720. Dutch wood carver, sculptor, working in Eng-land; employed by Wren to carve stalls in St. Paul's and other London churches; worked for king at Windsor and Whitehall.

EUROPE · *France*

Mansart, François. 1598-1666. Ba-roque architect; decidedly French style seen in country house (château) of *Maisons-Lafitte* (1642-50) and elegant Orléans wing at Blois; curved colon-nades give feeling of Rococo to château of *Maisons-sur-Seine;* many churches including Church of *Val-de-Grâce* (Paris), cupola intended imitation of Dome of *St. Peter's* (1645, Rome); in-fluenced Wren.

Hardouin-Mansart, Jules. 1646-1708. Outstanding Baroque court architect; distinctly French grandeur, elegance; dome of *Hôtel des Invalides* (1675-1706); two wings of *Versailles Palace,* including the famed *Hall of Mirrors;* *Maison de St. Cyr,* Grand Trianon; *Place des Victoires* (1684-86) and *Place Vendome* (1699); *Château de*

PALACE OF VERSAILLES, LOUIS LE VAU
AND HARDOUIN-MANSART

CHURCH OF THE INVALIDES,
PARIS,
BY HARDOUIN-MANSART

Clagny, residence of Madame de Montespan.

Levau, Louis. 1612-70. Leading Baroque architect; worked for Louis XIV; completed eastern and northern sides of *Versailles;* church of the *Collège des Quatre Nations* (now Institut de France, 1661); *Chapel de la Salpetrière* at the *Church of St. Sulpice* (Paris); *Hôtel Lambert;* rebuilt *Château de Vincennes.*

Perrault, Claude. 1613-88. Eminent architect, scientist, physician, scholar; colonnade, east façade of the *Louvre* (1667-70); added disciplined formality, classical balance to French architecture; *Paris Observatory* (1667-72); *Arc de Triomphe* for Porte Saint Antoine.

THE LOUVRE,
PARIS—PERRAULT, LE BRUN, LE VAU

Le Nôtre, André. 1613-1700. Brilliant landscape architect; *Gardens of Versailles,* celebrated work; established principles of formal gardens that dominated Europe; worked in Italy and England.

Lemercier, Jacques. 1585-1654. Noted architect; designed palace for Cardinal Richelieu (1631); commissioned by King Louis XIII to take charge of completion of *Louvre* (1624); *Church of the Sorbonne* (1635-52).

Brosse, Salomon de. *ca.* 1565-1627. Designer of the *Luxembourg Palace* (1615-24) for Marie de' Medici; façade of *Church of St. Gervais* (1616); main hall of the *Palace of Justice* (1618).

Puget, Pierre. 1622-94. Architect and sculptor; designed portico of *Hôtel de Ville* (Toulon); *Halle au Poissons* and *Hôspice de Charité* (Marseilles.).

197

Germany

Holl, Elias. 1573-1646. Leading architect of Augsburg; influenced by Palladio; secular buildings, particularly *Town Hall* (1615-20), one of the finest examples of German Renaissance architecture.

Schlüter, Andreas. 1660-1714. Court architect (Berlin); born Hamburg; worked Danzig and Warsaw; *Berlin Castle* (destroyed during World War II), excellent example of North German Baroque, was largely his design (see Sculpture).

England

Jones, Inigo. 1573-1652. Great master of early 17th century; studied in Italy, influenced by Palladio; *Queen's House* (Greenwich) considered first important building; *Lindsay House,* Lincoln's Inn Fields; *Covent Garden Piazza* (begun 1630); *Banqueting House* (Whitehall, London, 1619-22); reconstruction of *St. Paul's Cathedral* (1633); *The Queen's Chapel,* St. James's Palace (now Marlborough House Chapel, 1623-27); *Wilton House* (Wilshire) for 4th Earl of Pembroke.

WHITEHALL PALACE, LONDON, BY JONES

Wren, Sir Christopher. 1632-1723. Great master of second half of 17th century; influenced by Palladio; doctor of astronomy, celebrated mathematician; studied in Paris; rebuilt *St. Paul's Cathedral* (1675-1716); after great fire of London, proposed plans for rebuilding city; built no less than 52 churches (1670-1711), many of which were destroyed during World War II; hospitals, libraries, great homes, theaters, etc., including *St. Stephen's,* Walbrook (London, 1672-87), *Sheldonian Theater* (1665-69), *Custom House* (1668), *Temple Bar* (1670-72), *Greenwich Hospital* and *Observatory,* library of Queen's College (Oxford, 1693-96), library of Trinity College (Cambridge, 1677-92); additions to *Hampton Court Palace.*

Webb, John. 1611-72. Outstanding pupil of Jones (possibly related to him); worked with master until his death; asked by Charles I to design a new *Whitehall Palace* (1647-49); *Lamport Hall* for Sir Giles Isham (1654-57); *Belvoir* for Earl of Rutland (1654); great houses of *Amesbury,* (Wiltshire, 1661), *Gunnersbury* (Middlesex, 1663), possibly *Ashburnham House* (Westminster, before 1662); edited Jones's tract on *Stonehenge.*

Italy

Bernini (Giovanni) Lorenzo. 1598-1680. Universal genius, considered greatest sculptor of period; great architect from Naples; invited by Louis XIV to Paris to design plans to add east front to *Louvre Palace;* followed Maderna as architect at *St. Peter's* (1629); introduced unique *Scala Regia* stairs adjoining the building; famous late church, S. *Andrea al Quirinale* (1658–78), for Clement IX; magnificent *Royal Staircase*, Vatican Palace (*ca.* 1665).

Borromini, Francesco. 1599-1667. Leading Baroque architect; worked with Bernini, Maderna, official architect of Rome (1644-55); church of *San Carlo alle Quattro Fontane* (begun 1633), clever spatial composition added startling façade (1667); *Tower of S. Ivo* (begun 1642); façade of *Sant' Agnese* in Piazza Navona (1653-63); many other works; important influence.

SANT'AGNESE, ROME, BY BORROMINI

Maderna, Carlo. 1556-1629. Outstanding early Baroque architect of Rome; completed *St. Peter's* (1603), altering Michelangelo's Greek cross plan to present Latin cross; *Palazzo Barberini* (begun 1628); *Palazzo Mattei di Giove, S. Giacomo al Corso* (1594); *S. Susanna*; completed *S. Andrea della Valle* (Rome).

Cortona, Pietro da (Berrettini). 1596-1669. Primarily a painter; designed churches of *S. Maria della Pace* (begun 1656-57); *S. Martina*; façade

of *S. Maria in Via Lata,* others, Rome.

Rainaldi, Carlo. 1611-91. Roman architect; known for work on S. *Agnese* in Piazza Navona (begun 1652); S. *Maria di Monte Santo* (1662).

Algardi, Alessandro. 1602-54. Versatile artist; succeeded Bernini as court sculptor; designed façade of *Church of S. Ignazio* and *Villa Doria-Pamphili* (Rome).

Fontana, Carlo. 1634-1714. Roman architect; pupil of Bernini; façade of *San Marcello,* fountain in Piazza di San Pietro, tomb of *Queen Christina, Library of Minervan Convent,* all in Rome.

Longhena, Baldassare. 1604-82. Leading Venetian architect; known for S. *Giorgio Maggiore* (1643-45); *Santa Maria della Salute; Santa Maria dei Scalzi;* palaces and churches.

Guarini, Guarino. 1624-83. Noted northern Italian architect; professor of mathematics and philosophy, and architectural designer; *Archiettura Civile* (1737); daring style an important influence; churches include *Ste. Anne* (Paris, 1662), *Divina Providencia* (Lisbon), *San Lorenzo* (1666, Turin).

Ponzio Flaminio. 1560-1613. With Giovanni Vasanzio (who designed for the Villa Borghese, Rome, 1613-15) built *Cappella Paolina* in S. *Maria Maggiore* (1605-11); *St. Sebastiano* (1608-13); *Acqua Paola* (1612, Rome).

Spain

Mora, Francisco de. *ca.* 1546-1610. Leading court architect; assistant to Herrera, who recommended him to Philip II; designed city of Lerma (1604-14) for favorite of Philip III, Francisco de Sandoval y Rojas; façade of *San José* (1608, Avila).

Gómez de Mora, Juan. 1586-1647. Leading architect; pupil, nephew, assistant of Francisco de Mora; *Encarnacion Church* (1611-16, Madrid); dormitory building for *Jesuit Clerecía* (1617, Salamanca); Italian influence seen in Jesuit church in Alcala de Henares (completed 1625); *Court Prison* (now Foreign Office, 1629-34) and *Town Hall* (1640, Madrid).

Others. Alonso Cano (1601-67), Francisco Bustista, S.J. (1594-1679), Alonso Carbonell (*fl.* 1620-60), Martin de Olinda (d. 1655), Sebastian de la Plaza (early 17th century).

Sweden

Tessin, Nicodemus, the Younger. 1654-1728. Master of Swedish Baroque tempered by French classical style; studied in Italy, influenced by Bernini and Fontana; famous for *Royal Castle* (Stockholm, from 1676).

Netherlands

Keyser, Henrik de. 1565-1621. Noted Dutch architect; built churches at Zuyderkerk and Westerkerk (begun 1620); court of the *East Indian House* (1606) and the *Stock Exchange* (Amsterdam); *Town Hall* (Delft).

Russia

Outstanding period of religious architecture; *Church of the Nativity of the Virgin* (1649-52, Moscow), *Church of the Trinity* and of the *Georgian Virgin* (1634-54); *Church of the Trinity,* (1688, Ostankino, near Moscow); *Church of St. John Chrysostom* (1649-54, Yaroslavl); *Church of St. John the Baptist* (1687, Yaroslavl); *Church of the Presentation,* Borisoglebsk Monastery (near Rostov).

ISLAM · *Persia*

The magnificent *Masjid-i-shāh* at Isfahān (begun 1590) was designed by the Ustād (Master) architect **Abu'l-Qasim**; the chief calligrapher, responsible for the beautiful inscription frieze, was **'Ali Riza,** who signed the work (1616); he was assisted by **'Abdal-Baqu Danishan;** the portal of the *Masjid-i-shāh* is one of the most imposing in Iran; the portal screen is flanked by slender minarets 110 ft.

TAJ MAHAL, AGRA, INDIA

MOSQUE OF AHMED I, ISTANBUL

high; the arch itself, nearly 90 ft. high, is framed by a triple cable mold in bright turquoise blue, rising from huge marble vases, and the half-dome is filled with stalactites.

THEATER

EUROPE · *England*

Shakespeare, William. 1564-1611. Great dramatic genius; this is the period of the incomparable tragedies: *Hamlet* (1601), *Othello* (1604), *King Lear* and *Macbeth* (1605-6); his last great work, *The Tempest* (1611), as well as *All's Well That Ends Well* (1603-4), *Antony and Cleopatra* (1607-8), and *Coriolanus* (1608-10). *See* previous period.

HAMLET AND HORATIO AT THE GRAVE-YARD, *Hamlet* (AFTER DELACROIX)

Jonson, Ben. 1572-1637. Great dramatist, poet; largely self-educated, he became one of the best classical scholars of his time; sought perfection of form, failed in attempt to establish "classical" tragedy; realistic comedy closely tied to the London world in which he lived; bold satire, unsurpassed vitality; *Every Man in His Humour* (1598), first important play; *Every Man out of His Humour* (1599); *Cynthia's Revels* (1600); *The Poetaster* (1601), brilliant satire, but loses in obvious personal bitterness; *Volpone: or, The Fox* (1606), masterpiece; *Epicoene: or, The Silent Woman* (1609); *The Alchemist* (1610); *Bartholomew Fair* (1614).

SCENE FROM *Volpone* BY BEN JONSON

Dekker, Thomas. *ca.* 1572-*ca.* 1632. Dramatist, pamphleteer; best-known work, *Shoemaker's Holiday* (1599), racy, realistic picture of master-journeymen and their apprentices in late-Elizabethan London; wrote satire, *Satiromastix* (1601); morality play, *The Whore of Babylon* (*ca.* 1605); *The Honest Whore* (with Middleton, *ca.* (1604-05); *The Virgin Martyr* (with

Massinger, *ca.* 1620); middle-class romantic emphasis.

Fletcher, John. 1579-1625. Chief dramatist for King's Men; collaborated with Francis Beaumont and with Philip Massinger in writing of tragi-comedies; Fletcher's own works include: *The Faithful Shepherdess* (printed *ca.* 1609), *Wit Without Money* (*ca.* 1614), *The Passionate Madman* (*ca.* 1616, printed 1647), *A Wife for a Month* (1624), and many others.

Beaumont, Francis. 1584-1616. Famed dramatist; collaborated with John Fletcher; wrote approximately 50 plays, including *The Knight of the Burning Pestle* (printed 1613), *The Scornful Lady* (printed 1616), *The Maid's Tragedy* (printed 1619), *The Philaster* (printed 1620), and *The Coxcomb* (printed 1637); produced *A Masque for the Inner Temple* (1613).

Massinger, Philip. 1583-1640. Dramatist; collaborated with John Fletcher, whom he succeeded as chief dramatist for the King's Men (1625); with Fletcher: *The Little French Lawyer* (*ca.* 1620); *The Lover's Progress* (printed 1647); *The False One* (*ca.* 1620), and others; alone he wrote *The Duke of Milan* (1621-22), a tragedy; *A New Way to Pay Old Debts* (*ca.* 1625-26), most popular play.

Congreve, William. 1670-1720. Leading dramatist of the Restoration period; great writer of comedies including *The Old Bachelor* and *The Double-dealer* (1693); *Love for Love* (1695), most popular play; *Way of the World* (1700), considered his masterpiece.

Wycherley, William. *ca.* 1640-1716. Leading Restoration dramatist; first comedy, *Love in a Wood* (1671), won recognition; *The Gentleman Dancing-Master* (1672), *The Country Wife* (1675), and *The Plain Dealer* (1676), all popular.

Etherege, Sir George. *ca.* 1635-*ca.* 1691. Witty playright; *Comical Revenge; or, Love in a Tub* (1664); *She Would if She Could* (1668) and *The Man of Mode; or, Sir Fopling Flutter* (1676) set tone for comedy of manners that Congreve perfected.

Dryden, John. 1631-1700. Leading poet, dramatist, critic; best-known works, *Conquest of Granada* (1670); heroic drama, *Aureng-Zebe* (1675); *All for Love; or, The World Well Lost* (1677), blank verse; comedies, *The Gallant* (1663) and *Marriage à-la-Mode* (1672).

Cibber, Colley. 1671-1757. Dramatist, actor; first play, *Love's Last Shift* (1696), considered a landmark in the history of the theater as the first sentimental comedy; *Careless Husband* (1704).

Otway, Thomas. 1652-85. Dramatist who attempted to develop a tragic style; influenced by Racine; *Alcibiades* (1675); *Don Carlos* (1676); *The Orphan; or, The Unhappy Marriage* (1680), domestic romantic tragedy; *Venice Preserved; or, A Plot Discovered* (1682), outstanding work.

Others. John Webster (*ca.* 1580-*ca.* 1630), Thomas Middleton (1580-1627), James Shirley (1596-1666), Thomas Heywood (1570-1640), John Marston (1576-1634), John Ford (1586-after 1639).

Masques

Ben Jonson and Inigo Jones brought the Jacobean and Carolean masque to new heights of performance; *Masque of Blacknesse* (1605) probably introduced the Italian intermezzo into England for the first time; Jones (see Architecture), a member of Prince Henry's court, brought Italian stage innovations to the English stage, including movable sets and the change of scenery before the eyes of the audience by means of machines; *Masque of Hymen* (1606, Whitehall) used a globe with moving clouds (believed to have inspired Shakespeare's imagery in *The Tempest*); *Hue and Cry After Cupid* (1608) used moving shutters for the first time; *Masque of Queens* (1609) attempted the first real change of scenes and emphasized the comic and burlesque elements of theater for the first time; *Oberon* (1611); outstanding poets of masque, besides Jonson, were Campion, Shirley, Carew, and Davenant.

France

Racine, Jean. 1639-99. Supreme master dramatist of classical French

RACINE

tragedy; exquisitely delicate sensibility to music of own language make works difficult to translate; brilliant epigrams; favorite of court; most works still performed; *Andromaque* (Andromache, 1667), first tragedy with female lead (after Euripides); *Phèdre* (1677); *Athalie* (1691); development of modern psychological drama owes a great deal to Racine; often called the "most French of French writers."

Corneille, Pierre. 1606-84. Great master of French classical tragedy; most famous works, *Médée* (1635) and *Le Cid* (1636), first French tragic drama of destruction, introduced new theme in which man creates his own destiny; *Horace* (1640); *Cinna* (ca. 1641); and many others.

CORNEILLE

Molière (Jean-Baptiste Poquelin). 1622-73. Great master of comedy; first important work, *The Blunderer; or, The Mishaps* (1655); *The School for Husbands* (1661); *The School for Wives* (1662); *Tartuffe; or, The Imposter* (1664), deepest, bitterest comedy; *Le Misanthrope* (1666), comic view of life darker, attitude toward

203

MOLIÈRE

SCENE FROM MOLIÈRE's *Tartuffe*

man more philosophic in what is considered his masterpiece; *The Doctor in Spite of Himself* (1666); *The Bourgeois Gentleman* (*Le bourgeois gentilhomme*, 1670), superb picture of middle-class shopkeeper.

Quinault, Philippe. 1635-88. Important as librettist; 14 operas with Lully; *Armide* (1686), outstanding work; first play, *The Rivals* (printed 1655), comedy; *The Comedy without Comedy* (1657).

Hardy, Alexandre. *ca.* 1575-1631. Dramatist; more than 600 plays; best-known tragedy, *Marianne* (1610); only important as forerunner of others.

Spain

Lope de Vega Carpio, Félix. 1562-1635. One of the greatest figures in Spanish literature; founder of Spanish national drama; author of some 1,700 plays, 470 extant; developed the most characteristic features of the Spanish

LOPE DE VEGA

theater: style of tragicomedy; cloak-and-sword drama; created *el gracioso*, comic character or clown, parody of heroic figure copied by many others; imaginative realism, great lyric quality; *Punishment Without Revenge* (printed 1635), tragedy; *Marriages of Convenience* (printed 1621), first theatrical work dealing with love and money; *The Peasant in his Acres* (printed 1617); *Fuente Ovejuna*, important dramatic form used later in "proletarian" theater.

Calderón de la Barca, Pedro. 1600-1681. Last important figure of Golden

CALDERÓN DE LA BARCA

Age of Spanish drama; superb craftsman; more than 111 plays; 70 *autos* (religious theme); *Life's A Dream* (*ca.* 1636), best-known work; *The Wonderworking Magician* (1637, translated by Shelley); extremely popular.

Alarcón y Mendoza, Juan Ruíz de. 1581-1639. Dramatic poet; outstanding literary figure; born in Mexico; strong characterization in his 27 plays; *Truth Suspected* (printed 1628), romantic comedy, popular work; *Cruelty for Honour* (*ca.* 1625); *Gaining Friends* (*ca.* 1630); *Walls Have Ears* (printed 1628).

Tirso de Molina (Gabriel Tellez). 1571-1648. Prolific playwright, almost 400 plays; first presentation of Don Juan on stage in his *The Deceiver of Seville,* and the *Stone Guest* (printed 1630).

Castro y Bellvís, Guillén de. 1569-1631. Leading Valencian dramatist; his masterpiece, *Las mocedades del Cid* (The Youth or Reckless Life of the Cid), used by Corneille as basis for his play.

Royas Zorilla, Francisco de. *ca.* 1607-48. Dramatist; created *comedia de figuren,* carried romantic intrigue and idea of honor to an extreme; presented exaggerated or ridiculous as-

pects of characters; *Del rey abajo ninguno* (All Equal below the King), *What Women Are,* and *The Boobies' Sport* (all printed 1640-54).

Moreto y Cavaña, Agustín. 1618-69. Dramatic poet of Golden Age; witty, skilful technician; vied in popularity with Lope; *Scorn for Scorn* (printed 1654), best-known work; influential.

Salazar y Torres, Agustín de. 1642-75. Poet, playwright; many comedies, including *Segunda Celestina,* still produced.

Germany

Gryphius, Andreas Greif. 1616-64. Jesuit dramatist; works include *Catherine of Georgia; or, True Constancy; Charles Stuart; or, Majesty Murdered* (both printed 1698), historical tragedies; *Cardenio and Celinde* (1649), tragedy of love; *The Beloved Thorny Rose* (performed 1660), comedy.

Netherlands

Vondel, Joost van den. 1587-1679. Outstanding Dutch dramatist; translated the classics; wrote 30 dramas in classical tragic style, mostly on religious subjects; most famous work, *Gysbreght van Aemstel* (1637); also wrote the dramatic poem, *Lucifer* (1654).

Bredero, Gerbrand Adriaanszoon. 1585-1618. Leading dramatist; *De Spaanische Brabander* (The Spaniard from Brabant, 1617), satirically realistic comedy of life in Amsterdam, noted work.

Bidermann, Jakob. 1578-1639. Jesuit playwright; *Cenodoxus* (1602), tragedy, considered best of nine dramas; excellent characterization.

ASIA · *Japan*

The **Kabuki** theater was started by a woman dancer, **O Kuni.** After her death (*ca.* 1610), her successors created the **Onna Kabuki** (Women's Kabuki). When women were barred

KABUKI THEATER

KABUKI DANCER

from the stage, the **Wakashu** (Young Men's Kabuki) was organized to take its place, but they, too, were banned (1652).

The **Ningyo Shibai** (puppet or doll theater) gained in importance during the Kanei era (1624-43) when dolls were made of wood instead of clay; with the establishment of **Takemoto za** theater (1684) by the *joruri* singer, **Takemoto Gidayu** (1650-1714) in Dotombori, Osaka, *ningyo shibai* reached its peak of creativity and activity, and became the center of the theatrical life of Japan for the next 80 years. Many of the finest Kabuki dramas were written for *Takemoto za*, including the work of Chikamatsu (see below) who wrote almost exclusively for this theater. New dramatic techniques were developed, and the three-stringed *samisen* was used to accompany the important narrative and recitative.

Chikamatsu, Monzaemon (Suginomori Nobumori). *ca.* 1653-1724. Great dramatist of the Edo period; wrote for the Kabuki theater, but primarily for the *Takemoto za* (puppet stage); vastly improved the *joruri*, dramatic ballad; extremely prolific; wrote *jidai-mono* (historical) and *sewamono* (domestic) dramas, combining classical and colloquial styles; introduced the romantic play to Japan; often referred to as the "Japanese Shakespeare," his influence was tremendous.

Ichikawa Danjuro I of Yedo. 1660-1704. Created the school of acting that emphasized symbolism; noted for the technique called *aragoto*, that developed into *mie*; this theater has been immortalized in the prints of Sharaku.

MUSIC

EUROPE · *Italy*

Monteverdi, Claudio. 1567-1643. Great master and first great figure in history of opera; violist in service of the Duke of Mantua (*ca.* 1590); maestro di cappella, St. Mark's (1613, Venice); priest (1632); church music includes three Masses, Vespers, Magnificats, and numerous motets; secular vocal music includes nine books of madrigals,

MONTEVERDI

MUSICIANS AND SOLDIERS
BY VALENTIN (BAROQUE MUSIC)

a book of *canzonette,* and two books of *Scherzi musicali*; created first modern opera, *Orfeo* (1607, Mantua) by combining counterpoint and harmony and making music and orchestra more important than drama; developed *bel canto arioso*; introduced orchestral effects, including tremolo, pizzicato; first to turn madrigal into *cantata de camera*; first opera house opened (1637, Venice), for which he wrote *Il Ritorno d'Ulisse* and *L'Incoronazione di Poppea* (1642); called "Father of the Art of Instrumentation"; very influential.

Scarlatti, Alessandro. 1660-1725. Master composer of opera; founder, Neapolitan School; developed *aria da capo* and Italian overture; master of chapel to Queen Christina of Sweden (1680-84); 115 operas, 150 oratorios, 600 cantata with continuo, and 61 with instrumental accompaniment; Masses, a Passion, motets, and other church music; concertos, chamber music, and pieces for harpsichord.

SCARLATTI

Frescobaldi, Girolamo. 1583-1643. Most famous organist of the period (St. Peter's, Rome); innovator in development of the fugue and notation; through his pupil, Froberger, strong influence on German organists and composers; keyboard compositions and madrigals.

Torelli, Giuseppe. 1658-1709. Famed violinist, composer; credited with the invention of the concerto form with his *concerto da camera* (1686) for two violins and bass.

Corelli, Arcangelo. 1653-1713. Important composer, violinist, who gave definite form to the *concerto grosso*; his work the basis for revolution in the form of the solo sonata and orchestral concerti of Bach and Handel; established the style of writing for violin both as a solo instrument and for orchestra; works exclusively instrumental.

Cavalli (Caletti-Bruni), Pietro Francesco. 1602-76. Pupil of Monteverdi, whom he succeeded as choirmaster, St. Mark's (1668, Venice); composed more than 40 popular operas including *Didone* (1641), in which the *bel canto* aria was fully developed; *Il Giasone* (1649), most popular; *Serse* (1654); *Ercole amante* (1662), written for performance in Paris.

Carissimi, Giacomo. 1605-74. Composed the earliest examples of true oratorios; developed the solo cantata; *Jephte, Jonas, Baltazar* (all with Latin texts).

Amati, Nicolo (Niccolò). 1596-1684. Most celebrated of famed violin-makers of Cremona; master of Stradivari and Guarneri; violins, violas, cellos known for superb tone and beauty of appearance.

Allegri, Gregorio. 1582-1652. Composer of church music; famous for *Miserere* in nine parts, for two choruses (singing four and five parts respectively) that is sung at Sistine Chapel during Holy Week.

Cesti, Marc'Antonio. 1623-69. Composer of operas; Franciscan monk; pupil of Carissimi (Rome); singer in Papal Chapel; contributed to development of the aria in opera; noted for *Il pomo d'oro* (The Golden Apple, 1667, Vienna), which was written to celebrate the marriage of the Emperor Leopold I to the Infanta Margarita of Spain; *La Dori* (1661), considered his masterpiece.

Bassani, Giovanni Battista. *ca.* 1657-1716. Organist, violinist, composer; believed to have been the teacher of Corelli; conductor of music, Bologna Cathedral (after 1677); composer of oratorios, operas, church and instrumental music; excellent violin sonatas.

Landi, Stefano. *ca.* 1590-*ca.* 1655. Composer; maestro di cappella (from *ca.* 1619, Padua); Papal Chapel (from 1629); composed madrigals, monodies, church music; unique opera, *Sant' Alessio* (1632, Rome), on sacred subject with comic scenes and dance songs; important in the history of opera (sets by Bernini).

Rossi, Salomone Ebrio. *fl.* 1587-1628. Violinist, composer at the court of Mantua; considered one of the most important instrumental composers of his time because of his early use of a form that developed into the trio sonata; published five books of five-part madrigals (1600-1622); two volumes of *Sinfonie e gagliarde* (1607-08).

Draghi, Antonio. 1635-1700. Composer of over 200 works; 67 operas, 116 festival plays and serenades, 32 oratorios, and others.

Others. Agostino Steffani (1654-1728), Alessandro Stradella (1642-82), Giovanni Legrenzi (1626-90), Luigi Rossi (1595-1653), Domenico Mazzocchi (1592-1665), Bernardo Pasquini (1637-1710), Paolo Quagliati (*ca.* 1555-1628), Maurizio Cazzati (*ca.* 1620-77), Antonio Abbatini (*ca.* 1597-1680), Adriano Banchieri (1568-1634), Carlo Farina (17th century), Giovanni Vitali (*ca.* 1644-92), Biagio Marini (*ca.* 1597-1665).

Spain

Cabanilles, Juan José. 1644-1712. Organist, composer; called "the Spanish Frescobaldi"; prolific; organist, Valencia Cathedral (from 1665); variety of form and spontaneity of expression apparent in many works.

Hidalgo, Juan. d. 1685. Famous harpist, composer of earliest Spanish operas (known as *zarzuelas*); several based on plays by Calderon, *Ni amor se libra de Amor* (1640) and *Celos aun del aire matan* (Jealousy, even of air, is fatal, performed 1660, Madrid).

Pujol, Juan Pablo. 1573-1626. Catalan master; maestro de capilla, Sargossa and Barcelona; bridge between classical choral music and early Italian baroque style; influential.

Netherlands

Sweelinck, Jan Pieterszoon. 1562-1621. Leading organist, composer; known as the "maker of German organists"; studied in Venice; important in the development of the fugue; first to give independent part to the pedals; published four books of metrical psalms (for four to eight voices, 1604-

23); *cantiones sacrae* (1619); important teacher, composer for the organ.

Luython, Karel. *ca.* 1556-1620. Composer; court organist to Emperor Maximilian II and his successor, Rudolph II (from *ca.* 1576, Prague); pioneer in use of chromatic modulation; published volume of madrigals (1582); motets (1603); Lamentations (1604); Masses (1609); redesigned the harpsichord.

Belgium

Du Mont (Dumont), Henry. *ca.* 1610-84. Composer, organist, St. Paul's (1639-84, Paris); director, Chapel Royal (1665, Paris); canon, Maestricht Cathedral; five Masses, motets, *chansons*, and instrumental music.

France

Lully (Lulli), Jean Baptiste. 1632-87. Virtual dictator of the musical world under Louis XIV; born in Italy; violinist; established the form of the French overture; composed many op-

LULLY

eras (lyric tragedies), creating a style that held the French operatic stage until the advent of Gluck; composed music for the comedy-ballets of Molière (from 1664), including *Le Bourgeois Gentilhomme* (1670) in which he appeared as an actor and dancer; leader of the *Académie royale de Musique*; unusual grasp of the dramatic; extremely versatile, talented, temperamental; *Alceste* (1674), *Cadmus et Hermione* (1673), *Thésée* (1675), among better-known works.

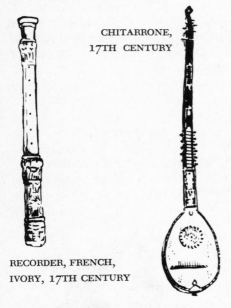

CHITARRONE,
17TH CENTURY

RECORDER, FRENCH,
IVORY, 17TH CENTURY

Chambonnieres, Jacques Champion de. 1602-72. Considered a founder of the French harpsichord school; influenced Couperin; a "father" of descriptive or programmatic music; works for the harpsichord (pub. 1670, though composed earlier); very influential.

Couperin, Louis. *ca.* 1626-61. Leading composer for the keyboard; one of the first French composers to write solo and trio sonatas for strings; viol-

player and organist; pupil of Chambonnières; uncle of François (Le Grand); organist, St. Gervais (1653); musician in royal service.

Charpentier, Marc-Antoine. 1634-1704. Composer; pupil of Carissimi in Rome; director of music, Sainte-Chapelle (1698); two operas, *Les Amours d'Acis et Galatée* (1678) and *Médée* (1693, libretto by Corneille); masterpiece, oratorio *Le Reniement de St. Pierre*; collaborated with Molière at the Théâtre Français (*Malade Imaginaire*, 1673).

Cambert, Robert. 1628-77. Composer (with Perrin) of *Pomone*, a pastoral in five acts and prologue (1671), considered the first French opera; obtained a patent (with Perrin, 1669) for first opera theater in France (taken away by Lully, 1672); went to London, and believed to have worked for Charles II.

Jeune, Claude Le. *ca.* 1528-*ca.* 1600. Prolific writer of *chansons*, instrumental fantasies, madrigals, and psalms; associated with the *Académie de Poésie et de Musique* of Jean-Antoine de Baïf (from 1570).

Sweden

Buxtehude, Dietrich. 1637-1707. Composer, organist; famous for music for the organ; organist, Lübeck (1668), most important music center in Northern Europe at the time; influenced Bach; church cantatas; sonatas for instrumental ensembles.

RECORDER, GERMAN, 17TH CENTURY

England

Purcell, Henry. 1659-95. Considered the greatest natural musical genius

PURCELL

England has produced; very imaginative, highly original; frustrated in working with materials not up to his talents; composed for the theater; six operas including *Dido and Aeneas* (1689) and *The Fairy Queen* (1692, based on Shakespeare's *Midsummer Night's Dream*); music for Dryden's *King Arthur* (1691); anthems are outstanding ones of the period; fantasies for viols, best of his instrumental music.

Gibbons, Orlando. 1583-1625. Last of the Elizabethan composers; organist, Chapel Royal (1605-19), Westminster Abbey (1623-25); chamber musician, James I (1619-25); worked for Charles I; compositions include 30 *Fantasies of Three parts for Viols* (ca. 1620); *The First Set of Madrigals and Motets of Five parts* (1612); large number of anthems; chamber music comprises several pavanes and gal-

liards; music for strings and keyboard pieces; music for four masques.

Blow, John. 1649-1708. Organist, Westminster Abbey; teacher of Purcell; masque *Venus and Adonis*; church music; harpsichord solos; anthems.

Locke, Matthew. 1632-77. Considered the father of English opera; *Psyche* (1675) earliest English opera written in imitation of French comedy-ballet; *The Tempest* (1673-74, based on Shakespeare's play); composer to Charles II; treatise *Melothesia* (1673), earliest extant English work on playing figured bass; influential.

Lawes, Henry. 1596-1662. Composer, highly respected in his own time; wrote *Comus*, based on Milton's masque (1634); part of music for Davenant's *Siege of Rhodes* (1656); coronation anthem for Charles II (1660).

Others. Pelham Humfrey (1647-74), Francis Pilkington (*ca.* 1562-1638), Thomas Tomkins (1572-1656), Thomas Weelkes (d. 1623), John Wilbye (1574-1638), Nicholas Laniere (1588-1666), Martin Peerson (*ca.* 1572-1650), Giovanni Battista Draghi (1667-1706).

Germany

Schütz, Heinrich. 1585-1672. Master composer; leading figure of North German music; forerunner of Bach and Handel; composed first German opera, *Daphne* (1627); pupil of Gabrieli (1609-12); established choral style evolved from Venetian polyphony and new dramatic style of Florence; Kapellmeister, Dresden (1617); Copenhagen (1633-35); *Twelve Sacred Songs* (1657); *Christmas Oratorio,* perfect balance between Italian style and Lutheran polyphonic tradition; important influence.

Scheidt, Samuel. 1587-1654. Organist, composer; studied with Sweelinck; important in the development of the chorale; *Tabulatura nova for organ* (3 vols., 1624), famous work.

Schein, Johann Hermann. 1586-1630. Adapted Italian monodic style to treatment of the Lutheran chorale; outstanding pre-Bach musician; much vocal music.

Others. Nikolaus Strungk (1640-1700), Michael Praetorius (1571-1621), Johann Pachelbel (1653-1706), Johann Kuhnau (1660-1722), Adam Krieger (1634-66), Johann Froberger (1616-67).

1700-1800

The first half of the 18th century in France was the Rococo period of Louis Quinze. The Rococo, essentially a refinement of the Baroque, was an all-inclusive style. The artists were concerned with the design of the entire interior decoration of a building, and the graceful, delicate curves of the paintings were carried out in the furniture, wallpaper, fabrics, silverware, china, etc.

The social satire that played a dominant role in the work of Hogarth, founder of the English school, contrasted sharply with the gay, elegant, and charming paintings of Watteau of France.

The second half of the period saw the emergence of a middle class with political power, an intellectual spirit of free scientific inquiry, and a faith in man's ability to reason individually and collectively.

PAINTING

EUROPE · *France*

Chardin, Jean-Baptiste-Siméon. 1699-1779. Considered the greatest French artist of the 18th century, Chardin's skilful, subtle color, amazing ability to balance figures against backgrounds, simplicity of rendition, which was, however, carefully planned and designed to give surprising power and

ITALIAN COMEDIANS BY WATTEAU

TEAPOT, CHARDIN

monumentality to the simplest subjects, account in part for his great influence, especially upon Manet and Cézanne; did not adhere to the Rococo style of the period; known for still-life studies, domestic scenes, and portraits; *House of Cards* (London); *Boy Spinning Top* (Louvre); *Kitchen Still Life* (Oxford); *Soap Bubbles* (Washington); from 1771, exhibited unusually fine pastel portraits.

Watteau, Antoine. 1684-1721. Master artist of Flemish origin; studied in Italy; famous for portrayal of Italian Commedia dell'Arte; strongly in-

fluenced by Rubens; true lyric painter; won little official recognition; great colorist; melancholy, poignant quality evident in work; magnificent drawings; *Jupiter and Antiope* (Louvre); *Le Mezzetin* (Met. Mus.); *Les Champs Élysées* (London); *A Pilgrimage to Cythera* (Berlin); *Fête in a Park* (Madrid); almost 800 etchings; décor for theater.

Boucher, François. 1703-70. Court painter to Louis XV; favorite of

DIANA AT THE BATH BY BOUCHER

Madame Pompadour; pupil of Lemoyne; studied in Italy; Rococo style at its height; interested in the nude, rustic pastorals; famous portraits of *Pompadour* and members of the court; tapestry cartoons; director of Gobelins (1765); works for porcelain; stage settings; large decorative paintings; *Venus in the Gorge, Diana After Bathing* (Louvre); *Cupid a Captive* (London); *Reclining Girl* (Munich); *The Toilet of Venus* (Met. Mus.); *Venus Consoling Love* (Washington).

Fragonard, Jean-Honoré. 1732-1806. Brilliant Rococo painter; apprenticed to both Chardin and Boucher; influenced by Rubens *(Bathers,* Louvre); won Prix de Rome (1752); became favorite of DuBarry; exemplified elegance, shallow sensuality of the court; later works warmer, more true feeling, expression of passion leading to romanticism of next century; *The Marionettes* anticipates Renoir's *Moulin de la Galette; The Swing* (London); *The Guitar Player* (Louvre); also domestic scenes, *Pastrycook, Washerwomen* (Amiens).

THE STOLEN KISS BY FRAGONARD

Greuze, Jean-Baptiste. 1727-1805. Popular painter of bourgeois genre studies; portraits and sentimental portrayals of women's heads; *The Village Bride* (1761, Louvre).

Nattier, Jean Marc. 1685-1766. Portrait artist at court of Louis XV; lost position to Boucher; some pastels best of Rococo period; painted royalty of Russia; *Mademoiselle de Clermont at the Bath* (London); many works at Versailles; died neglected.

Moreau, Louis-Gabriel, the Elder. 1739-1805. Known for small oils and *gouaches* done in tiny brushstrokes; views of Paris and suburbs favorite subjects; brother **Jean Michel** (1741-1814), engraver, illustrator, designer for court masques and fêtes.

La Tour (Latour), Maurice Quentin de. 1704-88. Pastel portraits of *Pompadour,* royal family, others.

Loitard, Jean-Étienne. 1702-89. Swiss artist; to Paris (1723), Rome (1736); known as the "Turkish painter" for red-chalk drawings of that country.

Robert, Hubert. 1733-1808. Famous for paintings of ruins and scenes of desolation and destruction; studied with Pannini in Rome.

Desportes, Alexandre François. 1661-1743. Animal and landscape painter known for hunting scenes; remarkable sketches; designs for Gobelins tapestries.

Oudry, Jean-Baptiste. 1686-1755. Famed director of Beauvais and Gobelins factories; pupil of Largillierre; noted for animal and landscape paintings; employed Boucher at Gobelins.

Perronneau, Jean-Baptiste. 1715-83. Excellent portrait artist; charm of pastels gained recognition in recent

215

years; worked in various world capitals; exceptional portrait of *Rousseau*.

Lancret, Nicolas. 1690-1743. Rococo painter, successful in his own time; many works owned by Frederick the Great; *Italian Comedy Scene* (London); *Fêtes Galantes* and *Seasons* (Louvre).

Natoire, Charles. 1700-1777. Tapestry designer of note; Rococo paintings rivaled those of Boucher; many works in the Louvre.

Lemoyne, François. 1688-1737. Excellent fresco painter; decorative ceiling of *Salon d'Hercule* at Versailles; influential teacher of Boucher and others; easel paintings.

Duplessis, Joseph-Siffred. 1725-1802. Portrait painter known for excellent study of the composer *Christoph Gluck* (1775, Vienna); admitted to Academy (1774); portrait of *Madame Lenoir, née Adam* (Louvre), considered by many his masterpiece; good draftsman, thoughtful use of color.

Vien, Joseph-Marie. 1716-1809. Prix de Rome (1743); Director of French Academy, Rome (1775); Director of Gobelins (1781); experienced with encaustic; important teacher of David; Vien's interest in antiquity prepared the way for the neoclassical style.

Pater, Jean-Baptiste-François. 1695-1736. Protégé of Watteau; individual Rococo style; boudoir and salon favorite; *The Bathers* (Grenoble); *Rustic Feast* (London); *The Hunting Party* (Munich).

Coypel, Antoine, 1661-1722. Baroque painter of large gallery and ceiling of *Palais-Royal*; influenced by Rubens; favorite of Duc d'Orleans; decorated vault of chapel of *Château de Versailles*.

Troy, Jean-François de. 1679-1752. Superficial, decorative painter of aristocracy at play; Director of French Academy (1738); cartoons for tapestries.

Vernet, Claude-Joseph. 1714-89. Painter of "heroic landscapes"; murals of French seaports.

Tocqué, Louis. 1696-1772. Portrait painter at courts of St. Petersburg and Copenhagen.

Van Loo (Vanloo), Carle (Charles). 1705-65. Court painter (1762); successful in Italy; painted churches and palaces in Turin.

Subelyras, Pierre Hubert. 1699-1749. Worked in Rome; best-known for religious paintings.

Russia

Levitski, Dmitri. 1735-1822. Portrait artist; influenced by prominent painters of Europe, but individual in use of unique quality of Russian icon in works; did not use dark background and light figure so popular at the time.

Losenko, Anton Pavlovich. 1731-73. First modern Russian painter to concentrate on historical subjects; studied in Paris; *St. Vladimir and Rogneda* (1770).

CAPRICCIO (DETAIL), BY CANALETTO

Italy

Tiepolo, Giovanni Battista (Giambattista). 1696-1770. Master Venetian artist; exceptional gift for composition; brilliant frescoes (Madrid, Würzburg); outstanding colorist in smaller works and sketches; attempted to delight the eye, create sensual and dramatic effects without thought to tragedy or the unpleasantness of life; masks and designs for Commedia dell'Arte (Ven-

COUNCIL OF THE KNIGHTS OF MALTA (DETAIL) BY TIEPOLO

ice); influenced by Veronese; spent last years in Spain, admired by Goya; *Adoration of the Kings* (Munich); *The Charlatan* (Barcelona); *Adoration of the Magi* (Met. Mus.); *The Martyrdom of St. Agatha* (Berlin); *Banquet of Cleopatra* (Venice); prized drawings and etchings.

Guardi, Francesco. 1712-93. Brilliant Venetian city landscape artist; brother-in-law of Tiepolo; pupil of Canaletto, however Guardi's style is looser, less precise; subtle color and clever use of black give painterly quality to work; *Gondola on the Lagoon* (Milan), considered masterpiece; *Venetian Courtyard* (London); *Grand Canal, Venice* (Washington); *Ascension Day* (Louvre); beautiful drawings and surprisingly free water colors; figure compositions; influenced the later impressionists.

Canaletto (Antonio Canale). 1697-1768. Master Venetian urban landscape artist; exceptional ability to represent buildings with precision, perfect perspective, and amazing use of light; studied ruins of Rome; worked in London (1746-55) and painted *Views of London from Richmond House* for the Duke of Richmond; influenced English

TRIUMPH OF FLORA BY TIEPOLO

artists; *Riva Degli Schiavoni* (Venice);
Stonebreaker's Yard (London); *The
Bridge at Walton* (Dulwich); *The
Bridge at Westminster* (London); fine
etchings.

Longhi, Pietro. 1702-86. Venetian
painter; contemporary scenes, figure
compositions; carnival and theatrical
scenes; excellent drawings, considered
better than oils, using brown chalk on
light chocolate-tinted paper, highlighted with white; also used black
splashes with blunted pencil similar to
Watteau; *The Rhinoceros* (Venice).

Magnasco, Alessandro. Known as
Il Lassandrino. 1667-1749. Genoese
painter; remarkably free; power, emotional intensity seen in small works;
forerunner of Goya and Daumier in
technique and subject matter; misfits
of society, monastic life, theatrical
scenes; *Scene of Inquisition* (Vienna);
Lunatic Asylum (Madrid); *Refectory
of the Monks* (Bassano del Grappa);
Puchinello Playing the Guitar (Venice).

Piranesi, Giovanni Battista (Giambattista.) 1720-78. Master etcher and
engraver; *Vedute di Roma,* views of
Rome; magnificent architectural drawings of ancient and contemporary
monuments; dramatic use of highlights and blacks; prints sold throughout Europe.

Pannini, Giovanni Paolo. *ca.* 1691/92-
1765. Architectural painter; famous
for scenes of interiors of Pantheon and
St. Peter's; Roman ruins and various
scenes of Rome.

Bellotto, Bernardo. 1720-80. Also
known as Canaletto; nephew and pupil
of Antonio Canale; noted for views
of Vienna, Poland; etchings.

Others. Giambattista Piazzetta

(1682-1754), Rosalba Carriera (1675-
1757), Luca Carlevaris (1665-1731),
Giuseppe Maria Crespi (Lo Spagnolo,
1664-1747), Giovanni Battista Pittoni
(1687-1767).

England

Hogarth, William. 1697-1764. True
founder of the English school; narrative, satirical, brilliant picture series:
Marriage à la Mode, Harlot's Progress,
and *The Rake's Progress;* great humor,
clever analysis of human foibles; also
portraits including *Self-Portrait, Lord
Loval, Captain Coram, Hogarth's Ser-
vants, The Graham Children; Masked
Ball at Wansted* and *Shrimp Girl*
(London); treatise on aesthetics, *The
Analysis of Beauty* (1753); engravings; silversmith.

THE SHRIMP GIRL BY HOGARTH

Blake, William. 1757-1827. Engraver,
poet, painter, water-color artist; mystic; published own illustrated poems;
large colored prints; employed new
process of printing from etched copper
plates; water colors for Young's *Night*

ILLUSTRATION FROM
Book of Job
BY BLAKE

court painter; knighted by George III; a founder of The Royal Academy (1768); historical compositions; more informal technique used for private commissions; influence of Rubens in late works; very successful, painting most famous people of his time; founded Literary Club with Dr. Johnson, Garrick, Goldsmith, Burke, Boswell, Sheridan, and others; wrote *Fifteen Discourses on Art*; works include *Mrs. Siddons as the Tragic Muse, Lord Heathfield, Governor of Gibraltar, Nelly O'Brien, Lady Cockburn and Her Sons, Lady Hamilton, Lady Elizabeth Delmé and Her Children*.

NEBUCHADNEZZAR GONE MAD BY BLAKE

MRS. SIDDONS AS THE TRAGIC MUSE,
REYNOLDS

Thoughts and Dante's *Divine Comedy*; illustrations for *Europe, a Prophecy* (1794) and *Book of Job* (1821); very original concept and technique that went unappreciated in his own time; many works in the British and Victoria and Albert Museums and Tate Gallery (London).

Reynolds, Sir Joshua. 1723-92. Leading portrait artist; studied in Italy;

Gainsborough, Thomas. 1727-88. Master portrait and landscape artist; rivaled Reynolds in success as court painter and portrait artist; first English landscape artist of real originality; *Cornard Wood, Landscape with a Bridge*; known for portraits of *Mrs. Siddons, The Blue Boy* (Young Mr. Butall), *Mr. and Mrs. Andrews, Sir William Blackstone, The Painter's*

219

ROBERT ANDREWS AND HIS WIFE,
GAINSBOROUGH

Daughters; *The Morning Walk* (London).

Lawrence, Sir Thomas. 1769-1803. Portrait artist; court painter to George III (1792); favorite of Queen Charlotte; succeeded West as president of the Royal Academy.

Romney, George. 1734-1802. Successful portrait artist; prolific (1800 portraits); still-life studies; dramatic compositions usually on themes from Shakespeare and Milton; *Lady Hamilton*, his favorite subject.

Stubbs, George. 1724-1806. Famous painter of horses; *Hambletonian, The Phaeton and Pair* (London), and *Gentleman Holding his Horse* (Tate, London); portrait of *Wedgwood* fired by famed ceramist; published illustrated *The Anatomy of the Horse*; worked on enamel, copper, and pottery.

Sandby, Paul. 1725-1809. Father of English landscape water-color school; first to use acquatint; founding member, Royal Academy; excellent handling of groups of people.

Fuseli, Henry (Johann Heinrich Fussli). 1741-1825. Popular Swiss artist, illustrator; worked in England; influenced by Blake; fine draftsman; dramatic intensity; *The Nightmare* (1783, Frankfort).

Thornhill, Sir James. 1675-1734. Decorative painter in Baroque style; best-known for ceiling of Great Hall at Blenheim; cupola of St. Paul's Cathedral; Hall of Greenwich Hospital.

Girtin, Thomas. 1775-1802. Outstanding water-color artist; used warm ground (or none) and painted directly with clear transparent washes; master at creating atmosphere of solitude; used limited range of colors; *Stepping Stones on the Wharfe, Rue St. Denis, Paris.*

Others. George Morland (1763-1804), Alexander Cozens (1717-86), George Lambert (1700-65), Joseph Wright (1734-97), Richard Wilson 1714-82), Thomas Rowlandson (1756-1827).

Germany

Mengs, Anton Raphael. 1728-79. Important in the introduction of the classical movement; associated with Winckelmann, whose enthusiasm for antiquity was shared by Mengs; studied in Rome; court painter, Poland; *Maria Luisa of Parma* (Prado), painted while in Madrid; gave Goya first commissions for Gobelins tapestries; author of treatise on aesthetics, *Thoughts on Beauty and Taste* (1765); successful painter of frescoes and easel paintings; *Parnassus*, representative work.

Chodowiecki, Daniel Nikolaus. *ca.* 1726/27-1801. Most popular illustrator of Prussia; engraver of exceptional ability; illustrated works by Goethe, Lessing, Schiller, Sterne, Goldsmith.

Zick, Januarius Rasso. 1730-97. Court painter, Munich; studied in Paris and Rome; influenced by Rembrandt and Watteau; grace, Rococo charm seen in *Dance at the Inn* (Munich); interesting use of light for dramatic effect in *A Tavern Brawl* (Stuttgart); religious paintings and frescoes; ceiling paintings in Swabian churches.

Desmarées, Georg. 1697-1776. Swedish-born artist; court painter, Munich for 46 years; Rococo portrait painter whose elegant, charming, and gay studies of women were very successful, if not great works of art.

Netherlands

Ruisch, Rachel. *ca.* 1664/65-1750. Outstanding Dutch flower painter; court painter to Elector Palatine; precise, detailed, delicate studies; use of elaborate architectural or traditional "black" backgrounds; represented in many museums of the world.

Huysum, Jan van. 1682-1749. Noted still-life and flower painter; bold, flamboyant compositions; unusual use of landscape backgrounds; partial to heavily sculptured urns in still-life paintings.

Haverman, Margareta. *fl.* 1716-*ca.* 1795. Excellent flower and still-life painter; gained fame in Paris; admitted to French Royal Academy, but dismissed for supposed imitation of master Huysum; brilliant use of color, elegant composition.

Pesne, Antoine. 1683-1757. French portrait artist who gained fame at the court of Frederick II of Prussia; very influential Rococo artist in Germany; elaborate, decorative, mythological ceiling paintings filled palaces.

Austria

Maulbertsch, Franz Anton. 1724-96. Painter of wall and ceiling frescoes as well as altarpieces that are very representative of Austrian Baroque painting; decorated many churches and palaces of Upper Danube.

NORTH AMERICA · British Colonies

Copley, John Singleton. 1738-1815. First really important American artist; excellent portraits; gained early recognition in Boston for painting realistic study of *Paul Revere* in his work clothes; painted *John Adams, John Hancock, Mrs. Theodore Atkinson, Jr., Mrs. Thomas Boylston,* and many others; forerunner of Romanticism with *Brook Watson and the Shark,* that created a sensation; settled in

MRS. SYLVANUS BOURNE
BY COPLEY

London (from 1774); influenced by West, he lost some of his individuality; *The Death of Lord Chatham* established his reputation for historical compositions.

West, Benjamin. 1738-1820. First American artist to gain recognition in Europe; successful portraitist at twenty; studied in Italy; settled in London (1763); became court painter; succeeded Reynolds as President of the Royal Academy; *Death of General Wolfe* (1771) introduced soldiers in more realistic contemporary costumes and attitudes; not master painter himself, but excellent teacher and adviser to Americans such as Copley, Stuart, C. W. Peale, and Allston, who studied in England; *Penn's Treaty with the Indians, The Return of the Prodigal Son,* representative.

UNFINISHED PAINTING OF "FOUNDING FATHERS" BY WEST

Stuart, Gilbert Charles. 1755-1828. Portrait artist best-known for studies of *Washington*; studied in England with West, influenced by Reynolds; excellent studies of *Jefferson, Madison,*

JOSEPH BRANT (THAYENDANEGEA), STUART

Portrait of Mrs. Yates (Washington), and others.

Trumbull, John. 1756-1843. Historical painter; small canvases, detailed accuracy with surprising breadth and movement; studied in England; *Death of General Montgomery at the Siege of Quebec, Signing of the Declaration of Independence,* well-known works; served in Washington's army and executed many important studies of the American fight for independence and the growth of the nation; excellent portraits.

Peale, Charles Willson. 1741-1827. Portrait artist, inventor; officer in Revolution; studied with West in London; many sketches of military figures; *Staircase Group* (1795, study of two sons), considered one of the best portraits by an American; coachmaker, dentist, taxidermist, silversmith, inventor of stoves, eyeglasses, and false teeth; established one of the world's first scientific museums of natural history; portraits of *Washington, Adams,* and *Madison.*

Smibert, John. 1688-1751. Portrait painter; born in Scotland; studied in Italy; worked in London; considered first really trained artist in New England; dominated Boston area (from 1730); *Dean Berkeley and Entourage* (Yale).

Hesselius, Gustavus. 1682-1755. Portrait painter known for his studies of Indian chiefs commissioned by the Penn family; *Lapowinsa,* best-known work.

Feke, Robert. *ca.* 1705-*ca.* 1750. First American to give three-dimensional effect to portraits; *Isaac Royall and Family* (Harvard); *Samuel Waldo* (Maine).

Others. Joseph Badger (1708-65), William J. Williams (1750-1823), Matthew Pratt (1734-1805).

ASIA · *India*

Kishangarh. In the middle of the 18th century the most beautiful paintings of the period were produced here. They represented the climax of a combined Rajasthani-Delhi style. The Vaishnava ruler, Savant Singh, a poet, was the patron of **Nihal Chand**, a great genius who, after 1730, painted larger pictures than the usual miniatures. Emphasis was placed on landscape, human figures were idealized, and color was restrained. Popular subjects were the princely image of Krishna and the delicate beauty of Radha.

In the state of Guler, an exquisitely cool, romantic style developed that was based on the Basholi style of *ca.* 1720 and that of the Delhi-trained artists.

Japan

Ritsuo, Ogawa. d. 1747. Great master; famed for brilliant lacquer work; rivaled Korin in use of raised decoration, process requiring exceptional facility and ingenuity.

Choshun, Myagawa. 1683-1753. Master technician; noted genre painter of the Edo period; individual style seen in *ukiyo-e*; no woodcuts, though influenced by Moronobu.

Masanobu, Okumura. 1686-1764. Master printmaker; credited with the invention of secondary wood blocks to print color; outstanding draftsman.

PUPPET ACTOR, MASANOBU

Kaigetsudo, Ando. *fl.* early 18th century. Famous painter of lovely women in graceful standing poses; elaborately patterned, decorative kimonos, bold use of color.

Utamaro, Kitagawa. 1753-1806. Outstanding color printmaker; works among first-known in Europe, brought west by Dutch traders; *ukiyo-e* technique with unusual use of red and black; painted in Kano manner; fine color, exquisite women.

Harunobu, Suzuki. *ca.* 1725-70. Noted printmaker; introduced multiple-color printing with wood blocks (1765); delicate, subtle draftsman; unusual strength in landscape background for figures; *Young Lovers in a Snowy Landscape.*

Kiyonaga, Torii. 1752-1815. Leading figure of the 1780's; large diptychs, triptychs; illustrated over 100 books; unusual quality of work.

Kokan, Shiba (Harushige). 1747-1818. First to use European method of oil painting; produced unique copper-plate landscape in perspective (1784); influential.

Taiga, Ikeno. 1723-76. Noted artist of the Edo period; first artist of the Nanga school of romantic, subjective painters of poetic landscapes.

Okyo, Maruyama. 1733-95. Leader of the realistic school of painters of the Edo period.

Kiyotada, Torii. *fl.* 1710-40. Printmaker; exceptional portrayal of Kabuki actors.

Toyonobu, Ishikawa. 1711-85. Printmaker; influenced by Masanobu; prints of Kabuki theater.

China

Emperor K'ang Hsi ordered the writing of the *Imperial Encyclopedia of Calligraphy and Painting* (1705); task of great magnitude requiring the work of 11 artists and scholars; 100 books (64 volumes), produced in three years; contained material on the history and practical applications of pictorial art.

Kao Ch'i-P'ei. 1672-1734. Famous "finger painter"; Manchu from Mukden; unique master of the difficult art of painting directly onto silk with one's fingers; delicate, lovely work; subtle use of color.

Chou, Shang-kuan. 1664-1752. Portrait and landscape artist; impressionistic ink-wash technique; bold strokes, unusually modern in quality.

SCULPTURE

EUROPE · *France*

Houdon, Jean Antoine. 1741-1828. Leading portrait sculptor; Prix de Rome; worked in Italy for ten years; excellent studies include seated figures of *Voltaire, Washington, Jefferson, Franklin, Catherine of Russia, Rousseau, Molière, Gluck,* and many others; *Écorché*; *Morphée*; Sophie Arnould as *Iphigenia.*

VOLTAIRE
BY HOUDON

Lemoyne, Jean Baptiste. 1704-78. Noted portrait sculptor; terra-cotta busts; three statues of *Louis XV* (destroyed during the Revolution); studies of *Voltaire, Pompadour*; tomb of *Cardinal Fleury.*

Falconet, Étienne Maurice. 1716-91. Court artist; pupil of Lemoyne; equestrian statue of *Peter the Great* (Leningrad); *Bathing Girl* (Louvre); studies of *Louis XV* (destroyed).

Clodion (Claude Michel). 1738-1814. Rococo artist known for small terra-cotta statuettes and decorative friezes of nymphs, fauns, children.

Pajou, Augustin. 1730-1809. Decorative sculpture for Opera at Versailles; portrait busts of *Pascal, Descartes, Buffon, Mme du Barry; Psyche* (Louvre).

Coustou, Nicolas. 1658-1733. Baroque artist; *Descent from the Cross* (Notre Dame, Paris); portraits include *Louis XV as Jupiter.*

Coustou, Guillaume. 1677-1746. Later works show naturalism that led to classicism; *Horse Tamers,* Champs Élysée.

Pigalle, Jean Baptiste. 1714-85. Successful works commissioned by Pompadour; *Love and Friendship; Mercury;* also tombs, genre, portraits.

Others. Antoine Chaudet (1763-1810), Jean Caffieri (1725-92), Edmé

VENUS AND ADONIS, PORCELAIN FROM VINCENNES, 1750-55

Bouchardon (1698-1762), Jacob S. Adam (1670-1747), and sons, Lambert (1700-1759), Nicolas (1705-78), François (1710-61).

Portugal

Machado, Joachim de Castro. 1731-1822. Last great Portuguese Baroque sculptor; most famous work the equestrian figure of *Dom José* in the Terreiro do Paco (Lisbon).

Denmark

Abilgaard, Nicolai Abraham. 1743-1809. Classical sculptor, painter; studied in Rome; historical, Norse mythological subjects; important teacher of Runge and Thorvaldsen.

Sweden

Sergel, Johan Tobias von. 1740-1814. Classical works include *Diomedes Stealing the Palladium, Faun,* colossal *Muse of History Recording the Deeds of Gustavus Adolphus;* portrait busts.

Low Countries

Delvaux, Laurent. 1695-1778. Flemish sculptor; works in bronze and marble for Westminster Abbey (London); court artist to Charles, Duke of Lorraine (1750-78).

Tassaert, Pierre Antoine. 1729-88. Court sculptor to Frederick the Great (from 1775).

Russia

Kozlovsky, Mikhail. 1753-1802. Classical sculptor; studied in Paris and Rome; imitated Michelangelo; *Apollo* shows influence of antiquity.

Shubin, Fedor. 1740-1805. Portrait sculptor; emphasized characterization rather than ornamentation.

Austria

Donner, Georg Raphael. 1693-1741. Leading late Baroque sculptor; successfully combined delicacy with classicism; fountains, decorations for staircases; sculptural groups in lead.

Grassi, Anton. 1755-1807. Viennese sculptor known for statues and portrait busts of *Haydn, Joseph II,* and others; porcelain designer.

Germany

Asam, Egid Quirin. 1692-1756. Brilliant Baroque sculptor of Munich; studied in Rome; decorated churches and palaces (stucco work); altars; *The Assumption of the Virgin,* altarpiece, monastic church (Rohr); brother, **Cosmos Damian** (1686-1739), worked with him.

Straub, Johann Baptist. 1704-84. Rococo sculptor of Bavaria; court artist, Munich; altars and tabernacles.

Gunther, Ignaz. 1725-75. Bavarian Rococo sculptor, woodcarver of delicately colored madonnas, angels; graceful movement; charming works in interiors of churches of South Germany and Austria.

Others. Johann Peter Wagner (1730-1809), Johann August Nahl (1710-81), Johann Michael Feichtmayr (*ca.* 1709-72), Johan J. Kuchel (1703-69).

Czechoslovakia

Braun, Matthias Bernard. 1684-1738. Successful Baroque sculptor; introduced subjective, dramatic element; influenced by Bernini; *Column of the Holy Trinity* (Teplice); *Crucifix,* in church at Plasy, woodcarving; *Faith, Wisdom, Anger, Frivolity,* etc., (alleys of Vices and Virtues, Kuks); *Annunciation; St. Mary Magdalene; St. Sebastian.*

England

Bacon, John. 1740-99. Famed for monuments to *Dr. Samuel Johnson,* (St. Paul's Cathedral, London), *William Pitt* (Guildhall, Westminster Abbey), *Sir William Blackstone* (All Souls, Oxford).

Banks, Thomas. 1735-1805. Sculptor to Catherine II of Russia; statue of *Shakespeare Attended by Painting and Poetry* (Stratford-on-Avon).

Others. Louis Roubillac (1695-1762), Anne Seymour Damer (1748-1828), Joseph Nollekens (1737-1823).

Italy

Canova, Antonio. 1757-1822. Leader of classical revival in Italy; very important influence; worked for several countries; marble statue of *Perseus,* typical example of his work.

PAULINE BORGHESE AS VENUS
BY CANOVA

Caracchi, Giuseppe. 1751-1802. Famed portrait sculptor; works include busts of *Sir Joshua Reynolds, George Washington, Benjamin Franklin,* and *Alexander Hamilton.*

Verschaffelt, Pierre Antoine (also known as Pietro Fiammingo, Peter the Fleming). 1710-93. Flemish sculptor working in Italy; noted for marble statue of *Pope Benedict XIV* (Rome).

Others. Carlo Rastrelli (d. 1744), Niccolo Salvi (1697-1751).

AMERICAS · *Brazil*

Aleijadinho (Antônio Francisco Lisbôa). 1730-1814. Great mulatto Rococo sculptor of Brazil; called *O Aleijadinho* which means little cripple; illegitimate son of Portuguese architect; considered greatest architect and sculptor of Brazil; from Minas Gerais area; stone pulpits, portals, caryatids, open-air group of twelve statues of prophets at Church of Congonhas do campo (1800-1805), masterpiece of sculpture; *capela mor* (apsidal chapel) of Saô Francisco (1773-94, Ouro Preto), outstanding work of architecture.

PROPHET ISAIAH BY ALEIJADINHO, CHURCH OF CONGONHAS DO CAMPO, BRAZIL

ARCHITECTURE

EUROPE · *Spain*

Churriguera, José Benito de. 1665-1725. Famed architect, who gave his name to a decorative (ornate scrolls, thick moldings) Baroque style (although actually his work is now considered conservative); born in Barcelona; influenced by Herrera and Palladio; original urban plan for new town of Nuevo Baztan (1709-13) for Juan de Goyeneche, considered the most ambitious attempt made by a single person in Spain during the 18th century; town house from there now *Academia de San Fernando* (Madrid); sacristy of the *Charterhouse* (1727-64, Granada); important influence on

HOSPICIO DE S. FERNANDO (PORTAL), CHURRIGUERESQUE STYLE, RIBERA

the Spanish colonial style of the southwestern part of the United States and of Mexico; brother **Joaquin** (1674-1724) responsible for the crossing dome of the Salamanca Cathedral (1714-24). **Alberto** (1676-1750), most

227

talented of the brothers, but always in José's shadow; designed the *Plaza Mayor* of Salamanca (1728), upper façade of the *Valladolid Cathedral* (1729-33); chief architect of the *Salamanca Cathedral* (from 1738).

Hurtado, Francisco. 1669-1725. Leading architect of Granada where he added two lateral chambers to the *Charterhouse* (1713); *Charterhouse at El Paular* (designed 1718, Segovia).

Díaz, Diego Antonio. *ca.* 1680-1748. Noted architect of Seville; masterpiece, the parish church at Umbrete (1725-33); influenced younger men.

Ribera, Pedro de. *ca.* 1683-1742. Called a madman; exuberant, explosive; probably a pupil of Teodoro Ardemanns (1664-1726); rival of Churriguera; riverside park of the *Virgen del Puerto* (1718); chapel of *N.S. de la Porteria* (1731, San Antonio); *Toledo Bridge* (1723-24, Madrid); *Montserrat Church* (1720, incomplete); portal of *Hospicio de San Fernando* (1722), most celebrated and disliked work.

Rodríguez, Ventura. 1717-85. Outstanding Baroque architect; studied under Marchand at Royal Palace, Aranguez (1731) and under Juvara and Sacchetti in Madrid (from 1735); parish church, *San Marcos* (1749-53), first major work; remodeled *Pilar Church* in Saragossa (1750); influenced by Blondel's writing and Herrera's works; operating theater for *Royal College of Surgery* (1761, Barcelona); professor in Roman Academia di S. Luca (1746); palace for the Infante Don Luis at *Boadilla del Monte* (before 1776), considered one of his best works; rivaled Villanueva.

Villanueva, Juan de. 1739-1811.

Leading architect of Madrid; worked as draftsman for Sacchetti at Royal Palace (until 1754); seven years in Italy (1759-65); court of Charles III, Escorial (1768); cathedral of *Brugo de Osma* (1770), first evidence of an individual style; greatest work, *Prado Museum* (1785-87); *Madrid Observatory*, final important building; influential.

Austria

Fischer von Erlach, Johann Bernhard. 1657-1723. Leading Baroque court artist; designed palaces, including that of Prince Eugene (1705, Vienna); *Castle Schönbrun* (1695-1700); *Royal Library* (begun 1722, Vienna); worked with Hildebrandt on *Belvedere Palace* (1695-1724) for Prince Eugene; private chancellery of Kingdom of Vienna; *Karlskirche* or Church of St. Charles, noted for twin towers, important work (1716-37); influential.

KARLSKIRCHE, VIENNA, FISCHER VON ERLACH

Hildebrandt, Lucas von. 1668-1745. Master of the Baroque; born in Italy;

worked with von Erlach on *Belvedere* (Winter) *Palace;* rebuilt grand stairway of *Mirabell Palace* (1719, Salzburg); palace for Prince Scwarzenberg; domed church of *St. Lawrence* at Gabel (Bohemia); *St. Peter's* and *Church of the Piarists* (Vienna).

Prandtauer, Jacob. 1658-1726. Outstanding Baroque architect; influenced by Italians, but developed individual style; most famous work, the remarkable *Abbey Church of Melk* (1702-38), shoots out of rocks, overhanging the Danube River; undulating front, towers, bulbous spires; also designed important buildings of *St. Florian's.*

MONASTERY, MELK ON THE DANUBE, AUSTRIA, PRANDTAUER

Germany

Knobelsdorff, Baron Georg Wenzel von. 1699-1753. Leading Rococo court architect; in charge of castles and gardens for Frederick II of Prussia; studied in Italy and France; worked on gardens of the palace at *Rheinsberg* (1734-39); designed east wing of *Charlottenburg* (1740-43);

magnificent *San Souci Palace* (1751, Potsdam), considered his best work; *Berlin Opera House.*

Dientzenhofer, Johann. 1665-1726. Bavarian master; famous for the *Pommersfelden Palace* (1711-18), built for the Bishop of Bamberg; also the *Fulda Cathedral.*

Neumann, Johann Balthasar. 1687-1753. Baroque master architect; famous for parts of the *Würzburg Palace,* particularly the staircase; many churches; staircase in *Electoral Palace* (1730, Bruchsal), excellent example of German Baroque; pilgrimage church of *Vierzehnheiligen* (1743-72 Franconia), Rococo in style; monastic church of Neresheim.

Gilly, Friedrich. *fl.* 1772-1800. Built national monument to *Frederick the Great* (1797); second *National Theater* for Berlin (1798) suggests Romantic style; published designs for medieval castles for German lords of East Prussia.

Cuvilliés, François de. 1698-1767. French architect who gained fame in Germany; introduced Rococo style of decoration in Nymphenburg park, Amalienburg (1734-37); worked for Charles VII at Munich; succeeded by son François (1731-77).

Others. Johann Conrad Schlaun (1694-1773), Johann Fischer (1692-1766), Cosmos Damian Asam (1686-1739), Dominikus Zimmermann (1685-1756), Karl Gontard (1731-91), Daniel Poppelmann (1662-1736), Georg Baehr (1666-1738), Maximilian von Welsch (1671-1745), Karl Langhans (1732-1808).

England

Vanbrugh, Sir John. 1664-1726. Versatile dramatist, Baroque architect; Flemish ancestry; studied in France; successful plays produced; built *Haymarket Theater*; best-known for magnificent *Blenheim Palace* (1705-24), that the nation presented to the Duke of Marlborough; influenced by Wren; designed *Castle Howard* (1699-1712, Yorkshire); *Vanbrugh Castle* (1717, Greenwich); *Goose-pie House* (1699, Whitehall); *Grimsthorpe* (begun 1722, Lincolnshire); *Seaton Delaval* (1720-29, Northumberland).

BLENHEIM PALACE, OXFORDSHIRE, VANBRUGH

Hawksmoor, Nicholas. 1661-1736. Leading architect; assistant to Wren at *St. Paul's Cathedral, Chelsea* and *Greenwich Hospitals;* worked with Vanbrugh on *The Mausoleum, Castle Howard;* built *Christ Church* (1723-29, Spitalfields); *St. George-in-the East* (London), and other churches; library and south quadrangle, *Queens College* and *All Souls' College* (completed 1734, Oxford).

Kent, William. 1684-1748. One of the early English landscape artists; protégé of Lord Burlington for whom he designed gardens at Chiswick (*ca.* 1720); influenced by Palladio's *Villa Rotunda;* designed *Devonshire House* in Piccadilly; *Holkham Hall* (begun 1734, Norfolk); *No. 44 Berkeley Square* (1742-44); interior designs for *Kensington Palace.*

Adam, Robert. 1728-92. Scottish artist; with brothers **James** and **William,** built many public buildings and private mansions; court architect to George III (1762-68); considered the leader of classical revival in England; introduced the principle of palace façade for a row of houses in his *Adelphi Terrace* (1768-72, London); *Edinburgh University* (1789-92); *Syon House* (begun 1762, Middlesex), and others; furniture design; William Adam designed *Hopetown House* (Linlithgowshire) and the *Royal Infirmary* (1738, Edinburgh).

Archer, Thomas. 1668-1743. Baroque architect; influenced by Bernini and Borromini; built great house of Duke of Shrewsbury (Heythrop); *St. Philip's Church* (now Cathedral, 1709-15, Birmingham); *St. Paul's* (1712-30, Deptford); *Monmouth House* (Soho); two garden buildings for the Earl of Kent at Wrest; extremely successful.

Gibbs, James. 1682-1754. Leading architect; studied with Fontana in Rome; most important works include the *Church of St. Martin's-in-the-Fields* (1721-26), steeples influenced American colonial church architecture; *St. Mary-le-Strand* (1714-17); circular *Radcliffe Camera* (1739-49, Oxford), influenced by Wren; *Sudbrook Lodge* (*ca.* 1718, Petersham); *Ditchley* (1720-22, Oxfordshire); *Fellows' Building* (1724, King's College, Cambridge).

Dance, George, the II. 1741-1825. Noted architect; rebuilt *Newgate Prison* (begun 1769), *All Hallows, London Wall* (1765-67); *Council Chamber,* Guildhall (1777, London, demolished 1906).

Others. Lancelot Brown (1715-83), John Wood (*ca.* 1700-1754), Thomas Cooley (1740-84), James Gandon (1743-1823), Sir William Chambers (1723-96), William Robinson (*ca.* 1720-75).

France

Gabriel, Jacques-Ange. 1698-1782. Considered outstanding French architect of the 18th century; first to turn to more classical forms; Premier Architect du Roi; *École Militaire* (begun 1751); two buildings, north side, Place de Concorde (begun 1757); *Petit Trianon* in garden of Versailles (1762-68); *Hermitage,* Fontainebleau; restoration of the *Louvre; Hotel Crillon* (after 1755).

Soufflot, Jacques-Germain. 1713-80. Leading architect; famous for *Pantheon* (Ste. Genevieve, Paris, 1755-92); influenced by Piranesi while in

THE PANTHÉON (STE-GENEVIÈVE), SOUFFLOT

Italy; also designed *Hôtel de Ville* (Bordeaux) and cathedral in Rennes.

Ledoux, Claude-Nicolas. 1736-1806. Builder of the city gates (toll houses) of Paris (Barrières, 1784-89); plan for complete city for saltworks at Chaux; *Theater* at Besançon (1778-84), semi-circular amphitheater with Greek Doric columns; published theories in *L'Architecture considerée sous le rapport de l'art, des moeurs et de la legislation* (1804, Paris).

Boulée, Étienne-Louis. 1728-99. Important for drawings rather than actual works; broke with Baroque tradition; invented new forms largely based on elementary geometrical shapes; attempted to express emotion through form.

Chalgrin, Jean François Therese. 1739-1811. Noted designer of the church of *St. Philippe du Roule,* the *Arc de Triomphe, Luxembourg Palace,* and the *College de France.*

Servandoni, Giovanni Niccolo. 1695-1766. Italian working in Paris (from 1724); court architect (from 1732); façade of the *Church of Saint Sulpice, Church of the Charteux* (Lyons).

Others. Jacques-François Blondel (1705-74), Robert de Cotte (1656-1735), Jacques Antoine (1733-1801).

Italy

Piranesi, Giovanni Battista. 1720-78. Venetian architect; settled in Rome; famous for architectural etchings and "portraits" of Roman antiquity; own architectural works inferior; influential. (*See* Painting.)

Bibbiena, Antonio Galli da. 1700-1744. Noted architect, designer; employed at the imperial court of Vienna; best-known works, *Academia Virgili-*

ana (Mantua) and *Teatro Comunale* (Bologna).

Piermarini, Giuseppe. 1734-1808. Milanese architect; *La Scala Theater, Porta Orientale,* and the façade of *Belgioso Palace,* outstanding works.

Bonomi, Giuseppe. 1739–1800. Worked in England (from 1767); influential in revival of classical style there.

Rinaldi, Antonio. *ca.* 1709-after 90. Worked in Russia (from 1755), court architect to Grand Duke; built Rococo *Chinese Palace* (1762-68); *"Sliding Hill"* (Oranienbaum); *Marble Palace* (1768-72); *Gatchina Palace* (1766-72); most important church, *Cathedral of St. Isaac.*

Russia

Starov, Ivan. 1744-1808. Leading architect; influenced by Palladio; adapted classical style to Russian architecture; *Taurida Palace* (Leningrad), most important work.

Rastrelli, Bartolomeo Francesco. *ca.* 1700-1771. Born in Paris of Italian descent; chief architect to Imperial Court of Russia (from 1736); palaces. Brilliant example of great wooden architecture of Russia seen in famous octagonal *Church of the Transfiguration* (1714, Kizhi).

Others. Jean Baptiste Michel Vallin de la Mothe (1729-1800), Yuri Matveevich Velten (1730-1801), Vasili Ivanovich Bazhenor (1737-99), S. I. Chevakinski (1713-83).

AMERICAS

Many examples of Colonial Baroque in Latin America showing the influ-

CHURCH OF THE ROSARY, OURO PRETO, BRAZIL

SAN LORENZO, POTOSÍ, BOLIVIA

ence of Churriqueresque style; *Chapel of the Church of St. José,* Tepotzotlán, Mexico; *Church of St. Francis of Assisi,* Ouro Preto, Brazil; small church of *Nossa Senhora de Gloria de Outerro,* bay of Guanabara, Rio de Janeiro.

Mexico

Balbas, Jeronimo de. *fl.* 1718-37. Introduced Churriqueresque with the *Altar of the Chapel of the Kings* (Mexico Cathedral), Sagrario retable of *Seville Cathedral.*

Bueno, Pedro. *fl.* 1734-53. Designed *Vizcainas,* school for girls.

Escobar y Llamas, Cristobal de. Designed Jesuit *Colegio de San Ildefonso* (*ca.* 1740).

Rodriguez, Lorenzo. *ca.* 1704-74. Built *Cathedral of Sagrario* (1749, Mexico City).

Guerrero y Torres, Francisco Antonio. *ca.* 1740-92. Architect; born in Guadalupe; designed the *Valparaiso House* (1769, now the Bank of Mexico); *Pocito Chapel* (1779).

Brazil

Fonseca e Silva, Valentim da. 1750-1813. Mulatto architect of important buildings in Rio de Janeiro.

MUSIC

EUROPE · *Austria*

Mozart, Wolfgang Amadeus. 1756-91. Great master; child prodigy, toured Europe; wrote first three symphonies (by 1766); wrote first stage works (by 1768); studied with Martini in Italy (1769-71); although influenced by others (Bach, Handel, Haydn), his was an unrivaled individuality; magnificent dramatic sense made him a great master of the classical style; important in the development of the concerto; wrote over 1,000 works includ-

MOZART

ing the operas *Marriage of Figaro* (1786), *Don Giovanni* (1787), *Così fan tutte* (1790), *Magic Flute* (1791); 41 symphonies, concertos, chamber music, works for piano, and church music; considered by Goethe and many others one of the greatest creative geniuses of all time.

Haydn, Franz Joseph. 1732-1809. First master composer of the symphony; gave concrete form to the sonata, string quartet, and symphony orchestra; Kapellmeister with Esterhazy family (1760-90); friendship with Mozart (began 1781); teacher of Bee-

HAYDN

thoven; to England (1791-92, 1794-95); influenced by Handel; at home of Prince Nicolaus II wrote *The Seasons* (1801); composed 104 symphonies, 13 keyboard concertos, 18 operas, 8 oratorios, 84 string quartets, etc; called "Papa Haydn."

Dittersdorf, Karl Ditters von. 1739-99. Composer, violinist; one of the most prolific composers of his time; considered Mozart's equal by contemporaries; 44 operas, including popular *Doktor und Apotheker* (1786); oratorios, Masses, symphonies, concertos, chamber music, and piano sonatas.

Haydn, Johann Michael. 1737-1806. Overshadowed by older brother, Joseph, but deserving of recognition; director of orchestra, organist at Salzburg; composed some 30 symphonies, several operas, chamber music, very fine sacred works often attributed to his brother; influenced Mozart; excellent teacher of many, including von Weber.

Fux, Johann Joseph. 1660-1741. Composer, theorist; Kappellmeister, court of Vienna (1715); supreme master of counterpoint; compositions include operas, much church music, and instrumental works; influenced Mozart and Haydn with his treatise on counterpoint, *Gradus ad Parnassum* (1725).

Germany

Bach, Johann Sebastian. 1685-1750. Great master composer, organist, contrapuntist; *Well-Tempered Clavier* (1725) established the scale system of most subsequent music; fugues represent the consummation of the form; chief influences in his music are the Lutheran chorale, church and organ music of predecessors, and French and

BACH

Italian styles of contemporaries; prolific genius; composed church, vocal, instrumental music including *B Minor Mass* (1733-38), *St. John* (1723), and *St. Matthew* (1729) *Passions*, oratorios, sonatas, chorales, concertos (*Brandenburg*, 1721), preludes, fugues, chamber and orchestral music; rescued from oblivion by later musicians, now considered one of the greatest creators in the history of music.

Handel, George Frederich. 1685-1759. German-English master com-

HANDEL

poser; famed organ virtuoso; most famous for oratorios including the *Messiah* (presented in Dublin, 1742); operas (*Rinaldo*, first produced in London, 1711), Passions, church music, concertos, chamber music, works for harpsichord and songs; powerful influence on English music (lived there from 1712).

Gluck, Christoph Willibald. 1714-87. Outstanding master; considered "father of modern opera"; studied in Italy; in London (1745), influenced by Handel; *Orfeo* (1762) embodied new ideas and marked the turning point in opera composition; rival of Piccini; one of his most dramatic works was *Alceste* (1767), considered his masterpiece; *Iphigénie en Aulide* (1774); *Armide* (1777); *Iphigénie en Tauride* (1779); more than 100 operas (many lost); 11 symphonies, seven instrumental trios.

GLUCK

Bach, Carl Philipp Emanuel. 1714-88. Leading master of late Rococo; influenced Haydn and Mozart; son of J. S. Bach; important in the development of instrumental music and in the introduction of the sonata form; harp-

sichordist to Frederick the Great (1740); remarkable skill in improvisation; treatise on playing keyboard instruments, invaluable guide; vocal and instrumental works, two oratorios, etc.

Graun, Karl Heinrich. 1704-59. Dominated opera in Berlin; composed *Rodelinda* (1741), first Italian opera performed in that city; court Kappellmeister; conductor of Royal Opera under Frederick (1740); composed 30 operas, dramatic cantatas; *Der Tod Jesu* (1755, Passion Cantata), church music.

Schulz, Johann Abraham Peter. 1747-1800. Most important composer of *leder* prior to Schubert; conductor, composer, author; music director, French Theater, Berlin; Danish court, Copenhagen (1787-95); book of songs (1782-90), first of their kind and still used; five operas to French texts.

Telemann, George Philipp. 1681-1767. Prolific composer; music director, Hamburg (from 1721); 12 cycles of cantatas for the church year, 44 Passions, 40 operas, 600 French overtures, etc.

Others. Georg Joseph Vogler (1749-1814), Reinhard Keiser (1674-1739), Johann Hasse (1699-1783), Johann Stamitz (Czech, 1717-57).

Italy

Scarlatti, (Giuseppe) Domenico. 1685-1757. Late Baroque master composer, harpsichordist; considered father of modern piano playing; greatest composer for harpsichord of the period; equaled Handel in playing of harpsichord, but Handel was a better organist; court composer and teacher of Polish Queen Maria Casimira (1709), wrote eight operas for her private theater in Rome; musical director, St. Peter's (1715-19); in service of the King of Portugal (*ca.* 1721-25), Madrid Court (1729-57); wrote 600 pieces (now generally called sonatas, though in his time called *Essercizi*); universal influence.

Vivaldi, Antonio. *ca.* 1675-1741. Leading late Baroque composer; violinist; called *il prete rosso* (red-haired priest); very prolific; enlarged solo passages in *concerto grosso* until solo violin became dominant instrument; concertos for a wide variety of solo instruments (one of the first to write for the clarinet); chamber music, secular cantatas, church music, oratorios, operas; compositions for violin expanded technique; influenced many, including Bach.

Pergolesi, Giovanni Battista. 1710-36. Neapolitan composer; comic intermezzo *La serva padrona* (The Maid as Mistress), first performed between the acts of his serious opera *Il prigionero superbo* (The Proud Prisoner, 1733) along with *Il maestro di musica* (1731), became the prototype of later *opera buffa*; *Stabat Mater* (1729) for treble voices and other great church music; trio sonatas cultivated the style of the allegro movement later used by Bach in the development of the sonata form; instrumental music.

Piccini, Nicola. 1728-1800. Leading opera composer; rival of Gluck; 120 operas, including very popular *La Cecchina* or *La buona figliuola* (1760, Rome, to libretto by Goldoni, based on Richardson's *Pamela*); to Paris (1776); wrote operas to French texts; oratorios, church music, instrumental pieces.

Boccherini, Luigi. 1743-1805. Cellist, prolific composer; Paris (1768);

published first six-string quartets; Madrid (1769); chamber composer to Friedrich Wilhelm II of Prussia (1786-97); important in the development of chamber music and symphonic writing.

Stradivari, Antonio. 1644-1737. Famed violin-maker of Cremona; pupil of Amati; best violins made (1700-*ca.* 1725); superb quality of tone; used by virtuosi of the instrument to this day.

STRADIVARI VIOLINS

Farinelli, Carlo. 1705-82. Remarkable male soprano; most famous of *castrati*; prominent at Spanish court.

Others. Giovanni Paisiello (1740-1816), Domenico Cimarosa (1749-1811), Niccolo Jommelli (1714-74), Vincenzo Righini (1756-1812), Antonio Sacchini (1730-86), Giovanni Sammartini (1698-1775), Giuseppe Tartini (1692-1770), Antonio Caldara (1670-1736), Benedetto Marcello (1686-1739), Antonio Lotti (1667-1740), Baldassare Galuppi (1706-85), Francesco Durante (1684-1755).

France

Rameau, Jean Philippe. 1683-1764. Most French of composers; master theorist, harpsichordist, organist; earliest works include harpsichord suites;

RAMEAU

important treatise on harmony (1722) laid the foundation of modern theory; formulated system of chord building in thirds and introduced doctrine of inversion of chords; composer of operas *Castor and Pollux* (1737), *Hippolyte et Aricie* (1733), and others.

Couperin, François (le Grand). 1668-1733. Leading Rococo composer; organist, Versailles; influenced by Corelli; first to introduce trio sonata into France; excelled as a clavecinist and composer of music for the keyboard; works for instrumental ensembles, secular songs, and church music; author

COUPERIN (LE GRAND)

of *L'Art de toucher le clavecin* (1716), method of playing music for the keyboard (influenced Bach); superb, decorative, imaginative compositions of great delicacy and charm.

Philidor, François-André (Danican). 1726-95. Composer of opéra comique; first to employ *a capella* quartet in lyric comedy; adaptation of Fielding's *Tom Jones* (1764); *Requiem for Rameau* (1766); motets, operas.

Méhul, Étienne Henri Nicolas. 1763-1817. Opera composer; influenced by Gluck; master of the overture; *Joseph* (1807), *Uthal* (1806), most mature works; prominent composer during the period of the revolution.

Grétry, André Ernest Modeste. 1741-1813. Leading Belgian composer, active in Paris (from 1768); founder of the opéra comique; studied in Rome (1759-66); one of the original members of the Institute (1795); many operas, most successful being *Richard Coeur-de-Lion* (1784); six small symphonies (1758), church and instrumental music.

Gossec, François Joseph. 1734-1829. Belgian composer; active in France (from 1751); one of the first teachers at the Paris Conservatoire (founded 1795); sonatas for harpsichord; experimented with elaborate orchestration; introduced horns and clarinets; influential.

Others. Jean Lesueur (1760-1837), Jean Joseph Mondonville (1711-72), Jean-Marie Leclair (1697-1764), André-Cardinal Destouches (1672-1749), André Campra (1660-1744), Sebastien de Brossard (*ca.* 1654-1730), Nicolas Bernier (1664-1734).

Spain

Soler, Antonio (padre). 1729-83. Composer; organist, Monastery of the Escorial (1753); influenced by teacher, D. Scarlatti; composer of church music; brilliant sonatas for the harpsichord, incidental music for plays; six quintets for strings and keyboard, and other chamber music; wrote theoretical treatise, *Llave de la modulación* (1762).

England

Arne, Thomas Augustine. 1710-78. Leading English composer; first opera setting of Addison's *Rosamund* (1733); other works for stage include *Masque Alfred* (1740) that included famous song, *Rule Britannia*; noted for using female voices in oratorio chorus, an innovation first introduced in the production of *Judith* (1773); setting of songs to Shakespeare's works include *Where the Bee Sucks, Under the Greenwood Tree*, and others.

Gay, John. 1685-1732. Librettist of first English ballad-opera, *The Beggar's Opera*, lyrical drama (1728), a caricature of Sir Robert Walpole.

Boyce, William. 1710-79. Organist, composer; church music, eight symphonies; chamber music and works for the stage; famed compiler of three volumes of *Cathedral Music*.

Others. John Smith (1712-95), Samuel Webbe (1740-1816).

NORTH AMERICA

Hopkinson, Francis. 1737-91. Generally considered first American composer; songs, *The Temple of Minerva* (1781) called "oratorical entertain-ment"; *My Days have been so Wondrous Free* (1759), first-known song by native American; *Seven Songs* (1788), first book of music published by Anglo-Saxon composer in the New World; *Collection of Psalm Tunes with a few Anthems* (1770); leader of musical life in Philadelphia.

Billings, William. 1746-1800. Composer; compiled and published six volumes of psalms and church music in New England; considered first musician of note; wrote *Chester*, sung by American troops during the Revolutionary War; introduced use of pitchpipe and accompaniment of doublebass and cello in church services; important chiefly as pioneer musician; said to have given the first concert in America.

Reinagle, Alexander. 1756-1809. Composer, pianist, conductor; of Austrian parents, educated in Scotland; to U.S. (1786); first to introduce four-hand piano music to America; built theater in partnership with Thomas Wignell in Philadelphia (1793); most music composed for the theater.

THEATER

EUROPE · *England*

Sheridan, Richard Brinsley. 1751-1816. Leading Irish dramatist, politician; famous writer of bourgeois comedies of manners; *The Rivals* (1775) and *The School for Scandal* (1777), skilful handling of plot and characters; *The Critic; or, A Tragedy Rehearsed* (1779), brilliant satire on the follies of the theater; M.P., undersecre-

SCENE FROM *School for Scandal*
BY SHERIDAN

tary for foreign affairs (1782); famous for speeches at the impeachment trial of Hastings (1787-88).

Goldsmith, Oliver. 1727-74. Poet, dramatist; objected to excessive sentimentality of comedy in *Essay on the Theatre; or, A Comparison between Laughing and Sentimental Comedy* (1772); *The Good-natured Man* (1768), first play; most popular play, *She Stoops to Conquer; or, The Mistakes of a Night* (1773).

Farquhar, George. 1678-1707. Restoration dramatist; *The Recruiting Officer* (1706); and well-known play, *The Beaux' Stratagem* (1707).

Gay, John. 1685-1732. Playwright, poet; famous for *The Beggar's Opera* (1728); owed success to burlesque atmosphere and delightful lyrics.

Garrick, David. 1717-79. Great actor, manager of Drury Lane Theater; with Colman wrote the excellent comedy, *The Clandestine Marriage* (1766).

Siddons, Sarah (née Kemble). 1755-1831. Famed tragic actress; noted for Shakespearean roles.

Burgoyne, John. 1722-92. Army officer and dramatist; wrote satires directed against the administration of the elder William Pitt; worked for Garrick; wrote *The Maid of the Oaks* (1775) and the very successful comedy, *The Heiress* (1786).

Steele, Sir Richard. 1672-1729. Most famous as copartner with Joseph Addison of *The Spectator*; also writer of sentimental, highly moral bourgeois comedies including *The Funeral; or, Grief à la Mode* (1701); *The Lying Lover; or, The Ladies' Friendship* (1703); *The Conscious Lovers* (1722).

Denmark

Holberg, Ludvig, Baron. 1684-1754. One of the most important figures in the literature of Denmark; born in Norway; first to use Danish language as literary medium; *Peder Paars*, burlesque epic; *Jeppe on the Hill; or, The Peasant Metamorphosed* (performed 1722); *Erasmus Montanus* (printed 1731); best-known play outside of Scandinavia, *No Time to Waste* (1728), excellent characterization.

Ewald, Johannes. 1743-81. National lyric poet, dramatist; wrote first original Danish tragedy and heroic drama; *Balders Dod*, well-known play.

Bruun, Thomas. 1742-1800. Stage designer; worked for the State Theater, Copenhagen (1782-1800).

Holland

Langendijk, Pieter Arenz. 1683-1756. Poet, playwright; comedies, *Lovers' Deceits* and *The Braggart* (1712); *The Mathematicians* (1715).

GOETHE,
FROM PAINTING BY
ANGELICA KAUFFMANN

Germany

Goethe, Johann Wolfgang von. 1749-1832. Great romantic of *Stürm und Drang* (Storm and Stress) period; first work for stage, tempestuous *Goetz von Berlichingen* (1773), revolutionary hero fighting against oppression; *Stella* (1775), unconventional theme of *ménage à trois; Iphigénia in Tauris* (completed 1787); *Egmont* (1787); *Faust* (1808, 1831).

Schiller, Johann Christoph Friedrich von. 1759-1805. Outstanding dramatist; member *Stürm und Drang* group;

SCHILLER

not as imaginative as Goethe, but more successful theatrically; *Die Rauber* (The Robbers, 1781); great Wallenstein trilogy (1798-99); *Die Jungfrau von Orleans* (1801); *Die Braut von Messina* (1803); *Wilhelm Tell* (1804); many historical works; translated Shakespeare into German; important influence.

Lessing, Gotthold Ephriam. 1729-81. Important essay on theater (1769); better critic than playwright, but produced *Miss Sarah Simpson* (1755), *Minna von Barnhelm* (1767), and influential *Nathan the Wise* (1779), that raised the issue of freedom of thought.

Kotzebue, August Friedrich von. 1761-1819. Important in the development of the melodrama; 36 of his plays have been translated into English; *Pizarro* (1799), adapted by Sheridan; *Stranger* (1798); *The Child of Love* (printed 1791), bold theme.

Spain

Cruz, Ramón de la. 1731-94. Prolific dramatist; over 500 *sainetes,* one-act representations of scenes from everyday life; popularly exploited the resources of farce and melodrama; first translation of Shakespeare's *Hamlet* into Spanish.

Hungary

Bessenyei, Gyorgy. 1747-1811. Considered the leading figure in the modern era in Hungarian literature; first to use native tongue in the writing of plays and other works; *Philosophus* (The Philosopher, 1790), satire on sentimentalism.

Russia

Sumarokov, Alexander Petrovich. 1718-77. Leading dramatist; regarded as the "father of Russian drama"; strongly influenced by the French; *Khorev* (1747); *Zemir* (1751); introduced Shakespeare to the Russian public.

Volkov, Fedor. 1729-63. Founded the court theater at St. Petersburg (1756); leading actor and director; honored by Catherine the Great.

France

Beaumarchais, Pierre-Augustin Caron de. 1732-99. Well-known dramatist; sentimental first play, *Eugénie* (1767); *The Two Friends* (1770), thoroughly bourgeois; *The Barber of Seville* (1775, used by Rossini for opera); *The Marriage of Figaro* (1784, opera by Mozart).

Regnard, Jean-François. 1655-1709. Successor and imitator of Molière; emphasis on monetary aspects of social milieu; earliest comedies written for Théâtre Italien, later one for Comédie Française; *The Gamester* (1696); *The Absentminded Lover* (1697); *The Lover's Madness* (1704), best-known works.

Crébillon, Prosper Jolyot de. 1674-1762. Playwright, tragic poet; combined classic chill and gruesome incident; *Rhadamiste et Zénobie* (1711), most successful work; *Catilina* (1748).

Voltaire (François-Marie Arouet). 1694-1778. Earliest play an imitation of Racine, *Oedipe* (1718); *Zaïre* (1732), most important work; also wrote *Brutus* (1730), *Mérope* (1743), *Tancrède* (1760); contributed content rather than form to drama; other writings more important.

Marivaux, Pierre-Carlet de Chamblain de. 1688-1763. Dramatist, novelist; 25 plays, including *The Game of Love and Chance* (1730), *False Confidences* (1737); fresh style of comedy; influential.

Talma, François Joseph. 1763-1826. Great actor-manager; established the theater first known as Théâtre Français de la Rue de Richelieu (1791), later the Théâtre de la République; greatest tragedian of his time; instituted the most important reforms in costuming and acting techniques.

Lesage (Le Sage), Alain-René. 1668-1747. Dramatist of bourgeois comedies of intrigue; *Crispin, Rival of his Master* (1707); *Turcaret* (1709); famous for novel, *Gil Blas de Santillane* (1715-35).

Chaussée, Nivelle de la. 1692-1754. Considered "father of *comedie larmoyante*" (pathetic or sentimental play combining comedy and tragedy); *The False Antipathy* (1733); *Fashionable Prejudice* (1735); *Mélanide* (1741); *The Man of Fortune* (1751).

Italy

Goldoni, Carlo. 1707-93. Dramatist; versatile, prolific, imaginative, amus-

GOLDONI

ing; influenced by Molière; *The Housekeeper* (1751), *The Mistress of the Inn* (1753), superb examples of characterization; *The Fan* (1765), one of the best-known of 250 plays (in French), used an inanimate object as the center of action, a unique device.

Alfieri, Count Vittorio Amadeo. 1749-1803. Dramatist; best works based on Greek themes; *Oreste* (1776), most powerfully conceived work; *Antigone* (1783); influenced Italian nationalism.

Maffei, Marchese, Francesco Scipione di. 1675-1765. Playwright, archaeologist, scholar; tragedy, *Merope* (produced in 1713); *Verona illustrata* (1731-32); stimulated development of the Italian theater.

Metastasio, Pietro (Trapassi). 1698-1782. Poet; universally admired in his own time; lyric dramas (with music); *Adriano* (1731), *Issipile* (1732), *La clemenza di Tito* (1734).

Gozzi, Count Carlo. 1720-1806.

STUDIES OF ITALIAN ACTORS, CHALK ON GRAY PAPER, WATTEAU

Commedia dell'arte, Venice; *fiabe* (fairy tales with a purpose), slightly grotesque, but with a touch of reality; first important work, *The Love of Three Oranges* (1761); *The King Stag* (1762); *The Magic Bird* (1765); exceptionally witty; excellent sense of theater.

Bibiena, Ferdinando da. 1657-1743. Celebrated throughout Europe for theatrical designs, magnificent decorations for public and court festivals.

NORTH AMERICA

Tyler, Royall. 1757-1826. Playwright, jurist; *The Contrast*, produced at the John Street Theater, New York (April 16, 1787), first comedy written by an American.

Godfrey, Thomas. 1736-63. Playwright, poet; member of Philadelphia group; *Prince of Parthia* (1765), tragedy, first professionally produced play by an American (Southwark Theater, Philadelphia, 1767).

Dunlap, William. 1766-1839. Playwright; *The Father; or, American Shandyism*, a comedy (produced 1789); *Leicester* (produced 1794); *Fontainville Abbey* (produced 1795), *The Italian Father* (produced 1799), first Gothic-type plays written in the United States.

ASIA · *Japan*

Izumo, Takeda. 1688-1756. Leading Kabuki playwright; author of *Chushingura* (1748), very popular play; prolific but shallow; success of his works due largely to the exceptional production they received at the hands of the actors and directors of the *Takemoto* *za;* credited, however, with the advancement of playwriting technique.

Ki no Kaion. *ca.* 1663-1742. Dramatist; collaborated with **Tokotake Wakatayu** (1680-1764), a pupil of **Takemoto Gidayu,** who established a rival theater, the *Tokotake za;* some of his 40 plays have survived.

Namiki Sosuki. 1694-1750. Very popular playwright; succeeded Ki no Kaion at *Tokotake za;* influenced the style of succeeding dramatists.

Jisuke, Sakurada. 1734-1806. Poet; known for many plays with social background; dances performed as part of his plays are still popular.

China

Kao Tse-ch'eng. Playwright; known for *P'i Pa Chi* (Story of a Guitar, 1704).

1800-1850

The first quarter of the 19th century was dominated by Napoleon who shared the contemporary enthusiasm for antiquity and was portrayed in pure classical grandeur as Alexander and Caesar by David and Canova.

The Romantic movement that followed was a strong reaction against both the rationalism of the 18th century and against Napoleon. Delacroix, leading artist of the Romantic period, expressed the growing concern with individual freedom and the plight of mankind. While he expressed emotional intensity through color and movement, Turner relied on unusual technique to create atmosphere and dramatic effect.

The Gothic revival that dominated the architecture and sculpture in England and Germany was an expression of a growing nationalism and a violent reaction against Napoleon.

244

PAINTING

EUROPE · *France*

David, Jacques Louis. 1748-1825. Founder of the French neoclassical school; winner of the Prix de Rome (1776); early Rococo gave way to simpler style and new interest in antiquity; inspired by Winckelmann; *The Oath of Horatio, Death of Socrates,* early examples of work; *The Sabine Women* (Louvre) considered by the artist his best work; painted coronation and several exceptionally fine portraits including *Napoleon, Madame Récamier, Portrait of Madame de Verninac, Death of Marat,* noble expression of the faith of a martyr, *The Gerard Family, Pope Pius VII*; great influence as a teacher.

BONAPARTE ON MOUNT ST. BERNARD
BY DAVID

Ingres, Jean Auguste Dominique. 1780-1867. Superb draftsman; leader of neoclassical school following the death of David, his teacher; Prix de

Rome (1801); influenced by Raphael; outstanding portraits: *Riviere family, François Granet, the Leblancs, Madame Devauçay, Duke of Orleans, Louis Bertin the Elder, Madame Moitessier*; nudes: *The Source, The Turkish Bath*; odalisques; brilliant drawings.

LA SOURCE
BY INGRES

Géricault, Théodore. 1791-1824. Early leader of the Romantic revolt against the Academy; caused a sensation at the Salon of 1819 with his *Raft of the Medusa* (Louvre); studied in Italy and London; superb studies of horses including *Horse Frightened by Thunder and Lightning* (London), *The Derby* (Louvre), *Cavalry Officer of the Imperial Guard* (Louvre); *Death of Hippolytus; The Bull Market*; powerful portraits of the insane including the wonderful *La Folle* (The Madwoman, Lyons), *The Madman* (Ghent).

Corot, Jean-Baptiste-Camille. 1796-1875. Master landscape artist; worked in Rome; *Old Man Sitting on a Trunk*; *The Colosseum*; *Claudian Aqueduct* and *View near Volterra,* best works of this period.

Rousseau, Théodore. 1812-67. Leading member of Barbizon school of landscape artists; deep respect for nature and love of solitude expressed in paintings of woods, groups of trees, countryside; many drawings, etchings; *The Little Fisherman*; *Edge of the Forest at Fontainbleau*; *Sunset.*

Gros, Antoine-Jean, Baron. 1771-1835. Historical painter; studied with David; influenced by Van Dyck and Rubens; painted portraits of Napoleon: *Bonaparte at the Battle of Arcola, Napoleon on the Battlefield of Eylan*; *Charles X*; *Hercule et Diomède*; intensified color.

Gérard, François, Baron. 1770-1837. Neoclassicist; favorite pupil of David; court painter to Napoleon.

Chassériau, Théodore. 1819-56. Creole of San Domingo; pupil of Ingres; influenced by Delacroix; attempted to

MASSACRE AT CHIOS BY DELACROIX

blend romanticism with Ingres' emphasis on line; visited Algeria, sketched Arab and Jewish life there; *Ali Hamed, Caliph of Constantine*; *The Toilet of Esther*; *Susanna Bathing*; *Venus of the Sea*; decorated churches.

Delacroix (Ferdinand Victor), Eugène. 1798-1863. Outstanding master of the period; leader of the Romantic school of French painting; compositions based on historical, mythological, and literary subjects; vibrant, voluptuous color used as a primary means of expression; exceptional draftsman and illustrator (Goethe's *Faust*); effects of the color and dramatic, emotional intensity of North Africa, where he spent time, are apparent in his work; *The Massacre at Scio* (Chios), *Dante and Virgil in Hell, Death of Sardanapalus, Women of Algiers in Their Apartment*; *Liberty Leading the People, Hamlet and Horatio, Medea* (all at the Louvre); *Combat Between Giaour and the Pasha, Arab Rider Attacked by a Lion, Lion Hunt,* and the *Wounded Lioness* (Chicago); *The Abduction of Rebecca, Christ on Lake Gennesaret* (Met. Mus.); perceptive, romantic studies of *Chopin* and *George Sand* are among his best-known portraits.

Daumier, Honoré Victorin. 1808-79. Social satirist of genius, painter, lithographer; considered leading caricaturist of the century; almost 4,000 lithographs for *La Caricature* and *Le Charivari*; imprisoned for political satire; turned to poking fun at the middle class, lawyers, doctors, etc.; superb water colors, drawings, woodcut illustrations; paintings such as *The Washerwoman, Painter at His Easel, Advice to a Young Artist* (Washington), *Man on the Rope* (Boston), *Third-Class Carriage* (Met.

THE AMATEURS, WATER COLOR,
BY DAUMIER

Mus.) anticipated realism; free treatment not appreciated until later when his works influenced modern artists.

Prud'hon, Pierre-Paul. 1758-1823. Historical and portrait painter; studied in Rome; successful portraits include *Empress Josephine;* sensuous nudes; *Rape of Psyche, Divine Wrath, Justice and Vengeance Pursuing Crime* (Louvre), *Triumph of Bonaparte* (sketch); exceptionally fine drawings.

Gavarni, Paul Sulpice Giulliame, Chevalier. 1804-66. Satirist who worked with Daumier on *Le Charivari*; witty, clever ironic drawings; over 3,000 lithographs concerned primarily with social problems; excellent book illustrations.

Charlet, Nicolas Toussaint. 1792-1845. Lithographer and painter; important series of lithographs of Napoleonic Wars; genre and street scenes; military canvases; over 2,000 lithographs; *The Retreat from Russia,* large oil.

Others. François Marius Granet, water-colorist (1775-1849), Adrien Dauzats (1804-68), Horace Vernet (1789-1863).

England

Turner, Joseph Mallord William. 1775-1851. Master Romantic landscape and seascape artist; extraordinarily prolific, leaving almost 300 paintings and 19,000 drawings and water colors; honored by contemporaries for amazingly effective use of light, atmosphere, and brilliant colors; forerunner of impressionism with barest suggestion of form and subject and spontaneity of response to scene; traveled widely; *Rain, Steam and Speed* and *Snowstorm* considered most

THE FIGHTING TÉMÉRAIRE BY TURNER

revolutionary paintings; *Calais Pier, Crossing the Brook, Dutch Ships, Interior at Petworth, The Slave Ship, Yacht Approaching the Coast,* and *The Founding of Carthage* among many works.

Constable, John. 1776-1837. Outstanding landscape artist; one of the first to paint directly from nature; brilliant play of color and light; influenced

Delacroix; spontaneity, splashes of color applied with a palette knife influenced the French Impressionists; *Salisbury Cathedral* (several versions), probably best-known work; *The Hay Wain; Stoke-by-Nayland;* large oil sketch, *Leaping Horse; Weymouth Bay, Dedham Mill, The Grove, Hampstead, Summer Afternoon After a Shower, Fording the River* are other works.

Crome, John. 1768-1821. Early master landscape artist, known as "Old Crome"; simple yet bold composition; great love of nature gives depth of feeling to work; outstanding water colors and etchings; leader, founder of Norwich Society of artists (1803); *Mousehold Heath; Moonrise on the Marshes of Yare; Shadowed Road,* outstanding water color.

Bonington, Richard Parkes. 1801-28. Famed water-color artist, genre and landscape painter; friend of Delacroix; credited with the introduction of the work of the French Romantics to England; *On The Balcony; Scene in Normandy; Rosny-sur-Seine.*

Palmer, Samuel. 1805-81. Exceptional water-color artist; poetic, visionary; influenced by Blake; highly individual; unconventional drawing and color; combined oil tempera and water color, adding layers of varnish; surprisingly modern in concept; romantic oils; *Cornfield by Moonlight,* suggestive of Van Gogh; *Oak Tree and Beech; Lullingstone Park; Coming from Evening Church.*

Cotman, John Sell. 1782-1842. Brilliant Norwich water-color artist; superb draftsman; simplicity and serenity of compositions unusual; abstract quality of design appreciated today but not

in Cotman's own time; etchings, lithograps; works include *Château Gaillard, Chirk Aqueduct, New Bridge, Durham, Greta Bridge.*

Wilkie, Sir David. 1785-1841. Important Scottish genre artist; succeeded Lawrence as court painter; president of the Royal Academy; influenced by Ostade and Teniers in the painting of rural scenes.

Martin, John. 1789-1854. Fantasy important element in his work; inspired by Turner; strange effects of light; *Sadak in Search of the Waters of Oblivion,* best-known work; rare illustrations for Milton's *Paradise Lost.*

Others. John Varley (1778-1842), Peter De Wint (1784-1849), David Cox (1783-1859), Samuel Prout (1783-1852), James Holland (1799-1870), William Etty (1787-1849).

Germany

Friedrich, Caspar David. 1774-1840. Leading artist of North German Romantic school; mystical approach surprisingly akin to Blake; interested in showing the mysterious infinity of the world and the relative insignificance and solitude of the individual; *Mountain Landscape with Rainbow; Man and Woman Gazing at the Moon; The Wreck of the "Hope";* concern with the transitory nature of life evidenced in paintings of cemeteries, ruins; *The Cross and the Cathedral;* bleak, lyrical poetry of *Landscape in Silesian Mountains* suggests Oriental influence; important in the development of the German school.

Menzel, Adolph. 1815-1905. Outstanding lithographer, illustrator, painter; famous for 400 wood-block illustrations for Kugler's *History of*

Frederick the Great (1840); self-taught historical and genre painter; considered founder of realistic painting in Germany with *Rolling Mill* and other studies of the interiors of factories; modern approach to light and motion, elimination of narrative detail, and atmospheric emphasis anticipated impressionists by 40 years; illustrated works by Frederick the Great, Goethe, and Kleist; pen-and-ink drawings; *Frederick Playing the Flute*; *The Artist's Sister*.

Runge, Philipp Otto. 1777-1810. Important Romantic painter; excellent portraits; studied in Hamburg and Copenhagen; unfinished allegorical series of paintings, *The Hours of the Day*, attempted to symbolize the cycles of nature and of man's life.

Blechen, Karl. 1798-1840. Romantic artist; worked in Italy; interesting use of light; best-known for landscapes; *Women Bathing in a Wood*.

Cornelius, Peter von. 1783-1867. Muralist; member of the Nazarenes; *Story of Joseph* for Casa Catholdy; also frescoes for Casino Massimo, Rome; illustrations for the *Nibelungen* and Goethe's *Faust*.

Carus, Carl Gustav. 1789-1869. Romantic landscape artist; pupil of Friedrich; best-known for theoretical works; *Letters on Landscape Painting*.

Belgium

Navez, François Joseph. 1787-1869. Neoclassical painter; studied with David; director of the Royal Academy of Beaux-Arts, Brussels; *Resurrection of Lazarus; Hagar in the Desert*.

Wiertz, Antoine. 1806-65. Historical, allegorical paintings; portraits; government has established the Wiertz Museum to house his works.

Norway

Cappelen, August. 1827-72. Outstanding Romantic painter of Norway; excellent landscapes.

Dahl, Johan Christian Clausen. 1788-1857. Landscape artist; worked and taught in Germany; subtle use of gray; famous for studies of Norwegian mountains.

Spain

Goya y Lucientes, Francisco José de. 1746-1828. Great master; extremely versatile artist; studied with Luzán at Saragossa, in Madrid and Rome; designed cartoons for the royal tapestry factory (Madrid); court painter (1786); period of outstanding portraits including many of the royal family, *Don Sebastián Martínez, Don Manuel Osorio Manrique de Zuñiga*, a very popular painting of a young boy and his pets, *Don Bernardo de Yriarte* (all in the Met. Mus., although the outstanding collection of his work is at the Prado);

ETCHING FROM *The Disasters of War* BY GOYA

The Reader and *The Marquesa de Pontejos* (Washington); Goya painted seven portraits of the *Duchess of Alba,* and she may have been his model for the well-known *Maja Nude* and *Maja Clothed* (1800-1802); with the invasion of Spain by Napoleon, Goya protested with the brilliant series of etchings, *The Disasters of War* (1810-13, pub. 1863), and the powerful painting, *Third of May* (1808); the great series of etchings *Los Caprichos* (The Caprices), exposing the corruption and superstitions of the time, is political and social satire of intense power; as a true Spaniard, Goya painted several

THE
BOOKSELLER
BY GOYA

pictures and produced a series of etchings, *La Tauromachia,* on bullfighting; later works include *Majas on a Balcony* (ca. 1810-15), *The Bewitched* (1815), and the excellent portrait of his friend *Don Tiburcio Pérez* (1820); Goya, who had started to lose his hearing earlier, became stone-deaf following a serious illness in 1792 and retired to his country house and then to Bordeaux; his last

work showed his preoccupation with demons, fantasy, and the fantastic; one of the outstanding draftsmen in the history of art, his wash drawings rank with Rembrandt's.

Alenza, Leonardo. *fl.* early 19th century. Portrait and graphic artist of note; life of Spanish lower classes in a style not unlike that of Goya.

AMERICAS · *United States*

Allston, Washington. 1779-1843. Pioneer American Romantic artist; studied with West in London; work in Rome shows influence of Venetian school; biblical, historical, classical works; *The Deluge,* painted in Paris (1804), thought his masterpiece; teacher of Samuel Morse; important for the introduction of a subjective, romantic style.

Audubon, John James. 1785-1851. Famed artist-naturalist; ornithologist; studied with David in France; watercolor and crayon mixture (possible overlay of pastel), best medium; occa-

TURKEY BY AUDUBON,
PLATE 1 OF *Birds of America*

sionally used oil colors for the ground in studies; not always scientifically accurate, but exciting, charming, highly decorative studies of birds and animals; published *The Birds of America* (4 vols. 1827-38) in London with hand-colored aquatints by Robert Havell, and *Quadrupeds of America* (1845); particular favorites from among 435 plates of birds include his studies of the *Gyrfalcon, Collie's Magpie-Jay, Great Blue Heron, Great Black-Backed Gull*, and the sophisticated presentation of the *Snowy Egret*.

Cole, Thomas. 1801-48. Landscape artist, born in England; pioneer of the Hudson River school; large allegorical paintings, *The Expulsion from Eden, Voyage of Life*, popular, but fame rests on landscape studies of New York State and New England; using romantic realism he was able to create a dramatic, yet lyrical mood; *In the Catskills, The Roman Campagna, A View of New Hampshire, The Titan's Goblet, Valley of the Vancluse*, among best-known works.

Morse, Samuel Finley Breese. 1791-1872. Artist, inventor; studied with Allston; portrait painter; *Mrs. Daniel De Sassure Bacot*; founder of the National Academy of Design (1825); invented electric telegraph and Morse code; with Draper introduced the daguerreotype into the United States.

Vanderlyn, John. *ca.* 1775-1852. Neoclassical historical painter, portrait artist; studied with Stuart under the patronage of Aaron Burr; worked with Allston in Rome; first American to study in Paris; *Massacre of Miss McCrea* (Conn.); *Caius Marius Amidst the Ruins of Carthage* (Phil. Mus.);

portraits of *Madison, Monroe, Calhoun*, others; died in poverty.

Bingham, George Caleb. 1811-79. Outstanding frontier artist; self-taught; dramatic simplicity, strong technique seen in studies of frontier life; *Stump Speaking, Jolly Flatboatmen, Emigration of Daniel Boone, Fur Traders Descending the Missouri, Raftsmen Playing Cards*, among favorites; portraits.

Sully, Thomas. 1783-1872. Successful portrait painter; brilliant technique but lacking in emotional depth or understanding of sitters; influenced most by Sir Thomas Lawrence; *Young Queen Victoria, Commodore Stephen Decatur, Jefferson*, among others.

Catlin, George. 1796-1872. Outstanding studies of Indians and the early West.

Others. Matthew Harris Jouett (1788-1827), Rembrandt Peale (1778-1860), Edward Hicks (1780-1849), William S. Mount (1807-68).

ASIA · *Japan*

Hokusai, Katsushika. 1760-1849. Great master artist, draftsman, innovator; created the landscape school of color printmakers that greatly influenced Western painters of later periods; foremost figure of the *ukiyo-e* school; pupil of Shunso; over 30,000 superb drawings; entirely individual portrayal of contemporary life and people; famous for color-print series: *Hundred Views of Mount Fuji, Views of Famous Bridges, Views of Lu-chu Islands; The Great Wave*, probably his best-known single print; very influential.

FUJI FROM KAJIKAZAWA, BY HOKUSAI

Hiroshige, Ando. 1797-1858. Master printmaker, painter; combined landscape motifs with genre painting and ancient scroll painting with modern realistic techniques; landscapes, snow scenes, or studies of rain, mist, and moonlight, most popular subjects; powerful portrayal of birds, fish, and delicate flowers; unusual knowledge of perspective.

PINE TREE IN EVENING RAIN BY HIROSHIGE

Kazan, Watanabe. 1792-1841. Samurai painter; introduced Western techniques; exceptional portraits.

Buncho, Tani. 1765-1842. Artist, art historian; painted with large brush strokes in vigorous manner; sophisticated technique; used lateral-dot method; exceptional portraits.

Hoitsu, Sakai. 1767-1833. Noted for beautiful screens in the style of Korin.

India

Period of powerful Sikh painting of portraits; *Gulab Singh of Jammu* (1820-57, London), an example.

SCULPTURE

EUROPE · *Denmark*

Thorvaldsen, Bertel. *ca.* 1768/70-1844. Leading neoclassical sculptor working in Rome (1798-1838) and in Copenhagen (1838-41); influence of Canova and mythological antiquity: *Jason, Ganymede with the Eagle of Jupiter, Venus, Psyche and the Graces*; designed the colossal lion cut into rock

HEBE
BY THORVALDSEN

at Lucerne; bas reliefs include *Entry of Alexander into Babylon* for Napoleon; *Night and Morning*; *Christ and the 12 Apostles*; influential.

Bissen, Hermann Wilhelm. 1798-1868. Student of Thorvaldsen, director of the academy at Copenhagen; neoclassicist; works in Copenhagen.

Germany

Schadow, Johann Gottfried. 1764-1850. Considered the founder of the modern Berlin school of sculptors; worked for the Prussian court; statue of *Frederick the Great*; group entitled *Quadriga of Victory* for Brandenburg Tor (Berlin); many portrait busts and groups.

Rauch, Christian Daniel. 1777-1857. Neoclassicist; influenced by Thorvaldsen during his stay in Rome; portraits include life-sized marble study of *Goethe*, busts of *Von Bülow, Dürer*; equestrian statue of *Frederick the Great*; reclining statue for the sarcophagus of *Queen Louise* of Prussia; large groups.

Dannecker, Johann Heinrich von. 1758-1841. Württemberg court sculptor; portrait busts of friends, *Schiller, Goethe, Herder, Canova*, etc.

Rietschel, Ernst Friedrich August. 1804-61. Dresden artist; bronze studies of *Goethe, Lessing, Schiller, Frederick Augustus I* of Saxony, *Luther*; works for the Leipzig University and the Berlin Opera House.

Wolff, Emil. 1802-79. Classical school; worked in Rome; pupil of Schadow; portrait busts of *Thorvaldsen, Niebuhr*, others; also Greek mythological and genre subjects.

Schwanthaler, Ludwig von. 1802-48. Bavarian sculptor; large works for buildings in Munich.

Spain

Álvarez de Pereira y Cubero, José. 1768-1827. Portrait busts of *Charles IV* and *Queen Maria Luisa*; statue of *Ganymede*.

Sweden

Fogelberg, Bengt Erland. 1786-1854. Classicist; worked in Rome; large statues, mythological subjects including *Venus and Cupid, Odin, Thor, Balder*; portrait statues of *Gustavus Adolphus, Charles IV*, and others.

Byström, Johan Niklas. 1783-1848. Classicist; worked in Rome; excellent small portraits of women and children; heroic statues of kings of Sweden to be seen in Stockholm.

France

Barye, Antoine Louis. 1796-1875. Famous animal sculptor; gained fame with *Tiger Devouring a Crocodile* in the exhibition of 1831; *Jaguar Devouring a Hare* (Louvre); remarkable realism, movement, strength seen in works.

JAGUAR DEVOURING A HARE, BARYE

Rude, François. 1784-1855. Combined sentimental Gothic with naturalistic, free-moving Baroque; known for *Neapolitan Fisherboy, Joan of Arc Listening to the Voices, Mercury*

Fastening his Sandal; relief for the Arc de Triomphe; large statue of *Napoleon*.

Bosio, François Joseph. *ca.* 1769-1845. Noted for carved bas reliefs on the Column Vendôme, Paris; portrait busts of *Napoleon, Josephine,* and others.

Belgium

David D'Angers, Pierre Jean. 1788-1856. Portraitist; born in Antwerp; influenced by Canova; famous for portraits, reliefs, and medallions: *Chateaubriand, Hugo, Jeremy Bentham, Lamartine, Goethe, Ney, Rossini, David, Paganini,* many others.

Italy

Tenerani, Pietro. 1789-1869. Classicist; *Deposition from the Cross* (Lateran, Rome); tomb of *Pius VIII* (St. Peter's, Rome); *Bolivar's* statue for the monument to him in Colombia; portrait busts.

Bartolini, Lorenzo. 1777-1850. Studied in Paris; excellent portrait busts of *Napoleon, Madame de Stäel, Lord Byron, Lizst*; *Charity*; group statues in Florence.

Vela, Vincenzo. 1822-91. Decorative figures for the tomb of *Donizetti*; statue of *Spartacus*.

England

Flaxman, John. Neoclassicist; portraits of *Burns* and *Kemble*, Westminster Abbey; *Shield of Achilles*; Greek influence seen in relief models used as designs for Wedgwood ware.

Baily, Edward Hodges. 1788-1867. Famed for statue of *Nelson* in Trafalgar Square, London; studied under Flaxman; *Eve at the Fountain*.

Chantrey, Sir Francis Legatt. *ca.* 1781-1841. Equestrian statue of *George IV*; portrait busts.

Gibson, John. 1790-1866. Portrait statues of *Queen Victoria* and *Sir Robert Peel*.

Others. Patrick MacDowell (Irish, 1799-1870), Matthew Cotes Wyatt (1777-1862), Sir Richard Westmacott (1775-1856).

AMERICAS · *United States*

Greenough, Horatio. 1805-52. Neoclassicist; first American sculptor of any importance; studied with Thorvaldsen in Rome, later worked in Florence; introductd classicism to the United States; seated statue of *Washington*; *The Rescue, Venus Victrix*; portrait busts of *Hamilton, Lafayette,* and others.

GEORGE WASHINGTON BY GREENOUGH

Rush, William. 1756-1833. First native-born sculptor; self-taught; life-sized statue of *Washington*, carved of wood, originally for the prow of a ship; founder of the Pennsylvania Academy of Fine Arts, Philadelphia; portraits of *Washington, Franklin, Joseph Wright, Samuel Morris.*

Frazee, John. 1790-1852. Portrait busts of *Daniel Webster, Nathaniel Bowditch, John Marshall,* and other prominent early Americans.

Stone, Horatio. 1808-75. Portrait studies of *Roger Brooke Taney, Alexander Hamilton, John Hancock,* and *Thomas Jefferson.*

Clevenger, Shobal Vail. 1812-43. Portrait busts of *Henry Clay, Edward Everett,* and *Daniel Webster.*

ARCHITECTURE

EUROPE · *England*

Nash, John. 1752-1835. Brilliantly successful architect, town planner; frontages of old Regent Street, terraces, including *Carlton House* and *Cumberland* (begun 1827), around *Park Crescent* in Regent's Park (1811-25); not devoted to one style, he built one of his own houses in neoclassical and another in Gothic; built *Cronkhill* (1802, Shropshire) as an Italianate villa; *Blaise Castle* (1809, near Bristol), cottage in Old-England style; *Luscombe* (1800, Devonshire); used Indian Gothic in building the *Royal Pavilion* (1818-21, Brighton); developed Marylebone region; designed the *Haymarket Theater.*

Soane, Sir John. 1753-1837. Noted architect; influenced by the classic revival, but forerunner of the Romantic movement in style; to Rome (1776);

influenced by Piranesi; appointed architect of the *Bank of England* (1788); *Dulwich College Art Gallery* (1811-14) and his own house in Lincoln's Inn Fields (1812-13), best works.

Barry, Sir Charles. 1795-1860. Leader in the Gothic revival in architecture; famous for his design of the *Houses of Parliament* (1836, built 1840-60); *Travellers' Club* (1831), *Reform Club* (1837), and *Bridgewater House* (1847), all in London; *Royal Institution* (now Art Gallery, Manchester, 1824-35).

HOUSES OF PARLIAMENT, LONDON, BARRY AND PUGIN

Wyatt, James. 1747-1813. Versatile, successful architect; famous for *Fonthill Abbey,* built for William Beckford in Gothic style (1796-1814); designed great house for the Earl of Bridgewater; *Oriel College Library* (Oxford); *Dodington House* (Gloucester); *The Pantheon,* Oxford Street (London).

Smirke, Sir Robert. 1781-1867. Successful, influential designer of the first Greek Doric building in London; *Convent Garden Theater* (rebuilt 1808); traveled widely; with Nash and

Soane, architect to the Board of Works; *British Museum* (begun 1823); *Eastnor Castle* (*ca.* 1808-15, Herefordshire); *General Post Office* (1824-29, London).

Pugin, Augustus Welby Northmore. 1812-52. Important in the Gothic revival; author of the influential work, *The True Principles of Pointed or Christian Architecture* (1841); worked with Barry on the *Houses of Parliament* (façade, interior decoration); designed churches.

Wilkins, William. 1778-1839. Leading architect; worked in Italy and Greece; *Downing College* (1806-11, Cambridge).

Others. Charles Cockerell (1788-1863), Edward Blore (1787-1879), Thomas Rickman (1776-1841), Benjamin Wyatt (1775-1850), Sir Joseph Paxton (1801-65).

France

Percier, Charles. 1764-1838. Leading architect (with Fontaine) under Napoleon; designed the *Arc de Triomphe du Carrousel* (1806); worked on the *Opéra* (1794); palaces of *Louvre* and *Tuileries* (1802-12), designed the entire interiors, including the furniture, fabric, wallpaper, etc., all to conform to the Empire motif; finesse, elegance, in everything he did.

Fontaine, Pierre. 1762-1853. After Napoleon's fall (1814) partnership with Percier was dissolved; court architect in reigns of Louis XVIII, Charles X, and Louis Philippe.

Vignon, Barthélemy. *ca.* 1762-1828. Noted for the design of the *Church of the Madeleine* that he converted for Napoleon into the *Temple of Glory*, using Corinthian colonnade.

Labrouste, Henri. 1801-75. Daring architect; experimented with the use °of exposed iron framework in the *Library of Sainte Geneviève* (1845-50) and at *St. Eugène* (begun 1854, Paris).

Duban, Felix Louis Jacques. 1797-1870. Neoclassicist; among the first to revive an interest in architectural polychromy; enlarged the *École des Beaux-Arts* (from 1834); architect of the *Louvre* (1848-54).

Others. François Gau (1790-1853), Jacques Hittorff (1792-1867), Jean Chalgrin (1739-1811).

Italy

Cagnola, Marchese Luigi. 1762-1833. Milanese architect; famed for two triumphal arches; *Arco della Pace* and the *Porta di Marengo*; campanile (Urgnano) and the chapel of *Santa Marcellina*.

Germany

Schinkel, Karl Friedrich. 1781-1841. Neoclassicist; pupil of Frederich Gilly; considered the most creative, sensitive architect of the Germany of his period; built castles and country houses, surrounded by gardens landscaped in the English style, for the nobility of Prusia; classicism more Greek than Roman; *Schloss Babelsberg* (1834); built church in the Werder Market, *Old Museum, Royal Theater, School of Artillery and Engineering* (all in Berlin.)

Gärtner, Friedrich von. 1792-1847. Bavarian architect; court of Ludwig I; director of the Munich Academy of Art; best-known work, the *National Library* (1831, Munich).

Klenze, Leo von. 1784-1864. Bavarian architect; studied under Gilly in Berlin; visited France, Italy, and Greece; noted works include the "Walhalla" (near Regensburg), *Beauharnais Palace, Glypothek, Odeon,* and *Alte* (Old) *Pinakothek* (all in Munich).

Russia

Zakharov, Adrian Dmitrievich. 1761-1811. Studied and worked with Chalgrin in Paris; traveled in Italy; worked and taught at Academy, St. Petersburg; noted for the new *Admiralty* (1806-15); *The Church of the Ascension; Razumovski Estate* (1793, near Moscow); *Church of St. Andrew* (Kronstadt).

Stasov, Vasili Petrovich. 1769-1848. Sent by Tsar Alexander to study in England, France, and Italy for six years (1802-08); renovated the royal palaces at *Oranienbaum, Peterhof,* and *Tsarskoe Selo*; built high school adjoining the latter palace; *Belfry at Gruzino* (*ca.* 1815, near Novgorod), considered best work; *Moscow Triumphal Arch* (1833–38, St. Petersburg).

Voronikhin, Andrei Nikiforovich. 1760-1814. Influenced by Italians; country house for Count Alexander Stroganov; *Cathedral of the Virgin of Kazan* on the Nevski Prospekt (1801-11) and *Academy of Mines* (1811), both in St. Petersburg.

Rossi, Karl Ivanovich. 1775-1849. Prominent architect of Italian origin; *New Michael Palace* (1819-23, now Russian Museum), shows individuality of style; excellent city planner; *Alexandra Theater* (1827-32); arches of the *General Staff Building* (1819-29,

Leningrad); *Senate* and *Synod* (1829-34, St. Petersburg).

AMERICAS · *United States*

Latrobe, Benjamin Henry. 1764-1820. Considered the first professional architect in this country; born in England; to the U.S. (1796); designed the *Bank of Pennsylvania* building (Philadelphia); proposed, designed, and built the first city water supply system in America in Philadelphia; after the burning of the Capitol during the War of 1812, Latrobe was commissioned to

CATHOLIC CATHEDRAL, BALTIMORE, LATROBE

CAPITOL BUILDING, WASHINGTON, D.C., LATROBE

257

redesign and rebuild the *Capitol* and made several important alterations; designed the first American Roman Catholic cathedral in Baltimore (1805-18); important in the introduction of the Greek Revival style; interested (with Fulton) in steam navigation (1812).

Upjohn, Richard. 1802-78. One of the founders and the first president of the American Institute of Architects (1857-76); came to the U.S. from England (1829); leader of the early American Gothic Revival; famous for *Trinity Church* (1839-46, New York).

Bulfinch, Charles. 1763-1844. Succeeded Latrobe as architect of the *National Capitol,* Washington; carried it to completion (1818-30), mostly working on the western front; also designed the *Massachusetts State House* (completed 1800, Boston), *Connecticut State House* (Hartford), *India Wharf* (Boston); introduced styles of Wren and Adams to America.

Mills, Robert. 1781-1855. Leading architect of public buildings including the *Treasury Building, Patent Office Building, General Post Office,* and *Washington Monument* (1839); state house, Harrisburg (1810, Pennsylvania).

MUSIC

EUROPE · *Germany*

Beethoven, Ludwig van. 1770-1827. Great master composer, virtuoso pianist; studied violin, viola, harpsichord, and organ; to Vienna (1792), where he remained; first public ap-

BEETHOVEN

pearance as a performer (1795); studied with Haydn; although influenced by his predecessors, he was a creative genius, believed by many to be the greatest composer in musical history; developed the sonata form, made innovations in the orchestra, freed the variation from a rigid form with his uniquely brilliant imagination; most famous works include nine symphonies (*Eroica* #3, *Pastoral* #6, and the *Ninth* with chorus) most popular; *Rasoumowsky quartets*; *Pathétique* (1799); *Kreutzer* (1802) and *Waldstein* (1805), *sonatas*; *Coriolanus* overture (1807); *Emperor* piano concerto (#5, pub. 1811); opera, *Fidelio* (pub. 1810); chamber and instrumental music and choral works.

Schumann, Robert Alexander. 1810-56. Leading Romantic composer; married Clara Wieck (1840), who gained fame as the interpreter of his music; wrote nearly 150 songs to poems by Heine, Goethe, and others; first symphony (1841); three string quartets (1842); famous *Quintet in E Flat Major* (opus 44); choral works; opera, *Genoveva* (1850); music for the piano; teacher of composition (1843, Leipzig); championed young composers,

SCHUMANN

including Brahms and Chopin; remarkable *D minor* symphony (revised form pub. 1851); often referred to as the most literary composer.

Mendelssohn, Felix (Ludwig Felix Mendelssohn-Bartholdy). 1809-1847. Outstanding Romantic composer; boy protégé; traveled widely; conductor, Leipzig (1835); with Schumann and others founded Leipzig Conservatorium (1842); earliest mature works, overtures, *A Midsummer Night's Dream* (1826) and *The Hebrides* (1830-32); symphonies, concertos, oratorios, choral music, chamber music, piano works, songs; performance of *St. Matthew Passion* (1829) gave impetus to revival of Bach's music, an important contribution to music; *Violin Concerto in E, "Italian"* and *"Scotch"* symphonies, most often performed works.

Weber, Carl Maria von. 1786-1826. Noted composer, pianist, conductor; laid the foundation for German romantic opera; best-known for *Der Freischütz* (1821), *Oberon* (1826); *Euryanthe* (1823), that influenced Wagner, outstanding; works for the piano, including the popular *Invitation to the Dance* (1819); nine cantatas, four piano sonatas, eight sets of variations, two piano concertos, two symphonies, over one hundred songs, Masses; *Concertstück in F Minor* (1821).

Austria

Schubert, Franz Peter. 1797-1828. Master Romantic composer; studied violin, piano; wrote over 600 songs; great composer of German *lieder;* brilliant symphonies, including the *Unfinished* (#8, 1822); chamber music (*A Minor, G Major, D Minor, Tod und das Madchen,* 1824-26, best-known quartets); incidental music for *Rosamunde* (1823); church music, piano sonatas; died very young without having achieved warranted success.

MENDELSSOHN

SCHUBERT

259

Russia

Glinka, Mikhail Ivanovitch. 1804-57. Founder of nationalist school and Russian opera; composer, pianist; famous for the opera *Russlan y Ludmilla* (book by Pushkin, 1842), first with characteristically Russian style; in orchestral fantasia *Kamarinskaya,* he showed how folk song could be used as the basis of an instrumental composition; *A Life for the Tsar* (Ivan Sussanin, 1836); very important influence.

Ireland

Field, John. 1782-1837. Romantic composer; distinguished pianist; apprenticed to Clementi; honored as a teacher in St. Petersburg; works include seven piano concertos, four sonatas, a number of works for the piano, including nocturnes that influenced Chopin.

France

Berlioz, (Louis) Hector. 1803-69. Leading Romantic composer; introduction of important innovations that influenced orchestration of later composers; built up musical forms by the use of tone color; brilliant originality, intense feeling, and sense of the dramatic; first of great orchestra conductors, and the forerunner of today's "maestro"; used *idée fixe* in unifying and telling a story in sound; called symphonies "instrumental dramas"; won Prix de Rome (1830); famous for *Symphonie Fantastique* (1830), *Damnation of Faust* (1846), *Harold in Italy* (for viola and orchestra, 1834); operas,

BERLIOZ

Benvenuto Cellini (1838), *Les Troyens* (1865-69); dramatic symphony, *Romeo et Juliette* (1838-39); church music, *Requiem Mass*; wrote exceptional *Memoires* and a treatise on instrumentation.

Chopin, Frédéric François. 1810-49. Polish-French composer and virtuoso pianist; master of romantic compositions for the piano including outstanding concertos, nocturnes, études, mazurkas, polonaises, rondos, preludes with charming melody, multicolored harmony; subtle master of the art of suggestion.

CHOPIN

Liszt, Franz. 1811-86. Hungarian-French pianist, composer; period of great virtuosity and transcriptions for the piano; retired from the concert stage (1847) and turned to composition (*see* next period).

LISZT

Auber, Daniel François Esprit. 1782-1871. Successful operatic composer; collaborated with Scribe; director, Paris Conservatory (1842); first of 45 operas, *Les Bergères châtelaines* (1820); *La Muette de Portici* (1828), first romantic "grand opera" of the 19th century; *Fra Diavolo* (1830), still popular; called "Prince of Opéra Comique."

Boieldieu, François Adrien. 1775-1834. Composer of opera; studied with Cherubini; conducted Imperial Opera, St. Petersburg (1803-11); teacher at Paris Conservatoire (1817); first real success, *Le Calife de Bagdad* (1800); *La Dame blanche* (1825), considered one of the best examples of French comic opera, and his masterpiece.

Meyerbeer, Giacomo (Jakob Liebmann Beer). 1791-1864. Leading composer of opera during brilliant period in Paris; born in Germany; worked with Scribe; *Robert le Diable* (1813), *Les Huguenots* (1836), *Le Prophète* (1849), best-known works.

Cherubini, Maria Luigi. 1760-1842. Musical dictator of Paris (settled there, 1788, from Italy); new dramatic style greatly influenced French stage; *Les deux journées* (1800, Water Carrier in English), best-known work; church music (after 1813); six string quartets and six piano sonatas.

Adam, Adolphe Charles. 1803-56. Composer of comic operas and ballets; pupil of Boieldieu; *Le Postillon de Longjumeau* (1836), most popular opera; *Giselle* (1841), most successful ballet.

Herold, Louis. 1791-1833. Referred to us as the "French von Weber"; composed operas and ballets.

Halévy, Jacques François (Fromental Elias Lévy). 1799-1862. Pupil of Cherubini; teacher of Gounod and Bizet; *La Juive* (1835), famed opera.

England

Balfe, Michael William. 1808-70. Irish composer, violinist, baritone; appeared as Figaro in Rossini's *Il barbiere de Siviglia* (1827, Paris); wrote first opera *I rivali di se stessi* (1829, Palermo, Italy); most works written for London, including best-known, *The Bohemian Girl* (1843).

Wallace, William Vincent. 1812-65. Irish composer; left Ireland (1835); traveled widely; conducted Italian opera in Mexico (1841); to London (1853); composed piano music; opera, *Maritana* (1845), brought success; *Lurline* (1860), most popular work.

Spain

Arriaga y Balzola, Juan de. 1806-26. Composer of excellent string quartets; opera, *Los Esclavos Felices* (performed when he was 13); studied violin, harmony in Paris (1821-24); admired by Cherubini.

Portugal

Bomtempo, João Domingo. 1775-1842. Composer; director of Conservatory in Lisbon (1833); studied in Paris and England; influenced by Haydn and Mozart; opera, *Alessandro in Efeso; Requiem* in memory of Camoëns (four voices and orchestra); four piano concertos; *Missa solemne* (1821); other church music.

Italy

Clementi, Muzio. 1752-1832. Last (with Cherubini) great Italian master of classical instrumental music; pianist, composer; studied in Italy and London; three piano sonatas (1773), said to have established the sonata form for the piano; conducted Italian opera in London; achieved a remarkable union of artistic expression with technical instruction in *Gradus ad Parnassum* (1817); concert tours; called "father of modern piano-playing"; influenced Beethoven; famous teacher; symphonies and other works.

Bellini, Vincenzo. 1801-35. Composer of Romantic opera; studied with Haydn, Mozart, Pergolesi; elegance, lyrical charm, and dramatic effect characterize his operas: *Norma, La sonnambula* (1831); *I puritani* (1835), most successful works; exponent of pure *bel canto.*

BELLINI

Rossini, Gioacchino Antonio. 1792-1868. Last great master of *opera buffa;* outstanding representative of the *bel canto* school; lavish, romantic melody; 40 operas in 15 years including *Barber of Seville* (1815), *Semiramide* (1823), *William Tell* (1828); *Stabat Mater* (1842); *Petite Messe solennelle* (1864); songs, piano pieces, and six woodwind quartets.

ROSSINI

Donizetti, Gaetano. 1797-1848. Opera composer; influenced by Rossini; composed over 65 operas, including *Lucia di Lammermoor* (1835), *The Daughter of the Regiment* (1840,

Paris), *Don Pasquale* (1843), best-known; six Masses and string quartets.

Paganini, Niccolò. 1782-1840. Violin virtuoso and composer; use of harmonics extended the range of the instrument; able to play pizzicato and bow passages simultaneously; wrote 24 caprices for solo violin.

PAGANINI

Spontini, Gasparo Luigi Pacifico. 1774-1851. Successful composer of operas *La Vestale* (1807) and *Fernand Cortez* (1809), first important historical operas; director Italian opera in Paris (1810-12); director of music at Court Opera (1820-41, Berlin); influenced German opera.

Viotti, Giovanni Battista. 1753-1824. Violin virtuoso, composer; toured Germany, Russia (1780), Paris (1782-92), London (1794-95); composed 29 violin concertos; other instrumental music; teacher.

AMERICAS · *United States*

Mason, Lowell. 1792-1872. Called "father of American church music";

organist, composer, conductor; important collector of psalms extracted from music of the great masters; a founder of the Boston Academy of Music (1832); received Doctor of Music degree, New York University (1835), first of its kind offered by an American university.

THEATER

EUROPE · *Spain*

Zorrilla y Moral, José. 1817-93. One of the great Romantic writers of Spain; poet, dramatist; fame rests on *Don Juan Tenorio* (1844), one of the best-loved plays of Spanish literature; *El Zapatero y el rey* (The Shoemaker and the King); others.

ZORRILLA Y MORAL

Martínez de la Rosa, Francisco. 1787-1862. Leading dramatist of the Romantic school; *La conjuración de Venecia* (The Venetian Conspiracy, 1834), first successful play; *Aben Humeya; or, The Rebellion of the Moors* (written in France, 1830, produced in Paris, translated into Spanish, 1836); influential.

García Gutiérrez, Antonio. 1813-84. Romantic playwright; *El trovador* (The Troubadour, 1836), best-known play (used by Verdi for opera *Il Trovator*, 1852); Verdi's *Simon Boccanegra* (1843) also based on a play of that name by Guitiérrez; *Juan Lorenzo* (1865), considered a masterpiece.

Rivas, Ángel de Saavedra, Duke de. 1791-1865. Poet, dramatist of the Romantic school; *Don Alvaro la fuerza del sino* (1835), first triumph (used by Verdi as libretto for *La Forza del Destino*, The Force of Destiny, 1862).

Vega, Ventura de la. 1807-65. Argentine dramatist; introduced realism to the Spanish theater adding a purely Castilian attitude in *El hombre del mundo* (The Man of the World, 1845).

Bretón de los Herreros, Manuel. 1796-1873. Prolific playwright and poet; 350 witty plays of middle-class life in Madrid.

Italy

Manzoni, Alessandro. 1785-1873. Leader of the Romantic school; novelist, dramatist, poet; early work, *Adelchi* (printed 1822), characters half-real and half-symbolic; *The Count of Carmagnola* (1820), tragic drama.

Foscolo, Niccolò Ugo. 1778-1827. Romantic poet, dramatist; *Tieste*; *Aiace*; *Ricciarda*.

Niccolini, Giovanni Battista. 1782-1861. Dramatic poet; historical dramas with political overtones; *Antonio Foscarini* (1827); *Giovanni de Procida* (1830); *Arnaldo da Brescia* (1843).

England

Lytton, Lord Edward George Bulwer. 1803-73. Popular novelist, poet, dramatist; politician; influenced by the realism of the French theater in *Money* (1840); popular "gentlemanly melodrama" in *The Lady of Lyons* (1838); *Richelieu; or, The Conspiracy* (1839), romantic historical play.

France

Musset, Alfred de. 1810-57. Romantic poet, dramatist; most famous exponent, but not originator, of *proverbe dramatique* or *comédie-proverbe*: comic short playlets with serious undertones; published eight volumes of them (from 1840); *No Trifling with Love* (printed 1834); *The Decoy* (printed 1835); *You Can't be sure of Anything* (printed 1836); peak of unreality reached in *Carmosine* (printed 1850); exceptional dramatic quality, delicate yet penetrating character studies.

Scribe, Augustin Eugène. 1791-1861. Dramatist, outstanding librettist of his day; over 350 plays; libretti for Verdi, Meyerbeer, Auber, Halèvy, etc.; exciting, popular works with little depth.

Pixérécourt, Guilbert de. 1773-1844. Popular writer of melodramas; *Selcio; or, The Magnanimous Slaves* (1793); *The Spanish Moors* (1804); *Christophe Colomb* (1815).

Denmark

Oehlensläger, Adam Gottlob. 1779-1850. Most influential Danish dramatist; influenced by Schiller; *Earl Hakon* (1807), defense of barbaric religion; *Palnatoke* (1809), based on a tragic Teutonic (Nordic) myth; *Axel and*

Valborg (1810), medieval love-drama; *Correggio* (1809), a play written in German, based on an artist's life, a theme often used in later works of the century.

Heiberg, Johan Ludvig. 1791-1860. Popular poet, dramatist; *The Hill of the Elves* (1828), romantic drama, one of the most frequently performed Danish plays; *A Soul After Death* (printed 1841).

Portugal

Almeida-Garrett, Visconde João Baptiste da. 1799-1854. Leader of the Romantic movement; dramatist, poet; considered one of the great Portuguese dramatists; *The Armourer of Santarem* (1842) has people's rights as the theme; *Frei Luiz de Souza* (1843).

Russia

Pushkin, Alexander Sergeyevich. 1799-1837. Great literary figure of Russia; playwright, poet, short story writer, novelist; most important poetic drama, *Boris Godunov* (1825), reaches tragic grandeur (used by Mussorgsky for opera); *Four Short Dramatic Scenes* (1830); *Rusalka* (1832), folk

drama; *The Golden Cockerel* (1833, used by Rimsky-Korsakov for opera).

Lermontov, Mikhail Yuryevich. 1814-41. Leading dramatist, poet; influenced by Schiller and Shakespeare; lyrical tragedies, *The Spaniards* (1830) and *Maskerad* (Masquerade, 1835), still performed.

Gogol (Gogol-Yanovsky), Nikolai Vasilievich. 1809-52. Father of Russian realism; dramatist, novelist, short story writer; social satire; *Revizor* (The Inspector-General, 1836), genuine basis of characteristically Russian comic realism; *Marriage* (printed 1847).

GOGOL

SCENE FROM *Diary of a Madman,* GOGOL

PUSHKIN

Hungary

Kisfaludy, Károly. 1788-1830. Founder of Hungarian national drama; *Tatars in Hungary* (1812), first genuine dramatic Hungarian play, the first of many successes including *The Suitors* (1819), *Irene* (1821), *Maiden's Guard* (1827), *Illusions* (1828), and *Disappointments* (1829); used peasants for the first time as dramatic material.

Germany

Kleist, Heinrich Bernt von. 1777-1811. Leading dramatist, poet, and novelist; tragic dramas include *The Schroffenstein Family* (1803), penetrating characterization; *Penthesilea* (1808); *The Prince of Homburg* (1811); comedy, *The Broken Jug* (1811).

Büchner, Georg. 1813-37. Dramatic poet; powerful force for democratic principles; sympathy for man's forced subjection to his fate; *Danton's Death* (1835); *Woyzeck* (also spelled *Wozzeck*, 1836, unfinished, from which Alban Berg derived his opera); comedy, *Leonce and Lena* (1836).

Schinkel, Karl Friedrich. 1781-1841. Architect, famed stage designer, Royal Theater, Berlin; created a new medieval Germany as fitting background for the *Sturm und Drang* drama.

Gutzkow, Karl. 1811-78. His play, *Uriel Acosta* (1846), represented the new trend toward naturalism combined with romanticism.

Austria

Grillparzer, Franz. 1791-1872. Noted dramatist; Romantic works inspired Hauptmann, Maeterlinck, and others; *The Ancestress* (1817); *Sappho* (1819); trilogy, *The Golden Fleece* (1812).

Raimund, Ferdinand. 1790-1836. Popular writer of *Zauberpossen*, fairytale farces; *The Peasant a Millionaire; or, The Maid from the World of Fairies* (1826) mingles world of reality with the unreal; *The Spendthrift* (1834) emphasizes bourgeois concern for money and material gain.

Bauernfeld, Eduard von. 1802-90. Master of high comedy; political, social satire; *The Acknowledgements* (1834); *Simple and Romantic* (1835).

Poland

Fredro, Count Aleksander. 1783-1876. Noted Polish playwright; famed for excellent comedies; *Husband and Wife* (1822), *The New Don Quixote* (1826), *Ladies and Hussars* (1826); *Mr. Jowialski* (1833), considered a minor masterpiece; *The Revenge* (1835), excellent characterization.

Slowacki, Juliusz. 1809-49. Poet, dramatist; inspired by Shakespeare; *Mindowe* (1841); *King Spirit* (1847); poetic power influenced younger Polish writers.

ASIA · Japan

Namboku Tsuruya IV. 1755-1829. Brilliant playwright; prolific writer of many plays that are still performed; famous for ghost plays; wrote for noted actors: Matsumoto Koshiro IV, Onoe Matusuke, Onoe Kikugoro III; played a leading role in the success of the Kabuki theater in his time; called "*dai* Namboku," or the "Great Namboku."

1850-1900

Reacting against the status quo, the French artists of the second half of the 19th century established two revolutionary movements in art. Realism, a study of nature "as it is" and the portrayal of people "as they are," developed into Objective Realism in the strong, direct canvases of Courbet and into Romantic Realism in the peasant paintings of Millet. Impressionism was inspired by the work of Manet, who also foreshadowed the work of Cézanne when he created planes by juxtaposing small flat areas of pure color applied directly to the canvas.

By the end of the century, with the invention of the camera and the scientific discoveries involving the nature of light, the artists were forced to create new means of expression and to explore the possibilities of new techniques.

The greatest artist of the period was Paul Cézanne who, as the leader of the Post-Impressionists and the forerunner of Cubism and abstract form, is considered the real founder of "modern art."

PAINTING

EUROPE · *France*

Manet, Edouard. 1832-83. Pioneer master Impressionist and *plein-air* painter; although not interested in effects of light as such, and although he did not break up color, his influence on his contemporaries was profound through his strong dramatic use of flattened planes and increased tonal values; achieved depth by subtle use of color intensities rather than by linear perspective; influenced by Courbet, Velásquez, Goya, and Japanese prints; only achieved a limited recognition during his lifetime; outstanding works include *Le Déjeuner sur l'herbe, Olympia, The Boat, The Guitar Player, Torero Saluting, The Old Musician, Le Bon Bock, Ball at the Opera, Boy with a Sword, Woman with a Parrot;* portraits of *George Moore, Zola,* and *Mallarmé.*

Monet, Claude-Oscar. 1840-1926. Leading Impressionist; painted directly from nature; important studies of the effects of light on buildings,

REGATTA BY MONET

haystacks, water, and flowers at different times of the day; completely eliminated black and brown from his palette; tones divided into pure color to produce intensity; almost completely abstract studies of water lilies an important influence on modern painters; studies of *Rouen Cathedral, Venice, Chrysanthemums,* the *Gare St. Lazare, Snow Effect at Vetheuil, Bridge at Argenteuil, Garden at Giverny,* among better-known works.

Pissaro, Camille. 1830-1903. Master Impressionist; brilliant landscapes;

KNEELING MONK
BY MANET

LE DÉJEUNER SUR L'HERBE (LUNCHEON ON THE GRASS) BY MANET

Bather in the Woods, Côte du Jallais, Pontoise; Paris street scenes: Street in Rouen, Versailles Road at Louveciennes, Boulevard des Italiens, Morning Sunlight; important influence on younger artists.

Renoir, Pierre Auguste. 1841-1919. Famed Impressionist; brilliant colors, delight in beauty, and enjoyment of life apparent in his works; magnificent studies of nudes, flowers, and children; *Mme Charpentier and Her Children, By the Seashore, On the Terrace, After the Bath, Le Moulin de la Galette, Box at the Theater, Girl with a Cat,* etc.

SLEEPING BATHER BY COURBET

THE JUDGEMENT OF PARIS BY RENOIR

Corot, Jean Baptiste Camille. 1796-1875. Painted outstanding figure studies, mostly of young women, in his last period: *Agostina, The Letter, Interrupted Reading* are examples.

Courbet, Gustave. 1819-77. Objective realist; direct, forceful expression of nature; individualist whose absolute honesty was resented by his contemporaries; *Burial or Funeral at Ornans,* considered his masterpiece; *The Painter's Studio, The Quarry of Optevoz, Sleeping Bathers, The Meeting,* and

The Stream in the Forest.

Sisley, Alfred. 1839-99. Impressionist; English; born in Paris and worked in France; sky important in his radiant landscapes; calm, serene studies of nature as seen in the valley of the Seine and in the area around Fontainbleau.

Post-Impressionists:

Cézanne, Paul. 1839-1906. Great master; achieved minor recognition at the close of his life, but considered today one of the greatest painters of his century; early work with Impressionists in Paris; more mature works after 1882, when he retired to the south of France; believed all nature could be divided into certain basic forms: cube, cone, cylinder (led to Cubism); color used as a means of describing masses and forms, separating space into receding vertical planes, creating the illusion of depth, achieving solidity and calm monumentality; distortion added dramatic expression, energy, life to landscapes, still lifes, portraits, card players, bathers, self-

SELF PORTRAIT, CÉZANNE

THE STAR
(PASTEL) BY DEGAS

STILL LIFE WITH APPLES BY CÉZANNE

THE TUB BY DEGAS

portraits; extraordinary sense of design and composition; tremendously important; outstanding works include *Portrait of Victor Chocquet, Gulf of Marseilles Seen from L'Estague*, views of *Montagne Sainte-Victoire, The Artist's Wife* (Hortense), *The Card Players, Boy Wearing a Red Waistcoat, Harlequin, The Great Bathers, Still Life: Oranges and Apples*; water colors, with their clarity of design, delicacy of transparent color, and abstract quality, are thought by some critics to be the most original of his works.

Degas, Hilaire Edgar. 1834-1917. Master linear Impressionist; influenced by the late pastels of Chardin, the works of Ingres, and Japanese prints; superb studies of nudes and ballet dancers; exceptional draftsman; *The Rehearsal; Woman with Chrysanthemums; Four Dancers; Horses with Jockeys*; small sculptures.

Gauguin, Paul. 1848-1903. Pioneer expressionist; influenced by Manet and the Japanese; flat areas of brilliant color, decorative design; worked in Tahiti, painted magnificent studies of native women, landscapes: *Ia Orana*

Maria, Manao Tupapau, The Call, Two Tahitian Women; studies of Breton peasants; *The Yellow Christ*; penetrating portraits and self-portraits; exceptional woodcuts; *The Spirit of the Dead Watching*; *Noa Noa*.

THE JOCKEY
(DRAWING) BY TOULOUSE-LAUTREC

THE MOON
AND THE EARTH
BY GAUGUIN

Seurat, Georges Pierre. 1859-91. Neoimpressionist; creator of pointillism; intellectual, scientific approach to problems of color and light; attempted to restore balance and deliberate design to painting; important in foreshadowing preoccupation with geometry and formal structural elements in art; *Sunday Afternoon on the Island of La Grande Jatte*, his masterpiece; *La Parade*; *Les Poseuses*; *Le Chahut*; *Bathing at Asnières*.

Toulouse-Lautrec, Henri de. 1864-1901. Master of Post-Impressionist period; influenced by Degas and the Japanese; superb draftsman, noted lithographer; *gouaches*, water colors; important in the development of the art of the poster; studies of performers, prostitutes, dancers, circuses, and horses; *Artistide Bruant, Jane Avril,*

Yvette Guilbert, posters; *The Artist's Mother, The African Countess,* scene at the *Moulin Rouge, Woman in a Studio*, among many oils.

Bonnard, Pierre. 1867-1947. Post-Impressionist; member of Nabis group; "Intimist," noted for colorful, deceptively simple, often delicate studies of everyday life; *Luncheon Table* (*ca.* 1900, Baltimore), *Bourgeois Afternoon* (1902-03); portraits, nudes, landscapes, and excellent graphics.

Redon, Odilon. 1840-1916. Master of atmosphere; created a world of fantasy and dreams; flower studies using brilliant color, stark design; excellent haunting lithographs and drawings.

Rousseau, Henri. 1844-1910. Called *Le Douanier*; primitive; visionary; exotic, bright colors, jungle scenes; *The Sleeping Gypsy*, his masterpiece.

Others. Edouard Vuillard (1868-1940), Paul Signac (1863-1935), Jean Louis Forain (1852-1931), Jean-

François Millet (1814-75), Charles-François Daubigny (1817-78), Henri Fantin-Latour (1836-1904), Constantin Guys (1805-92), Pierre Cecile Puvis De Chavannes (1824-98), Eugène Boudin (1824-98), Berthe Morisot (1841-95), Rodolphe Bresdin (1822-85), Gustave Moreau (1826-98), Gustave Doré (1832-83).

Netherlands

Gogh, Vincent van. 1853-90. Post-Impressionist; pioneer expressionist; dynamic, brilliant color and impasto technique; very personal, highly emotional expression of feeling for people and nature; carefully, intellectually planned compositions that gave the effect of spontaneity, passionate abandon; tragic, unsuccessful life; works include Self-Portraits, *Starry Night, Church at Auvers, Potato-Eaters, Cypresses, Sunflowers, Wheat Field, Bedroom at Arles, La Berceuse; The Drawbridge* shows influence of Japanese prints.

CORNFIELD AND CYPRESS TREES
BY VAN GOGH

Jongkind, Johann Berthold. 1819-91. Landscape and seascape painter; worked in Paris; importance of the effect of light showed him to be a precursor of Impressionism; influenced Sisley and Pissaro; *Rue des Francs-Bourgeois, Paris*; excellent water-color and graphic artist.

Switzerland-Germany

Böcklin, Arnold. 1827-1901. Leader of neo-Romantic group of German artists working in Italy and Germany; born in Switzerland; symbolic, atmospheric, poetic allegorical landscapes; painted in realist technique; *The Island of the Dead*, best-known work; influenced German realists.

Sweden

Zorn, Anders. 1860-1920. Impressionist; landscapes, genre, nudes, portraits; one of the most successful artists in Europe at the end of the century; traveled widely; successful *plein-air* studies of Swedish life; *Girls Bathing; The Artist in His Studio; King Oskar*; self-portraits; excellent etchings.

Italy

Segantini, Giovanni. 1858-99. Impressionist; paintings of Swiss and Italian Alps; peasants, fishermen; bright color, impasto technique.

England

Rossetti, Dante Gabriel. 1828-82. Founder and guiding spirit of Pre-Raphaelite Brotherhood; studied with Ford Madox Brown, worked with Hunt, Millais, others; use of medieval religious subject matter; romantic, poetic, over-sentimental, static works; considered poet-painter; *The Annunciation; Girlhood of the Virgin Mary; Lady Lilith; Beata Beatrix; The Beloved*; numerous water colors; illustrated the *Life of Dante*; important influence.

ROSSETTI

Millais, Sir John Everett. 1829-96. Pre-Raphaelite painter of exceptional technical competence; sentimental, shallow emotion expressed in *Christ in the House of His Parents, Lorenzo and Isabella*; turned to more lucrative, popular material with *The Blind Girl.*

Hunt, William Holman. 1827-1910. Pre-Raphaelite painter; photographic realism; stiff, humorless, colorless yet popular works include *The Light of the World, The Hireling Shepherd, The Awakening Conscience,* and *Finding of Christ in the Temple.*

Brown, Ford Madox. 1821-93. Associated with the Pre-Raphaelite group, but not a member; social criticism saved him from weak sentimentality; *Work,* his masterpiece, inspired by Carlyle's thinking; *The Last of England*; murals in Manchester.

Burne-Jones, Sir Edward. 1833-98. Pre-Raphaelite; influenced in early works by Rossetti and Botticelli; *Cophetua and the Beggar-Maid; Days of Creation; Mirror of Venus*; later worked with Morris; illustrations for the Kelmscott Press.

Sickert, Walter Richard. 1860-1942. Impressionist; studied with Whistler; founder of the Camden Town Group; organized the London Impressionists exhibition, 1889; *The Old Bedford; Ennui; Cicely Hay.*

Beardsley, Aubrey. 1872-98. Illustrator, outstanding graphic artist; influenced by Morris; drawings for *The Studio,* Malory's *Morte d'Arthur,* Wilde's *Salome, Lysistrata,* and many magazines.

Dyce, William. 1806-64. Landscape artist; worked with Nazarenes in Rome; fresco decorations in government buildings and churches in England; seascape, *Pegwell Bay,* shows influence of Pre-Raphaelite movement.

McTaggart, William. 1835-1910. Leading Scottish painter of the 19th century; landscapes; influenced by Impressionists; *The Storm; The Young Fishers.*

Watt, George Frederick. 1817-1904. Portrait artist; popular painter of allegorical works.

Leighton, Lord Frederick. 1830-96. Successful neoclassical painter, sculptor; first painter to become a peer; *The Bath of Psyche; Andromache Captive.*

Frith, William Powell. 1819-1909. Academic painter; *Paddington Station; Derby Day*; popular realism.

Haden, Sir Francis. 1818-1910. Graphic artist.

Germany

Corinth, Lovis. 1858-1925. Leading Impressionist, illustrator; late period very free impasto technique, *Walchensee Landscape*; considered an important bridge between Impressionism and Expressionism in Germany; studied in Paris; influenced by Liebl and Courbet; sensual nudes; portraits, *Graf Keyserling, Gerhart Hauptmann*;

water colors; early epic works include *Temptation of St. Anthony* and *Lament for the Dead.*

Liebermann, Max. 1847-1935. Founder of Berlin *Sezession* (1899); leading Impressionist; influenced by Hals and Dutch masters; studies of beach at Scheveningen and of Wannsee near Berlin show his interest in the effects of light on nature and his affinity with the French Impressionists; *Women Mending Nets*; influence of Manet seen in *Papageienallee*; portrait artist of note.

Slevogt, Max. 1868-1932. Outstanding Impressionist; illustrator; studied in Paris, Italy, Munich; taught, worked in Berlin; frescoes for public buildings; gay, humorous paintings; outstanding lithographs and etchings; illustrations for Cooper's *Last of the Mohicans* and many other books.

Marées, Hans von. 1837-87. Romantic historical painter; fresco for the Aquarium, Naples; worked in Rome; influenced by classical antiquity; interest in mythology seen in *The Judgment of Paris*; many drawings.

Uhde, Fritz Karl Hermann von. 1848-1911. Early Impressionist; known for attempt to paint religious subjects in modern setting; excellent group portraits.

Spitzweg, Karl. 1805-55. Romantic painter; influenced by French school; known for humor in interpretation of human follies; prominent in Munich; *The Cactus-fancier.*

Schwind, Mortiz von. 1804-71. Historical painter, illustrator, muralist; known for cycles: *Seven Ravens* (Weimar), *Melusine* (Vienna), *Cinderella.*

Leibl, Wilhelm. 1844-1900. Natural-ist; influence of Courbet on trip to Paris seen in *The Cocotte*; scenes of Upper Bavarian peasant life; portraits.

Richter, Adrian Ludwig. 1803-84. Late Romantic school; teacher, Dresden; best-known for book illustrations and *Memoirs of a German Painter.*

Thoma, Hans. 1839-1924. Poet-painter; lyrical studies of the Black Forest; excellent lithographs.

Trübner, Wilhelm. 1851-1917. Influenced by Courbet; landscapes, portraits.

Feuerbach, Anselm. 1829-80. Romantic, classical artist; literary subject matter; sensitive works.

Austria

Alt, Rudolf von. 1812-1905. Viennese landscape, architectural painter; exceptionally fine water-color artist.

Russia

Repin, Ilya Efimovich. 1844-1930. Leader of the naturalist movement in second half of the 19th century in Russia; widely traveled; genre, historical works show social awareness; famous for discerning, perceptive portraits of *Tolstoy, Mussorgsky, Gogol, Borodin, Turgenev, Rimsky-Korsakov,* and others.

Korovin, Konstantin. 1861-1939. Important theatrical designer; first to reflect the art of French Impressionists in Russia; teacher.

Vrubel, Mikhail. 1856-1910. Leading water-color artist; traveled widely; excellent draftsman; little recognition during his lifetime.

Surikov, Vassily. 1848-1912. Realist; famous for *The Boyarina Morosova* depicting the persecutions of the "Old Believers" by patriarch Nikon.

Scrov, Valentin. 1865-1911. Outstanding portrait artist of the late 19th century; landscapes.

AMERICAS · *United States*

Whistler, James Abbott McNeill. 1834-1908. Decorative Impressionist; lived in London; influenced by Velásquez' color, Courbet; first to be attracted by Japanese color woodcuts; concerned primarily with color, form, design, and elegance of style: famed for "arrangements," "symphonies," and "nocturnes"; *Arrangement in Gray and Black* (portrait of his mother), *Nocturnes in Black and Gold, Blue and Green, Harmony in Grey and Green, Arrangement in Flesh Color and Black* (Theodore Duret); *The Falling Rocket*; *The White Girl*; excellent portrait of *Carlyle*; superior series of etchings

THE WHITE GIRL
BY WHISTLER

of the Thames River, of London, and of Venice.

Eakins, Thomas. 1844-1916. Outstanding objective realist; unconven-

MAX SCHMITT IN A SMALL SCULL,
EAKINS

tional, pessimistic approach to life; photographic detail with little emotion; penetrating portraits of *Walt Whitman, Signora Gomez D'Arza, Margaret in Skating Costume*; famed *Clinic of Dr. Gross, The Chess Players, Cowboy Singing*; water colors: *John Biglen in a Single Scull, Young Girl Meditating*.

Ryder, Albert Pinkham. 1847-1917. Romantic artist of unusual ability; imaginative small canvases; able to create poetic atmosphere of loneliness and isolation; subtle, uncomplicated color, luminous design; *Toilers of the Sea; Death on a Pale Horse; Flying Dutchman*.

Homer, Winslow. 1836-1910. Objective realist; land and seascapes, genre;

THE GULFSTREAM BY HOMER

charming scenes of life in America; brilliant, imaginative water colors; *High Tide*; *Breezing Up*; *Snap the Whip*; *The Carnival*; water colors include *Rum Cay, Gulf Stream, Palm Tree,* and *Nassau,* examples of many works.

Cassatt, Mary. 1845-1926. Impressionist painter; worked in Paris; influenced by Manet and Degas; excellent studies of children, interiors.

Sargent, John Singer. 1856-1925. Portrait artist working in London; facile handling of texture; *Madame X: Portrait of Madame Gautreau,* best-known work; excellent water colors include *Venetian Canal, Idle Sails, Tyrolese Crucifix.*

Inness, George. 1825-94. Landscape painter; early works influenced by Barbizon school; later works show an unusual ability to create atmosphere typical of American Impressionism: *Autumn Oaks, Niagara Falls, Sunset, The Lackawanna Valley.*

Courier & Ives prints of contemporary scenes by the lithographers Nathaniel Currier (1813-88) and J. Merritt Ives (1824-95).

Durand, Asher. Romantic realist of the Hudson River school; one of the first Americans to paint directly from nature; excellent portraits, genre paintings.

Others. John Kensett (1818-72), John La Farge (1835-1910), William Harnett (1848-92), Frederick Church (1826-1900), William Merritt Chase (1849-1916), Albert Bierstadt (1830-1902), Worthington Whittredge (1820-1910), Seth Eastman (1808-75), Frederick Remington (1861-1909), Matthew Brady, pioneer photographer (1823-96).

Argentina

Pueyrredón, Prelidiano Paz. 1823-83. Excellent portrait and landscape artist.

ASIA · *Japan*

Kyosai, Shofu. 1831-89. First political cartoonist in Japan; subject matter usually based on native folklore; also popular as a painter and illustrator; free, strong, simple, and direct style.

SCULPTURE

EUROPE · *France*

Rodin, Auguste (François Auguste René). 1840-1917. Great master of the late 19th, early 20th centuries; considered the father of modern sculpture; expressive realist; basic concern with everlasting sculptural relationships of volumes and voids; fluidity of movement, intensely dramatic; psychological depth and atmosphere surrounding forms provided originality of conception; studied with Barye; first exhibited at Paris Salon of 1877 where his *Le'âge d'airain* (The Bronze Age) raised a storm of criticism; also criticized were his great *Saint John the Baptist* and *Man Walking* (both 1877); *The Burghers of Calais* (1894-96), considered masterpiece; outstanding portraits of *Laurens* (1881), *Mirabeau* (1889-95), *Balzac* (1893, 1897), *Hugo* (1897), *Geffroy* (1905), *Becque* (1907), *Clemenceau* (1911); other

THE THINKER
BY RODIN

THE KISS
BY RODIN

THE DANCE BY CARPEAUX

well-known works include *The Think-er* (1880), *The Kiss* (1886), *Woman Crouching* (1882), *The Hand of God* (1898), *The Jugglers* (1909); many superb drawings; very influential.

Carpeaux, Jean Baptiste. 1827-75. Favorite of Second Empire period; studied in Paris and Rome; worked mainly in Valenciennes; *La Danse* (on façade of Paris Opera House); portrait busts of *Napoleon III, Dumas fils,* and others.

Rosso, Medardo. 1858-1928. Italian sculptor, lived in Paris (from 1889); first active as a painter; met Rodin (1884-85); influenced by him; *Lady with a Veil* (1896); *Sick Man at the Hospital* (1889); *Conversation in a Garden* (1893); subtle, rich plastic impressionist; worked in wax.

Others. Paul Bartholomé (1848-1928), Frederic Bartholdi (1834-1904), Emmanuel Fremiet (1824-1910), Jules Dalou (1838-1902), Paul Dubois (1829-1905), Leonard Morel-Ladeuil (1824-88), Henri Iselin (1826-1905), Jean Falguiere (1831-1900), Cyprien Godebski (1835-1909), Henri Chapu (1833-91).

Russia

Antokolski, Mark Matveevich. 1843-1902. Outstanding portrait studies of *Ivan the Terrible, Turgenev,* and others; lived in Paris (from 1880); represented in many museums.

Germany

Hildebrand, Adolf von. 1847-1921. Noted portrait sculptor; worked in Florence, Italy (1874-92); famed for *Brahms* monument; studies of *Clara Schumann, Ludwig of Bavaria,* others.

Begas, Rheinhold. 1831-1911. Monuments to *Schiller* and *Alexander von Humboldt;* portraits of *William I, Frederick III,* and *Bismarck; Pan Consoling a Deserted Nymph;* colossal groups.

NIKE EIRENE
BY SAINT-GAUDENS

AMERICAS · *United States*

Saint-Gaudens, Augustus. 1848-1907. Leading American sculptor of the period; born in Dublin, Ireland; studied in New York, Paris, and Rome; first recognized work, *Hiawatha* (1871); *Farragut* monument, Madison Square, New York (1880); statues of *Abraham Lincoln, General Sherman; The Puritan,* Springfield, Massachusetts; *Adams* Memorial, Rock Creek Cemetery, Washington; *Adoration of the Cross,* bas relief, St. Thomas' Church, New York; important influence.

ADMIRAL FARRAGUT,
SAINT-GAUDENS AND S. WHITE

French, Daniel Chester. 1850-1931. Famed for colossal *Statue of the Republic,* World's Columbia Exposition, Chicago (1893); bronze doors of the Boston Public Library; *The Minute Man* (modeled 1874); portraits of *John Hancock, Dr. Gallaudet and His First Deaf-mute Pupil* (1888), *Lewis Cass* (1887); influential.

EMERSON
BY FRENCH

Powers, Hiram. 1805-73. Worked in Washington (from 1835-37); portraits of *Jackson, Franklin, Jefferson* in Capitol; to Florence (1837-73); gained recognition with *Greek Slave* (1843);

Il Penerosa; *The Fisher Boy*; *America*; *California*; others.

Rimmer, William. 1816-79. Stonecutter, sculptor, painter; born in England; to the U.S. (1818); *Head of Saint Stephen* and *Falling Gladiator* (1861); *Dying Centaur* (*ca.* 1871); portrait of *Alexander Hamilton*; author of *Art Anatomy* (1877); taught at Museum of Fine Arts, Boston.

Potter, Edward Clark. 1857-1923. Worked with French; excellent studies of animals; noted for *Lions* in front of the New York Public Library.

ARCHITECTURE

AMERICAS · *United States*

Richardson, Henry Hobson. 1838-86. Leading innovator, architect; studied in Paris with Labrouste; won competition for the *Church of the Unity*, Springfield, Mass. (1866);

TRINITY CHURCH, BOSTON, BY RICHARDSON

Trinity Church, Boston (1872-77); *Austin Hall*, Harvard University (1883); *Library*, North Easton, Mass. (1881); *Marshall Field Wholesale Warehouse*, Chicago (1885-87), his outstanding building.

Burnham, Daniel Hudson. 1846-1912. Leading architect and city planner; member of the architectural firm of Burnham and Root (1873-91); helped rebuild Chicago after the fire of 1871; *Montauk Building* there considered first "skyscraper"; chief of construction, World's Columbian Exposition, Chicago (1890); served on the commission to improve Washington, D.C. (1901); designed the *Masonic Temple*, Chicago; *Union Station*, Washington; *Flatiron Building*, New York.

Post, George Browne. 1837-1913. Pioneer in the introduction of elevators, the use of iron floor beams, and steam heat in buildings; *Western Union Telegraph Building* (1873-75); *New York Produce, Cotton and Stock Exchange* (1905); *New York World* (Pulitzer) *Building* (1890); *St. Paul's* (1897-99), the tallest in New York at the time; *Wisconsin* and *Montreal State Capitols*.

Hunt, Richard Morris. Outstanding 19th-century architect; one of the first American students of architecture in Paris; *Lenox Library, Tribune Building*, main part of the *Metropolitan Museum of Art* (all in New York); *Fogg Art Museum*, Cambridge, Mass.; administration building for the World's Columbian Exposition, Chicago (1893); great mansions including *The Breakers* at Newport and William K. Vanderbilt's home, Fifth Avenue, New York.

McKim, Charles Follen. 1847-1909. Successful architect; studied in Paris; worked for H. H. Richardson; organized his own firm (McKim, Mead and White; W. R. Mead joined in 1877, and Stanford White in 1879); organized the American Academy in Rome (1901); buildings by his firm include: old *Madison Square Garden* (White), *Boston Public Library, Metropolitan Club,* N.Y.; group of buildings for *Columbia* and *New York Universities;* reconstruction of the *White House,* Washington, D.C.; *Battle Monument* at West Point; many private residences.

Olmsted, Frederick Law. 1822-1903. Leading landscape architect; superintendent of *Central Park* (1857); in association with Calvert Vaux, designed plans for building the park; also planned *Prospect Park* (Brooklyn), *South Park* (Chicago), grounds of the national Capitol, Washington, D.C.

Others. Bruce Price (1845-1903), John Wellborn Root (1850-91), Thomas Walter (1804-75), William Jenney (1832-1907), Paul Johannes Pelz (1841-1918), Russell Sturgis (1836-1909), George Lewis Heins (1860-1907), Frank Miles Day (1861-1918), Alexander J. Davis (1803-92).

Brazil

Araujo Porto-Alegre, Manuel de. 1806-79. Designed the church of *Sant 'Ana* and the *Bank of Brazil,* Rio de Janeiro.

EUROPE · *France*

Garnier, (Jean Louis) Charles. 1825-98. Leading Neo-Baroque architect; one of the earliest and best examples

OPÉRA, PARIS, GARNIER

of this style being his *Paris Opera House* (1861-74); also designed the *Nice Conservatory, Monte Carlo Casino;* author of several works on theater architecture.

Eiffel, Alexandre Gustave. 1832-1923. Engineer, bridge, and viaduct builder, authority on aerodynamics; designed the famous *Eiffel Tower* which is 984 feet high and was erected for the Paris Exposition of 1889.

EIFFEL TOWER, PARIS

Viollet Le Duc, Eugène Emmanuel. 1814-79. Leader in the Gothic revival in France; designed the restoration of many medieval buildings, including the cathedrals of *Notre Dame* (Paris), *Amiens, Laon;* restored the *Cité de Carcassone*, and several châteaus; wrote and illustrated several art books.

Bernard, Henri Jean Emile. b. 1844. Noted designer of churches; won first prize (1899) for design in international competition for plans for the *University of California.*

Others. Hector Lefuel (1810-81), Gabriel Davioud (1823-81).

Belgium

Poelaert, Joseph. 1817-79. Renowned architect who designed the *Palace of Justice*, Brussels (1866-83), largest building in modern Europe.

Netherlands

Cuypers, Petrus Josephus Hubertus. 1827-1921. Famed prize-winning designer of the *Rijksmuseum* (built 1877-85), Amsterdam; studied in Antwerp; restored the *Mainz Cathedral* (1872-75) and other medieval buildings.

Denmark

Hansen, Hans Christian. 1803-83. Leading Danish architect; built the *University of Athens*; navy yard at Trieste; municipal hospital, Copenhagen; brother **Theophilus** (1813-91) built the *Academy of Science* and astronomical observatory at Athens.

Germany

Semper, Gottfried. 1803-79. Noted for his design of the *Opera House* and synagogue in Dresden; imperial palace, museums, and theaters in Vienna.

Wallot, Paul. 1841-1912. Designed the *Reichstag Building* in Berlin.

Olbrich, Joseph Maria. 1867-1908. Leader of the Vienna Secession movement.

Hungary

Steindl, Emmerich von. 1839-1902. Designer of the parliament building, Budapest (1883-1902).

Czechoslovakia

Zitek, Josef. 1832-1909. Famed designer of the museum at Weimar; *National Theater* of Prague.

England

Scott, Sir George Gilbert. 1811-78. Led the Gothic revival in England; built or restored cathedrals, churches, schools, monuments, colleges, public buildings, and *St. Pancras Station.*

Shaw, Richard Norman. 1831-1912. Influential designer of *New Scotland Yard* on the Thames Embankment; stores and inn at Bedford Park Garden Suburb, Acton, London (1878).

Waterhouse, Alfred. 1830-1905. Gothic adherent; designed Manchester assize courts and town hall; *Girton College*; *Natural History Museum*; used terra cotta and one of the first to use structural ironwork; son **Paul** (1861-1924), town planner.

Barry, Edward Middleton. 1830-80. Son of Sir Charles; built *New Covent Garden Theater, Charing Cross Hotel,* and extensions to the *National Gallery.*

Bodley, George Frederick. 1827-1907. Noted for his designs of Gothic style cathedrals.

Others. John Bentley (1839-1902), Joseph Pearson (1817-97), George Street (1824-91).

MUSIC

EUROPE · *Germany*

Wagner, Richard. 1813-83. Great master composer of romantic opera or music drama; brilliant dramatic power, amazingly pure tonal effects; great gift for melody more evident in mature works; unusual mastery of orchestration; established the festival theater,

BRAHMS

WAGNER

synthesis of coldness of north Germany and the sensuous charm of Vienna; composed four symphonies; chamber music; concertos for piano, violin, cello; choral works, including the impressive *German Requiem*; *Academic Festival Overture*; many other works.

Strauss, Richard. 1864-1949. Master composer of symphonic or tone poems and opera (*see* next period, Vienna Opera, 1919-24); influenced by Wagner and Liszt; conductor, Munich Opera (1896); Berlin Opera (1898);

RICHARD
STRAUSS

Bayreuth (1872); famous operas include *Flying Dutchman* (1841), *Tannhauser* (1845), *Lohengrin* (1846-48), *The Ring* (1854-76), *Tristan and Isolde* (1857-59), *Die Meistersinger* (only comic opera, performed 1868); orchestral music, works for piano and choral groups; tremendous influence.

Brahms, Johannes. 1833-97. Leading composer; romantic neoclassicist; supreme master of German *lieder*; lived in Vienna (1863) and music reflects

highly imaginative, superb mastery of orchestral technique; tone poems include *Aus Italien* (1887), *Macbeth* (1887), *Don Juan* (1888), *Till Eulenspiegel* (1894), *Also sprach Zarathustra* (1895), *Ein Heldenleben* (1898); chamber music, works for piano, and orchestral music.

Others. Hans von Bülow (1830-94), Max Reger (1873-1916).

Austria

Mahler, Gustav. 1860-1911. Czech-Austrian composer, conductor; great master of the art of orchestration; very individual expression; composer of nine symphonies (second, *Resurrection,* 1894; fourth, *Ode to Heavenly Joy,* 1900; eighth, *Symphony of a Thousand,* 1907), with parts for voices, songs, and song-cycles; *Das Lied von der Erde* for solo voices and orchestra (1908), masterpiece; brilliant director of the Vienna Opera (1897); conductor, New York Philharmonic (1908).

MAHLER

Bruckner, Anton. 1824-96. Composer, organist; compositions romantic in style, and an unusual mixture of simplicity and Catholic mysticism; nine symphonies (last unfinished),

three Masses, a string quintet (1879); teacher of Mahler.

Wolf, Hugo. 1860-1903. Leading composer of over 300 *lieder*; admired Wagner; choral works, symphonic poem, string quartet, and opera.

Strauss, Johann, Jr. 1825-99. Viennese composer of famous waltzes, including *The Blue Danube* (1866), *Tales from the Vienna Woods* (1868); operettas, *Die Fledermaus* (The Bat, 1874) and *Der Zigeunerbaron* (The Gypsy Baron, 1885).

Russia

Tchaikovsky, Peter Ilyich. 1840-93. Extremely successful, popular composer of romantic symphonies, concertos, music for piano, violin, opera, and ballet; studied with Anton Rubinstein at St. Petersburg; best-known works include fantasy overture, *Romeo and Juliet* (1869); ballets, *Swan Lake* (1876) and *Sleeping Beauty* (1889); opera, *Eugene Onegin* (1879); *Nutcracker Suite* (1891).

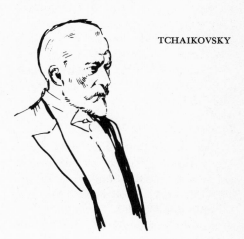

TCHAIKOVSKY

Moussorgsky, Modest Petrovich. 1839-81. Leading composer of the Nationalist school and of the "Five"; original, penetrating, direct style; gained fame with opera, *Boris Godunov* (based on Pushkin's drama, 1868-69; produced 1874); symphonic poem, *Night on Bald Mountain; Pictures from an Exhibition* (1874), popular work for piano; comic opera, the *Fair at Sorochinsk* (1874, completed by others); influenced 20th-century music.

Borodin, Alexander P. 1833-87. Composer of the Nationalist school; member of the "Five"; inspired by Russian folk songs; gained recognition for *In the steppes of Central Asia*; opera, *Prince Igor* (completed by Rimsky-Korsakov and Glazunov); string quartets, chamber music, and songs.

Rimsky-Korsakov, Nicolas Andreievich. 1844-1908. Famed composer of operas, including *The Snow Maiden* (1881) and *Le Coq d'Or* (The Golden Cockerel, 1907), *Scheherezade* (1888), for orchestra; *Spanish Capriccio*, remarkable *tour de force* of virtuoso orchestration (1887); teacher of Stravinsky; wrote *Principles of Orchestration*.

Others. Mily Balakirev (1837-1910), Alexander Glazunov (1865-1936), César Cui (1835-1918), Alexander Dargomijsky (1813-69), Nicolai Tcherepnin (1873-1945).

Czechoslovakia

Dvorak, Antonin. 1841-1904. Leading composer; second symphony considered an outstanding work of late 19th century; works include nine symphonies (*No. 2 in D minor* and *No. 5 in E minor, New World*, 1893), most famous; chamber music, solo songs; oratorio, *St. Ludmilla* (1886); operas, symphonic poems, etc.

DVORAK

Smetana, Bedrich (Friedrich). 1824-84. Creator of a national style; inspired by Czech songs; best-known operas, *The Bartered Bride* (1866) and *Dalibor* (1868), a great tragic work; symphonic cycle, *Ma vlast* (My Country), set of six musical landscapes.

Poland

Moniuszko, Stanislaw. 1819-72. Creator of Polish art song and national opera; studied in Germany; *Halka* (1847), first Polish opera on a national theme; 17 others, choral works, church music, symphonic poem, *Bajka* (The Fairy Tale).

France

Franck, César Auguste. 1822-90. Belgian-French composer, organist; interest in "pure music" changed the pattern of French instrumental music, reviving the polyphony that had been overlooked; harmonic modulations freer; influenced by Bach; many works include famed *Symphony in D minor* (1886-88), oratorios, operas, church music, symphonic poems, chamber music, works for organ, piano, and songs.

FRANCK

Liszt, Franz. 1811-86. Hungarian-French Romantic composer, virtuoso pianist; considered early exponent of the symphonic poem, *Les Preludes* (1856); freedom of construction, elaboration on motif creating a free form; acknowledged greatest pianist of his day; director, music court at Weimar (1848-61); 20 *Hungarian Rhapsodies* (1851-86), 12 symphonic poems, piano concertos; supported younger composers.

Gounod, Charles François. 1818-93. Opera composer; organist, choirmaster; works were uneven in quality, lacked dramatic vitality, but had appealing lyrical charm; 13 operas including the famed *Faust* (1859) and *Romeo and Juliet* (1867); oratorios, church music, cantatas, symphonies, and piano works.

Saint-Saëns, Charles Camille. 1835-1921. Neoclassicist; prolific composer, pianist, organist; "cyclic" design in symphonies, influenced by Liszt; chamber music has clarity of form; famous for opera, *Samson and Delilah*

(1877), symphonic poem, *Danse Macabre* (1874), and well-known *Third Symphony.*

Indy, Vincent d'. 1851-1931. Influential teacher; pupil of Franck; author of *Cours de composition musicale* (3 vols., 1897-1933) on teaching methods; *Symphony on a French Mountain Air* for piano and orchestra (1886); operas, symphonies, chamber music.

Bizet, Georges. 1838-75. Opera composer; most famous for *Carmen* (1875); revitalized the theater.

Fauré, Gabriel. 1845-1924. Outstanding writer of lyrical songs; masterpiece, *Requiem* (1887); notable teacher; *Pénélope* (1913), poetic originality.

Dukas, Paul. 1865-1935. Bridge between Franck and Debussy; *The Sorcerer's Apprentice* (1897).

Delibes, Léo. 1836-91. Noted composer of the opera, *Lakmé* (1883), and ballet, *Coppélia* (1870).

Lalo (Victor) Edouard. 1823-92. Individuality, skilled orchestration; *Symphonie espagnole* for violin and orchestra (1875); opera, ballet.

Offenbach, Jacques. 1819-80. Creator of French operetta; *La Vie Parisienne* (1866); *Tales of Hoffman* (1881), masterpiece.

Others. Jules Massenet (1842-1912), Emmanuel Chabrier (1841-94), Ambroise Thomas (1811-96).

Spain

Barbieri, Francisco. 1823-94. Composer of 80 comic operas (*zarzuelas*); best-known, *Pan y Toros* (1864, Madrid); edited an important collection of Spanish part songs of the 15th and 16th centuries.

Norway

Grieg, Edvard Hagerup. 1843-1907. Combined national idioms with German romanticism; use of dissonance unique; lyrical gift seen in small forms; *Piano Concerto in A Minor* (1868); *Peer Gynt* suites; chamber music, choral and piano works.

GRIEG

SCENE FROM *Rigoletto* BY VERDI

Italy

Verdi, Giuseppe. 1813-1901. Master composer of opera; passion, dramatic intensity, lyrical quality all combine in great operas including *Rigoletto* (1851), *Il Trovatore* and *La Traviata*

VERDI

(1853), *Aida* (1871); maturity of style and importance of orchestra evident in *Otello* (1887), *Falstaff* (1893); *Requiem* (1874); string quartet (1873).

Leoncavallo, Ruggiero. 1858-1919. Opera composer; *Pagliacci* (1892, Milan), most successful work; ballet, symphonic poems, and other operas.

Mascagni, Pietro. 1863-1945. Composer of famed one-act opera, *Cavalleria rusticana* (1889).

Finland

Sibelius, Jan. 1865-1957. Composer of seven symphonies, orchestral music, many tone poems, *En Saga* (1892), and the well-known *Finlandia* (1899); chamber music; works for the piano; important original force in contemporary music.

England

Sullivan, Sir Arthur. 1842-1900. Composer, organist, conductor; wrote music to lyrics by William Gilbert for *Trial by Jury* (1875), *Pirates of Penzance* (1879), *The Mikado* (1885); oratories; opera; *The Lost Chord*

(1878); hymn, *Onward Christian Soldiers* (1871).

Grove, Sir George. 1820-1900. Noted musicologist; *Dictionary of Music and Musicians* (1879-89), standard reference work.

Denmark

Gade, Niels Wilhelm. 1817-90. Most famous composer of his country; eight symphonies, six overtures, violin concerto, chamber music; influenced by Mendelssohn and Schumann; skilled instrumentation.

AMERICAS · Brazil

Gomes, Antonio Carlos. 1836-96. Composer; studied in Milan, Italy; influenced by Verdi; operas include *Il Guarany* (1870), *Maria Tudor* (1879), and *Lo Schiavo* (1889); cantatas, songs, piano pieces.

Argentina

Berutti, Arturo. 1862-1938. Known for operas *Pampa* (1897) and *Yupanqui* (1899), on an Incan theme, (Enrico Caruso sang tenor role); pieces for piano and violin.

United States

MacDowell, Edward Alexander. 1861-1908. Leading composer of programmatic piano sonatas; studied in Paris and Germany; head of the newly founded Department of Music, Columbia University (1896-1904); *Woodland Sketches* (1896); *Indian Suite* (1897); concertos.

Parker, Horatio William. 1863-1919. Noted composer of outstanding church music of the period; oratorios include *Hora Novissima* (1893); operas.

Foster, Stephen Collins. 1826-64. Sentimental writer of 200 popular songs; *Oh! Susanna* (1848), *Beautiful Dreamer* (1864); works might be called folk songs.

Others. Arthur Foote (1853-1937) and Louis Gottschalk (1829-69).

JAPANESE WOMAN PLAYING GEKKIN

THEATER

EUROPE · Norway

Ibsen, Henrik. 1828-1906. Great master dramatist of the period; important contribution in dramatic technique, use of penetrating characterization to present ethical and moral problems in realistic social dramas; name "Ibsenism" given to the establishment of human values as seen in the individual's struggle in a complex society; best-known works include *A Doll's House* (1879), *Ghosts* (1881), *An Enemy of the People* (1882), *Wild Duck* (1884), *Rosmersholm* (1886), *Hedda Gabler* (1890), *The Master Builder* (1892), *John Gabriel Bork-*

IBSEN

man (1896), and his last play, *When We Dead Awaken* (1899).

Bjornson, Bjornstjerne. 1832-1910. Lyric poet, teller of peasant tales, dramatist; first social-reform play, *A Bankruptcy* (1874), influenced Ibsen; dramatic trilogy, *Sigurd the Bastard* (1862); best historical work, *Mary Stuart of Scotland* (1864); *The Newly-Weds* (1865), first prose play on a contemporary theme in modern Norwegian drama; *The Editor* (1874), an attack on the evils of powerful and unscrupulous journalism; *Beyond Human Power*; his most popular play, *A Gauntlet* (1883).

Sweden

Strindberg, August. 1849-1912. Outstanding dramatist, novelist; influenced by Nietzsche; mystic; play of the subconscious, emphasis on subjectivity of art; *Master Olof* (1872), first masterpiece of the Swedish theater; works of realism started with *The Father* (1887); *Miss Julie* (1888), first naturalistic tragedy, and his most popular play; *Debit and Credit* (printed 1893); late historical plays, *Gustav Vasa* (1899) and *Queen Chris-*

tina (1903); developed new form of "dream play," *To Damascus* (Parts 1 and 2, 1898); *The Dream Play* (1902); *The Spook Sonata* (1907), surrealist theater.

Ahlgrennsson, August Frederick. 1838-1902. Leading stage designer; worked in Paris, Vienna; engaged by State Theater of Copenhagen and Stockholm.

Denmark

Gyllich, Svend Ludvig Valdemar. 1837-95. Important scenic designer; imaginative décor for ballet; use of illusion; realism adapted to plays.

Italy

Cossa, Pietro. 1830-81. Dramatic poet; considered the leading Italian dramatist of the transition from romanticism to naturalism; historical plays, *Monaldeschi* (1861), *Nerone* (1871), and *The Borgias* (1878).

Giacosa, Giuseppe. 1847-1906. Dramatic poet; wrote librettos for Puccini's operas *La Boheme, Tosca,* and *Madame Butterfly*; plays include *Il conte Rosso* (1880), *A Game of Chess* (1873), and *Sad Loves* (1888).

Russia

Chekhov, Anton Pavlovich. 1860-1904. Great writer of the 19th century; first play, *Ivanov* (1887); *The Sea Gull* (unsuccessfully produced, 1896); achieved fame when his works were performed at Stanislavsky's Moscow Art Theater; *Uncle Vanya* (1897); *The Three Sisters* (first performance, 1901); *Cherry Orchard* (first performance, 1904); excellent one-act plays include *The Bear, The Marriage Proposal* (1888), and *The Wedding* (1889).

CHEKHOV

Turgenev, Ivan Sergevich. 1818-83. Master novelist, short story writer, dramatist; greatest play, *A Month in the Country* (1850); influenced Chekhov; one-act plays include *The Lady from the Provinces, Poor Gentleman*, and *The Bachelor*.

TURGENEV

Ostrovski, Alexander Nikolaevich. 1823-86. One of the most important dramatists of his period, although not well-known outside Russia; influenced Chekhov, others; developed native realistic style; strong characterization emphasized rather than plot; 40 or 50 plays still produced; *Enough Stupidity*

in Every Wise Man (1868), considered masterpiece; best-known play, *The Storm* (1860); *Snow Maiden* (1873, used by Rimsky-Korsakov as libretto for his opera).

Tolstoi, Count Leo (Lev) Nikolayevich. 1828–1910. Great novelist; first play, *The First Distiller* (1886); *The Power of Darkness* (1889), tragic naturalistic drama; *The Fruits of Enlightenment* or *Culture* (1889), satire on the so-called cultured classes; *The Living Corpse* or *Redemption* (written 1900, produced 1911), tragedy of the upper classes; *And Light Shines in Darkness* (published 1911), autobiographical.

Goldfaden, Abraham. 1840-1908. Father of the modern Yiddish Theater; poet, composer; directed theater in Russia by the order of the Tsar (1883); *Aunt Sosie* (published 1896), considered his best play; light, comic touch; text and music for many operettas; best historical play, *Shulamith* (1880); musical dramas include *Dr. Almosado* (1882) and *Bar Kochba* (1883).

Tolstoi, Count Alexei Konstantinovich. 1817-75. Playwright, poet; historical dramas, *The Death of Ivan the Terrible* (1866), *Tsar Feodor Ivanovich* (1868), and *Tsar Boris* (1870); colorful, intense plays; successful productions at the Moscow Art Theater.

Pisemski, Alexei. 1820-81. Playwright, novelist; *Bitter Destiny* (1859), violent, gloomy drama in the tradition of Tolstoi and Gogol.

Krylov, Alexandrovich. 1838-1906. Wrote more than 100 plays, including many translations from the French; emphasis on social problems.

289

England

Wilde, Oscar. 1854-1900. Flamboyant, romantic dramatist, novelist, poet; extremely versatile; witty drawing-room comedies: *The Duchess of Padua* (1891), *Lady Windermere's Fan* (1892), *A Woman of No Importance* (1893), *An Ideal Husband* (1895), and *The Importance of Being Earnest* (1895, really a farce); sophisticated play, *Salome* (1893).

Gilbert, Sir William Schwenk. 1836-1911. Famed satirist; collaborated with Sir Arthur Sullivan in the writing of many brilliant, clever, and very popular light operas for the impresario Richard D'Oyly Carte (1844-1901) at the Savoy Theater: *Trial by Jury* (1875), *H.M.S. Pinafore* (1878), *Pirates of Penzance* (1879), *Iolanthe* (1882), *The Mikado* (1885), *Ruddigore* (1887), *The Yeomen of the Guard* (1888), and *Gondoliers* (1889).

Robertson, Thomas William (Tom). 1829-71. First English writer of successful realistic comedies; established reputation with *Society* (1865); *Caste* (1867), best-known work.

Pinero, Sir Arthur Wing. 1855-1934. Playwright; known for *The Second Mrs. Tanqueray* (1893) which attempted to shock the audience; wrote many so-called problem plays.

Spain

Echegaray y Elizaguirre, José. 1832-1916. Nobel Prize (1909) dramatist; often called the "Spanish Ibsen" (although he never knew Ibsen's work), because he dealt with social problems and the struggle between the individual and a hostile society; *El gran Galeoto* (1881, translated into English as *The World and His Wife*), anticipates the form used by Pirandello; *Lunatic or Saint* (1877), most popular play in Spain; important influence.

Tamayo y Baus, Manuel. 1829-98. Popular dramatist; attempted to re-establish strong national theater in Spain; *Madness of Love* (Love's Fool, 1855) and *A New Play* (1867), most interesting works.

Hungary

Szigligeti, Ede. 1814-78. Writer of plays based on Hungarian folk life; *The Pretender* (1867), tragic drama set in the 13th century; *The Deserter* (1845), a comedy-drama; *The Foundling* (1863).

Poland

Wyspiánski, Stanislaw. 1869-1907. Outstanding playwright; used folk material; *The Wedding* (presented in Cracow, 1901), unique achievement; designed sets.

Kalewski, Kazimierz. 1849-1918. Dramatist; plays concerned with misdirected affection; domestic dramas of realist school: *Without a Dowry* (1869), *Ours on Top* (1883), and *The Apfel Marriage* (1887).

Austria

Anzengruber, Ludwig. 1839-89. Dramatist; attempted to develop the use of more realistic dialogue in popular, fairly melodramatic plays; *The Fourth Commandment* (1871), best-known work; *The Worm of Conscience* (1874) used sardonic humor.

Germany

Hauptmann, Gerhart. 1862-1946. Master poet, dramatist; naturalism; individual style; emphasis on social problems; atmospheric, descriptive stage directions; *Before Sunrise* (1889), first play, created a sensation; *The Weavers* (1892), romantic, unique in concept and technique; first introduction of the lower classes to the German stage; *The Sunken Bell* (1897), symbolic allegory of artist's struggle, most popular play; important influence.

HAUPTMANN

Hebbel, (Christian) Friedrich. 1813-63. Dramatic poet; considered most powerful tragic dramatist of the period; links last of Romanticism to Realism; *Judith* (1841); *Maria Magdalena* (1844); *Agnes Bernauer* (1855); *Gyges and his Ring* (1855, performed 1898), most poetic; trilogy in which the story of *Die Nibelungen* (1862) is a part is recognized as his outstanding work.

Wedekind, Frank. 1864-1918. Forerunner of the expressionists; moves from naturalism to symbolic abstractions (similar to Strindberg); *The World of Youth* (1890), frank, bold; *Spring's Awakening* (1891), strangely beautiful; *Earth Spirit* (1895); *The Dance of Death* (1906), violent; propagandist against the hypocrisy of sex.

Sudermann, Hermann. 1857-1928. Dramatist, novelist; influenced by Ibsen, Nietzsche; first play, *Honor* (1889), won fame; *The Destruction of Sodom* (1891); *Home* (usually played as *Magda*, 1893), most successful.

Hirschfeld, Georg. 1873-1935. Experimental dramatist; *The Mothers* (1896), first play with conflict between father and son as theme; *Agnes Jordan* (1898); disciple of Hauptmann.

Halbe, Max. 1865-1944. Dramatist; *Youth* (1893), first real success; many other works.

France

Dumas, Alexandre (*fils*). 1824-95. Popular dramatist, novelist; *Le demi-monde* (1855) established modern comedy of manners; most famous work, *La dame aux camelias* (Camille, 1852); *A Question of Money* (1857); *The Illegitimate Son* (1858), modern thesis-play; influential.

Rostand, Edmond. 1868-1918. Poet, dramatist; *Cyrano de Bergerac* (1897), classic work.

Sardou, Victorien. 1831-1908. Dramatist; excellent comedies of intrigue, historical plays, include *A Scrap of Paper* (1860), *The Fatherland* (1869); *La Tosca* (1887), considered his best play; *Madame Sans-Gene* (1893, written with Moreau).

Augier, Émile. 1820-89. Dramatist, satirist; pioneer in modern realism, presenting social problems from an ethical and moral point of view; *The Adventuress* (1848); *Gabrielle* (1849); *The Son-in-law of M. Poirier* (1854, from Jules Sandeau's novel, *Sacs et parchemins*), minor masterpiece; *Olympia's Marriage* (1855); others.

Zola, Émile. 1840-1902. Novelist, dramatist; naturalism, objectivity; ideas more important than dramatic technique; *Thérèse Raquin* (1873).

Antoine, André Leonard. 1858-1943. Theatrical manager; formed *Théâtre Libre,* France's first naturalistic theater (to 1894); formed *Théâtre Antoine* (1897-1906), served as the model for experimental theaters in Europe and America.

Becque, Henry. 1837-99. Called the "Flaubert of the theater"; powerful, gloomy atmosphere in *The Vultures* (1882), keen satire, ancestor of the modern triangle comedy; *The Woman of Paris* (1885).

Hervieu, Paul. 1857-1915. Dramatist of "problem bourgeois tragedies"; *Words Remain* (1892); *The Pincers* (1895), first real success; *The Passing of the Torch* (1901).

SARAH BERNHARDT,
FRENCH ACTRESS

Porto-Riche, Georges de. 1849-1930. Dramatist; theme of eternal triangle; subtle, skilful characterization; *The Luck of Françoise* (1889); *A Loving Wife* (1891), delicate play of words.

Brieux, Eugene. 1858-1932. Dramatist of "idea" plays with social significance: *Blanchette* (1892), *The Philanthropists* (1896), *The Three Daughters of Mr. Dupont* (1897); *Damaged Goods* (1902), best-known play, discusses the taboo subject of venereal disease.

Donnay, Maurice. 1859-1945. Dramatist; concentrated on the theme of love; *Lovers* (1896), popular.

AMERICAS · *United States*

Aiken, George L. 1830-76. Playwright, actor; dramatization of Harriet Beecher Stowe's novel, *Uncle Tom's Cabin* (1852), which had an unprecedented run of 200 performances.

Boker, George Henry. 1824-90. Dramatist; *Francesca da Rimini* (1855), tragedy; *Anne Boleyn* (1850); *Widow's Marriage* and *Poems of War* (1864).

ASIA · *Japan*

Mokuami, Kawatake. 1816-93. Leading Kabuki playwright of at least 50 *sewamono* (lives of the common people) plays; extremely versatile in variety of plot and characterization.

Tsubouchi Shoyo. 1859-1935. Outstanding dramatist; introduced realism into the Kabuki theater; attempted to create a new school of historical playwrighting; important in presentation of Western masterpieces in Japan.

Shimpa or "New School." In the 1890's an important theatrical group presented contemporary events and dramatized versions of popular novels in dramatic form.

India

Ghosh, Girish Chandra. 1844-1911.

Bengali dramatist; produced more than 90 plays; best-known works: *Bilwamangal, Sirajaddaula, Aśoka*.

Vasu, Amritalal (Bose or Basu). 1853-1929. Popular actor-dramatist; writer of popular comedies.

1900-TODAY

The tremendous advances made in science and technology in the 20th century have been reflected in the many changes in experimental style made by the artists in a constant search for a new visual language. Cubism developed into geometric abstraction, nonobjective painting, and constructivist sculpture. An increased interest in Freud, psychology, symbolism, and the subconscious produced many new schools, styles, and interpretations.

Artists revolted against the space age, automation, and the dehumanization of the individual, as well as against the inhumanity of man to man and against the commercialism of an "other directed" society. In general the artist of this century has attempted to interpret experience, emotional response, and mood rather than to portray reality, and in so doing, to regain a true sense of identity, a new individualism.

With the remarkable new means of communication, artists of the world, in all the arts, tend to express universal rather than regional concerns, and there is an increasing awareness of and response to new expressions of creativity in many parts of the world.

PAINTING

EUROPE · *France*

Picasso, Pablo. 1881- . Great Spanish master of 20th-century art; worked in Paris; influenced in early work by Cézanne and Toulouse-Lautrec; "blue-period" (1903); "rose period" (1905); meeting with Matisse, Braque, Kahnweiler (1906); interest in design, form, texture rather than objects; *Les Demoiselles d'Avignon* (1909); leader (with Braque and Gris), analytical cubism (1907-17); interest in collage and synthetic cubism (1912); works for Diaghilev's ballet (1917); "neoclassical period" (1920); *Woman in White* (1923); interest in surrealism (1925-27); abstract-sculptural-form "bone" pictures; stained glass still-life studies in brilliant color; series of "simultaneously clothed, nude, and X-rayed" works, *Girl Before a Mirror* (1932); etchings, *Minotauromachy* (1935); antiwar protest, *Guernica* (1937); double-faced portraits, simultaneous vision (1938-44); sculpture, *Man with Sheep* (1940's); pottery works (1946, Vallauris); graphics (1947-50); extremely influential.

Braque, Georges. 1882-1963. Master modern artist; restrained color; intellectual approach; cubist (*see* Picasso); leading exponent of collage, primarily still-life subjects; illustrations for Hesiod's *Theogony* (1932); sculpture (1939); Grand Prize, Venice Biennale (1949); decorated ceiling in Salle Henry II (1953, Louvre); late works: poetic studies, birds, sea.

Matisse, Henri. 1869-1954. Leading expressionist; famous for drawings and lithography; master of the nude; highly decorative, flat surface technique; brilliant color; leader of the Fauves (1905); "odalisques" (1920-25).

Léger, Fernand. 1881-1955. Noted cubist; famed for machinelike forms; *Le Grand Déjeuner* (1921), considered masterpiece; large work for the United Nations; mosaic for façade of the church at Assy (1946).

Modigliani, Amedeo. 1884-1920. Italian artist, worked in Paris; sensitivity; master of line; unique style; sculpture influenced by cubism and African art; noted for nudes, portraits.

Rouault, Georges. 1871-1958. Expressionist; vivid use of color outlined in black; primarily religious subjects, flowers, and clowns; graphic series, *Miserere* (1914-27); popular.

Gris, Juan (José Victoriano Gonzalez). 1887-1927. Spanish cubist working in Paris; studied in Spain; important friendship with Picasso (1906); first showed at Independents and Section d'Or (1912); primarily cubist still-life studies and portraits.

Duchamp, Marcel. 1887- . Dadaist; member of Section d'Or; famous for painting *Nude Descending a Staircase* (1912) that created a sensation at the Armory Show (1913, New York), considered a "blueprint of movement" by the artist; influenced Italian futurists; first mobiles, "ready-mades", *The Fountain* (1917); produced extra-

ODALISQUE WITH MAGNOLIAS
BY MATISSE

WOMAN IN WHITE
BY PICASSO, 1923

THE TABLE
BY BRAQUE, 1928

SEATED WOMAN
BY PICASSO, 1926-27

PICASSO

THREE WOMEN (DETAIL)
BY LÉGER, 1921

ANNA DE ZBOROWSKA
BY MODIGLIANI, 1917

CHRIST MOCKED BY SOLDIERS,
ROUAULT

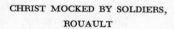

TIME IS A RIVER WITHOUT BANKS,
CHAGALL

ordinary film, *Anemic Cinema;* rotore-
liefs (1930); to United States (1941).

Chagall, Marc. 1887- . Russian expressionist; worked in Paris and the
United States; noted illustrator, Gogol's
Dead Souls, La Fontaine's *Fables*
(1927-1930); use of brilliant color;
strong element of autobiographical
fantasy, closely connected with folk
art; décor for Stravinsky's *Firebird
Ballet* (1946); stained glass windows
for Jerusalem (1961-62).

Villon, Jacques (Gaston Duchamp).
1875-1963. Leader of Section d'Or
(1911-12); associated with cubism;
turned to abstraction; showed at first
Salon des Réalitiés Nouvelle (1939);
winner, Carnegie Award (1950); sensitive, intellectual approach to art.

Vlaminck, Maurice de. 1876-1958.
Fauvist; self-taught; shared studio in
Paris with Derain.

Derain, André. 1880-1954. Fauvist;
"Gothic period" (1912); sets for Ballet
Russe (1919); graphics.

Soutine, Chaim. 1894-1943. Russian
artist, worked in Paris (1913); expressionist; brilliant color; portraits.

Ernst, Max. 1891- . Dadaist sculpture; co-founder of Surrealist Movement (1922); *La Belle Jardiniere,
Children Frightened by a Nightingale*
(1922, Dusseldorf); "ready-mades."

Delaunay, Robert. 1885-1941. Neoimpressionist (1905); cubist (1909);
worked with Kandinsky; Orphic Cubism (1912); abstract "Formes Circu-
lairs" (1913); reliefs (1930); influential.

Masson, André. 1896- . Associated with the surrealists (1925-29);
exhibited with Miró (1933).

Picabia, Francis. 1878-1953. Cubist
(1909); helped found Section d'Or

(1911-12); associated with Dadaists
and surrealists (from 1924).

Dufy, Raoul. 1877-1953. Decorative,
colorful, light scenes of Paris; tapestries (1921); popular.

Others. Marcel Gromaire (1892-),
Marie Laurencin (1885-1956), Albert
Gleizes (1881-1953), Léon Gischia
(1903-), Amédée Ozenfant (1886-),
Othon Friesz (1879-1949), Roger
de la Fresnaye (1885-1925), Maurice
Utrillo (1883-1955), André Lanskoy
(1902-), André Lhote (1885-),
Jean Lurçat (1892-), René Magritte
(1898-), Felix Del Marle (1889-
1952), Albert Marquet (1875-1947),
Jean Metzinger (1883-), Pierre Roy
(1880-), André Dunoyer de Segon-
zac (1884-), Paul Serusier (1864-
1927), Yves Tanguy (1900-1955),
Felix Vallotton (1865-1925), Louis
Marcoussis (1883-1941), Franz Kupka
(1871-1957), Camille Bombois (1883-),
Tsugouharau Foujita (1886-).

Germany

Kandinsky, Wassily (Vasili). 1866-
1944. Great pioneer abstract artist;
Russian, worked in Germany and
Paris; with Klee, initiated German expressionism; outstanding figure at the

IMPROVISATION, KANDINSKY, 1914

Bauhaus, Dessau; introduced the notion that art should reflect the abstract quality of absolute music; emphasis on pure line and color rather than form; painted numbered, untitled *Improvisations, Compositions*; author of very influential work, *The Art of Spiritual Harmony* (1910).

Klee, Paul. 1879-1940. Important Swiss nonrepresentational artist; abstract expression of nature, human values; subtle color; stressed importance of creating with the "innocent eye" of a child; worked with Kandinsky at Bauhaus; showed at first surrealist exhibit, Paris (1925); exceptional pen-and-ink drawings and water colors.

TWITTERING MACHINE,
WATER COLOR, PEN AND INK BY KLEE

Moholy-Nagy, László. 1895-1946. Hungarian artist, designer; great teacher at Bauhaus, Weiman, and Dessau (1923-28) and Chicago Institute of Design (from 1929); invented "light modulator," play of light and shadow over moving shapes of metal and plastic; important influence.

Nolde, Emil (Hansen). 1867-1956. Expressionist; leader of *Die Brücke* (The Bridge) group (1906-8); member of the *Der Blaue Reiter* (1912).

Kirchner, Ernest Ludwig. 1880-1938. Co-founder of *Die Brücke*; beginning of abstract period (1926); excellent graphics; brilliant, sensitive.

Macke, August. 1887-1914. Member of *Der Blaue Reiter* group (1911); expressionist; influenced by Kandinsky and cubism; individual style.

Beckmann, Max. 1884-1950. Expressionist; member of Berlin secession group; symbolism strong; important work, triptych, *The Departure* (1932-35).

Grosz, George. 1893-1959. Brilliant satirist; famous for pen-and-ink drawings in postwar Germany; antiwar paintings in Bosch tradition; delicate studies of nature; superb draftsman.

Others. Franz Marc (1880-1916), Willi Baumeister (1889-1955), Heinrich Campendonk (1889-1957), Otto Müller (1874-1930), Erich Heckel (1883-), Otto Dix (1891-), Kurt Schwitters (1887-1948), Hans Richter (1888-), Johannes Itten (1888-), Carl Hofer (1878-1955), Adolf Hoelzel (1853-1934), Paula Modersohn-Becker (1876-1907), Karl Schmidt-Rottluff (1884-), Sophie Tauber-Arp (1889-1943).

Netherlands

Mondrian, Piet. 1872-1944. Master of geometrical abstraction movement known as Neoplasticism; leader, with Van Doesburg, of *De Stijl* (Style) group (1917); influenced Bauhaus artists; published influential articles on

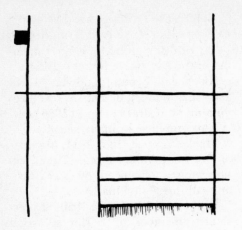

COMPOSITION IN WHITE, BLACK AND RED
BY MONDRIAN, 1936

theories (1920); also worked in Paris, London, and New York.

Doesburg, Theo van (C. E. M. Kupper). 1883-1931. Leading member of *De Stijl* (1917); founded magazine with Mondrian on subject of Neoplasticism; participated in Dada movement in Holland (1922); beginning of Elementarism (1924); collaborated with Arp (1926-28); published *Art concret* (1930).

Domela, César. 1900- . Abstract paintings first shown in Berlin (November Group, 1923); relief-like decorative montages in various materials (1928); worked with Abstraction-Crèation group, Paris (from 1933).

Leck, Bart van der. 1876- . Cofounder of *De Stijl* movement (1917); broke with group (1919); flat, powerful, geometrical, figurative compositions in three primary colors.

Norway

Munch, Edvard. 1863-1944. Leading early expressionist; created sensation with exhibition in Berlin (1892); brilliant graphics.

Russia

Malevich, Casimir. 1878-1935. Founder of Suprematism (1913); cubist (1910-13); met Kandinsky at Bauhaus (1926); important influence as a teacher.

Jawlensky, Alexej von. 1864-1941. Expressionist; studied in Munich; group of paintings with "mystical faces" (1917); joined *Die Blauen Vier* group, (1924, Kandinsky); small, "abstract heads" (1934).

Goncharova, Natalya. 1881- . With husband, **Larionov,** founded Rayonism (1912-13); sets for the theater and ballet.

Tatlin, Vladimir. 1885- . First relief constructions (1913); important teacher.

Lissitsky, El (Lasar Markovitch). 1890-1947. Constructivist; worked in Germany with Doesburg and Miës van der Rohe (1922-23); influenced Moholy-Nagy and others.

Italy

Chirico, Giorgio de. 1888- . Surrealist painter; in Paris (1911-15); founded *Pittura Metafisica* with Carrà (1917); moved to Paris (1924), worked with surrealists; dream fantasies, expressionism of time, space, and solitude.

Boccioni, Umberto. 1882-1916. Futurist; worked with Balla, Severini, Marinetti (1909); met Apollinaire and cubists in Paris (1911); published *Technical Manifesto of Futurist Sculp-*

ture (1912); exhibited at Futurist shows; died in the war.

Severini, Gino. 1883- . Cubist, neoclassicist; to Paris (1906); associated with Modigliani, Jacob, and Braque; signed *Futurist Manifesto* (1910); influenced by Picasso and *Valori Plastici*; winner Biennale prize (1950).

Carrà, Carlo. 1881- . Influential teacher, Milan; futurist, cubist periods; with de Chirico, *Pittura Metafisica*; developed archaic realism based on Masaccio; helped young artists.

Balla, Giacomo. 1871-1958. One of the founders of futurism (1910); influential.

LEASH IN MOTION BY BALLA, 1912

Sironi, Mario. 1885- . Founder, member of *Novecento*; influenced by Léger and *Pittura Metafisica* group; large frescoes for Milan Triennale.

Soldati, Atanasio. 1896-1953. Developed abstract, strictly geometrical style (1930-35); founder, member of *Movimento Arte Concreta*.

Others. Luigi Russolo (1885-1947), Felice Casorati (1886-), Giuseppe Santomaso (1907-), Enrico Prampolini (1894-1956), Mario Radice (1900-), Mauro Reggiani (1897-),

Ottone Rosai (1895-1957), Scipione (1904-33), Luigi Spazzapan (1890-).

Austria

Kokoshchka, Oscar. 1886- . Expressionist; taught at Dresden Academy (1920-24); popular.

Belgium

Ensor, James. 1860-1949. Forerunner of expressionism; one of the founders of experimental *Group des XX* (1883); famous for use of masks and masked figures; influential.

Spain

Miró, Joán. 1893- . Although he has worked in Paris, strong Catalan heritage apparent in his works; showed at first surrealist exhibition (1925); worked with Max Ernst; influenced by Klee; mural for Spanish pavilion at Paris World's Fair (1937); highly individual symbolic "ideogrammatic" style combining surrealism and linear abstraction in such works as *Person Throwing a Stone at a Bird* (1926), and *Dutch Interior* (1928).

PERSON THROWING A STONE AT A BIRD, MIRO, 1926

Dali, Salvador. 1904- . Successful surrealist painter; studied in Madrid; to Paris (1928); joined surrealist movement (1929); influenced by Freud; called his own work "paranoiac painting"; *The Persistence of Memory* (1931) and *The Enigma of William Tell* (1934), best-known works of the period; technique of "Dutch masters" combined with dreamlike (often double) images; barren landscapes; religious subjects.

PERSISTENCE OF MEMORY BY DALI, 1931

England

Nash, Paul. 1889-1946. Founding member of "Unit I" (1933); showed with the surrealists; intellectual painter; metaphorical approach.

Spencer, Stanley. 1891-1959. Visionary; showed with post-impressionists (1912); dry, primitive realism.

Lewis, P. Wyndham. 1882-1957. Founded Vorticist group (1914); influenced by poets Pound, Eliot, and Joyce; founded "Group X" (1920); important as an influence on young artists.

Wadsworth, Edward. 1889-1949.

Member of Vorticist group (1914-15); influenced by Kandinsky; member of "Unit 1."

Others. C. R. W. Nevinson (1889-1946), David Bomberg (1890-1957), William Roberts (1895-).

AMERICAS · *Mexico*

Rivera, Diego. 1886-1957. Pioneer of monumental art of new Mexican School; brilliant murals of historical and social importance; use of peasants, laborers; portrayal of war, poverty.

Orozco, José Clemente. 1883-1949. Powerful, dramatic muralist; political and social themes; murals in the United States (1930-34).

Siqueiros, David. 1898- . Social realism with elements of surrealism; founder of magazine, *Machete*; social protest; technical innovator in use of pyroxylin paints on masonite; influential.

Posada, José Guadalupe. 1851-1913. Important leader of first independent movement in Mexican art of social and political protest; 15,000 engravings used as illustrations by the opposition newspapers during dictatorship of Porfirio Díaz; vigorous, passionate technique expressing sorrows, aspirations, and joy of Mexican people.

Others. Carlos Merida (1893-), Julio Castellanos (1905-), Miguel Covarrubias (1904-1962), Jesus Guerrero Galvan (1910-), Maria Izquierdo (1906-), Fernando Leal (1900-).

Chile

Matta (Roberto Sebastian Matta Echaurren). 1912- . Studied and worked in Paris; joined surrealist

20TH CENTURY—LATIN-AMERICAN PAINTING

MURAL (DETAIL)
PRADO HOTEL, MEXICO CITY,
BY RIVERA

AGRARIAN LEADER ZAPATA
BY RIVERA, 1931

REVOLUTION BY OROZCO

ECHO OF A SCREAM BY SIQUEIROS, 1937

group (1937); began to paint demonic fantasies (1945); mythical metaphorical vision of reality.

United States

Weber, Max. 1881-1962. Leading expressionist; worked in Paris, influenced by Cézanne, Matisse; subtle, sensitive color; complex composition, various styles; belonged to "291" group in New York (from 1910); retrospective show at Museum of Modern Art (1930) and Whitney Museum (1949) in New York.

THE GERANIUM BY WEBER, 1911

Marin, John. 1870-1953. Noted for semi-abstract water colors; seascapes, Manhattan skyline, and scenes of Maine.

Feininger, Lyonel. 1871-1956. German-American; master at Bauhaus, Weimar, Dessau (1919-33); co-founder of *Die Blauen Vier* group (1924); cool, semi-abstract studies.

Davis, Stuart. 1894-1964. Early non-objective painter (1919); Paris (1928-29); influenced by cubism; well-known teacher; use of brilliant color; works

have a poster quality and show interest in jazz, calligraphy.

Shahn, Ben. 1898- . Expressionist; flat color; interest in social and religious themes.

Prendergast, Maurice Brazil. 1859-1924. Impressionist; influenced by Cézanne, Seurat, and French school; member of "The Eight" or Ashcan School; work shown in Armory Show of 1913; landscapes and beach scenes in short strokes of broken, pure color: *May Day, Central Park, Boston Street Scene, Landscape with Figures,* and many others.

Bellows, George Wesley. 1882-1925. Leading member of Ashcan School; intense interest in motion, strength, as seen in *Dempsey Through the Ropes*; excellent lithographer, illustrator; an organizer of the Armory Show of 1913.

Henri, Robert. 1865-1929. Leader of "The Eight"; important teacher; emphasized importance of the artist expressing his own personality and not relying on technique alone; *A Dutch Girl in White.*

BACKYARDS, GREENWICH VILLAGE, BY SLOAN, 1914

Sloan, John. 1871-1951. Leader of Ashcan School; reportorial approach; famed *McSorley's Bar, The City from Greenwich Village, Six O'Clock, Wake of the Ferry*; later works glazed, striped nudes.

Glackens, William. 1870-1938. Leading colorist of "The Eight"; landscape, genre painter; influence of Renoir; *The Promenade; Chez Mouquin.*

Luks, George Benjamin. 1867-1933. Portrait, genre painter; member of "The Eight"; *Otis Skinner, White Clowns,* among best-known works.

Davis, Arthur B. 1862-1928. Painter, lithographer; largely responsible for famous Armory Show of 1913 that introduced modern art to the United States.

Shinn, Everett. 1876-1953. Member of "The Eight"; love of theater seen in *London Hippodrome* and *London Music Hall.*

Lawson, Ernest. 1873-1929. Excellent landscape artist; influenced by French Impressionists; *Harlem River at High Bridge*; scenes of New York.

Others. Stanton MacDonald-Wright (1890-), Morgan Russell (1886-1953), Charles Sheeler (1883-), George Bellows (1882-1925), Marsden Hartley (1878-1943), Joseph Stella (1877-1946), Yasuo Kuniyoshi (1893-1953), Charles Burchfield (1893-), Thomas Hart Benton (1889-), Edward Hopper (1882-), Alfred Maurer 1868-1932), Niles Spencer (1893-1952), Georgia O'Keefe (1887-), Man Ray (1890-), John S. Curry (1897-1946), Abraham Walkowitz (1880-), Fritz Glarner (1899-), Arthur Dove (1880-1964), Grant Wood (1891-1942), Louis Guglielmi (1906-).

ASIA · *Japan*

Takeuchi Seiho. 1864-1942. Attempted to introduce modern techniques to Japanese painting; excellent *sumi-e*; used fresh sense of color along with light, delicate line.

Yamamoto Kanae. 1882-1946. Pioneer in new movement of creative printmakers; worked in Europe; with Hakutei Ishii and others published magazine *Hosun* (1907); organizer of the *hanga* artists.

Onchi, Koshiro. 1891-1955. Leading abstract printmaker; influenced by Kandinsky, Munch; poet; subtle, witty, daring; magnificent technique.

Sekino, Jun'ichiro. 1914- . Printmaker; designer, illustrator; excellent portraits.

China

Hüang, P'ing-hung. 1864-1955. One of the most famous painters of the period; from the province of Anhwei; professor Pei-p'ing Academy of Art (1937-48); master landscape artist; *Landscape with Small Bridge; Landscape in Neighborhood of Peking* (1942).

Ch'i, Pai-shih. 1861-1957. Master painter; highly individual although most works in tradition of the Ming painters; represented in several museum collections.

Hsü, Pei-hung. 1895-1953. Studied in Paris; professor Academy in Nanking; influenced young artists; water-color drawings of horses very popular; organized exhibitions in Europe.

Chang, Su-chi, Dr. 1898-1957. Noted for delicate paintings of birds and flowers; to United States (1949).

India

Roy, Jamini. 1887- . Leading modern west Bengali painter; studied in Calcutta; *Santal Girl* (*ca.* 1930), period of interest in Santal subjects (similar to Picasso's interest in primitive art); Byzantine, Christ period (1937-40); individual style combines Indian past with Picasso; popular.

Tagore, Rabindranath. 1861-1941. Famed poet; painted late in life; influenced by Klee, Munch, and Picasso; best work (1928-30); influential.

Tagore, Abanindranath. 1871- . Learned Western techniques at Calcutta School of Art; influenced by Mughal miniatures and Japanese; attempted to create a national style; lack of emotional power.

Others. Amrita Sher-Gil (1913-37), Ravi Varma (d. 1905), Gogonendranath Tagore.

Ceylon

Keyt, George. 1901- . Combines Dutch and Indian backgrounds; pictures of Sinhalese people; dramatic, strange, expressive grandeur; primarily interested in poetic love.

NO. 34, POLLOCK, 1949

GARDEN IN SOCHI BY GORKY, 1941

1945–Today · United States

Jackson Pollock (1912-56), Arshile Gorky (1904-48), Morris Graves (1910-), Hans Hofmann (1880-), Willem de Kooning (1904-), Leonard Baskin (1922-), William Baziotes (1912-63), James Brooks (1906-), Richard Diebenkorn (1922-), Sam Francis (1923-), Leon Golub (1922-), Adolph Gottlieb (1903-), Balcomb Greene (1904-), Philip Guston (1913-), Grace Hartigan (1922-), Franz Kline (1910-62), Wilfredo Lam (1902-), Rico Lebrun (1900-1964), Robert Motherwell (1915-), Jan Muller (1922-58), Barnett Newman (1905-), I. Rice Pereira (1907-), Mark Rothko (1903-), Clyfford Still (1904-), Mark Tobey (1890-), Bradley Walker Tomlin (1899-1953).

Europe

France: Jean Bazaine (1904-), Bernard Buffet (1928-), Nicholas

De Stael (1914-55), Jean Dubuffet (1901-), Jean Fautrier (1898-), Hans Hartung (1904-), Bernard Lorjou (1908-), Georges Mathieu (1921-), Edouard Pignon (1905-), Serge Poliakoff (1906-), Pierre Soulages (1919-), Pierre Tal Coat (1905-), Victor de Vasarely (1908-), Marie-Helene Vieira Da Silva (1908-).

Italy: Afro (Basaldella, 1912-), Alberto Burri (1915-), Massimo Campigli (1895-), Antonio Corpora (1909-), Lucio Fontana (1899-), Renato Guttuso (1912-), Osvaldo Licini (1894-1958), Alberto Magnelli (1888-), Giorgio Morandi (1890-), Armando Pizzinato (1910-), Emilio Vedova (1919-), Giuseppe Zigaina (1924-).

Great Britain: Francis Bacon (1910-), Alan Davie (1920-), Duncan Grant (1885-), Peter Lanyon (1918-), Ben Nicholson (1894-), Victor Passmore (1908-), John Piper (1903-), William Scott (1913-), Graham Sutherland (1903-), Bryan Wynter (1915-).

Germany: Fred Theiler (1916-), Theodor Werner (1886-), Fritz Winter (1905-), Wolfgang Schulze, known as Wols (1913-51).

Others

Netherlands: Corneille (Cornelis van Beverloo, 1922-), Karel Appel (1921-).

Denmark: Asger Jorn (1914-), K. Sonderborg (1923-).

Canada: Jean-Paul Riopelle (1924-).

Spain: Antonio Tapies (1923-), Manolo Millarès (1926-).

Australia: Sidney Nolan (1917-).

Sweden: Endre Nemes (1909-).

Austria: Fritz Hundertwasser (1928-), Carl Unger (1915-), Karl A. Wolf (1908-).

SCULPTURE

EUROPE · *France*

Maillol, Aristide. 1861-1944. Leading exponent of return to classical antiquity and emphasis on female form; first one-man show (1902); exceptional collection of works at Museum of Modern Art (New York) includes *Mediterranean* (*ca.* 1901), *Young Cyclist,* and plaster relief, *Desire* (*ca.* 1904); *Chained Action* (*ca.* 1906); *Ile de France* (1910); *Seated Figure* (*ca.* 1930); *The River* (*ca.* 1939-43).

Brancusi, Constantin. 1876-1957. Leading pioneer in use of abstract forms (organic abstraction); influenced by primitive art, principally in wood carvings; born in Rumania; to Paris (1904); *The Kiss* (1908); *The Prodigal Son* (1914); *Mlle Pogany* (1920, polished brass; and *ca.* 1928-29, marble); *Bird in Space* (1919); *The New Born* (1915); *The Fish* (1930); *Adam and Eve* (1925); extremely influential.

Pevsner, Antoine. 1886-1962. Constructivist; studied in Russia; with brother, **Naum Gabo,** published the *Realist Manifesto* (1920); in Paris (from 1923); concerned with function of sculpture in human society; *Torso* (1924-26, brass and plastic); *Construction in Space* (1929, brass, steel, and glass, Kunstmuseum, Basle); *Portrait of Marcel Duchamp* (1926, celluloid with zinc, Yale); *Developable Column* (1942, brass and oxidized bronze); *Oval Fresco* (1945, brass, Amsterdam Museum); spatial construction, *Bird Soaring* (1956, General Motors Company, Detroit).

Arp, Jean (Hans). 1887- . Noted sculptor of "concretions" (1931-32), forms suggestive of organic growth; connected with *Der Blaue Reiter* group (1912); one of the founders of the Dada movement (1916); settled in Switzerland; *Birds in an Aquarium* (*ca.* 1920); *Relief* (1938-39, relief wood construction); *Human Concretion* (1935); participated in first surrealist show, Paris (1925); abstract reliefs in wood (from 1929).

Gonzalez, Julio. 1876-1942. Brilliant abstract sculpture in wrought iron; Spaniard; moved to Paris (*ca.* 1900); primarily a painter (until 1927), although engraved metal figures; worked with and influenced Picasso (1930-32); *Angel* and *Maternity* (1933); *Dancer with Flowing Hair* (1934) represents important invention of the "sign in space" that has had profound influence on younger sculptors; *Head* (1936); *La Montserrat,* moving figure in sheet iron; *Woman Combing Her Hair* (1937).

Vantongerloo, Georges. 1886- . Constructivist; member of *De Stijl* and Abstraction-Création group; Belgian; settled in Paris (from 1927); abstract constructions of interlocking prismatic forms, sometimes with mathematical equations as titles; transformed Mondrian's designs into three-dimensional form; *Sculpture in Space* ($y=ax^3 - bx^3 + cx$, Basel), representative work.

Laurens, Henri. 1885-1954. Leading sculptor; introduced to cubism by Braque (1911); *Head* (1918, painted wood construction); *Bottle and Newspaper* (1919, painted wood and metal collage, cross between relief and sculpture; *Le Grand Poseur* (1920); turned to organic forms (1925); works for Paris World Exhibition (1937); *Mermaid* (1945); *Luna* (1948) shows influence of Arp; *Great Amphion* (1952, bronze), powerful work.

Duchamp-Villon, Raymond. 1876-1918. Cubist; *The Lovers* (1913, plaster); *Rider* (*ca.* 1913); *The Horse* (1914), first drastic transformation of the animal in modern sculpture.

Others. Antoine Bourdelle 1861-1929), Charles Despiau (1874-1946); Henri Gaudier-Brzeska (1891-1915); famous painters who were also sculptors include Picasso, Matisse, Modigliani, Braque, Derain, Degas.

1945—Today

Richier, Germaine. 1904-59. Leading "sculptor of the terrible"; tragic outlook in her conception of man and space; strange fantasies, hybrids, monsters, surrealist in feeling; *Don Quixote with the Sail of a Windmill* (1949, gilt bronze); influence of Giacometti in skeleton like figures; *The Top* (1953, lead, coloring by Hans Hartung).

Zadkine, Ossip. 1890- . Russian; to Paris (1909); Grand Prix at Venice

MODERN EUROPEAN SCULPTURE

ILE DE FRANCE
BY MAILLOL, 1910

THE KISS,
BRANCUSI, 1908

TORSO
BY PEVSNER,
1924-26

SEATED WOMAN
BY MAILLOL, *ca.* 1901

HEAD
BY GONZALEZ, *ca.* 1935

Biennale; influenced by Brancusi, cubism; *Maenads* (1932); *Small Orpheus* (1948); expressionist, "personnage-instrument"; *The Destroyed City* (1951-53, Rotterdam), most celebrated public monument of postwar years.

César (Baldacchini). 1921- . Italian; lives in Paris; creates weird characters that combine nature and technology; *The Devil* (1956).

Penalba, Alicia. 1918- . Argentine; lives in Paris (from 1948); studied with Zadkine; *Homage to Vallejo* (1957), cactiform structure.

Teana, Marino di. 1920- . Argentine; worked in Italy, lives in Paris (since 1953); *Architectonic Conception No. 1* (1959); (forged steel).

Ubac, Raoul. 1910- . Belgian, lives in Paris (from 1929); slate reliefs (from 1942); nature subjects.

Others. Henri-Georges Adam (1904-), Étienne Béothy (1906-), Willy Anthoons (1911-), Robert Jacobsen (1912-), Claude Viseux (1927-), Sergio Signori (1906-), Nicolas Schoeffer (1912-), Pablo Picasso (1881-), Marta Pan (1923-), Maurice Dipsi (1898-), Samaï Haber (1922-), Étienne Martin (1913-), Robert Müller (1920-).

England

Moore, Henry. 1898- . Considered by many the leading sculptor of the period; first one-man show (1928); figure style built on fluid transitions from solids to voids; strong emphasis on exploitation of great inherent potential of materials; initial influence African and pre-Columbian sculpture; works include *Two Forms*

FAMILY GROUP BY MOORE, 1945

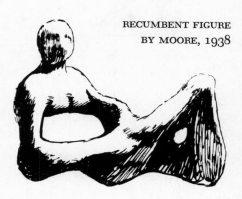

RECUMBENT FIGURE
BY MOORE, 1938

(1934, Pynkado wood), *Reclining Figure* (1935, Elmwood), *Square Form* (1936, Green Hornston stone), *Reclining Figure* (1937, Hoptonwood stone), *The Bride* (1940, cast lead and copper wire), *Madonna and Child* (1943-44), *Family Group* (1945-49), *Double Standing Figure* (1950), all bronze; drawings, *gouaches*; extremely influential.

Epstein, Jacob. 1880-1959. Important architectural sculpture and penetrating portraits; influenced by vorticism and African art; *Mother and Child* (ca. 1913); *Admiral Lord Fisher* (1915); *Jacob Kramer* (1921); *Oriel*

PORTRAIT OF
ORIEL ROSS
BY EPSTEIN, 1931

national Prize for Sculpture, Venice
Biennale (1956); first mobile composition (1945); *The Fisheater* (1950-51);
studied architecture; *The Stranger II*
(1956), fantastic half-bird, half-man
suggesting "geometry of fear"; *Two
Watchers* (1958).

Armitage, Kenneth. 1916- . Concerned with simplified human figure,
alone or in groups; *Seated Woman
with Arms Raised* (1953-57); introduced to United States (1954); *The
Seasons* (1956); *Diarchy* (1957).

Paolozzi, Eduardo. 1924- . Leading metal sculptor; *The Cage* (1950-
51); *St. Sebastian IV* (1957).

Martin, Kenneth. 1905- . First
screw mobiles (1953); equilibrium
and movement in space; experiments
with contemporary materials and me-
chanics.

Ross (1931); *Tomb of Oscar Wilde,
Ecce Homo* (1933); *Adam* (1939);
Lazarus (1949).

Hepworth, Barbara. 1903- . Abstraction-Création group, Paris, (1933-
35); influenced by Moore and Arp;
purely abstract works (1934-47); *Discs
in Echelon* (1935); *Cobden Head*
(1949); *Figure in Landscape* (1952).

Nicholson, Ben. 1894- . Member
of Abstraction-Création group, Paris
(1933-35); painter; abstract relief
sculpture outstanding; *Relief* (1939,
painted wood, Mus. Mod. Art), representative work.

Germany

Lehmbruck, Wilhelm. 1881-1919.
Outstanding German expressionist;
worked in Paris (1910-14); influenced
by Maillol; slender, elongated, almost

1945—Today

Butler, Reg. 1913- . First prize in
international competition for *Monument to Unknown Political Prisoner*
(1953); studied architecture; sculpture
(1950); *Boy and Girl* (1950-51, iron);
Girl (1954-56), intense vitality of
erotic suggestion; *Figure in Space*
(1959), wires support flying figure;
relationship of form and space uppermost.

Chadwick, Lynn. 1914- . Inter-

STANDING YOUTH
BY LEHMBRUCK, 1913

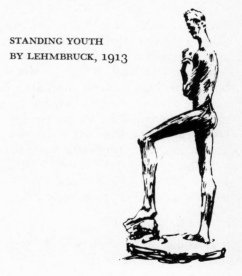

Gothic figures; *Standing Woman* (1910); *Kneeling Woman* (1911); *Standing Youth* (1913); *Attacking Figure* (1914-15); *Seated Youth* (1918).

Barlach, Ernst. 1870-1938. Leading expressionist; style influenced by Russian folk carvings and Gothic sculpture; worked mainly in wood; *Man Drawing a Sword* (1911); *Man in the Stocks* (1920); *Ehrenmal* (1927, cathedral, Gustrow); *Singing Man* (1928); war monuments, Magdeburg (1929) and Hamburg (1930); woodcuts; drama.

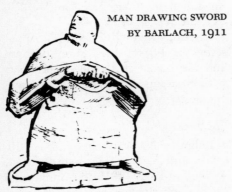

MAN DRAWING SWORD
BY BARLACH, 1911

Schwitters, Kurt. 1897-1948. Constructivist; famous for MERZ building (begun Hanover, 1920); combined all arts; best-known for collages.

Marcks, Gerhard. 1889- . Member of Bauhaus (1919); *Seated Girl* (1932); *Man of Sorrows,* ceramic figure for church of St. Catherine, Lübeck; *Pair of Runners* (1923); exotic animal statuettes; important teacher.

Kolbe, Georg. 1877-1947. Best-known for over 15 public monuments; *The Dancer* (1912); *Assunta* (1921).

1945—Today

Hartung, Karl. 1908- . Influential leader; combining sculpture with ar-

chitecture his chief concern; worked in Paris, Italy, and Berlin (since 1936); *Sculpture* (1947, mahogany); *Thronoi* (1958-59), over-life-sized figure enthroned; capacity for creating feeling of extreme tension.

Uhlmann, Hans. 1900- . Important sculptor in metal; many commissions for modern buildings; *Figuration* (1951, iron); *Suspended Sculpture* (1957, brass and chrome steel); *Rondo* (1958-59, brass), two movements of dance; staircase of University Library, Freiburg; excellent example of ability to relate highly individual sculpture to architecture.

Heiliger, Bernhard. 1915- . Leading teacher; *Portrait of Ernst Reuther* (1954, cement); *Vegetative Sculpture* (1955, bronze), portrayal of organic growth.

Werthmann, Friederich. 1927- . Prize for Young German artists (1959); *Struktur Remanit* (1959, steel); spatial, "floating" structures of rhythmical steel bands suggest plants, foliage, living matter.

Ris, Günter-Ferdinand. 1928- . Sculptor, architect, painter; steel reliefs from preformed sections; *Relief in Concrete* (1959), important integration of sculpture and architecture; also uses steel.

Others. Hans Mettel (1903-), Emil Cimiotti (1927-), Guido Jendritzko (1925-), Otto H. Hajek (1927-), Hans Kock (1920-), Norbert Kricke (1922-), Brigitte Meier-Denninghoff (1923-), Emy Roeder (1890-), Hans Steinbrenner (1928-).

Italy

Boccioni, Umberto. 1882-1916. Leading exponent of futurism (*see* Painting); *Unique Forms of Continuity in Space* (1913), representative work; *Grief* (1921).

Manzù, Giacomo. 1908- . *Crucifixion* reliefs (1939-43, bronze).

1945—Today

Italy

Marini, Marino. 1901- . Leading sculptor; gained recognition in 30's for portraits and figures of wrestlers and acrobats; in Switzerland (1942-46); *Quadriga* (1941, terra cotta sculptured frieze); *Dancer* (1949, polychrome bronze); portrait study of *Stravinsky* (1950); famed *Horse* (1951); *Miracolo* (1954), collapsing horse and rider, symbolic of dying humanity; *Equestrian Monument* (1958-59), synthesis of abstract architecture and sculpture at its height.

HORSE AND RIDER
BY MARINI

Campoli, Cosmo. 1922- . Closed, blocklike, massive works with birth and death central themes; *Birth of Death* (1950) supernatural god quality; *Return of the Prodigal Son* (1957-59).

Mirko (Balsadella). 1910- . Worked in Rome; director of Harvard University Workshop; expressionist works; *The Great Mask*, cement; influential.

Consagra, Pietro. 1920- . Founded the group known as Forma (1947); published *Necessita della scultura* (1952); works in Rome; *Human Colloquium* (1958, form of wood relief); linear frieze effect.

Mastroianni, Umberto. 1910- . Influenced by Arp and futurism; *The Rider* (1953), sense of controlled motion.

Others. Berto Lardera (1911-), Luciano Minguzzi (1911-), Arnaldo Pomodoro (1926-), Gio Pomodoro (1930-).

Sweden

Milles, Carl. 1875-1955. Extremely popular sculptor; famous for *Mermaid*; *Triton Fountain*; decorative memorials.

Spain

Gargallo, Pablo. 1881-1936. Teacher in Barcelona; studied in Paris; *Prophet* (1933); use of positive and negative forms; concave and convex surfaces; interesting work.

Switzerland

Giacometti, Alberto. 1901- . Leading Swiss artist; in Paris (from 1922); worked with Bourdelle; influenced by surrealists; *Head* (1928, marble); *Slaughtered Woman* (1932); *The Palace at 4 a.m.* (1932-33, construction in wood, wire, glass, and string); *Hands Holding the Void* (1934); famous for elongated, skeletal heads and figures; *Man Pointing* (1947); *Venice VII*

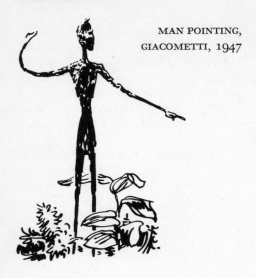

MAN POINTING,
GIACOMETTI, 1947

(1957); *City Square* (1948); *Leg* (1959).

Bill, Max. 1908- . Member Abstraction-Création group (1932); studied Zurich, Bauhaus; geometrical abstract style; first prize; São Paolo Biennale; *Construction* (1937); *Tripartite Unity* (1947-48, chrome-nickel-steel).

Tinguely, Jean. 1925- . Compositions involve movement generated by motor devices; *Yokohama in Metamorphosis* (1956, oil on mechanisms).

Linck, Walter. 1903-65. Steel and iron in motion; *Sculpture Mobile* (1959), steel coils unwind like clock springs; movement tense, restricted.

Kemeny, Zoltan. 1907- . Rumanian; in Switzerland (from 1942); metal relief paintings; *Banlieu des Anges* (1958, copper).

Austria

Wotruba, Fritz. 1907- . Important teacher; in Switzerland during World War II; in Vienna (since 1945); monumental works combine brilliantly with architecture of buildings for which they are intended; *Marble Figure* (1959, Municipal Hall, Vienna).

Hoflehner, Rudolf. 1916- . Works in metal; *Doric Figure* (1958, iron); colossal, solid figures.

Bertoni, Wander. 1925- . Co-founder of Art Club of Vienna; studied with Wotruba; *Icarus* (1953, aluminum); *Movement* (1955-58, stainless steel).

Others. Toon Kelder (1894-), Jaap Mooy (1905-), Hans Verhulst (1921- , The Netherlands), Eduardo Chillida (1924-), Manuel Rivera (1927- , Spain), Drago Trsar (1927- Yugoslavia), Takis (1925- Greece).

AMERICAS · *United States*

Calder, Alexander. 1898- . Famed creator of "mobiles" and "stabiles," abstract constructions made of wire and sheet metal; Paris (1926); influenced by Arp, Mondrian, and Miró; member Abstraction-Création group (1931), first mobiles; since 1938 has also created stationary sheet-metal constructions; *Steel Fish* (1934);

LOBSTER TRAP
AND FISH TAIL,
MOBILE,
BY CALDER, 1939

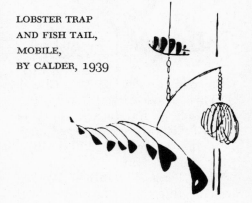

Whale (1937); *Thirteen Spines* (1940);
Lobster Trap and Fish Tail (1939);
Constellation with Red Object (1943);
Bifurcated Tower (1950); *Streetcar*
(1951); uses combination of materials.

Gabo, Naum. 1890- . Constructivist; brother of A. Pevsner; worked in
Berlin, Russia, Paris, London; since
1946 in United States; *Column* (1923,
wood, metal, plastic, glass); *Construction in Space* (1937, light-blue plastic);
Spiral Theme (1941, plastic); *Study
for Construction in Space* (1951, brass
net, plastic, and stainless-steel wire);
Rotterdam Construction (1954-57, concrete, steel, bronze wire, 85 ft. high);
important influence.

FIGURE
BY LIPSCHITZ, 1926-30

HEAD OF A WOMAN,
CELLULOID AND METAL,
BY GABO, 1917

Lipchitz, Jacques. 1891- . Leading
Polish-French sculptor; to United
States (1941); influenced by African
Negro art, cubism, surrealism; first
"transparent" sculpture important in
opening up of form (1927); *Man with
a Guitar* (ca. 1915); *Woman Standing
with Guitar* (1926); *Reclining Nude
with Guitar* (1928); *Song of the
Vowels* (1931-32); *Mother and Child
II* (1941-45); *Benediction* (1945);
Sacrifice (1948).

Archipenko, Alexander. 1887-1964.
Pioneer abstract sculptor; born in Russia, settled in Paris (1908); first one-
man show, Germany (1910); first
"sculpture-paintings" (1914); emigrated to United States (1931); cubist
element seen in *Woman Combing her
Hair* (1915).

Lachaise, Gaston. 1882-1935. French-
American; to United States (1906);
figure style of unique vitality and
power; *Standing Woman* (1912-27);
Floating Figure (1927); *Portrait of
John Marin* (1928); *Standing Woman*
(1932); *Two Floating Figures* (ca.
1925-28); *Acrobat* (1934); *Torso*
(1930).

Others. William Zorach (1887-),
José de Creeft (1884-), Gutzon Bor-
glum (1867-1941), George Gray Bar-
nard (1863-1938), Paul Manship
(1885-), Elie Nadelman (1885-
1946), Oronzio Maldarelli (1892-),
John Flannagan (1895-1942), Hugo
Robus (1885-), Chaim Gross
(1904-).

315

Noguchi, Isamu. 1904- . Outstanding sculptor; Brancusi's assistant in Paris (1927-29); exhibited abstract metal construction (1929, New York); terra-cotta techniques; large-scale architectural sculpture (colored cement reliefs); large interlocking constructions gained world acclaim; *Cronos* (1949, balsa wood), *Night Voyage* (1948), *The Self* (1957), representative works.

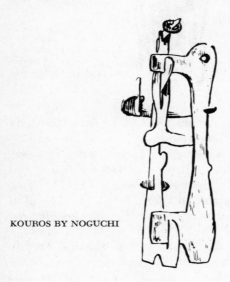

KOUROS BY NOGUCHI

Rivera, José de. 1904- . Leading sculptor of works in chromium-plated steel; harmony of movement in space;

CONSTRUCTION #4 BY DE RIVERA

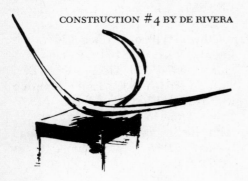

gliding rhythm, brilliant symplicity; *Yellow Black* (1946-47, painted aluminum); *Construction 8* (1954); influential.

Lippold, Richard. 1915- . Leading creator of geometric wire constructions; *Variation No. 7; Full Moon* (1949-50, nickel-chromium wire, stainless-steel wire, and brass rods; *Variations within a Sphere No. 10; The Sun* (1953-56, gold wire); decorations for important buildings, including Philharmonic Hall, Lincoln Center, New York.

THE SUN BY LIPPOLD, 1956

Roszak, Theodore. 1907- . Polish-American; to United States (1909); first steel sculptures (1945); interest in organic growth; exotic, baroque, abstract quality; *Thorn Blossom* (1947, steel with nickeled silver); *Spectre of Kitty Hawk* (1946-47, welded with hammered steel, brazed with bronze and brass); *Turret and Belfry* (1955, aluminum), Chapel of M.I.T., Boston; important architectural sculpture.

Smith, David, 1906- . First steel sculpture (1933); influenced by Gonzalez; *The Banquet, Austria*, two powerful works in steel (1951).

Lipton, Seymour. 1903- . Abstract expressionist; first sculpture show (1938); *Cerberus* (1947, lead); *The Hero* (1957, nickeled silver on steel); powerful forms.

Hare, David. 1917- . First sculpture (1942); influenced by surrealism, Giacometti; *Man with Drum* (1948); *Figure with Bird* (1951, steel, iron).

Ferber, Herbert. 1906- . Abstract expressionist; first show (1937); *The Bow* (1950); important architectural sculpture for synagogues.

Lassaw, Ibram. 1913- . Russian, emigrated to United States (1921); works in metal; *Monoceros* (1952, bronze); *Counterpoint Castle* (1957, bronze and copper); open architectonic patterns creating sculptural space.

Others. Louise Nevelson (1900-), Mary Callery (1903-), Constantino Nivola (1911-), Bernard Rosenthal (1914-), Cornelia Runyon (1887-), Day Schnabel (1905-), Shinkichi Tajiri (1923-), Peter H. Voulkos (1924-).

Brazil

Vieira, Mary. 1927- . Constructivist; studied with Max Bill; works in Switzerland; *Sphere-Tension* (1956-58); harmony of movement in space.

Argentina

Kosice, Gyula. 1924- . Constructivist; Czech-Hungarian; to Argentina (1928); founded Madi group (1946); influenced by Gabo; *Sculpture* (1959, plexiglass).

ARCHITECTURE

EUROPE · *Germany*

Miës van der Rohe, Ludwig, 1886- . Leading modern architect; pupil of Peter Behrens; influenced by Berlage; in charge of Weissenhof Settlement, Stuttgart (1927), model housing project; first use of steel construction in domestic dwellings; designed *German Pavilion*, Barcelona Exposition (1929); director of Bauhaus (1930-33); exponent of glass and steel frame construction; to Chicago (1938).

SEAGRAM BUILDING, NEW YORK, MIES VAN DER ROHE, 1957-58

Gropius, Walter. 1883- . Brilliant educator; co-founder of Bauhaus, director (1919-28); designs for Weissenhof housing development, Stuttgart (1927); to England (1934); to United States (1937); head of School of Architecture, Harvard University (1937-

317

GROPIUS

BAUHAUS,
DESSAU, GERMANY, GROPIUS, 1925-29

53); worked with Breuer (1937-41); extremely influential teacher.

Behrens, Peter. 1868-1940. Leader and founder of German *Jugenstil* movement; considered important pioneer in modern architecture; teacher of Miës van der Rohe, Gropius, and Le Corbusier; director of architecture department, Vienna Academy (1922-36); noted designer of factories, including *General Electric Buildings,* Berlin (1909); workers' apartment buildings, Vienna.

Italy

Nervi, Pier-Luigi. 1891- . Master architect; famous for concrete constructions and introduction of new ways to vault large open spaces with ribbed, reticulated, and corrugated systems of reinforced concrete; cantilevered roofs and tiers; *Stadium,* Florence (1932).

Boni, Giacomo. 1859-1925. Architect and archaeologist; known for restorations of the *Doge's Palace* and campanile in Venice; excavations of *Roman Forum* and *Palatine.*

Netherlands

Oud, Jacobus Johannes Pieter. 1890- . Leader of the *De Stijl* group (1917); studied in Germany; influenced by Wright; spokesman for modern architecture; chief architect, city of Rotterdam (1918-33); influential.

Berlage, Hendrik. 1856-1934. Pioneer in modern architecture; designed *Amsterdam Bourse* (1903).

Austria

Wagner, Otto. 1841-1918. Viennese architect of Secessionist group; combined iron construction with *Jugenstil* in elevated and underground railway system in Vienna; used ferroconcrete; *Postal Savings Bank, Palace of Justice,* Vienna; hospital, Hutteldorf; *Steinhof Church*; apartment houses; author of several books on architecture.

Belgium

Velde, Henry van de. 1863-1957. Painter turned to applied arts and architecture; designed *Folkwang Museum,* Hagen; director, Weimar School of Art.

France

Le Corbusier (Charles Edouard Jeanneret). 1887- . Leader of international importance in the development of modern architecture; born in Switzerland; trained as engraver, Paris (1908); studied with Behrens, worked with Perret; first experimental studies (1915); emphasis on functionalism; settled in Paris (1917); edited periodical, *Esprit nouveau* (1920).

NOTRE-DAME-DU-HAUT,
RONCHAMP, FRANCE,
LE CORBUSIER, 1950-55

Perret, Auguste. 1873- . Teacher of Le Corbusier and others; engineer.

Great Britain

Voysey, Charles F. Annesley. 1857-1941. Pioneer modern architect in England; stress on simplicity of line; excellent designer.

Mackintosh, Charles Rennie. 1868-1928. Scottish architect and designer; influenced leading architects on continent; *Glasgow School of Art* building; *Music Room*, Vienna.

Luytens, Sir Edwin L. 1869-1944. Successful architect of government buildings, New Delhi, India; *British School,* Rome; *Cenotaph,* Whitehall, London; new *British Embassy,* Washington, D.C.

Others. Basil Champneys (1842-1935), Sir Giles G. Scott (1880-), Sir Aston Webb (1849-1930), Sir Thomas Jackson (1835-1924), Henry V. Lanchester (1863-), Sir Herbert Baker (1862-).

Sweden

Ostberg, Ragner. 1866-1945. Leading architect; designer of *Stockholm Town Hall, Marinmuseum,* and other important buildings.

Finland

Aalto, (Hugo) Alvar Henrik 1899- . Collaborated with wife, Aino Marsio (1894-1949) for 25 years; building for *Turun-Sanomat,* newspaper in Turku (*ca.* 1930), gained international recognition; *Viipuri Library* (1927-35); *Tuberculosis Sanatorium,* Paimio (1929-33); Finnish pavilions at Paris Exposition (1937), New York (1939); successful industrial designer in Finland (from 1936); influenced by nature and wood of native land; several interesting churches.

TUBERCULOSIS SANATORIUM,
PAIMIO, FINLAND, AALTO,
1929-33

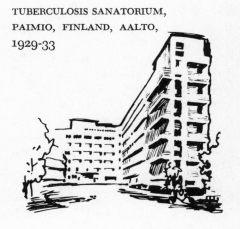

UNITED STATES

Wright, Frank Lloyd. 1869-1959. Great figure in American architecture; important international influence; first to produce open planning in houses; desire to use nature and blend outdoors with interiors; studied engineering at University of Wisconsin; joined firm of Adler and Sullivan, Chicago, and helped design *Chicago Auditorium*; Sullivan great influence in life; went on own (1893); designed series of "Prairie Houses" including famed *Robie House,* Chicago (1909); architect for *Larkin Building,* Buffalo, N.Y.

WRIGHT

(1904), for which he also designed the first metal office furniture; *Imperial Hotel,* Tokyo, Japan (1916-22, earthquake-proof, reinforced concrete and brick); *Millard House,* Pasadena, California (1923), first of "textile block" houses; the famous *"Falling Water"* home designed for E. J. Kaufmann, Bear Run, Pennsylvania (1936), most publicized house; *Johnson Administration Building,* Racine, Wisconsin (1939).

Sullivan, Louis Henri. 1856-1924. Leading pioneer in modern American architecture; emphasized "functional-ism"; studied in Paris; partner in firm of Adler and Sullivan (1881); *Auditorium Building,* Chicago (1887-89); use of steel frame construction; *Wainwright Building,* St. Louis (1890-91); *Guaranty Building,* Buffalo, N.Y. (1894-95); *Bayard Building,* New York City (1897-98); famed *Carson, Pirie, Scott Department Store,* Chicago (1899-1904); *National Farmers' Bank,* Owatonna, Minnesota (1907-8); important influence, although not accorded enough recognition during his lifetime.

Fuller, R. (Richard) Buckminster. 1895- . Brilliant "Comprehensive Designer," educator, creative engineer, architect, inventor, writer; invented Energetic and Synergetic geometry (1917); designed *Wichita House* (1926); *Dymaxion House* (1927) and *Geodesic Dome* to provide mass-production shelters that give optimum, usable space at minimum cost.

FULLER
WITH GEODESIC DOME

Breuer, Marcel. 1902- . Leading architect, furniture designer, teacher; at Bauhaus (1920-24, 1926-28); to United States (1937) to teach at Harvard University; worked in collaboration with Gropius; born in Hungary; designed famous steel-tube chair; famed houses; butterfly-roof exhibition house, Museum of Modern Art, N.Y. (1949); influential.

Saarinen (Gottlieb) Eliel. 1873-1950. Leading Finnish-American architect; with partners Gesellius and Lindgren designed *Finnish Pavilion* at Paris Exposition (1900), *National Museum,* Helsinki; to United States (*ca.* 1927); built *Cranbrook School,* Bloomfield Hills, Michigan, and became its director; important teacher.

Others. Albert Kahn (1869-1942), John Carriere (1858-1911), Charles A. Coolidge (1858-1936), Cass Gilbert (1859-1934), Frederick Kiesler (1896-   ), Fiske Kimball (1888-   ), Christopher La Farge (1862-1938), John Pope (1874-1937), James Rogers (1867-   ), William Tuthill (1855-1929), William Ware (1832-1915), Whitney Warren (1863-1943).

ASIA · *Japan*

Raymond, Antonin. 1889-   . Pioneer of modern architecture in Asia; born, Prague, Czechoslovakia; to United States (1914); accompanied F. L. Wright to Japan and remained there (1921-37).

Sutemi Horiguchi designed the *Okada House* and *Gardens* (1933) and the *Wakasa House* (1939), both in Tokyo; **Junzo Sakakura** worked with Le Corbusier; designed *Japanese Pavilion,* Paris Exposition (1937) and *Museum of Modern Art,* Kamakura (1951).

1945–Today · United States

Wright, Frank Lloyd. (See above.) Designed laboratory for *Johnson Wax Company* (1949), store for *V. C.*

Morris, San Francisco (1949), *Wayfarers' Chapel,* Palos Verdes, California (1951), *Price Tower,* Bartlesville, Oklahoma (1956); many private homes and buildings all over the United States; last important work, *Guggenheim Museum of Non-Objective Art,* Fifth Avenue, New York City (1943-58); of poured and sprayed concrete in the form of a great cantilevered spiral; the main gallery is in the form of a spiral ramp with pictures hung on one side and a great interior space rising 90 feet from the floor to a glass-domed roof on the other.

Miës van der Rohe, Ludwig. (See above.) *Dr. Edith Farnsworth House,* Plano, Illinois (1950); *Lake Shore Drive Apartments,* Chicago (1951); *Commonwealth Promenade Apartments,* Chicago (1957); *Crown Hall;* architectural department of Illinois Institute of Technology, Chicago (1957); *Cullinan Hall of the Museum of Fine Arts,* Houston, Texas; *Seagram Building,* New York (with Philip Johnson, 1958).

Saarinen, Eero. 1910-62. Finnish-American; son of Eliel (see above); to U.S. (1923); studied Paris and Yale School of Architecture; won furniture design prizes (with Eames, Mus. Mod. Art); designed *General Motors Technical Center* (1948); *Kresge Auditorium* and *Chapel,* M.I.T. (1955); *Emma Hartman Noyes House,* Vassar College (1954-58); *London Embassy* (1956); *University of Chicago Law School* (1956-60); *I.B.M.,* Rochester, Minnesota and Yorktown, N.Y. (1956); *T.W.A. Terminal,* Kennedy Airport, N.Y. (1956-62), model for *World Health Organization Building* (1959); *Yale University Colleges* (under construction, 1962); *Dulles International Airport*, Washington, D.C. (1962).

Fuller, R. Buckminster. (See above.) Dome for *Ford Rotunda Building*, Dearborn, Michigan (1953); *Restaurant Dome*, Woods Hole, Mass. (1954); famed *"Air-Ocean World Map"* (1954); *Kaiser Aluminum Company Dome*, Honolulu (1957); *Union Tank Car Company Dome*, Baton Rouge, Louisiana (1958-59); "Golden Dome" *Kaiser Aluminum Company*, Moscow (1959); exhibition of work (1959, Mus. Mod. Art).

Harrison, Wallace K. Leading industrial designer, architect; Director of Planning of *United Nations Secretariat*, N.Y. (1950); assisted by **Max Abramovitz** (Deputy Director, with whom he built the *Alcoa Building*, Pittsburgh, 1952 and *The Lincoln Center for the Performing Arts*, New York); **Oscar Niemeyer** (Brazil), **Le Corbusier** (France), **G. A. Soilleux** (Australia), **Gaston Brunfaut** (Belgium), **Sven Markelius** (Sweden), **N. D. Bassov** (U.S.S.R.), **Howard Robertson** (United Kingdom), **Julio Vilamajo** (Uruguay), **Ernest Cormier** (Canada) and **Ssu-Ch'eng Liang** (China), all leading architects in their respective countries.

Neutra, Richard J. 1892- . Austrian-American; studied with Otto Wagner; worked with Eric Mendelsohn, Berlin; important in design of modern homes that blend with natural landscape surrounding them (influenced by Wright); excellent example of his work is the *Warren Tremaine House*, Montecito, California (1949).

Mendelsohn, Eric. 1887-1953. German-American; leader of New Objec-

tivity in Germany; to United States (1933); noted industrial architect; famed for concrete and glass structure, the *Maimonides Health Center*, San Francisco, California (1950).

Aalto, Alvar. (See above.) Taught at M.I.T., where he designed (with others) the *Baker House Dormitory* (1947-49); *Finnish Pavilion* for Venice Biennial (1956); interested in organic architecture and city planning.

Others. Edward D. Stone (1902-   ), Philip Johnson (1906-   ), Louis Kahn (1901-   ), Pietro Belluschi (1899-   ).

ASIA · *Japan*

Tange, Kenzo. 1913- . Leading architect; professor of architecture, Tokyo University; winner of many prizes and awards; author of several important publications; designed *Hiroshima Peace Hall*, (1949-56); *Tokyo City Hall* (1952-53); *Tsuda College Library* (1953-54) and *Sogetsu Art Center*, Tokyo (1955-58); *Shizuoka Convention Hall* (1955-57); *Housing Project*, Takamatsu (1959); main, covered stadium for 1964 *Olympics*, Tokyo.

KENZO TANGE

MODERN UNITED STATES ARCHITECTURE

ROBIE HOUSE, CHICAGO, WRIGHT, 1909

TWA TERMINAL, J. F. KENNEDY AIRPORT,
NEW YORK, SAARINEN, 1956-62

"FALLING WATER," KAUFMANN HOUSE,
BEAR RUN, PENNSYLVANIA, WRIGHT, 1936

UNITED NATIONS BUILDING,
NEW YORK, 1949-51

WAINWRIGHT BUILDING, ST. LOUIS,
SULLIVAN, 1890

FORD HOUSE, AURORA, ILLINOIS, GOFF, 1950

MUSIC

EUROPE · *Russia*

Stravinsky, Igor. 1882- . Master composer of symphonic poems, orchestral music, works for the ballet, television; pupil of Rimsky-Korsakov; wrote music for Russian ballet under Diaghilev in Paris; *L'Oiseau de feu* (The Fire Bird, 1910); *Petrushka* (1911); *Le Sacre du printemps* (Rite of Spring, 1913); *The Soldier's Tale,* for narrator and seven instruments (1918); *The Song of the Nightingale* (1919); outstanding influence on other composers.

Shostakovich, Dmitri. 1906- . Leading Soviet composer; studied St. Petersburg; first symphony performed Leningrad (1926); satirical opera, *The Nose* (1927-28); ballet, *The Golden Age* (1930); *Fifth Symphony* (1937), most popular; *Seventh Symphony* (1951, Siege of Leningrad); influenced by Mahler, Beethoven; represents the problem of the creative individual in a collective society; 11 symphonies, operas, works for piano, chamber music.

SHOSTAKOVITCH

Prokofiev, Sergei. 1891-1953. Outstanding modern composer; studied with Glière; in United States (1918-

PROKOFIEV

21) to conduct first performance of his *Love for Three Oranges* (1919); in Paris, wrote ballets for Diaghilev, including *Chout* (The Buffoon, 1922); most celebrated work for piano, *Concerto No. 3; Classical Symphony* (1916-17); music for film *Lt. Kije* (1934), satirical quality; seven symphonies; eight piano sonatas, considered most characteristic work; *Peter and the Wolf* (1936); *Alexander Nevsky* (1938).

Rachmaninoff, Sergei. 1873-1943. Virtuoso pianist, composer; influenced by Tchaikovsky; four piano concertos (*Second,* 1901, best-known); *Rhapsody on a Theme of Paganini* (1934) for piano and orchestra; orchestral tone poem, *Isle of the Dead* (1907).

Scriabin, Alexander Nikolaievich. 1872-1915. Mystic impressionist; pianist, composer; introduced "mystic chords" built in fourths, instead of conventional major and minor triads, in superb piano compositions; subtle sense of harmony.

Glière, Reinhold Moritzovich. 1875-

1956. Composer; Belgian origin; important teacher in Kiev and Moscow; known for ballet, *Red Poppy*, based on Russian Revolution (1927); three symphonies, violin and harp concertos; four string quartets; *The Bronze Horseman*, based on Pushkin's story (1949); *Ilya Murometz* (1911).

Khatchaturian, Aram Ilyich. 1903- . Armenian composer; use of colorful folk music adds excitement to compositions; two symphonies; concertos for piano, violin, and cello; chamber music; popular ballet, *Gayane* (Happiness, 1942); conductor, teacher in Moscow.

Poland

Paderewski, Ignace. 1860-1941. Statesman, virtuoso pianist; famed for *Minuet in G* for piano; wrote opera, *Manur* (1901), and two symphonies.

Szymanowski, Karol. 1883-1937. Composer; director State Conservatoire (1926); two operas, ballets, three symphonic works for solo voices, chorus, and orchestra; violin concertos; chamber music.

Austria

Schönberg, Arnold. 1874-1951. Foremost composer, teacher; noted for introduction of 12-tone technique, first presented in *Serenade* (1924); *Kammersymphonie* (1906), first use of chords built in fourths, foreshadows his later use of atonality; *Second String Quartet* (1907); to United States (1933); taught in California; *String Suite in G Major* (1935); *Violin Concerto, Op. 36* (1936); *A Survivor from Warsaw*, narrator, male chorus, and orchestra, Op. 46 (1947); *Orchestral Variations, Op. 31*, and unfinished op-

SCHÖNBERG

era, *Moses und Aron*, leading works.

Berg, Alban. 1885-1935. Leading pupil of Schönberg; important composer of modern music; great originality and technical facility; operas include very evocative, expressive *Wozzeck* (1914) and unfinished *Lulu* (1928); orchestral works; *Lyric Suite for String Quartet* (1925-26), one of his outstanding successes; chamber music; works for the piano.

Webern, Anton von. 1883-1945. Composer, editor; pupil of Schönberg; used 12-note system and various ingenious contrapuntal devices; very original atonal style; wrote symphony for small orchestra, three cantatas, string quartet, concerto for nine instruments, songs; *Three Sacred Folk Songs*, for voice, clarinet, bass clarinet, and violin (1924), beginning of dodecaphonic system.

Germany

Hindemith, Paul. 1895- . Extremely versatile musician; conductor, Opera Orchestra, Frankfort (1915-23); one of leading figures in festivals of

HINDEMITH

contemporary music (1921-26); to United States (1939); one-act expressionist operas (1921-29); six chamber concertos; opera, *Mathis der Maler* (own libretto, performed 1938); ballets, *Nobilissima Visione* (1938) and *The Four Temperaments* (1944); author of several books.

Strauss, Richard. 1864-1949. Outstanding operas of late period include *Electra* (1909), *Der Rosenkavalier* (1911), *Ariadne auf Naxos* (1913); influenced by Hugo von Hofmannsthal, his librettist.

Orff, Carl. 1895- . Noted conductor; composer; important works for theater include *Der Mond* (The Moon, 1937-38) and *Die Kluge* (Wise Woman, 1942); *Carmina Burana*, dramatic cantata (1936), best-known work.

Netherlands

Pijper, Willem. 1894-1947. Composer, pianist, leading teacher; three symphonies, string quartets, concertos for piano, cello, and violin; choral works, including *Heer Halewijn* (1920), *Heer Danielken* (1925, unaccompanied eight-part chorus); chief figure among modern Dutch composers; influenced by Mahler; head of Rotterdam Conservatory where he trained younger generation of Dutch composers.

France

Debussy, Claude Achille. 1862-1918. Outstanding leader of impressionist movement in music; although first compositions date from 1890's, his work and influence belong to early 20th century; as impressionist artists allowed the eye to blend color, Debussy allowed the ear to bridge the silences and harmonize the chords to create "impressions" or picture images; *Prélude à l'Après-Midi d'un faun* (1892, written to poem by Mallarmé); *Pelléas et Mélisande* (1902, opera based on Materlinck's play); *Printemps* (1887); *La Mer* (1905); *Images* (1912); chamber music, choral works, and songs.

DEBUSSY

Ravel, Maurice. 1875-1937. Postimpressionist; polytonality; subtle, restrained music; master of piano; exceptional orchestration; *Pavane pour une Infante Defunte* (Pavane for a

RAVEL

Dead Princess, 1899); *Jeu d'eau* (1901); *Concerto for Left Hand* (1931); *Daphnis and Chloe* (1909-12, ballet for Diaghilev); *G Major Piano Concerto* (1931); *L'Enfant et les Sortileges* (1925, one-act fantasy on text by Colette); *Bolero* (1928), popular work.

Satie, Erik Alfred Leslie. 1866-1925. Composer; pioneer in original, simplicity of style as reaction against impressionism; ironic humor; leader of group known as "Les Six"; *Parade* (1917), ballet produced by Satie, Cocteau, Picasso, and Diaghilev in Paris; symphonic drama, *Socrate* (1919); important influence.

Milhaud, Darius, 1889- . Composer; member of "Les Six"; 13 operas, ballets, 8 symphonies, 28 choral works; concertos, chamber music, and music for the piano; polytonality, lyrical clarity; *Poems juifs* (1916); *La Création du monde* (1922, ballet); *Scaramouche* (1937, two-piano suite), best-known works.

Honegger, Arthur. 1892-1955. Swiss-French composer; one of "Les Six"; polytonal style marked by incisive rhythms and sharp dissonances; *Pacific 231* (1923, for orchestra); *Judith* (1926, ballet); *King David* (1921, oratorio); *Concerto da Camera* (1923-25, for flute, *cor anglais,* and strings); *Antigone* (1927, lyric tragedy by Cocteau, after Sophocles); of five symphonies, 4th the most popular, 5th considered his most mature work.

Others. Albert Roussel (1869-1937), Georges Auric (1899-).

Spain

Falla, Manuel de. 1876-1946. Composer, pianist; romantic impressionist; brilliant adaptation of Andalusian themes to modern style; *Nights in the Gardens of Spain* (1916, for piano and orchestra); ballets, *El amor brujo* (1915) and *Three-cornered Hat* (1919); later works neoclassical.

Albéniz, Isaac. 1860-1909. Founder of modern Spanish "national school"; composer of *Iberia* (1906-9), 12 pieces for the piano, published in four books, popular work.

Hungary

Bartók, Béla. 1881-1945. Master composer, considered by many the most "professional"; possessed of one of the great rhythmic imaginations of the century; with Kodály, collector of genuine Hungarian folk music; six concertos for piano and violin; chamber music; one-act opera, *Duke Bluebeard's Castle* (1911); choral, *Cantata profana* (1930); *Mikrokosmos* (1926-37), collection of 153 pieces for piano; important innovator; very influential.

327

BARTOK

Dohnányi, Ernö (Ernst von). 1877-1960. Composer, pianist, conductor of Budapest Philharmonic Society (1919); in United States (1949-60); four rhapsodies, chamber music; *The Tower of Voyvod* (1922), portraying Hungarian national spirit; symphonies and operas.

Kodály, Zoltán. 1882- . With Bartok, collected and published Hungarian folk songs that influenced his compositions; *Psalmus Hungaricus* (1923), brought success; *Háry János*, play with music (1926), gained world recognition; choral works, concertos, chamber music, etc.

Czechoslovakia

Martinu, Bohuslav. 1890-1959. Outstanding composer; operas, ballets, four symphonies, symphonic poems, chamber music; *First Symphony* commissioned by Koussevitsky, performed by Boston Symphony Orchestra (1942); *Partita for Strings* (1931), *Memorial to Lidice* (1943), best-known works.

Janácek, Leos. 1854-1928. Composer; directed school of organists; *Jenufa*

(1916), one of ten operas; *Taras Bulba* (1918), symphonic poem; orchestral works, choral music; chamber music; created "dynamic leitmotifs" in musical dramas; collections of Moravian folk songs; treatise on theory of harmony.

Hába, Alois. 1893- . Composer, theorist; adherent of quarter-tone music, written in quarter and sixth tones; quarter-tone piano, clarinets, and trumpets made especially for first performance of his opera *Die Mutter* (The Mother, 1931, Munich); *The Unemployed* (1932); half-tone compositions: *New Earth* (1935), *The Way of Life*, symphonic fantasy; string quartets; work for strings.

Switzerland

Burkhard, Willi. 1900-1955. Composer; studied in Berne, Germany, Paris; two symphonies, two string quartets; *Ulenspiegel Variations* for orchestra; *Musikalische Ubung* (1934, for chorus and orchestra); *Das Gesicht Jesajas* (1935, oratorio); very prolific; austere simplicity seen in style that is linear and contrapuntal in almost Baroque way; *Das Jahr* (1942).

Italy

Puccini, Giacomo. 1858-1924. Famed composer of operas *Manon Lescaut* (1893), *La Bohème* (1896), *La Tosca* (1900), *Madame Butterfly* (1904), *The Girl of the Golden West* (1910), and *Turandot* (produced 1926); superb sense of dramatic theater; romantic, sensuous melody; very popular.

Busoni, Ferrucio Benvenuto. 1866-1924. Virtuoso pianist, composer; published *A New Aesthetic of Music*

(1907), that has had profound influence on contemporary composers, particularly those of electronic music; compositions for orchestra, chamber music; music for piano, violin, voice; operas.

Respighi, Ottorino. 1879-1936. Excellent viola player, composer; studied with Rimsky-Korsakov; romantic symphonic poems: *The Fountains of Rome* (1917), *Pines of Rome* (1924), *Roman Festivals* (1929); opera, *La Fiamma* (1934); chamber music.

Malipiero, Gian Francesco. 1882- . Exponent of neo-Baroque; composer; *Pause del Silenzio* (1917), "impressions" for orchestra; 11 symphonies; over 20 operas, including *Fable of the Changed Son* (1933, text by Pirandello); chamber music, oratorios.

Casella, Alfredo. 1883-1947. Composer, conductor, pianist, critic; studied in Paris, pupil of Gabriel Fauré; teacher in Rome (1915-23); furthered the cause of modern music in Italy; organized Biennale festivals, Venice; three symphonies, concertos, operas, ballets, chamber music, etc; *Concerto Romano* (1926), most important work; very influential.

Toscanini, Arturo. 1867-1957. Maestro; brilliant interpreter of great masters; world famous.

England

Delius, Frederick. 1862-1934. Composer; studied in Germany; lived in Paris; works made famous by Sir Thomas Beecham; intimate, rhapsodic works for orchestra, choral works, operas, chamber music; *Sea-Drift* (1906, to Whitman's words), considered masterpiece of passionate yet sedate expression; *In a Summer Garden* (1908).

Elgar, Sir Edward William. 1857-1934. Composer; *Pomp and Circumstance* marches (1902-30); *Enigma Variations* for orchestra (1899); oratorios: *The Dream of Gerontius* (1900) and *The Apostles* (1903).

Walton, William Turner. 1902- . Leading figure of postwar England; *Violin Concerto* (1939, written for Heifetz); excellent work for films, including Shaw's *Major Barbara* (1941), Olivier's production of Shakespeare's *Henry V* (1944) and *Hamlet* (1947); gained fame for instrumental pieces designed to be played with Edith Sitwell's *Façade* (1922); *Belshazzar's Feast* (1931), oratorio.

Vaughan Williams, Ralph. 1872-1958. Prolific popular composer with considerable range of expression; *London Symphony* (1914, rev. 1920), most popular work; *Flos campi* (1925, for viola, orchestra, and voice), used polytonality; very English style.

Holst, Gustav Theodore. 1874-1934. Composer; experimented with five- and seven-beat bars; suite of seven tone poems for large orchestra; best-known works include *The Planets* (1916), *The Hymn of Jesus* (1917, for two choruses, semi-chorus, and orchestra); opera-ballet parody, *The Perfect Fool* (staged 1923); *Hammersmith* (1930), polytonal orchestral work.

Bax, Sir Arnold. 1883-1953. Romantic composer; influenced by Irish folklore; master of King's Music (1942); knighted (1937); seven symphonies, chamber and orchestral music, choral works, songs.

Denmark

Nielsen, Carl August. 1865-1931. One of the leading symphonic composers and inspired innovators in Scandinavian music; director of Conservatoire and conductor of Musical Society (1915-27), Copenhagen; works include two operas, six symphonies, three concertos, four string quartets, cantatas, songs, and piano pieces; two volumes of his writings have been translated into English.

IVES

AMERICAS · *Brazil*

Villa-Lobos, Heitor. 1887-1959. Foremost composer of Latin America; incredibly prolific; influenced by Brazilian folk music; five operas, six symphonies, *choros* (serenades), choral works, piano solos, songs, symphonic poems, cello concertos, etc; best-known work, *Bachianas Brasileiras No. 5* (in two parts)—*Aria* (1938) and *Dansa* (1945).

Mignone, Francisco. 1897- . Studied in Italy; intensely emotional works; opera, *The Diamond Merchant* (1924); *Fantasias Brasileiras* (1931-37, for piano and orchestra); ballet, *Amazonian Pictures* (1949); *Sextet* (for piano, flute, oboe, clarinet, bassoon, and horn) greatly admired.

Fernandez, Oscar Lorenzo. 1897-1948. Established and directed Conservatorio Brasileiro de Musica in Rio de Janeiro; opera, *Malazarte* (1941); ballet, *Amaya* (1939); orchestral works; songs.

United States

Ives, Charles Edward. 1874-1954. One of the most prolific, original, and neglected composers of his time; polytonal writing with use of polychords and occasional atonal passages pre-

dated many better-known Europeans; symphonies, chamber music, songs, and choral works; won Pulitzer Prize (1947) for *Third Symphony* (1911); gained recognition with *Second Piano Sonata*; influenced young composers.

Gershwin, George. 1898-1937. Composer; musical comedies, popular songs; folk opera, *Porgy and Bess* (1935), considered masterpiece; *Rhapsody in Blue* (1924, for piano and jazz orchestra), classic example of symphonic jazz; *Piano Concerto in F* (1925); *American in Paris* (1928).

GERSHWIN

Copland, Aaron. 1900- . Considered most representative of American

COPLAND

music of this period; *Music for the Theater* (1925), idiom of jazz introduced into work; ballets: *Billy the Kid* (1938), *Rodeo* (1942), *Appalachian Spring* (1944), *El Salón Mexico* (1936); music for movies.

Loeffler, Charles Martin. 1861-1935. Composer; first violinist with Boston Symphony; very individual style; *Pagan Poem* (1905-6, for orchestra) shows influence of impressionists; *Canticle of the Sun* (1925, for solo voice and orchestra); *Five Irish Fantasies* (1922, for voice and orchestra); choral works, chamber music, and songs.

Bloch, Ernest. 1880-1959. Swiss-American composer of *Schelomo* (Solomon, 1915, for cello and orchestra) and *Israel Symphony* (1916); important teacher in America; pathos, intensity of emotion, orchestral color; both admired and denounced.

Griffes, Charles Tomlinson. 1884-1920. Composer; pupil of Humperdinck; *The Pleasure Dome of Kubla Khan* (1920), symphonic poem; *Roman Sketches* (1915); *Piano Sonata* (1921), representative of mature style.

Barber, Samuel. 1910-   Composer; winner of Prix de Rome, Pulitzer Prize (1935, 36); symphonies, chamber music, choral works; overture, *The School for Scandal* (1933); *Adagio for Strings* (1936); *Dover Beach* (1931, for voice and string quartets).

Piston, Walter. 1894-   . Composer; neoclassicist; teacher at Harvard (since 1932); seven symphonies; string quartets: *Concerto for Orchestra* (1933) and witty *Concertino* for piano and chamber orchestra (1937).

Harris, Roy. 1898-   . Prolific composer of seven symphonies, orchestral works, chamber music, many choral works; *When Johnny Comes Marching Home* (1934).

Carpenter, John Alden. 1876-1951. Composer; influenced by French Impressionists; *Adventures in a Perambulator* (performed 1915); *Skyscrapers* (1926); two symphonies, violin concerto, chamber music, choral works, songs; song-cycle to poems of Tagore, *Gitanjali*.

Others. Virgil Thomson (1896-   ), Ernst Krenek (1900-   ), Randall Thompson (1899-   ), Marc Blitzstein (1905-64), Howard Hanson (1896-   ), Daniel G. Mason (1873-1953), William Grant Still (1895-   ), Vittorio Rieti (1898-   ).

Mexico

Chávez, Carlos. 1899-   . Composer; conductor-founder of Orquesta Sinfónica de Mexico (1928-52), one of the best in the Hemisphere; used Indian instruments and music; four symphonies, piano concerto, three string quartets, and other chamber music; ballets; choral works; *Sinfonia India*

(1936); author of *Toward a New Music* (1938).

Ponce, Manuel. 1882-1948. Composer, conductor; studied in Europe; *Chapultapec*, symphonic triptych for orchestra; famous for song, *Estrellita*; orchestral works, concertos, chamber music; collected and arranged Mexican folk songs.

Carillo, Julián. 1875- . Composer; proponent of fractional divisions of accepted intervals; split half-tone into infinite number of smaller parts; *Revolution of the Sound Thirteen* (beyond conception of quarter-tone); invented special instruments for performance of his music, including *octavina* (eighth-tones) and *arpa citera* (sixteenth-tones); *Concertino*, world première, Philadelphia Symphony Orchestra under Stokowski (1927); operas, symphonies, chamber and choral music.

Revueltas, Silvestre. 1899-1940. Composer, conductor; melodic imagery steeped in Mexican folklore; many orchestral works, chamber music, songs.

Argentina

Paz, Juan Carlos. 1897- . Leader of modern school of music; atonal composer; founder of Nueva Musica, group dedicated to the performance of contemporary music; *Passacaglia*, for orchestra (twelve-tone technique, performed Paris, 1937); chamber and orchestral music; music for piano; very influential.

Ginastera, Alberto. 1916- . Leading musical figure in Argentina; advanced harmonic idiom based on folklore; ballets, *Panambi* (1940) and *Estancia* (1941); orchestral works.

Williams, Alberto. 1862-1952. Composer, pianist, conductor, poet; studied under Franck in Paris; founded conservatory, Buenos Aires (1903); works include nine symphonies and other orchestral music; chamber music; unaccompanied choral music; piano pieces and songs.

Chile

Santa Cruz (Wilson), Domingo. 1899- . Composer; educated in Madrid; neoclassicist; called "Chilean Hindemith"; *Vinetas* (1927, for piano); chamber music; *Cantata de los Rios de Chile* (performed 1942, for chorus and orchestra); set poems of Gabriela Mistral (1928).

Allende, Humberto. 1885- . Pioneer of modern music in Chile; toured Europe; symphonic poems, music for piano; later works include *La Despedida* (1934, for two sopranos, contralto, and large orchestra); music for violin and cello.

Cuba

Roldan, Amadeo. 1900-1939. Composer, conductor; studied in Spain; conductor of orchestra of Havana (1932-39); *La Rebambaramba*, Afro-Cuban ballet in one act; *Miracle of Anaquille*, choreographic Afro-Cuban mystery in one act; *Negro Dance*, poem for high voice and seven instruments; *Overture on Cuban Themes*; orchestral works, string quartet, etc.

1945–Today · Europe

France: **Poulenc,** Francis. 1889-1963. Composer, pianist; member of "Les Six"; irrepressible satirical expression; classical clarity of style; outstanding works include *Le Bal masque*

POULENC

teacher; with Baudrier, Lesur, and Jolivet formed group, *La jeune France* (1936); important influence as professor of harmony at Paris Conservatoire; credited with breaking hold of neoclassicism on Paris school; introduction of Oriental elements into Western music; *Turangalîla Symphony* (1948); religious works; contributions to music for the organ; noted for use of new instruments; symphonic poems, vocal, piano music with complex rhythmic patterns.

(1932), song-cycle "secular cantata" on surrealist verses of Max Jacob; *Banalités* on poems of Apollinaire (1940); *Le travail du peintre* (The Painter's Work, 1957), impressions of seven contemporary painters; ballet, *Les Biches* (House Party, 1923); *Les Dialogues des Carmélites* (1953-55), serious opera, often performed; with Cocteau, tour de force opera in one act, *La voix humaine* (1958); chamber music; concerto for two pianos, choral works, and piano pieces.

Boulez, Pierre. 1925- . Leading younger composer of contemporary France, though his compositions have been both praised and denounced; studied Paris Conservatoire; pupil of Leibowitz who initiated him into serial technique; influenced by Messiaen; musical director of Barrault and Renaud theatrical company (1947); committed to dodecaphonic; orchestral music; *Le Marteau sans Maître* (The Hammer Without a Master, 1953-54, for contralto and six instruments based on three short poems of René Char), best-known work.

Messiaen, Oliver. (Eugene Prosper Charles). 1908- . Composer, organist,

Switzerland: **Martin**, Frank. 1890- . Outstanding composer of unusual originality and power; interested in Schönberg's 12-note serial technique, but did not adopt it; *Petite Symphonie Concertante* (for two string orchestras, harp, harpsichord, and piano), delightful, popular work; cantatas, Mass, chamber music; *La Vin herbé* (1938-41, dramatic oratorio), most famous work; *Sonnets of Cornet Rilke* (for low voice and chamber orchestra); works for stage: *Golgotha* (1945-48), *The Tempest* (1956), *La Mystère* de la *Nativité* (1960), *Monsieur de Pourceaugnac* (1962-63).

Liebermann, Rolf. 1910- . Leading Swiss exponent of 12-tone system; musical staff of Radio-Zurich; eclectic style that combines classic, romantic, and 12-tone elements; *Concerto for Jazzband and Symphony Orchestra* (1954); *Penelope* (1954), successful opera.

Beck, Conrad. 1901- . Composer; outstanding choral works including *Der Tod des Oedipus, Angelus Silesius* (oratorio), *Der Tod zu Basel*; six symphonies, concerto.

England: **Britten,** (Edward) Benjamin. 1913- One of the most prolific and popular English composers today; operas; *Peter Grimes* (1945), *Rape of Lucretia* (1946), *Billy Budd* (1952), *Turn of the Screw* (1954); considerable dramatic power; essentially an exceptional lyrical talent; choral works, chamber music, successful compositions for solo voices, and works for orchestra; recent work, *War Requiem*, written for the dedication of Coventry Cathedral (1962, for alto voices, large chorus, boys' choir with organ, chamber group, and full symphonic orchestra).

BRITTEN

Tippett, Michael Kemp. 1905- Unusual intellectual, technically expert, original musical talent; although influenced by Stravinsky and Bartok, owes much to cross-rhythms of Purcell and madrigalists; *A Child of our Time* (1941, oratorio); *The Midsummer Marriage* (1952, opera); two symphonies, concerto for double-string orchestra, choral works, chamber music, and piano pieces.

Rawsthorne, Alan. 1905- Versatile composer; individual style; studied Royal Manchester College of Music; settled in London (1935); compositions include *Symphonic Studies* (1938), concertos for clarinet (1942), violin (1947), piano (1951); chamber music, songs, orchestral music.

Maconchy, Elizabeth. 1907- . Composer; pupil of Vaughan Williams; most representative of highly individual treatment of contemporary idioms within traditional forms are string quartets and other chamber music; ballet music; orchestral works.

Germany: **Henze,** Hans Werner. 1926- . Considered one of the most talented of younger generation of German composers; unorthodox handling of 12-tone system; studied Heidelberg, Paris; influenced by Schönberg, Stravinsky; brilliant instrumentation, romantic lyricism, and flair for dramatic; excellent ballet music: *Ballet Variations* (1949), *Ballet Scenes for Orchestra* (1950); opera, *Boulevard Solitude* (1951), considered outstanding achievement in lyric theater; *Prinz von Homburg* (1959); most brilliant success, *Undine* (1959, ballet); orchestral, vocal music, chamber works, radio operas.

Stockhausen, Karlheinz. 1928- Leading avant-garde composer and considered most exciting musical figure in postwar Germany; editor *Die Reihe* (The Row), quarterly review of serial music, published in Vienna; studied physics and acoustics, Bonn; first published score of electronic music, *Electronic Studies* (1953-54); *Song of the Youths* (1956), combining sound of human voice with pure electronic sound, considered most important work.

Blacher, Boris. 1903- . Composer; influential teacher; free contrapuntal style; symphony and other orchestral works; dramatic oratorios: *Romeo and Juliet, The Grand Inquisitor*; ballets: *Hamlet* (1950), *Lysistrata* (1951); chamber music.

Klebe, Giselher. 1925- . Prolific composer; 12-tone system; operas, *The Robbers* (after Schiller, 1956) and *The Fatal Wish* (after Balzac, 1957); ability to create pervasive mood; orchestral works; chamber music.

Russia: **Stravinsky,** Igor. 1882- . Ballet, *Agon* (1953-57), shows influence of Webern; *Threni* (1958, for soloists, chorus, and orchestra); works for television.

STRAVINSKY

Italy: **Dallapiccola,** Luigi. 1904- . Leading composer; intellectual, literary emphasis apparent in style; influence of Schönberg, 12-note system without semitone; operas: *Volo di notte* (Night Flight, 1940) and the brilliant *Il Prigioniero* (The Prisoner, 1944-48, performed 1950); choral works, chamber music.

Maderna, Bruno. 1920- . Outstanding contemporary composer; one of founders of Studio di Fonologia Musicale at Milan Radio, one of the centers of new electronic music; *Studies for the Trial of Kafka* (1950, for recitation, soprano, and small orchestra); *Serenata No. 2 for 11 Instruments* (1955); *Sequenze e strutture, Notturno* and *Syntaxis*, electronic compositions; works widely performed; influential.

Nono, Luigi. 1924- . Talented composer of post-Webern generation in Italy; studied with Maderna; *Epitaph for Federico Garcia Lorca* (1952-54, for chorus and orchestra); *Cori di Didone* (1958); electronic music and works for conventional instruments.

Berio, Luciano. 1925- . Composer of absolutely controlled music; associated with Maderna; studied with Dallapiccola; chamber works; *Mutations* (1956, electronic work); *Différences* (1958, combines flute, clarinet, viola, cello, harp, with magnetic tape); *Hommage à Joyce* (1959) introduces work with reading of fragment of Ulysses by female voice, which is then reconstructed electronically and enlarged into composition.

Petrassi, Goffredo. 1904- . Composer; early works influenced by Hindemith and include religious work, *Psalm IX* (1934-36, for chorus, strings, brass, two pianos, and percussion); *Coro di Morti* (Chorus of the Dead, 1941, "dramatic madrigal" for four-part male chorus, three pianos, brass, double brasses, etc.); *Notte oscura* (Obscure Night, 1951) uses Schönberg's 12-tone technique; *Nonsense* (1952) on poems by Lear, choral work; concertos, piano, and vocal music, two operas and two ballets.

Denmark: **Bentzon,** Jørgen. 1897-1951. Leading composer of movement-construction technique known as "character polyphony"; *Second Symphony* (1946-47, with sections—Energy, Growth, Construction) combines musical architectonics and a lyrical, expressive mood in highly individual tone language.

Sweden: **Rosenberg,** Helding. 1892- . Prolific leader of modern Swedish music; exceptional string quartets, oratorios, dramatic musical works; song-cycle based on Mann's *Joseph and His Brethren;* important teacher.

Blomdahl, Karl-Birger. 1916- . Outstanding pupil of Rosenberg; *String Trio* (1946); *Violin Concerto* (1947); *Concerto Grosso* (1944); magnificent set of variations known as *Facetter* (Facets); *In the Hall of Mirrors* (1950), choral cycle based on modern Swedish poetry.

Belgium: **Poot,** Marcel. 1901- . Best-known contemporary Belgian composer; a founder of *Synthétistes*, group dedicated to propagation of musical modernism; influenced by Stravinsky;

three operas, two ballets, two oratorios, two symphonies, and other works.

Americas

United States: **Riegger,** Wallingford. 1885-1961. Composer, conductor, teacher; 12-tone system; studied with Bruch; managed to combine dodecaphonic techniques with classical tradition; *Dichotomy for Chamber Orchestra* (1932), strong early work; *Canon and Fugue for Strings* (1941), considered one of best compositions; excellent music for modern dancers including Graham, Weidman, and Humphrey; symphonies, orchestral, and chamber music.

Sessions, Roger. 1896- . Composer, teacher; studied under Parker, Bloch; lived abroad (1925-33); music lies between atonal chromaticism and 12-tone system; subtle expressionist; four symphonies; one-act opera, *The Trial of Lucullus* (play by Brecht, 1947); *Idyll of Theocritus* (1954); now experimenting with electronic music; influential.

Copland, Aaron. 1900- . Late works adapt serial techniques of 12-tone school to personal harmonic style; *Fantasia for Piano* (1958).

Bernstein, Leonard. 1918- . Conductor, composer; first American-born conductor of New York Philharmonic Symphony Orchestra (1958); studied under Piston, Koussevitsky; *Jeremiah Symphony* (1942); *Age of Anxiety* (Second Symphony for piano and orchestra, 1949, to poem by Auden); ballets and musical comedies.

Varèse, Edgar. 1885- . Founder and conductor of New Symphony Orchestra (1919), founder, International Composers' Guild (1921); born in Paris; studied under d'Indy; to United States (1915); geometric patterns of cubism reflected in *Amériques* (1922), symphonic poem; *Hyperprism* (1923, for chamber orchestra); started to compose electronic music (1952); *Deserts* (1954); *Poème Électronique* (1958); most celebrated work probably *Ionisation* (1931), using percussion and bell sounds, study in pure sonority and rhythm.

Weisgall, Hugo. 1912- . Czech-American composer, conductor, teacher; studied with Sessions, Reiner; expressionist theater; dissonant tension; sound dominated by major and minor seconds, sevenths, and ninths; *The Tenor* (1950, libretto, Karl Shapiro and Ernst Lert, from Wedekind's drama, *Der Kammersanger*); *Six Characters in Search of an Author* (1953-56, based on Pirandello), considered best work; *Purgatory*, using 12-tone row (1958, based on last play of Yeats).

Wolpe, Stefan. 1902- . Intellectual composer whose work is often compared to modern abstract painting; highly intellectual; to United States (1939); *Quartet for Trumpet, Saxophone, Piano and Drums* (1950) attests to interest in jazz; *Quintet with Voice* (1957).

Kirchner, Leon. 1919- . Composer; studied with Bloch and Sessions; *Piano Sonata* (1948), important early work; *Piano Concerto* (1953); chamber music.

Carter, Elliott Cook. 1908- . Leading composer; *Variations for Orchestra* (1955), considered excellent work; bold, original string quartets (1951,

1960), important contributions to chamber music.

Menotti, Gian Carlo. 1911- . Italian-American composer of operas; *Amelia Goes to the Ball* (1937), opera buffa; *The Medium* and *The Telephone* (1946), *The Consul* (1950), *Amahl and the Night Visitors* (1951), *The Saint of Bleecker Street* (1954), considered most important work; ballets, piano concerto.

Moore, Douglas. 1893- . Composer, teacher; studied with d'Indy, Bloch; head of music department, Columbia University; *Ballad of Baby Doe* (1956, opera in two acts); *Devil and Daniel Webster; Four Museum Pieces.*

Foss, Lukas. 1922- . German-American; to United States (1937); pianist of Boston Symphony; studied with Koussevitsky; full-length cantata, *The Prairie* (1944, based on Sandburg's poem); one-act opera, *The Jumping Frog of Calaveras County* (1950, based on Mark Twain's story); *Griffelkin* (1955); *Time Cycle* (1960).

Dello Joio, Norman. 1913- . Organist, pianist, composer; harmony is freely dissonant; achieved mature style with *Concert Music* (1944), symphonic rondo in three sections; *Meditations on Ecclesiastes* (1957) won Pulitzer Prize; *Blood Moon* (1961), opera.

Porter, Quincy. 1897- . Classicist, composer, important teacher; outstanding chamber music, including *String Quartet No. 8* (1950); Pulitzer Prize (1954).

Diamond, David Leo. 1915- . Composer; six symphonies, two violin concertos, cello concerto, four string quartets, and other chamber music; ballets.

Powell, Mel. 1923- . Composer, teacher at Yale; studied with Hindemith; influenced by Webern; outstanding chamber music; *Trio for Piano, Violin, Cello* (1957); *Piano Quintet* (1957); *Stanzas for Chamber Orchestra* (1959), *Filigree Setting for String Quartet* (1960).

Schuman, William. 1910- . Composer, teacher; president of Juilliard Music School (from 1945); seven symphonies, third (1941, most popular), seventh (1960, most mature); ballet, *Undertow* (1945); *American Festival Overture;* choral works, four string quartets.

Swanson, Howard. 1909- . Outstanding composer; *Short Symphony,* leading work; *Symphony No. 1* (1945); *Night Music for Chamber Orchestra* (1950); *Music for Strings* (1951).

Kay, Ulysses. 1917- . Brilliant composer of music for voice; influenced by Hindemith; *Suite for Orchestra* (1945); *Suite for Strings* (1947); *Concerto for Orchestra* (1948); cantata, *Song of Jeremiah* (1945); *Song of Ahab* (1950), for baritone voice and ten instruments); *Three Pieces after Blake,* for dramatic soprano and orchestra.

Argentina: **Castro,** Juan José. 1895- . Composer, conductor; studied with d'Indy; founded Renacimiento Orchestra in Buenos Aires (1929); ballet, *Mékhâno* (1934); opera, *Proserpina y el extranjero* (performed 1952, Milan, won Verdi prize of La Scala, 1951); recent vocal works include songs to poems of García Lorca; versatile, prolific, influential.

THEATER

EUROPE · *Great Britain*

Shaw, George Bernard. 1856-1950. Master Irish-English dramatist, essayist, critic; best-known for social satire or the "play with purposeful laughter"; *Arms and the Man* (1894); *Candida* (1895); *The Devil's Disciple* (1897); *Caesar and Cleopatra* (1899); *Major Barbara* (1905); *Androcles and the Lion* (1912); *Pygmalion* (1913); *Saint*

SHAW

SCENE FROM SHAW'S *Caesar and Cleopatra,*

Joan (1923), considered his masterpiece.

Synge, John Millington. 1871-1909. Master Irish dramatist, poet; influenced by Yeats; famous for interpretation of Irish peasant life in short plays, including *Shadow of the Glen* (1903, comedy), *Riders to the Sea* (1904, tragedy); *The Playboy of the Western World* (1907), bitter humor expressing what is real and what men think is real; *Deirdre of the Sorrows* (1910).

Yeats, William Butler. 1865-1939. Irish playwright, poet; with Lady Gregory produced plays at the Irish Literary Theatre (1899), that became the Abbey Theatre (Dublin Players); *The Countess Cathleen* (1892); *The Pot of Broth* (1902, short comedy); *Deirdre* (1906); *At the Hawks' Well* (1920); influence more important than work itself.

YEATS

O'Casey, Sean. 1884-1964. Master Irish dramatist; famous for realist plays: *Juno and the Paycock* (1924); *The Plough and the Stars* (1926); expressionist style emerges in *The Silver Tassie* (1928); *Within the Gates*

(1934); *The Star Turns Red* (1940); *Red Roses for Me* (1943), fantasy; *Purple Dust* (1945).

Galsworthy, John. 1867-1933. Dramatist, novelist; realist; *The Silver Box* (1906); *Joy* (1907); *Strife* (1909); *Justice* (1910), best-known work; concerned with social problems.

Barrie, Sir James Matthew. 1860-1937. Scottish playwright; sentimental realism in *The Admirable Crichton* (1902), *Peter Pan* (1904), *What Every Woman Knows* (1908), *Dear Brutus* (1917).

Colum, Padraic. 1881- . One of the founders of the *Irish Review* and the Abbey Theatre; first play, *The Broken Soil* (revised to *The Fiddler's House*, 1907); *Thomas Muskerry* (1910).

Carroll, Paul Vincent. 1900- . Irish playwright; problem drama with an element of the supernatural; *Shadow and Substance* (1934); *The White Steed* (1938).

Priestley, John Boynton. 1894- . English writer; psychological melodrama, *Dangerous Corner* (1932); *Laburnum Grove* (1933); *An Inspector Calls* (1946), good characterization.

Belgium

Maeterlinck, Maurice. 1862-1949. Symbolist; *Menna Vanna* (1902); *Joyzelle* (1903); *The Blue Bird* (1909); *The Betrothal* (1918); a drama set in medieval period, *Pelléas et Mélisande* (1892, opera by Debussy).

Crommelynck, Fernand. *ca.* 1885-/88- . Influenced by surrealists in combining scenes of striking contrast; best-known for *The Magnificent Cuckold* (1920, successfully produced in Paris, 1921); *Golden Tripe* (1925), social satire; *The Woman Whose Heart is Too Small* (1934).

France

Giradoux, Jean. 1882-1944. Leading dramatist; best-known works: *Amphitryon 38* (1929), *Électre* (1937), *Ondine* (1939, fairy tale), *The Madwoman of Chaillot* (1945); influential.

SCENE FROM *Madwoman of Chaillot,* GIRADOUX, 1945

Cocteau, Jean. 1889-1963. Dramatist, artist; influenced by surrealists; flight from reality; various styles; *The Couple of the Eiffel Tower* (1921); *Antigone* (1922); *Orphée* (1926); *The Infernal Machine* (1934), *The Typewriter* (1941), *The Eagle with Two Heads* (1946).

Claudel, Paul Louis Charles. 1868-1955. Considered greatest modern religious Christian dramatist in France; synthesized symbolist techniques with Catholicism; *The Midday Break* (printed 1906); *Tidings Brought to*

COCTEAU

Mary (produced 1912); *The Satin Slipper* (printed 1930); *The Father Humiliated* (1946).

Curel, François de. 1854-1928. Outstanding dramatist of realist school; *The Reverse of a Saint; The Fossils; The Dance Before the Mirror* (1914), precursor of psychological dramas.

Raynal, Paul. 1885- . Romanticist of psychoanalysis; *The Master of His Heart* (1920); *The Tomb beneath the Arc de Triomphe* (1924, translated as *The Unknown Warrior,* 1928), outstanding war drama; *In the Sunshine of Instinct* (1932); *La Francerie* (1933).

Lenormand, Henri-René. 1882-1951. Dramatist; important influence in introduction of psychoanalytic method to the stage; *The Eater of Dreams* (1922).

Italy

Pirandello, Luigi. 1867-1936. Leading dramatist, novelist; 300 stories, six novels, and about 50 plays; essentially a realist concerned with the contrast between the image and reality; portrayal of inner solitude; *Six Characters in Search of an Author* (1922).

D'Annunzio, Gabriele. 1863-1938. Flamboyant, passionately romantic novelist, dramatist; symbolic-realistic plays; *The Dead City, La Gioconda* (1898); *Francesca da Rimini* (1902); *Jorio's Daughter* (1904), probably his best work; *The Light Under the Bushel* (1905).

Chiarelli, Luigi. 1880-1947. Leading representative of the grotesque theater; *The Mask and the Face* (1916), brilliantly clever; *The Silken Ladder* (1917), humorous, though grotesque satire on politics; *Chimeras* (1919); *The Lovers' Death* (1921).

Rosso di San Secondo, Pier Maria. 1887- . Original, bizarre drama of the grotesque; *Marionettes, What Passion* (1918), three characters without names, moved by forces they cannot control; *The Sleeping Beauty* (1919).

Spain

Benavente y Martínez, Jacinto. 1866-1954. Nobel Prize dramatist (1922); extremely prolific; very clever dialogue, excellent characterization rather than strong plots; *La Malquerida* (The Passion Flower, 1913); *Los intereses creados* (Bonds of Interest, 1907, performed by Theater Guild, 1919); *The Evildoers of Good* (1905); *The Joyous and Confident City* (1916).

Martínez Sierra, Gregorio. 1881-1947. Dramatist, novelist, poet; social dramas; *Cancion de cuna* (1911, English version, *The Cradle Song,* 1917), often produced in New York and London; *The Kingdom of God* (1916); *The Romantic Young Lady* (1918).

Álvarez Quintero, Serafín. 1871-1938. With brother **Joaquín** (1873-1944) wrote many highly successful plays of all types; portrayed Andalusian middle-class life; *The Lady from Alfaqueque* (1914), best-known work outside of Spain.

Russia

Gorki, Maxim (Alexei Maximovich Peshkov). 1868-1936. Outstanding playwright, short story writer, novelist; great work, *The Lower Depths* (1903); *Summer Visitors* (1903); *Enemies* (1906); *The Last Oven* (1908); *The Judge* (1915); *Egor Bulichov and Others* (1932).

GORKI

Andreyev, Leonid Nikolaevich. 1871-1919. Leading playwright, short story writer; combined symbolism and melodrama; *Life of Man* (1906); *The Black Masters* (1908); *Anathema* (1909), considered masterpiece; *Samson in Chains* (1914), outstanding; *S.O.S.* (1919), denunciation of life under Communism.

Afinogenov, Alexander Nikolaevich. 1904-41. Gifted dramatist; revolutionary zeal; *Keep Your Eyes Open* (1927);

Fear (1931), important characterization; *Distant Point* (1935) shows influence of Chekov; *Raspberry Jam* (1928), comedy.

Bulgakov, Mikhail Afanasyevich. 1891-1940. Playwright, famed for *The Days of the Turbine* (1926); influenced by Chekhov.

Kirshon, Vladimir Mikhailovich. 1902-37. Dramatist; with Uspenski wrote *Konstantin Terekhin* (translated as *Red Dust*, 1927); *Bread* (1930); *The City of Winds* (1929); *Miraculous Alloy* (1934).

Evreinov, Nikolai Nikolaevich. 1879- . Playwright; best-known for short plays; *The Theater of the Soul* (1912); *The Fourth Wall* (1915).

Glebov, Anatol. 1899- . Playwright; *Inga* (1929), position of a woman in the new Socialist society.

Bakst, Leon Nikolayevich (Lev Rosenberg). 1866-1924. Scenic and costume designer, painter; studied in St. Petersburg and Paris; identified with beginnings of Russian modernism; sets for Diaghilev's Ballet Russe, Paris (1909); also sets for operas.

Others. Anatoli Lunacharski (1875-1933), Vladimir Maiakovski (1893-1930), Nikolai Pogodin (1900-).

Czechoslovakia

Capek, Karel. 1890-1938. Expressionist dramatist; famous for *R.U.R.* (1921), satire using robots; *The Macropulos Secret* (1922); with brother **Josef,** *The Insect Comedy* (1921); use of symbolism.

Hungary

Molnar, Ferenc. 1878-1952. Dramatist; noted for *Liliom* (1909), *The Guardsman* (1910), and *The Swan* (1920), all produced in the United States.

Sweden

Bergman, Hjalmar. 1883-1930. Leading dramatist of his country; influenced by Ibsen; short-realistic-poetic *Marionette Plays* (from 1917); most successful work, *The Nobel Prize* (produced in the United States, 1932); *The Rabble* (1928).

Austria

Schnitzler, Arthur. 1862-1931. Dramatist, novelist; part of group called "Young Vienna" opposed to German naturalistic school; concerned with individual happiness; *Liebelie* (*Light o' Love*, 1895), best-known work; *The Lonely Way* (1904), excellent; *The Vast Domain* (1910); *Prof. Bernhardi* (1912).

Billinger, Richard. 1893- . Leading dramatist; *The Perchten Play* (1928); *Rauhnacht* (1931); *The Witch of Passau* (1935), peasant revolt of the 17th century.

Iceland

Sigurjónsson, Jóhann. 1880-1919. Vigorous playwright; known for *Ejvind of the Hills* (1911); *Loft's Wish* (1915); use of folk tales.

AMERICAS · *United States*

O'Neill, Eugene. 1888-1953. Outstanding American dramatist; first full-length play, *Beyond the Horizon* (produced 1920), followed in the same year by the exciting work, *Emperor Jones; Anna Christie* (1921); *The Hairy Ape* (1922); *All God's Chillun Got Wings* (1924); *Desire Under the Elms* (1924); *The Great God Brown* (1926); *Strange Interlude* (1928); *Mourning Becomes Electra* (1931); *Ah, Wilderness* (1933); *The Iceman Cometh* (1946); *Long Day's Journey Into Night* (1956); *A Moon for the Misbegotten* (1957).

O'NEILL

SCENE FROM O'NEILL'S *Desire Under the Elms*, 1924

Anderson, Maxwell. 1888-1959. Popular, successful playwright; historical play his forte; *What Price Glory* (with Lawrence Stallings, 1924); *Elizabeth the Queen* (1930); *Mary of Scotland* (1933); *Valley Forge* (1934); *Winterset* (1935); *High Tor* (1936).

Others. S. N. Behrman (1893-), Marc Connelly (1890-), Elmer Rice (1892-), George Kelly (1887-), Sidney Howard (1891-1939), Sidney Kingsley (1906-), Robert E. Sherwood (1896-1955), Marc Blitzstein (1901-1964), Irwin Shaw (1913-), Clifford Odets (1906-1963), Thornton Wilder (1897-), William Saroyan (1908-), Lillian Hellman (1905-).

1945–Today · Germany

Brecht, Bertolt. 1898-1956. Outstanding playwright, poet; called "pessimistic anarchist"; considered by many leading dramatist of period; very influential; one-act farce, *The Wedding* (1923); *In the Jungle of the Cities* (1921-23), foreshadows Theatre of the Absurd; *Man Equals Man* (1924-

BRECHT

343

SCENE FROM BRECHT's *Mother Courage*

25), *Three-Penny Opera* (1928; music by Kurt Weill, adaptation of *Beggar's Opera*); *Good Woman of Setzuan* (1938-40); *Mother Courage* (pub. English, 1941); *Schweik in the Second World War* (1941-44); *Private Life of the Master Race* (1944); *Caucasian Chalk Circle* (1944-45); *Trumpets and Drums* (performed 1956); gained in popularity after World War II.

France: **Sartre**, Jean Paul. 1905- . Existentialist; *No Exit, The Flies* (1944); *The Respectful Prostitute* (1946); *Dirty Hands* (1948).

SARTRE

Camus, Albert. 1913-60. Nobel Prize novelist; *Caligula* (1945); *Les Justes* (1949).

Anouilh, Jean. 1910- . *The Waltz of the Toreadors* (1952).

United States: **Williams,** Tennessee (Thomas Lanier). 1914- . *Glass Menagerie* (1945), N.Y. Critic's Award; *Streetcar Named Desire* (1947); *Camino Real* (1953); *Cat on a Hot Tin Roof* (1955), Pulitzer Prize; *Sweet Bird of Youth* (1959), *The Night of the Iguana* (1962).

Miller, Arthur 1915- . *Death of a Salesman* (1949); *The Crucible* (1952-53); *After The Fall* (1963); *Incident at Vichy*.

SCENE FROM *Death of a Salesman,* MILLER

Theater of the Absurd. An international movement, similar to contemporary abstract art in its rejection of "literary" elements, that is, more concerned with "happenings" on stage and with concrete and objectified images that transcend and often contradict the language of the play. The desire or aim of the group is to present the ultimate absurdity of the human condition in order to make man come to terms with the world in which he lives.

Leading dramatists of the group include: Arthur **Adamov** (1908- , Russian-French), *La Parodi, L'Invasion, Le Ping-Pong, Paolo Paoli;* Edward **Albee** (1928- , United States), *The Zoo Story, The American Dream, Death of Bessie Smith, Who's Afraid of Virginia Woolf?;* Fernando **Arrabal** (1932- , Spanish-Moroccan, lives in France), *The Executioners, The Automobile Graveyard;* Samuel **Beckett** (1906- , Irish, lives in France), *Waiting for Godot, Endgame, Krapp's Last Tape, Happy Days;* Dino **Buzzati** (1906- , Italian), *Un Casa Clinico, Un Verme al Minstero;* Ezio **d'Errico** (1892- , Italian), *The Anthill, Time of the Locusts, The Forest;* Max **Frisch** (1911- , German-Swiss), *Biedermann and the Incendiaries;* Jean **Genêt** (1909- , French), *The Maids, The Balcony, The Blacks, The Screens;* Günter **Grass** (1927- , German), *Uncle, Uncle, The Wicked Cooks;* Wolfgang **Hildesheimer** (1916- , German-Israeli), *Pastoral, or Time for Cocoa, Landscape with Figures, The Clocks;* Eugène **Ionesco** (1912- , Rumanian, lives in France), *The Bald Soprano, The Lesson, Jack, or the Submission, The Chairs, Victims of Duty, The Killer, Rhinocéros,* others; Manuel **de Pedrolo** (1919- , Spanish, writes in Catalan), *Cruma, Humans and No;* Robert **Pinget** (1919- , Swiss-French), *Dead Letter, The Old Tune;* Harold **Pinter** (1930- , English), *The Room, The Dumb Waiter, The Birthday Party, The Caretaker;* Norman Frederick **Simpson** (1919- , English), *A Resounding Tinkle, One Way Pendulum;* Jean **Tardieu** (1903- ,

French), *The Lovers in the Subway, The A.B.C. of Our Life, A Voice Without Anyone;* Boris **Vian** (1920-59, French), *Knackery Made Easy, Les Bâtisseurs d'Empire.*

DANCE

At the beginning of this century, the dance as an art form was revitalized through the creative efforts of two important dancers: the Russian, Michel Fokine, and the American, Isadora Duncan. Fokine brought new life to the ballet and Duncan, in her pseudo-Greek, "back-to-nature" movement, introduced a new freedom of expression that led ultimately to the modern dance and the work of the supreme artist of the form, Martha Graham.

Ballet

Fokine, Michel. 1880-1942 (Russian). Dancer-choreographer; created *Les*

Les Sylphides, MARKOVA AND KRIZA

Sylphides (1909), *Prince Igor* (1909), *Carnaval* (1910), *Scheherazade* (1910), *The Firebird* (1910), *Petrouchka* (1911), *Daphnis and Chloe* (1912).

Bolm, Adolph. 1884-1951 (Russian). Dancer-choreographer; associated with the great impressario, Serge Diaghilev (1872-1929); dancing partner of Anna Pavlova; worked in the United States making excellent use of American material and recreating the American spirit in the dance; *Krazy Kat* (1920), *Apollo Musagetes* (1928), *Le Ballet Mechanique* (1932).

Massine, Léonide. 1884- (Russian). Dancer-choreographer; Diaghilev associate; *Parade* (1917), *Three-Cornered Hat* (1919), *La Boutique Fantastique* (1919), *La Symphonie Fantastique* (1936), *Seventh Symphony* (1938), *Gaité Parisienne* (1938), *Mam'zelle Angot* (1947).

Nijinsky, Vaslav. 1890-1945. Great Russian ballet dancer and choreographer; *Afternoon of a Faun* (1912), *The Rite of Spring* (1913), *Jeux* (1913), *Til Eulenspiegel* (1916); noted for interpretation of *Le Spectre de la Rose* (1910).

Balanchine, George. 1904- (Russian-American). Choreographer; Diaghilev associate; major figure in contemporary ballet; director, New York City Ballet; *Cotillon* (1932), *Card Party* (1937), *Danses Concertantes* (1944), *Ivesiana* (1955), *Divertimento #15* (1956), *Seven Deadly Sins* (1958), *Figure in the Carpet* (1960), *Electronics* (1961), *Midsummer Night's Dream* (1962).

BALLANCHINE'S *Apollo*

Valois, Ninette de (Edris Stanns). 1898- (Irish). Associated with Diaghileff; organizer of Sadler's Wells Ballet (Royal Ballet Company); *Job* (1931), *Rake's Progress* (1935), *Checkmate* (1937).

Ashton, Frederick. 1906- (British). Director, Royal Ballet; choreographer of *Façade* (1931), *Les Rendezvous* (1935), *Les Patineurs* (1937), *Wise and Foolish Virgins* (1939).

Tudor, Antony. 1908- . (British). *Lilac Garden* (1936), *Goyescas* (1941), *Romeo and Juliet* (1943).

De Mille, Agnes. *ca.* 1905- (American). Works for ballet, *Rodeo* (1942), *Tally-Ho* (1944); and for musical comedys *Oklahoma, Bloomer Girl*; also work for films.

BALLANCHINE

ULANOVA IN *Giselle*

LES BALLETS DE PARIS, *Carmen*

Petit, Roland. 1924-   (French). *Young Man and Death* (1946), *Don Quixote* (1950), *Sleeping Beauty* (1956).

Modern Dance

Duncan, Isadora. 1878-1927 (American). Created new dance form; sought to free dance from standard, prescribed choreography; used natural body movements to express human emotion.

Denishawn. American school created by Ruth St. Denis (1877-   ) and Ted

Shawn (1891-   ); mystics; admirers of human body and beauty of natural movement; Shawn later established dance center at Jacob's Pillow; influenced younger dancers.

Wigman, Mary. 1886-   (German). Exceptionally gifted dancer; more creative than Duncan, she was as great an influence on modern dance; extended concepts of movement and use of musical accompaniment.

Holm, Hanya. (German). Graduate of Wigman group; created an American style based on Wigman theories; *Trends* (1937), *Orestes and the Furies* (1943).

Humphrey, Doris. 1895-   (American). Denishawn associate; envolved what can be considered the kinetic laws of dance.

Weidman, Charles. 1901-   (American). Denishawn graduate; associated with Humphrey; concerned with movement derived from pantomime in which gesture is reduced to its essence; *Candide* (1933); *Inquest* (1944).

Graham, Martha. *ca.* 1894-   (American). Denishawn graduate; considered greatest creator of modern dance; *Bacchanale* (1931), *Appalachian Spring* (1944), *Death and Entrances* (1944), *Night Journey* (1947), *Diversion of Angels* (1950), *Canticle*

GRAHAM

GRAHAM IN *Legend of Judith*

for Innocent Comedians (1952), *Clytemnestra* (1953), *Entrance into the Maze* (1957), *Phaedra* (1963).

Limon, José. 1908- (Mexican). Choreographer-dancer; known for intensely emotional works; *The Moor's Pavane, The Emperor Jones.*

The young avant-garde group of American choreographers, **Merce Cunningham, Katherine Litz, Alwin Niko-**

AFRICAN DANCER

lais, **Paul Taylor** among many others, are striving to eliminate emotional motivation in the dance; not an attempt to dehumanize but to depersonalize.

Important figures in dance based on ethnic material include **Asadata Dafora** and **Pearl Primus** (African), **Uday Shankar** and **Ram Gopal** (Indian), **Azuma Kabuki Dancers** (Japan).

FILM

The creative film director is responsible for the great success of cinematic art. However, before this important 20th-century art form could compete for recognition, its tools and techniques had to be developed.

The motion picture has its genesis in the scientific inquiry of the 19th century. In 1824, Roget proposed the theory of "The Persistence of Vision." This states that the eye retains an image for a fraction of a second after it actually appears. By 1832 this theory was verified by animated drawings achieved with Plateau's phenakistoscope and von Stampfer's stroboscope. Paralleling these developments were Nicephore's experiments with photography. In 1839 he and Daguerre produced a practical photographic process. As early as 1861, Coleman Sellers animated a series of still photographs with his kinematoscope. Less than ten years later, Heyl projected similar photographs on a screen. In quick succession, there followed the experiments of Muybridge, Messonier,

Marey, Edison, and Dickson that culminated in the basic tools of the new art: the motion picture camera, film, and projector.

The motion picture was an immediate popular success. To maintain this popularity it quickly evolved from a device for recording reality to a means of presenting stories or drama. With the new film techniques employed by D. L. W. Griffith, the motion picture was raised to the level of an art form.

1895–1920

Méliès, George (French). Among first to develop narrative films: *The Doctor's Secret* (1900), *Trip to the Moon* (1902), *Conquest of the Pole* (1912).

Ince, Thomas H. (American). Enhanced the narrative film by using the techniques of close-up, cross-cutting; moved camera outdoors to use natural settings: *The Great Train Robbery* (1903), *Typhoon* (1914).

Griffith, David L. W. (American). Considered father of modern film; advanced graphic realism; evolved fluid

GRIFFITH,

Birth of a Nation,

1915

cinematic structure; created first American feature, *The Birth of a Nation* (1915); other important films: *Intolerance* (1916), *Broken Blossoms* (1919), *Way Down East* (1920).

Sennett, Mack (Michael Sinnott, American). Master of slapstick comedy; creator of the Keystone Cops, Sennett Bathing Beauties; *Tillie's Punctured Romance* (1914), *Dizzy Heights and Daring Hearts* (1916).

Chaplin, Charles Spencer (British-American). Graduate of Sennett school; created universally beloved figure, *The Tramp; Carmen* (1915), *The Immigrant* (1916), *The Cure* (1917).

1920–29

The Golden Era of the German silent cinema; work of the following directors greatly influenced American film of the period:

Weine, Robert. Created the startling expressionistic *The Cabinet of Dr. Caligari* (1919).

Lang, Fritz. Filmed *Doctor Mabuse* (1922), *Siegfried* (1924), *Metropolis* (1926).

Murnau, F. W. Gave camera a new and exciting mobility in *The Last Laugh* (1925).

Pabst, G. W. Captured *die neue Sachliehkeit* (the new realism) with socialistic flavor, *The Joyless Street* (1925), *The Loves of Jeanne Ney* (1927).

Avant-garde film experimentalists, in part influenced by surrealism in literature and the art of the period, created important, interesting films:

Richter, Hans (German). *Rhythmus 21* (1921), *Filmstudie* (1926).

Eggeling, Viking (German). Scroll-films (1919), *Symphonie Diagonale* (1921).

Dulac, Germaine (French). *The Smiling Madame Beudet* (1922), *The Devil in the City* (1924), *The Seashell and the Clergyman* (1927).

Clair, René (French). *Entr'acte* (1924), *The Phantom of Moulin Rouge* (1924).

Léger, Fernand (French). *Le Ballet Mécanique* (with Dudley Murphy, 1924-25).

Ray, Man (French). *The Return to Reason* (1923), *The Star of the Sea* (1928).

Bunuel, Luis (Spanish). *Un Chien Andalou* (1929).

Chaplin, Charles. Produced his feature-length masterpieces of the 20's: *The Kid* (1921), *A Woman of Paris* (1923), *The Gold Rush* (1925), *The Circus* (1928).

CHAPLIN,
The Gold Rush,
1925

Flaherty, Robert J. (American). Important and uncompromising maker of documentaries *Nanook of the North* (1920, released 1922), *Moana* (1923-4, released 1926), *Tabu* (1928-9, released 1931).

Stroheim, Erich von (German-American). Noted for savage social comment: *Foolish Wives* (1921), *Greed* (1923), *Wedding March* (1927).

Sternberg, Josef von (German-American). Noted for social commentary: *The Salvation Hunters* (1925), *Underworld* (1927), prototype of gangster film; directed German-produced *The Blue Angel* (1931).

The 20's marked the great period of the Russian film:

Eisenstein, Sergei. Exponent of the epic film; developed art of film editing: *Strike* (1924), *Battleship Potemkin* (1925), *Ten Days that Shook the World* (1928).

Pudovkin, Vsevolod. *Mother* (1926), *End of St. Petersburg* (1927), *Storm over Asia* (1928).

Dovzhenko, Alexander. *Arsenal* (1929), *Earth* (1930).

The last great silent film was created by **Carl Dreyer** (Danish) in France: *The Passion of St. Joan of Arc* (1929).

1929–World War II

Important introduction of sound added a new dimension to the motion picture.

Clair, Rene. *Sous les Toits de Paris* (1929), *A Nous la Liberté* (1931); *The Ghost Goes West* (1935).

Cocteau, Jean (French). *The Blood of the Poet* (1930).

Dali, Salvador (Spanish). *The Age of Gold* (1930).

Riefenstahl, Leni (German). *The Blue Light* (1933), *Olympiad* (1936-38).

STILL FROM ODESSA STEPS SEQUENCE, BATTLESHIP POTEMKIN, EISENSTEIN, 1925

MILESTONE, *All Quiet on the Western Front*, 1930

DE MILLE, *Ten Commandments*, 1923

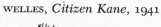

WELLES, *Citizen Kane*, 1941

GARBO, *Camille*, 1936

351

Korda, Alexander (British). *The Private Life of Henry VIII* (1933), *Rembrandt* (1936).

Grierson, John (Canadian-British). Noted for documentaries including *Drifters* (1929).

Vigo, Jean (French). *A Propos de Nice* (1930), *Zero de Conduite* (1933), *L'Atalante* (1934).

Renoir, Jean (French). *Madame Bovary* (1934), *The Grand Illusion* (1937).

Ford, John (American). *The Informer* (1935), *The Plough and the Stars* (1937), *Stagecoach* and *Young Mr. Lincoln* (1939), *The Grapes of Wrath* (1940).

Lorentz, Pare (American). Noted for excellent documentaries: *The Plow that Broke the Plains* (1936), *The River* (1937), *The Fight for Life* (1940).

Chaplin, Charles. *City Lights* (1931), *Modern Times* (1936), *The Great Dictator* (1940).

Welles, Orson (American). *Citizen Kane* (1941), *Magnificent Ambersons* (1942).

World War II–Today

Exciting neo-realist movement in Italy.

Rosselini, Roberto. *Open City* (1945), *Paisa* (1946), *Amore* (1948).

De Sica, Vittorio. *Shoe Shine* (1945), *The Bicycle Thief* (1948).

Successful development of the Japanese film industry seen in such films as *Rashomon* (1951) by **Akira Kurosawa.**

Satyajit Ray brought the Indian film to international attention with *Pather Panchali* (1956), *Aparajito* (1957), *The World of Apu* (1958).

Reed, Carol (British). *Odd Man Out* (1947), *The Third Man* (1949), *Outcast of the Islands* (1951).

Richardson, Tony (British). *Taste of Honey* (1961), *The Loneliness of a Long Distance Runner* (1962).

Huston, John (American). *Treasure of Sierra Madre* (1948), *Red Badge of Courage* (1951), *African Queen* (1951).

Bergman, Ingmar (Swedish). *The Seventh Seal* (1956), *Wild Strawberries* (1958), *The Virgin Spring* (1960), *Through a Glass Darkly* (1961), *Winter Light* (1962).

Resnais, Alain (French). *Hiroshima, Mon Amour* (1960), *Last Year at Marienbad* (1961).

Polanski, Roman (Polish). *Knife in the Water* (1963).

FURNITURE

ANTIQUITY · *Egypt*

The first piece of furniture was probably the Egyptian bed. The contents of Tutankhamen's tomb indicate that by the 14th century B.C. many more types of furniture had been developed, including stools, chairs, headrests, chests, and gaming tables. Dovetailing and doweling were used for joints; decorative details included inlaid glass, ivory, and gems; and there was frequent use of gilded plaster and detailed carving. Egyptian furniture is known for its elegance of design.

Greece and Rome

Few examples survive but vase paintings, reliefs, and literary descriptions help to give an adequate picture of the furniture of the period. The bed comprised a wood (rarely bronze or marble) frame, supported by four legs; mattresses were used; legs were turned, or carved to resemble animal legs; rosettes, volutes, and other decorative devices were common. Several types of chairs date from as early as the Greek Archaic period. Pieces worth mentioning are the *klismos* (*cathedra* of Roman period), a chair with a

FOLDING CAMP BED, WITH
LINEN STRETCHED OVER
WOODEN FRAME
EGYPTIAN, 14TH CENTURY
B.C.

GILDED WOOD AND GESSO THRONE CHAIR,
BACK DECORATED WITH RITUAL SCENES
AND HIEROGLYPHICS
EGYPTIAN, 14TH CENTURY B.C.

CHAIR
GREEK, 4TH CENTURY B.C.

BRONZE BED
ROMAN (POMPEII), 1ST CENTURY B.C.

rounded back and curved legs; the *dyphros*, a stool with turned legs; the Roman *sella curulis*, a type of folding chair. Greek oblong tables had three or four fluted or animal-form legs, while the most common table had a round top. Both round and oblong tables with a single pedestal leg also were used; tripods, footstools, chests, all variously decorated and made of diverse materials, are also known.

MIDDLE AGES

Today little furniture exists dated prior to the beginning of the 14th century. After the collapse of the Roman Empire, Europe lost the refinement of the Roman models. Nevertheless, the turnery technique continued to be used, despite primitive construction methods. New developments in the 14th and 15th centuries included cupboards, ambries, desks; folding chairs, stools, trestle tables with adjustable tops became more common. The best furniture was created for the monasteries. The invention of framed wood paneling in the 15th century made it possible to construct chests and other furniture without the need of large surfaces requiring the use of single planks of wood. Drawers came into usage and more practical joints in case furniture were invented. "Linen-fold" or "parchment" paneling was popular, while carved wood elements included tracery and other Gothic devices. Furniture was sometimes painted or gilded, while fabrics were draped over tables and cushions were used on seat furniture.

The chest, used as a desk, seat, table, or storage area, was the basic and most important piece of furniture of the Middle Ages until the cupboard came into common usage at the beginning of the 16th century. Originally hollowed-out logs with lids, chests were subsequently made with planks held together by dowels and strengthened by nails and iron bandings.

Seat furniture was rare during the Middle Ages. Two types were the X-shaped chair with fabric or leather seat and back, and the settle, developed from the chest. Bedsteads were considered important possessions because of their fabric hangings.

RENAISSANCE · *Italy*

A renewed interest in domestic architecture influenced the design of new furniture, and architectural details were the leading decorative motifs. The *cassone*, or coffer, was common; chairs included the *scabello*, an octagonal seat supported by two carved boards with a fan-shaped back; and the X-shaped or "Dante" chair of medieval origin. Tables were often supported by columnar legs, consoles, or sculptured figures, braced by a metal stretcher. Italian furniture had an important influence on the rest of Europe.

France

The medieval tradition lingered on until the second half of the reign of Francis I. Walnut replaced oak as a cabinet and chair wood. Many Italians were employed at Fontainbleau; French designers included **Androuet du Cerceau** and **Sambin.** Cabinet furniture was delicate, with inlays of marble, ivory, and different colored woods; chairs included the *caqueteuse*, or conversation chair. Tables were similar to the Italian models; chests continued to be used, while the armoire was created.

Spain

Islamic influences were strong and a half-Eastern, half-Western style known as *Mudejar* emerged. The vargueño, a fall-front chest or desk, is typically Mudejar. Frequent use of iron also characterized the Spanish style.

Holland and Germany

Northern Europe was much influenced by the prevailing Italian style. Heaviness of medieval furniture was generally retained. The pattern books of **Vredeman de Vries** and **Dietterlein** were of great influence.

England

Although many forms were still medieval, Italian decorative motifs gradually replaced medieval ornament in the first quarter of the 16th century. The pattern books of Northern Europe, as well as itinerant German cabinetmakers, influenced the over-all appearance of English furniture. The surfaces of cabinet furniture were elaborately decorated and "Nonesuch" chests were imported from Germany. The "farthingale" chair, with no arms and an upholstered seat and back, was introduced very late in the 16th century, following long attempts to create upholstered seat furniture. Bed frames were more decorated, tables with leaves were designed, and chests of drawers were introduced early in the

17th century. The English guilds became more specialized.

BAROQUE

The architecture of the baroque period had great influence on baroque furniture. Furniture details, while no less elaborate than those of the Renaissance, created an over-all dramatic effect, a harmonious whole. The importation of Oriental lacquers and tropical woods made possible many new innovations.

Italy

Flamboyantly carved, painted, and gilded details; broken pediments, moldings, spiral columns, and other architectural devices predominated. Cut velvets were popular; scrolls were used for the arms and legs of chairs, and inlaid marble for table tops. **Brustoloni** of Venice was an outstanding designer.

France

Louis XIV established the royal factory of Gobelins to produce furniture, as well as tapestries, for the royal buildings. Italian baroque influences were apparent in the case furniture veneered with tortoise shell or exotic woods, and inlaid with brass. Seat furniture was gilded and pieces in solid silver are known to exist. **Boulle** was the most celebrated *ébéniste*, while **Bérain** contributed many notable designs.

England

After the Restoration, French and Dutch influences prevailed. As elsewhere in Europe, many new forms of

14TH-16TH CENTURY-ENGLAND, ITALY, FRANCE

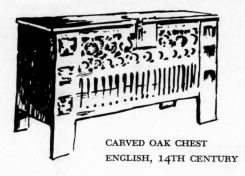

CARVED OAK CHEST
ENGLISH, 14TH CENTURY

CARVED OAK "DANTE" CHAIR
ITALIAN, 16TH CENTURY

LATE RENAISSANCE WALNUT TABLE
ITALIAN, LATE 16TH CENTURY

HENRI II
WALNUT *caqueteuse*
FRENCH, 16TH CENTURY

ARMCHAIR
ENGLISH, *ca.* 1530

UPHOLSTERED
"FARTHINGALE" CHAIR
ENGLISH, 16TH CENTURY

17TH CENTURY-ENGLAND, FRANCE, SPAIN

LOUIS XIV GILDED CONSOLE TABLE, WITH MARBLE TOP FRENCH, LATE 17TH CENTURY

WALNUT DROP-FRONT *vargueño*, INLAID WITH BONE SPANISH, *ca.* 1600

LOUIS XIV GILDED ARMCHAIR, WITH FLORAL TAPESTRY UPHOLSTERY FRENCH, LATE 17TH CENTURY

LOUIS XIV GILDED *torchère* (FOR HOLDING CANDELABRUM) FRENCH, LATE 17TH CENTURY

STATE BED WITH VELVET HANGINGS ENGLISH, *ca.* 1685

WILLIAM AND MARY CARVED WALNUT WINGED UPHOLSTERED TALL-BACK SETTEE ENGLISH, LATE 17TH CENTURY

WILLIAM AND MARY WALNUT DROP-
FRONT WRITING CABINET, INLAID WITH
OYSTERWOOD
ENGLISH, LATE 17TH CENTURY

furniture were designed, including day-beds, upholstered armchairs ("sleeping chairs"), sofas, etc. Varied decorative motifs, particularly in chairs, made their appearance. Scrolled legs on chairs, usually of polished walnut or gilded, were common during the reign of Charles II, while baluster legs became common later on. Elaborately carved state beds, with high testers and fabric hangings, were influenced by the French designer **Marot.** Important designers included **Moore, Jensen,** and **Pelletier.**

EIGHTEENTH CENTURY

Often referred to as the "Golden Age" of European furniture; the influence of French and English furniture designers was evident throughout Europe.

France

The style known as *Régence*, which came between the baroque of the Louis XIV period and the rococo of the Louis XV period, was named after the regent Philippe d'Orléans. The style that had been imposed by the rigid formality of the court of Louis XIV gave way to a lighter, more curvilinear style. Case furniture was mounted in *bronze doré*, a bronze gilded by a mercury process, and marquetry became a developed art. **Cressent** was the most famous *ébéniste.*

Rococo became the predominant style in France and the rest of Europe in the mid-18th century. Usually known as the *Louis XV* style, it is noted for sinuous, asymmetrical lines; over-all characteristics are grace and fluidity. Decorative devices include shells, volutes, C-scrolls, ribbons, flowers, and trophies. The number of types of furniture invented has never been equaled for diversity: *bibliothèques,* candelabra, upholstered armchairs with open and closed arms, *canapés* or sofas (of the many types each has a specific name), an endless variety of tables, commodes, and writing desks. Many influences from Near East and Far East; *chinoiserie.* Most case furniture richly mounted in gilded bronze; marquetry with floral or geometric patterns much used and widely imitated. Seat furniture usually of beechwood or walnut; while often left in natural wood state, chairs were frequently painted or gilded. Makers were many: **Delanois** and **Tilliard** for seat furniture; **Jacques Caffiéri** for bronze casting; **Oeben, Lacroix,** and **Bernard van Risen Burgh** for cabinet-

359

Régence CARVED
BEECHWOOD WINGED
bergère
FRENCH, EARLY 18TH CENTURY

LOUIS XVI PAINTED
AND UPHOLSTERED
fauteuil
FRENCH, *ca.* 1775

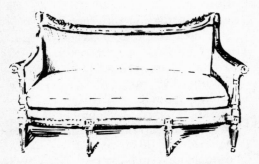

Régence EBONY *bibliothèque,*
WITH INLAID BRASS BANDINGS
FRENCH, EARLY 18TH CENTURY

LOUIS XVI PAINTED AND UPHOLSTERED
canapé
FRENCH, *ca.* 1780

LOUIS XVI CARVED AND GILDED
CONSOLE TABLE, WITH MARBLE TOP
FRENCH, *ca.* 1775

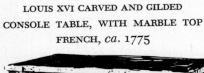

LOUIS XV CARVED BEECHWOOD
fauteuil,
SIGNED LOUIS DELANOIS
FRENCH, MID-18TH CENTURY

18TH CENTURY-FRANCE

LOUIS XV WRITING DESK, IN TULIPWOOD AND
KINGWOOD MARQUETRY, AND MOUNTED
IN *bronze doré*; SIGNED BERNARD VAN
RISENBURGH (B.V.R.B.)
FRENCH, MID-18TH CENTURY

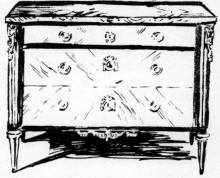

LOUIS XV COMMODE, DECORATED WITH
BLACK AND GOLD LACQUERS, AND
MOUNTED IN *bronze doré* ATTRIBUTED
TO JACQUES CAFFIÉRI
FRENCH, MID-18TH CENTURY

LOUIS XVI COMMODE, IN TULIPWOOD AND
KINGWOOD MARQUETRY, AND MOUNTED
IN *bronze doré*
FRENCH, *ca.* 1770

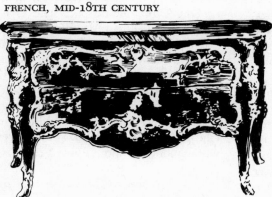

LOUIS XVI INLAID MARQUETRY DROP-FRONT
SECRETARY (*secrétaire à abattant*), IN THE
STYLE OF PIERRE ROUSSEL
FRENCH, *ca.* 1775

work; **Germain** for silvercasting. The richness and beauty of Louis XV furniture has never been rivaled.

In 1750's discoveries of Herculaneum and Pompeii and general interest in traveling and archaeology helped produce a classical reaction to the prevailing style. The new style, called *Louis XVI* (though occurring during the reign of Louis XV), evolved during 1760's; while adopting the richness of the Louis XV style, basic furniture design confined itself to rectilinear and more rigidly geometrical forms, using classical decorative devices (egg-and-dart and *guilloche* moldings, acanthus leaves, tapering fluted legs). While the Louis XV style is sinuous and free in its forms, the Louis XVI style tends to be more reserved, sober, and precise in outline. Many *ébénistes* and designers of the Louis XV period were equally famous for Louis XVI designs: **Georges Jacob, Boulard, J. B. Sené** for seat furniture; **Weisweiler, David Roentgen, Carlin, Roussel** for cabinet-work; and **Gouthière** in bronze foundry.

Just before and after the French Revolution, a style known as *Directoire* was in vogue and was followed by another minor style called the *Consulat*. Outlines in both styles are basically Louis XVI in design; but heavier reliance on Greek and Roman models, more frequent use of mahogany, infrequent use of marquetry are apparent. Both styles anticipated the Empire style.

England

At beginning of 18th century a new and simple style known as *Queen Anne* was created. Carving and ornament of the 17th century much reduced; cabriole leg, terminating in claw-and-ball or pad feet, was used for both cabinets and chairs; chairs had backs with splats; stretchers for chairs were soon abandoned. New types of furniture evolved, including tall- and lowboys, shelved cabinets, secretaries, and a variety of desks. Woods were carefully chosen for color and grain; mahogany, first imported into England in 1720's, became common. The diversity of English pieces, while not as rich in detail, rivaled those of France.

When taste for Palladian architecture was on the ascendant, more ample furniture was required. **William Kent,** the architect, designed a good deal of furniture for neo-Palladian interiors.

In the 1740's, the asymmetrical qualities of the Louis XV style influenced English furniture. Pattern books by **Lock** and **Copeland** were published. In 1754 **Chippendale** published *Gentleman and Cabinet-Maker's Director*; provided designs for a wide range of mid-18th century furniture, including two minor styles, the Chinese (usually known as *Chinese Chippendale*) and the Gothic. Innumerable chairs and cabinets were invented. In addition to Chippendale, **Vile, Cobb,** and **Shearer** were among the more famous cabinet-makers.

In a reaction to the rococo during 1760's, **Robert** and **James Adam,** whose inspiration was found in antiquity and the Italian Renaissance, created a new decorative vocabulary, assimilating such classical devices as paterae, husks, urns, and masks. More ordinary furniture, reflecting the classical style, was shown in **Hepplewhite's** *Cabinet-Maker and Upholsterer's Guide*

CARVED AND
GILDED STATE
ARMCHAIR
VENETIAN, EARLY
18TH CENTURY

CHIPPENDALE CARVED AND PARCEL-GILDED
CONSOLE TABLE, WITH GOAT-HEAD LEGS
AND MOSAIC MARBLE TOP
ITALIAN FOR THE ENGLISH MARKET, 18TH
CENTURY

COMMODE IN THE FRENCH TASTE, INLAID
WITH MAHOGANY AND SATINWOOD MAR-
QUETRY, AND MOUNTED IN *bronze doré*;
BY COBB
ENGLISH, *ca.* 1770

MAHOGANY PEDESTAL WRITING
DESK, IN THE STYLE OF THOMAS
SHEARER
ENGLISH, 18TH CENTURY

HEPPLEWHITE INLAID
MAHOGANY, CONCAVE-
FRONT SIDEBOARD
ENGLISH, 18TH CENTURY

363

HEPPLEWHITE UPHOLSTERED MAHOGANY
SETTEE
ENGLISH, 18TH CENTURY

HEPPLEWHITE GILDED
CONSOLE TABLE, WITH
INLAID SATINWOOD
MARQUETRY TOP
ENGLISH, 18TH CENTURY

ADAM CARVED AND GILDED SETTEE
ENGLISH, *ca.* 1775

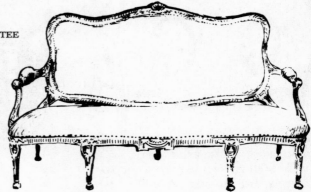

SHERATON ROSEWOOD SOFA TABLE
ENGLISH, LATE 18TH CENTURY

18TH CENTURY-UNITED STATES

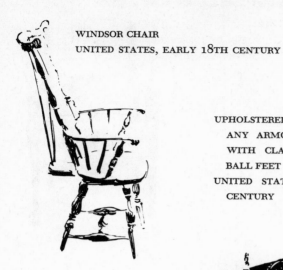

WINDSOR CHAIR
UNITED STATES, EARLY 18TH CENTURY

UPHOLSTERED MAHOG-
ANY ARMCHAIR,
WITH CLAW-AND-
BALL FEET
UNITED STATES, 18TH
CENTURY

MAHOGANY KETTLE-BASE
SECRETARY
UNITED STATES (MASSA-
CHUSETTS), 18TH CEN-
TURY

WALNUT HIGHBOY
UNITED STATES (PHIL-
ADELPHIA), 18TH
CENTURY

HEPPLEWHITE-STYLE
MAHOGANY CARD-
TABLE, BY JOHN
TOWNSEND
UNITED STATES (NEW-
PORT), LATE 18TH
CENTURY

EARLY 19TH CENTURY—FRANCE, ENGLAND, UNITED STATES

EMPIRE UPHOLSTERED
MAHOGANY *fauteuil*
FRENCH, *ca.* 1810

EMPIRE MAHOGANY ROUND
TABLE   (*guéridon*),
WITH MARBLE TOP
FRENCH, *ca.* 1810

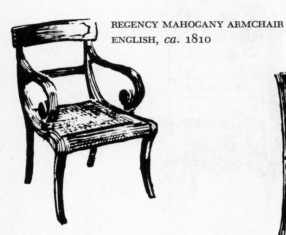

REGENCY MAHOGANY ARMCHAIR
ENGLISH, *ca.* 1810

DUNCAN PHYFE
MAHOGANY
SIDE CHAIR
UNITED STATES
(NEW YORK),
ca. 1805

Restauration "WATERED" ASHWOOD
BOAT-SHAPED BED (*lit en bateau*)
FRENCH, *ca.* 1830

PAPIER-MÂCHÉ SIDE CHAIR WITH GILT
AND LACQUER DECORATION
UNITED STATES, *ca.* 1860

CABINET, BY WILLIAM MORRIS
ENGLISH, LATE 19TH CENTURY

(1788). As the century drew to a close, the classical appearance of English furniture became even more delicate and restrained; **Thomas Sheraton's** *Cabinet-Maker and Upholsterer's Drawing Book* (1791) reflected this development.

United States

During the 17th century, settlers in America had few of the comforts known in the mother countries. What furniture did exist was conditioned by environment and outlook, and hence differs from contemporary European models. While rural areas retained more primitive aspects of early American furniture, many English and Dutch innovations were introduced into America during the 18th century. Chairs replaced stools; chest of drawers replaced box chest; daybeds, folding tables, cabinets appeared. Carving replaced painted decoration. The pad-footed cabriole leg in case and seat furniture was quite popular by 1725 and remained so until the American Revolution. The usual cabinet wood was walnut, with unseen interiors of pine; after 1755 the popularity of mahogany and the influence of Chippendale became apparent. Highly-skilled artisans were to be found in Boston, New York, Philadelphia, Newport, and Charleston, and included **Thomas Affleck**, **William Savery**, the **Townsend** and **Goddard** families, and **Jonathan Gostelowe**. The linear verticality of American furniture contrasted markedly with the massiveness of its English counterparts.

The classical tendency in England toward the end of the century is reflected in the United States by the work of **Samuel McIntire, James Seymour,** and **Duncan Phyfe**. French *Directoire* and Empire styles also had an influence on American furniture during the early years of the 19th century.

NINETEENTH CENTURY

The Empire style spread throughout Europe during the early part of the 19th century in direct proportion to the influence of Napoleon in continental politics. **Percier** and **Fontaine** were the outstanding designers. While following the general outlines of Louis XVI furniture, the Empire style relied more on direct copying of antique models, with added decorative motifs taken from Egypt. Sphinxes, acanthus leaves, upright sculptured bronze figures, and frequent use of mahogany characterize the style, which is monumental and somewhat heavy in scale.

In England, **Thomas Hope** and **George Smith** helped create the Regency style, which somewhat resembles the studied classicism of Empire; later a Gothic revival followed that had none of the delicacy of its 18th-century counterparts. In Germany and Austria during the period between 1815-50, a style known as *Biedermeier* was created (in France it was called *Charles X* or *Restauration*), using light fruitwoods, with scrolled arms on chairs and sofas. The Greek influence of the Empire style was apparent.

During the Victorian period in England, Europe, and America the widespread use of machinery led to a general decline in standards of furniture making, individual craftsmanship, and style; every previous period of furniture design was badly imitated and interpreted. General heaviness and eclecticism of Victorian furniture caused experiments in metal and bentwood furniture to be completely overlooked.

Taking cue from the Arts and Crafts Movement of **William Morris**, who deplored the shabbiness of Victorian furniture, **Ernest Gimson** and the **Barnsley** family revived the craft of handmade furniture in England toward the end of century. In Europe during the period between 1890 and 1910, the Art Nouveau movement created furniture known for its elongated and floriform lines.

TWENTIETH CENTURY

The Art Nouveau movement and the concepts of the Morris school of designers prefigured modern furniture design and manufacture. The German Bauhaus artists, with the aid of machinery, created well-designed furniture at moderate prices. Simple lines, the use of new materials (plywood, chrome, laminated board, etc.) and of bright colors for upholstery characterize the modern movement. Two leading exponents of the style, which has become basically international, have been **Ambrose Heal** and the architect **Miës van der Rohe**.

MING DYNASTY LACQUERED
BARREL STOOL
CHINESE, 17TH CENTURY

TUBULAR STEEL CHAIR,
BY LUDWIG MIES VAN DER ROHE
GERMAN, 1926

MING DYNASTY LACQUERED ARMCHAIR
CHINESE, 17TH CENTURY

ASIA · *China*

Chinese furniture has always been noted for its conservative tradition; models vary but slightly over centuries. By Western standards the types of Chinese furniture are quite limited; typical are altar tables, low tables, armchairs, screens, and cabinets. The usual materials are lacquered and plain woods, including sandalwood, rosewood, and burl. Noteworthy characteristics are luster, fine craftsmanship, simplicity of design, and minimal use of ornament; best furniture dates from the Ming dynasty (1368-1644).

MING DYNASTY ROSEWOOD
TABLE-TOP CABINET
CHINESE, 17TH CENTURY

369

GLOSSARY

Aaron's Rod. In architecture, a decorative molding having leaves or scrolls on either side of a straight, rounded rod.

Abacus. Molded or sculptured slab forming the top of the capital of a column used to support the superstructure.

Abbey. In religious architecture, a monastery or convent ruled by an abbot or abbess; church of a monastery.

Abhanga. In Indian music a term referring to devotional songs.

Absolute Music. Differing from program music, it has no association outside itself; devoid of extramusical content, self-derived, complete in its own form, it makes its appeal through tone and struc-

ture alone; sometimes called *abstract music.*

Abstract Expressionism. Following World War II artists, reacting against the abstract formalism of Mondrian and American regionalism, turned to more personal creative expression through the rejection of preconceived ideas before "attacking" a canvas, the use of intuitive calligraphy, and the exploitation of accidents of color and value patterns.

Abstraction. Art that is nonrepresentational in purpose, using lines, color, form, and space without reference to natural objects.

Abutment. Part of a buttress or wall

that supports the weight and takes the thrust of an arch, vault, or strut; support of any weight that tends to spread outward.

Acanthus. Carved ornament in the pattern of acanthus leaves; used mainly on capitals of Corinthian and Composite orders and in moldings.

A cappella (also *alla cappella*). "In the church style." Choral music for voices without instrumental accompaniment.

Acrolith. Statue made of two or more materials; torso usually of wood and extremities of stone.

Acropodium. Pedestal for a statue, raised from the substructure on supports or feet.

Acropolis. Fortified summit, usually on a hill, of a Greek city where temples and chief public buildings were erected.

Adad. Babylonian-Assyrian god of wind and storm; also known as *Ramman*, the roaring one.

Aegicranes. Sculptured heads of rams and goats used in symbolic decoration of Greek and Roman temples.

Agon. Argument, contest, debate between two actors introducing a Greek play, usually a comedy, each actor supported by half the chorus.

Aileron. Scroll-shaped ornament or device used at either side of or above a door or window.

Aisle. Wings or side divisions of church or temple, separated from the nave by arches or columns; passage between two rows of pews or seats.

Ajanta. Small town to the south of great plain of the Deccan, India, where a group of 29 chambers for Buddhist *viharas* and *chaityas* were hewn into the rocky sides of the hills; walls are decorated with magnificent frescoes and sculptures of life of the Buddha; frescoes constitute the most important document of Indian painting of period (2nd century B.C.-A.D. 7th century).

Akroterion. Tall marble shaft topped by a finial; common pattern is pair of volutes surmounted by a palmette; favorite kind of grave monument in ancient Greece.

Alabaster. Fairly soft crystalline stone varying in color from white to pale-yellow; a variety of gypsum; harder types are used for large figures, softer and semi-transparent types for smaller ornaments.

Alai Darwaza. Southern gateway of a proposed enlargement of Aibak's mosque (1311); represents the finest ornamental architecture of the early Delhi sultanate; style continued in Gujarat.

Alberti bass. Style of continuous, identical broken chords played by the left hand in piano music; suggests contrapuntal elaboration, but is purely harmonic; used but not invented by Domenico Alberti, Italian composer of music for the harpsichord.

Alcora. Brilliantly polychromed variety of Spanish porcelain made in the 18th century.

Alhacena. In Moorish architecture, an ornate recess or alcove of sculptured stucco.

Altarpiece. Decorated screen or series of panels on or at the rear of an altar; either painted or sculptured in relief.

Alto-relievo. High relief; figure stands out from background by at least half its depth.

Amalaka. Original Sanskrit word used internationally for bulbous, melon-shaped ornaments that top the turrets or sikharas of medieval Indian temples.

Ambry (also *aumbry, armarium*). Small recess, often built into the thickness of the wall of a church, to hold sacred vessels.

Amitābha (Sanskrit). Buddha who lives in the Western Paradise (*Sukhā-vatï*); worshiped by followers of the Pure Land (*Ching tu*) sect.

Amphitheater. Oval or circular building with rising tiers of seats around an open space; for spectacular public entertainment during the period of the Roman Empire.

Amphora. In architecture, a series of arches on columns or a colonnade supported on piers; in ceramics, a large Greek two-handled jar or vase with a narrow neck.

Amulet. Ornament, gem, scroll, or small package worn as protection against evil; originally a small part of the body of an ancestor; later representations of parts of the body were carved in ivory, gold, wood, etc.; used in Egyptian funerary practices.

Anta. Pier or pilaster produced by thickening a wall; usually having a capital and base not conforming with the other columns of the building.

Antefix. Ornament fixed at the eaves to conceal the end of the tiles; upright, decorated termination at the cornice.

Anthem. Formerly a hymn or psalm sung antiphonally or responsively; choral composition sung by church choir, with or without instrumental accompaniment; Anglican equivalent of the motet, but simpler in style, more like the choral.

Anthemion. Form of decoration based on the flower and leaves of the honeysuckle; arranged in radiating clusters.

Anthesteria. In ancient Greece, three-day festival, called *Feast of Flowers*, featuring songs, dances, and athletic competitions in honor of Dionysus; held in Athens during the month of *Anthesterion* (February-March).

Anubis. Jackal-headed god of the ancient Egyptians; entrusted with conducting the spirits of the dead to the judgment hall in Amenti and weighing their hearts against the feather of truth and right; popular figure in tomb painting and sculpture.

Apadana. Great columned judgment or audience hall in ancient Persian architecture; supported a wooden roof of heavy timbers and wattling.

Apis. Sacred bull believed by the Egyptians to be the embodiment of the god Ptah of Memphis; represented in paintings as black with distinctive white markings; new Apis was believed to be born upon the death of the old and the body of the dead Apis was embalmed and buried in the rock-cut Serapeum in the necropolis at Memphis; worship of Apis began as early as the 4th Dynasty and continued until the reign of Emperor Julian.

Apron. In theater, part of the stage in front of the proscenium arch and the curtain.

Apsaras (Sanskrit). Buddhist heavenly maiden; frequently represented in Indian art as a water nymph or dancer.

Apse. Semicircular alcove or recess located at the east end of the choir or end of the central aisle of a church.

Aquatint. Etching process invented by Jean Baptiste Le Prince (1734-84); produces a transparent quality of tone (not as deep or rich as mezzotint) resembling a wash drawing or water color; popular method used in conjunction with soft-ground etching, dry point, or other intaglio techniques; greatest master of aquatint was Goya.

Arch. Curved structure resting on supports at both ends used to sustain weight; pointed, semicircular or horseshoe arrangement of separate wedge-shaped blocks or *voussoirs*, arranged with their joints at right angles to the curve to span the opening; self-supporting; used to support the wall or other weight above an opening or as an ornamental feature in decoration; means of spanning an opening by resolving vertical pressure into horizontal or diagonal thrust; series of arches side by side known as a vault.

Architrave. Lowest division of an entablature; any horizontal beam resting across two upright columns; molded frame that surrounds a door or window.

Archmime. Chief jester in Roman courts, theaters, and festivals; particularly the mime who burlesqued the deceased in funeral processions.

Arch rib. Projecting band on the line of an arch, particularly in vaulting.

Armature. In architecture, iron bars or framing designed to brace or stiffen a weak part of a building; in sculpture, a framework or skeleton on which the work is modeled; stiff wire used for small pieces, wire mesh and iron pipes or wood used for larger works.

Arm stump. In furniture, the short and often decorative vertical piece of wood extending from the arm of a chair down to the seat frame.

Arras. Tapestry originating in Arras, northeastern France, known for its loose texture, complex, interwoven figures; tapestry used for hanging on walls of a room or as a screen.

Art Nouveau. International ornamental style (flourished 1890-1905); originated in England with the Arts and Crafts Movement sponsored by William Morris; found its expression in architecture, ceramics, the graphic arts, jewelry, painting, sculpture, silver, stained glass, and textiles; attempted to break with old traditions; interest shown in the new technology of the period and the potentials of new materials; known as *Jugenstil* in Germany, the *Yachting Style* in France, *Stile Liberty* in Italy, *Secessionstil* in Vienna, and in Belgium it was associated with the group known as *Les XX's* and called *Paling stijl*; Henry van de Velde (1863-1957, Belgian) leading figure of movement.

Atefcrown. Symbolic headdress of Upper Egypt worn by the deities Osiris and Khnum and by the Ramesside kings; tall, conical, white cap, flanked by a pair of ostrich feathers, with the solar disc and uraeus in front; occasionally omitted in works of art; mentioned in *The Book of the Dead*.

Atlante. Male figure used as column to support an entablature; not as frequently used as female figure (*see* Caryatid).

Atonal music. Refers to music without tonality, where there is no relationship of tones and chords to a central key or tonal center; although considered characteristic of Schönberg's music, he prefers to call his music *pantonal* or "the relation of all tones to one another"; Schönberg's style is based on the chromatic scale, a semitonal division of the octave, with each of twelve tones or degrees of equal value (atonal style preceded his twelve-tone system); although atonal music is not built exclusively in fourths, chords so constructed were one of several innovations.

Atrium. Main room in an early Roman house, usually open to the sky; courtyard, surrounded by colonnades, in front of narthex of early Christian basilicas or medieval churches.

Attic. Low story above main cornice; *attic base* frequently found in Greek and Roman orders of architecture.

Aubade (French). Morning serenade; short instrumental work performed at dawn or in the morning; originally more a troubadour love song then concert music; *Aubade in G Minor* for five wind instruments and five strings by Lalo and Wagner's *Siefried Idyll* are excellent examples.

Aubusson. Variety of hand-woven tapestries and rugs, with brilliant, sometimes ornate, designs and figures, originating in Aubusson, France.

Axminster. Hand-woven cotton or jute rug, with a cut-pile of woolen threads (tied in by hand), made in Axminster, Devon, England.

Bab. Exterior gate or arch in Moorish architecture.

Bachiru. Japanese style of carving ivory; tinted and decorated using graffito technique.

Bacile. Bowl or deep dish of (or similar to) enameled or lustered pottery; same as *bacino*, brilliantly colored pottery dishes built into the walls of medieval structures in Italy.

Bahut. Richly carved or decorated cabinet or chest; rounded top, often covered with leather; important article of furniture during medieval and Renaissance periods; in architecture, low wall raised above the main cornice of a building, supporting the roof behind the gutter and balustrade crowning the main walls.

Baldachin. In architecture, a fixed canopy of metal, stone, or wood above the isolated, high altar of a church or tomb; portable canopy of decorative nature, carried in ceremonial processions to protect and dignify important persons, relics, or sacred objects; stationary canopy of cloth over a dais; originally a rich, embroidered silk made in Baghdad for ceremonial canopies.

Ballade. Originally dance-song with improvised accompaniment used by the troubadours and *trouvères*; free style, romantic composition usually written for solo piano or orchestra.

Ball flower. Characteristic carved, circular ornament of English Gothic interior architecture of the 13th century; floral shape with a ball in the center.

Baluster. Small column, or pillarlike support for a railing, usually of a staircase.

Bamiyan Buddha. Enormous statue of Buddha (130 ft. high, almost in the round) carved into a cliff rock in the desert regions beyond the Khyber Pass, Afghanistan.

Banderole. Sculptured band bearing an inscription; used extensively during the Renaissance; also *banderol* and *bannerol*.

Bandurist. Ukrainian national singer-poet or troubadour; sang ballads, psalms accompanying himself on his instrument, the *bandura*.

Bänkelsänger. Wandering minstrel or troubadour of old Germany; sang romantic songs (often original compositions) of history, love, adventure, and chivalry; outside Germany, known as a *bench singer* because he invariably stood on a bench while performing to be better seen and heard.

Bar back. Heppelwhite chair with shield-shaped back and uprights carved to match the shield design.

Baritone. Adult male voice between bass and tenor; range from lower G on bass staff to lower F on treble; large, valved brass instrument used primarily in bands.

Basalt. Stone of volcanic origin widely used by the ancient Egyptians in sculpture, obelisks, and tombs; highly-prized basalt stoneware, usually black with a dull matte glaze, made by Josiah Wedgwood.

Base. In architecture, the part of the column on which the shaft rests; consists of plinth and moldings between the shaft and ground (pavement); terms *base* and *pedestal* have been synonymous since the Renaissance period.

Basilica. Oblong building with nave and aisles used by Romans for public assembly and hall of justice; early Christian churches similarly built with nave higher than the aisles.

Bas relief. Sculpture in low relief with the figures almost flat, protruding from the surface less than half the real proportion; in **demi-relief,** the figures are projected from the surface with medium prominence; also called *mezzo-relievo*; halfway between alto-relievo and bas-relief.

Basse-taille. Transparent enamel work on low relief; application of a fondant or flux to raised metal prior to firing.

Bauhaus. Grew out of a reorganization of the Weimar Art School by Walter Gropius, who designed and established the Bauhaus at Dessau (1919); emphasis on teaching basic nature of design as integral part of objects used in everyday living; developed experimental laboratories for new techniques and new materials of the Machine (Industrial) Age;

important effort to bridge the gap between pure and applied art; many famous artists and teachers continued the influence of Bauhaus ideas as teachers in other countries after the school was closed by Hitler in 1933.

Bautasteiner. Scandinavian memorial stone like a *menhir*, decorated with runic inscriptions; often 20 ft. high, placed at the top of barrows; common to the Viking culture of the 6th to 8th centuries.

Bay. Vertical unit of a wall or façade; compartments into which a nave is divided; in Gothic architecture, buildings were divided into bays by the use of transverse arches and priers of an arcade; **bay window,** curved or angled window or series of windows projecting beyond the normal line of the building; usually built on the ground floor level; also known as *bow* or *oriel* windows.

Bell beakers. Gracefully curved beakers with deeply incised designs; native to Spain during Neolithic period; spread to other areas and under the influence of geometric pottery designs, developed zonal decorative patterns.

Belleek ware. Fragile, highly translucent porcelain with a pale, pearly glaze; famous product of Belleek Porcelain Works of northern Ireland; first produced in the United States in 1882.

Belvedere. Building (usually a summer house) or upper story of any structure affording a beautiful view.

Bema. In early Christian and Orthodox churches, the raised area between the apse and the head of the nave reserved for the higher clergy; enclosed space surrounding an altar; pulpit in a synagogue; sanctuary or chancel.

Bench-table. Low stone seat built into the interior walls or around columns or pillars of medieval churches.

Beni-e. Early Japanese woodcut using three colors; usually rose-red and green added to black.

Biedermeier. German style based chiefly on French Empire designs; essentially appealed to bourgeoisie and lesser nobility; emphasis on simplicity and use of local materials; name derives from character in magazine, "Papa Biedermeier," who symbolized *gemütlichkeit*—comfortable, home-loving serenity; later considered old-fashioned and dull.

Blind arcade. Arcade of arches superficially fixed to a wall that has no opening; serves as decoration only; also known as *wall arcade.*

Bodegones. Spanish word meaning *indoor scenes*; Velásquez (early period) painted *bodegones* or pictures of ordinary people going about their everyday chores.

Bodhisattva (Sanskrit). Deity of Mahayana Buddhism; renounced Buddhahood and nirvana in order to act as a savior to all sentient beings; often portrayed in agony of physical suffering.

Bombé. Swelling or convex surface; bulging sides and front found in many Louis XV and later 18th-century Italian pieces of furniture.

Bone sculpture. Characteristic Eskimo art form; developed from decoration for handles of weapons and tools.

Book of the Dead. Name given to ancient Egyptian writings on rolls of papyrus found in tombs of the wealthy; contained collections of spells and funerary practices; believed to facilitate the passage of the dead person to the world beyond; placed within coffin or in special wooden box used as pedestal for statue of Osiris; some original texts found on walls of pyramid chambers.

Borobudur. Earliest (8th century) important Javanese Buddhist area under Indian influence; stone-faced earth mound forms core and supports six superimposed square terraces, with double projections on each side, surmounted by three circular platforms; large *stupa* (on top) 52 ft. in diameter, 504 statues of Buddha, 1,400 bas .reliefs, and 72 bell-shaped towers.

Buhl. Form of inlay or marquetry in furniture; brass, bronze, or unburnished gold inlaid into wood, or tortoise shell; also called *boule* or *boull* after André Charles Boulle (1642-1732), cabinetmaker for Louis XIV, who designed and executed inlaid paneling and pieces of marquetry for the Palace of Versailles.

Bun foot. Foot of a chair or table shaped like a flattened globe as distinguished from the purely spherical *ball foot* (which is often contained in a claw and known as *claw-and-ball foot*).

Buttress. Projecting structure (usually masonry) built against an outside wall to give support and stabilize or resist the pressure exerted by an inside vault or arch.

Byobu. Elaborately painted six-paneled Japanese folding screen.

Byōdōin. Temple in Uji, Japan; main building is famed Phoenix Hall.

Cabriole. Tapering, double-curved leg of a chair or table ending in an ornamental foot; frequently seen in Chippendale and Queen Anne furniture.

Caissons. Series of sunken panels in a vault, ceiling, or dome, forming a continuous pattern; also known as *coffers* and *lacunaria*.

Calligraphy. The art of elegant writing or penmanship; distinguished from ordinary writing by its artistic quality; regarded as a great art in China, and more creative than painting in Persia.

Canephora. In Greek sculpture, a female figure bearing a basket containing religious objects, usually for performance of sacrifices in special festivals.

Canon. A polyphonic composition in which the melody is sung by two or more voices at the same or different intervals (pitch); canons, when they lead back to the beginning without a break are "circular," "infinite," or "perpetual"; some are broken and completed by means of a coda.

Cantata. Choral composition either sacred, resembling a short oratorio, or secular, lyric drama with instrumental accompaniment (not performed as theater).

Canticum. In ancient plays, those parts that were to be chanted or sung; differing from the *diverbium* or *spoken verse*.

Cantoria. Balcony or gallery for a church choir.

Cantus firmus. Melody (usually not original) used by the composer as basis for polyphonic composition; traditional Gregorian chant prescribed by ecclesiastical rules, used as starting point of polyphonic or contrapuntal musical structures.

Canzone. Ballad or instrumental composition for two or more voices; set in polyphonic style similar to a madrigal.

Capital. Form, head, or top of a column or pilaster; crowning the shaft; often decorated; designed to support the weight of the entablature.

Carillon. Fixed bells in a church tower or other building (usually public or educational) played by striking the outer rims with hammers operated by a keyboard or by pegs on a rotating cylinder; usual range, three to four chromatic octaves.

Cartouche. Ornamental tablet (usually oval) with scrollwork; frequently decorated with armorial bearings; popular scroll decoration on Italian furniture (from the 15th century) and French furniture of the period of Francis I; used by Chippendale on cabinets; in ancient Egypt, an oblong or oval figure on a monument.

Caryatid. Draped female figure serving as a column to support an entablature; male versions, atlante or telemon; name thought to derive from *caryatis*, a Spartan dance performed by nude maidens in the Laconian woods or temples dedicated to Diana; later performed as dance of innocence at marriage feasts.

Cassone. Large decorated Italian hinged

trunk or chest, often with richly carved lid.

Catacombs. Subterranean places of burial with interconnecting sepulchral chambers; name referred originally to the tombs under the Church of St. Sebastian near Rome; centers of cults for Christian martyrs; most famous, discovered in 1578, are those on the Appian Way near Rome.

Catch. Round, written as one continuous melody, for three or four unaccompanied voices; popular during the Restoration period in England, they were sung everywhere, particularly in taverns, that accounted in part for their increasingly ribald lyrics; *Catch That Catch Can*, collection of catches published by John Hilton (1652-58), with words set to music by Purcell, required extensive editing for modern editions.

Caulicoli (*cauliculus*). Eight stalks rising out of the lower leaves and supporting the volutes on a Corinthian capital.

Cavetto. Concave molding in which the curve, usually a quarter circle, is cut back below a fascia; common in Egyptian and classical Greek architecture; in decorative art, any recessed pattern, the reverse of relief; usually found as important member of cornice.

Chamber Music. Instrumental (or vocal) music considered particularly suitable for a room or small audience hall; more intimate in character than larger works; written for a limited number of performers, one player to each part.

Chancel. Part of the church, usually east of the nave, including choir and sanctuary, reserved for clergy and choir; often separated from the rest of the church by a screen.

Chanson. French song for either a single voice or vocal ensemble; instrumental music of vocal character; **chansonniers** are collections of manuscript songs of French troubadours of the 13th century.

Château. French *seigneur*'s mansion combining the defense aspects of the castle with comforts and convenience; early château built with moat, massive walls, and tower; later, fortifications eliminated and, from the 17th century, became center of lavish entertainment and living.

Chattas. Series of ceremonial umbrellas surmounting dome of stupa in ancient Indian architecture; also *chatra*.

Chêng. In China, painting on silk, backed and edged with cloth; hung on temple walls during religious ceremonies (usually Buddhist); folded and stored away when not in use.

Chiaroscuro (literally, "light-dark"). Creation of form through the use of light and shadow in painting or drawing; chiaroscuro print, developed in 16th-century Europe, using one line and one tone block, gives effect of wash drawing.

Chih-hua. Chinese finger-painting technique: use of fingertip or fingernail instead of brush; originated during T'ang dynasty.

Ch'i-lin. Unicorn, king of the animals, in Chinese and Japanese mythology; appears frequently in art as symbol of good and wise government; called *kirin* in Japan.

Chippendale. Late 18th-century style of furniture made by or in the style of Thomas Chippendale (*see* Furniture).

Choir. In architecture, part of the church separated from the nave and the sanctuary, or arm of the cross between the transepts and apse; in music, originally an organized group of singers in church or temple services who rendered hymns, chants, etc.

Chorale (*choral*). Hymn or psalm sung in unison by choir or congregation usually with organ accompaniment; hymn tune of Lutheran Church; in Gregorian music, any part of concentus; used by Bach in church cantatas.

Chorale prelude. Organ music based on hymn tune; originated in Germany in the 17th century.

Choreography. Art of representing dancing by signs; notation of composed dances; composition and creation of dance forms.

Chorten. Small Tibetan roadside religious shrine or bottle-shaped stupa carved of stone.

Chryselephantine. Made of, or decorated with, gold and ivory; monumental cult statues in Greek temples had flesh of ivory and hair and draperies of gold; technique might have originated in Orient; statuettes in tomb of Tutakhamen similarly executed; other examples found in Crete and Mesopotamia.

Chüan chou. Rolled paintings or scrolls; considered outstanding form of painting in China; scroll is rolled onto a rod called a *chou*; ends carved, embellished with mosaic work in jade or ivory, or hung with tassels.

Ciborium. In medieval architecture, free-standing canopy supported by four columns, covering the high altar; goblet-shaped vessel covered with dome-shaped lid (containing the Eucharist vessel); drinking cup (usually covered) shaped like the Egyptian lotus or lily or its seed pod.

Cilery (*cillery*). Carved ornamentation at the head of a column; a volute (*q.v.*).

Circus. Entertainment area in ancient Rome for gladiatorial combats, chariot races, athletic games, public shows, etc., oval shaped, ringed by rising tiers of seats; also known as *stadium*.

Cire-perdue. Lost wax process used in casting bronze statues. Wax model coated with clay, then heated, melting wax and leaving cavity into which bronze is poured; when bronze cools, clay is chipped away, leaving cast form; introduced into Benin from Ife (Africa) about 1280 and used until early 18th century;

known in ancient civilizations of Central and South America, ancient Egypt, India, and the Malay Archipelago.

Clerestory (*clearstory*). Upper part of church or cathedral nave having windows, that provide additional light to the central part of the interior, rising above the roofs of the aisles.

Cloister. Covered passage separated from a court by columns or arches; monastery or convent.

Closet drama. Play or dramatic poem written to be read rather than for stage presentation.

Coffer. Recessed ornamental panel in a ceiling or vault.

Collage. Pasting paper, cloth, etc. into pictures or objects, creating an artistic work; introduction credited to Braque and Picasso, who in 1911 used newspaper, cuttings, laundry bills, bus tickets, stamps, etc. to devise a sophisticated, artistic expression of protest against conventional materials.

Colonnade. Series or continuous row of columns carrying or linked by beams or horizontal entablature; when in front of building called a *portico*, when around open court, square, or building, a *peristyle*; favorite motif of baroque and classic revival.

Colonnette. Small, often miniature, column; one of many groups in balustrade or clustered column; used ornamentally on furniture.

Colossus of Rhodes. Bronze statue of sun god, Helios; erected at port (*ca.* 280 B.C.) to commemorate the city's successful defense against Demetrius Poliorcetes (304 B.C.); 102 ft. high, considered one of the Seven Wonders of the World; execution credited to sculptor Chares of Lindus.

Combine-paintings. Oil paintings embodying ready-made objects.

Commedia dell'arte. Italian comedy, introduced during mid-16th century, performed by guild actors trained to improvise dialogue and action from a written plot.

Concerto. Musical composition for one or more solo instruments, with orchestral accompaniment, based on the sonata form; originally a work for one or more voices with instrumental accompaniment either for figured bass or with additional instruments.

Conductus. Metrical Latin song for one or more voices, either sacred or secular, not based on a Gregorian melody; 12th and 13th centuries.

Constructivism. Russian-French art movement of geometric-abstract painting and sculpture founded in 1920 by Naum Gabo and Antoine Pevsner; others include Moholy-Nagy, Tatlin, Lissitsky, and Rodchenko.

Corbel. Projecting wall block used to support a beam; small bracket used to support projecting cornices, balconies, or moldings (frequently curved and decorated); corbeled arch is made up of horizontal layers each protruding more than the one below.

Cornice. Projecting top portion of an entablature; projecting top course of a building, often in form of decorative railing; horizontal top or finish molding of pieces of furniture; molded angle formed by ceiling and wall.

Crocket. Gothic architectural ornament, often in the form of curved foliage, projecting from the edge of a gable or flying buttress.

Cupola. Small circular, polygonal, or square structure rising from the center of a roof or larger dome.

Cusp. Points separating foils of Gothic tracery; triangular projection from intrados of arch.

Daibutsu. Large image of Buddha; outstanding example in bronze at Kamakura, Japan.

Daiza (Japanese). Pedestal for carved figure, frequently decorated with design similar to sculpture.

Dancette. Moldings with a zigzag pattern; chevron molding; used in Norman and Romanesque architecture.

Debureau. Any pantomimist of remarkable ability; from stage name of Kolin nad Labem (1796-1846), great Slavonic artist internationally famous; immortalized in world literature.

Decastyle. Ten-columned portico.

Découpage (French, cutting out, cutting up). In collage, materials cut with scissors or knife; often decorated with added materials such as wire, string, cloth, etc. Art of paper cut-outs used in decoration; abstract paper forms used as art form by Matisse.

Dentils. Small, projecting rectangular blocks resembling teeth, closely spaced in horizontal rows; used to decorate cornices.

Devadasi. Dancing girls in Hindu temples; devoted to religious ceremonials.

Diastyle. Colonnade in which the space between each pair of the equidistant columns is three times the diameter of a column.

Diatonic. Chord, note, or progression confined to one major or minor key or scale; diatonic melody is one in which no flats or sharps foreign to the key are used.

Dienst. Long thin shafts, similar to a clustered pier, arranged around a column; used in German Gothic architecture to support and strengthen a column that bears the thrust of the vaulting.

Diptych. In Roman antiquity, two-leaved, hinged writing tablet; in painting, two-hinged panels considered single work; frequently used as altarpieces, or in displaying Japanese prints or paintings.

Dolmen. Neolithic or Bronze Age structure; monument of upright stones (megaliths) topped by cross slabs to form a chamber; usually place of burial; word, Celtic origin, meaning "stone table"; **cromlech** almost synonymous term.

Double axe. Double-headed axe used as a sacred symbol in Minoan Crete; used frequently on pottery of period.

Drolery. Satirical scenes or figures decorating empty spaces on Gothic buildings, furniture; featured imaginary humorous or bizarre creatures.

Drum. Circular or polygonal structure on which a dome is raised; one of horizontal stone pieces in a column.

Drypoint. Intaglio print process; long sharp needle used on polished copper plate; in engraving more burr thrown along sides of line and retained; rich, velvety line; no acid; limited prints.

Duncan Phyfe. Style of American furniture named after its designer (1768-1854).

Durga. In Hindu mythology, the consort of Siva; frequently represented with ten arms.

Eaves. Lower part of a roof, overhanging the tops of the walls.

Ecce Homo ("Behold the Man"). Title of many paintings depicting the suffering of Christ.

Eccyclema. Large wooden machine, mounted on wheels, used as early type of revolving stage by Greeks.

Echinus. Convex molding, sometimes decorated, beneath the abacus of the capital of a column.

E-gorai ware. Korean pottery of the Korai Dynasty; floral designs painted as underglaze.

E-kotoba. Japanese scroll painting featuring both painting and text; without text called *e-maki.*

Electronic music. Based on techniques that generate, manipulate, and transform sounds electronically; also called *concrete music, tape music,* and *soundtrack music* (lines drawn on film, Norman McLaren of Canada); composer freed from use of 70 or 80 pitch levels produced by conventional instruments and from traditional time values and dynamic levels; various systems of notation have been devised; first public concert of compositions for tape recorder, Museum of Modern Art (1952), when Vladimir Ussachevsky's *Sonic Contours* and Otto Luenings' *Low Speed, Invention,* and *Fantasy in Space* played; important experimental work also done by Pierre Schaeffer, Musique Concrete group in Paris, John Cage, the Northwest German Radio station in association with Bonn University (Cologne), and many others.

Elephanta. Rock temple on island near Bombay known as Indian Parthenon; built during post-Gupta period (4th-7th centuries A.D.).

E-makimono. Horizontally rolled Japanese picture scroll.

Embolimon. Choral interlude in Greek tragedies unrelated to the plot.

Encaustic painting. Pigments mixed with hot, refined beeswax; popular method of mural and easel painting during antiquity.

Engaged column. Column partly recessed in a wall or pier.

Engraving. Process of incising lines on a metal (usually copper) plate (or wood) with a graver or burin to produce intaglio prints.

Entablature. Horizontal top part of order of classical architecture; supported by columns; divided into architrave, frieze, and cornice.

Entasis. Slight curve on shaft of column; designed to counteract optical illusion of concavity; used in Greek and 7th-century Japanese architecture.

Entremes (Spanish, "interlude"). In Middle Ages, interlude inserted in mystery play; short classical play, similar to English interlude, frequently used by Cervantes; introduced into Spain by Dukes of Burgundy who presented short songs and dances between servings of lavish banquets (*entremets*).

Esnafs. Slavonic craftsmen's guilds comparable to those of the medieval

West; each member had to execute a masterpiece (*esnaf*) before he could advance further in his craft.

Espadaña. In Mexican architecture, pierced, arch-shaped gables in which bells were hung.

Espagnolette. Female busts used as ornaments on legs, posts of cabinets, etc.; seen in styles of Louis XIV, the Regency, and Louis XV.

Etching. Intaglio process; polished copper plate first covered with etching ground (a combination of gummy and resinous substances: varnish; asphalt, wax, Burgundy pitch melted together); grounded plate then held over lighted candles to form deposit of carbon; artist then draws design with etching needle and dips plate in acid bath as often as necessary to produce wanted depth of line; impressions produced by taking prints from inked plate.

Evangeliar. Illuminated, unabridged manuscript of the four Gospels; ornamented with decorative capital letters and illustrated texts.

Exodium (*exodos*). In Greek drama, all that followed final choral song in play; light, short farce played after tragedies presented at Roman contests and festivals.

Expressionism. To quote Herbert Read, "a form of art that gives primacy to the artist's emotional reactions to experience. The artist tries to depict, not the objective reality of the world, but the subjective reality of the feelings which objects and events arouse in his psyche, or self"; used more specifically to refer to movement originating in Germany during early years of this century (Die Brücke, 1905), whose aim was to embody the subjective content in powerfully symbolic imagery; for example, Van Gogh, Munch, Nolde, Beckmann considered expressionists.

Ezo. In Japanese art, portrait painting.

Fabula Praetexta. Roman historical drama; **fabula saltica,** Roman ballet

pantomime; actor gestures and dances to text chanted by chorus.

Façade (*face*). Exterior, main or front entrance of a building; faces of chests.

Fauves ("wild beasts"). Term of derision used by a critic after attending group exhibition (1906); referred to use of brilliant color in broad, unbroken areas expressing strong emotion; artists led by Matisse, included Derain, Rouault, Dufy, Vlaminck, Van Dongen, and Friesz.

Festoon. Ornamentation shaped like a suspended wreath; used on panels and friezes; in furniture, series of scalloplike loops forming a chain; painted or carved; also known as *swag*.

Filigree. Delicate ornamental wire work; usually gold, silver, or copper, used to decorate silver or gold.

Finial. Carved, molded, projecting ornament, often foliate, topping a spire, gable, etc. in Gothic architecture; also decorative vertical top of post, pediment, or intersection.

Flèche. Long, tapering spire above the transepts and nave of a church.

Flutes (*fluting*). Grooved or curved vertical section decorating pilasters or columns in classical architecture; in furniture, applied to legs, pilasters, etc. after the 16th century; ridge between flutes called *fillet*.

Flying buttress. Half or sloping arch between wall or piers of building (usually church or cathedral) and solid vertical masonry member designed to take thrust of roof or vault.

Fresco (from Italian, "fresh"). Two types of fresco painting: *buon fresco* and *fresco secco*, or dry fresco; **buon fresco,** used by Michelangelo, Giotto, Orozco, refers to painting on wet lime plaster with paints mixed with water or with lime and water; artists using **fresco secco** work on relatively dry wall using paint mixed with egg (closer to egg tempera) or pigments mixed with glue and applied to dry plaster treated with baryta water;

careful planning and execution required; term also refers to mural or painting done by this method.

Fret. In architecture, geometric ornament in relief made up of small straight lines and bars intersecting one another in oblique or right angles; in furniture, ornamental work of an interlaced design either cut in low relief or perforated on solid ground; flat fretwork, painted and inlaid, feature of Arabian and Moorish design.

Frieze. Flat, often decorated, middle band of an entablature, between architrave and cornice; ornamental band on a wall; any long, narrow sculptured band often referred to as a frieze.

Frottage. Rubbing; technique of transferring relief design to paper.

Fugue. Polyphonic, contrapuntal musical composition developed according to strict rules in which a subject (*theme*) is performed or proposed by one part (*voice*) and answered by other parts; generally divided into exposition, development, and conclusion; Bach and Handel considered great masters of form.

Gabri. Brilliantly decorated Persian pottery of 11th and 12th centuries.

Gaku. Framed Japanese panel painting; also *gakumen*.

Ganesa (*Ganesha*). Hindu god of wisdom depicted in art as a short, fat, red or yellow figure with a protruding stomach (belly) and an elephant's head.

Genre painting. Realistically portrayed scenes of everyday life.

Gesso. Ground used in painting; white gelatinous substance, mixture of plaster of Paris (or chalk) and size (specially refined glue) applied to wood, cardboard, etc. in series of thin, alternatingly smooth and rough coats; **gesso duro** more durable substance used for making bas-reliefs, statuettes, etc.

Giocolari. Jesters; buffoons and various performers who were employed by Tuscan princes as entertainers.

Giralda Tower. Adjoining the cathedral, Seville, Spain, built (1163-84) as minaret for mosque; converted into bell tower (1568).

Glaze. Cover with thin surface similar to glass; fused by firing in a kiln to earthenware, sealing the surface; in painting, application of transparent or semitransparent color to subdue tone of underpainting.

Gopura. High, elaborate gateway to Indian temples; also refers to massive pyramidal tower built above entrance gate.

Gouache. *See* water color.

Grisaille. Decorative painting in gray monochrome; popular in decoration of late 18th century.

Groin. Edge, projecting solid angle, or curved arris created at intersection of two vaults, growing more obtuse at the top.

Heppelwhite. Style of furniture named for cabinetmaker George Heppelwhite (d. 1786).

Herma. Square stone pillar topped by sculptured head of bearded god Hermes.

Hornacina. Niche for statue of patron saint or Virgin; Mexican churches and palaces of 17th and 18th centuries.

Hsiang. Annex on left and right of central apartment of Chinese mansion.

Hyoshigi. Hardwood clappers used in theaters in Japan; used to attract attention or indicate confusion on stage.

Hypostyle. Building with roof supported by many columns; example, great hall at Karnak, Egypt.

Icon. Representation of sacred person in paint, fresco, enamel, mosaic, etc. (not sculpture); famous Byzantine and Russian art form.

Iconostasis. In Eastern Church, partition (with doors) decorated with icons (sometimes called "icon-screen") that separated the bema of church from choir or nave.

Idée fixe. In music, constantly repeated theme, most often in symphonic poem; term suggested by Berlioz.

Imitation. In music, repetition of melodic theme, motif, or phrase by second part following original presentation by first part; if governed by strict rules, a canon.

Impasto. Heavy application of paint on canvas, wood, gesso panel, etc.; palette knife popular tool of this technique; used successfully by many expressionists.

Impost. Top section of wall, pillar, pier, column, etc., upon which the arch rests.

In. Japanese intaglio or relief seal impressed onto painting along with signature of the artist; similar to Chinese *yin chang.*

Incunabula. Refers to books printed from movable type prior to 1501.

Ink splash. Japanese technique, popular in 13th century, using very few brushstrokes to create simple but effective landscapes.

Inlay. In furniture, designs formed by inserting contrasting grains, colors, and textures of woods, ivory, metal, etc. flush into the piece of wood; outstanding work done by ancient Egyptians; used extensively during Renaissance; popular in Italy as **intarsia.**

In Nomine. Instrumental composition based on a plainsong theme; used by English composers of 16th and 17th centuries.

Intaglio. Drawing, figure, or design incised into metal or cut below the surface of an object; intaglio print pulls ink from furrows of plate; engraving, etching, dry point, mezzotint, aquatint, etc. are intaglio processes.

Intermezzo. Interlude, short musical composition; performed between the acts of an opera; short movement in symphony taking the place of the scherzo.

Intráda. Short prelude, introductory movement.

Intrados. Interior curve or face of an arch or vault.

Ivan. Open-ended vault in architecture of India and ancient Arabia.

Jamb. Vertical part of masonry of door, window, or fireplace.

Janus. Two-faced Roman god of gates and doors; *numen* of all beginnings.

Jasper ware. Stoneware with classic white designs in cameo relief on blue ground; used by Wedgwood.

Jiku. Ornamental knob at ends of round stick or rod used in rolling and mounting Japanese paintings.

Kakemono. Japanese painting or calligraphic scroll rolled on rod and suitable for hanging.

Kan pi. Dry-brush painting in China.

Kanshitsu. Dried lacquer sculpture technique popular during 8th and 9th centuries in Japan and China; excellent example, *Sakyamuni Buddha,* Jungo-ji temple near Kyoto, Japan.

Keystone. Top central *voussoir* of an arch; often projecting and decorated; important in that it "locks" arch.

Kobzar. Ukrainian troubadours of 17th and 18th centuries who traveled the countryside singing military songs.

Kondo. Central hall or chamber of worship in Buddhist temple.

K'uan. Colophon or signature in Chinese work of art; sometimes includes name of person for whom work was intended; often considered part of painting, therefore carefully designed.

Kuan Yin. Goddess of mercy in Buddhist art.

Lalique glass. Decorative glassware named for René Lalique, late 19th-century French jeweler; figures of animals, birds, flowers, etc., in relief.

Lantern. Small open or glazed structure designed to admit light crowning a dome or roof.

Leitmotiv. Identifiable, recurring leading themes connected with characters, ideas, or actions in modern music-dramas; Wagner credited with development.

Lich gate. Covered gateway to churchyard.

Lied. German song; originally folk song, developed into art form.

Limoges enamelware. Produced in 16th-century France; white decoration applied to dark-blue base.

Lintel. Horizontal beam or girder spanning opening or space between supports, designed to bear weight from above.

Lithoglyph. Engraving or carving on gem or precious stone.

Lithography. Graphic arts technique developed by Aloys Senefelder (1771-1834); drawing (usually with greasy lithographic crayon) on stone; treated with wash of dilute nitric acid, then washed, inked, and printed; various new techniques used and metal plates, synthetic materials, etc. have largely replaced stones; popular process developed by many great artists; color lithographs perfected by Toulouse-Lautrec, Kandinsky, and contemporary artists.

Loggia. Roofed open gallery; open on one or more sides; colonnade or arcade at one end.

Lunette. Semicircular space; opening in a vault for a window; in furniture, half-moon shape with carving, painting, or inlay; carved in Gothic oak furniture; inlaid or painted with fan-shaped designs in late Georgian English.

Luster. Pottery with metallic look, often having iridescent glaze.

Luxor Obelisk. One of famed obelisks of Ramesses II; placed in Place de la Concorde, Paris, by Louis Philippe (1833).

Lyre back. Chair with back in shape of lyre, or decorated with lyre motif; found in many styles.

Madrigal. Unaccompanied polyphonic song in three or more parts, using counterpoint and imitation; 14th-century Italian madrigal resembled *pastourelles* of the troubadours in structure and subject-matter; generally sung in chorus, upper voice more elaborate.

Magodi. Itinerant poet-musicians, singers of humorous songs and ballads in ancient Greece; later applied to singers and mimes who performed on the stage.

Magot. Japanese or Chinese small grotesque figure; usually cross-legged or crouching; used as knobs on covers of vases.

Maiolica (*majolica*). Originally the term was used to describe Spanish lustered pottery taken to Italy by way of Majorca; now refers to tin enameled pottery made in Italy from Renaissance period on; earthenware coated with opaque white enamel and decorated in various colors; technique long known in Near East, carried into Spain by the Moors.

Mandala. Temple painting in Islamic art; mystical, symbolic representation of pantheon; group of Hindu deities carefully arranged in symbolic circle.

Mandapa. In Indian architecture, series of terraced pavilions surmounting medieval temples.

Mañjuśrī (Sanskrit). Bodhisattva of wisdom; emblems are sword and lion; often placed to left of *Śākyamuni*.

Marquetry. Inlaid furniture; inlay of contrasting woods or other materials into background of veneer.

Mascaron. Grotesque, often in relief, used in decorative arts of ancient Romans, revived in classical styles of 16th century; seen on handles of large vases, etc.

Mask. Face or head covering used to disguise the wearer; used by Greeks and

Romans, ancient Chinese theater, primitive peoples; in architecture, keystone, fountain ornament; used in decorative arts, dance, etc.

Mass. Vocal composition performed during High Mass in Roman Catholic Church; setting of certain parts of the Mass to music, generally with instrumental accompaniment, including *Kyrie, Gloria, Credo, Sanctus*, etc.

Mastaba. Rectangular (or oblong with sloping sides) brick tomb with many internal compartments built over subterranean burial chamber; façades decorated with complicated arrangement of recesses and buttresses; Mesopotamian in character.

Matte. Dull, smooth finish; applied to pottery, tempera, glass, glaze, etc.

Meander motif. Interlocking fret or key pattern used by Greeks in period of geometric ornamentation (1000-700 B.C.); used by Chinese as symbol of lightning and thunder.

Megalith. Prehistoric monuments or large stone structures.

Megaron. Central hall in Minoan architecture; central room with fireplace used as living room and kitchen in ancient Greece; similar to Roman atrium.

Metope. Panel in Doric frieze between decorated triglyphs.

Mezzotint. Intaglio technique; tone process, works from dark background to highlights; metal surface is roughened with rocker tool that creates small burr indentations; lighter effects made with scraper; rich black tones produced; developed in 17th century, used to reproduce famous portraits in 18th-century England.

Miao. Originally ancestral shrine, later any non-Buddhist temple.

Mihrab. Recess or niche in mosque indicating direction of Mecca; generally contains copy of the *Koran*.

Minaret. High, slender tower or turret of mosque with one or more projecting balconies; *muezzin* calls people to prayer (five times daily).

Mizu. Japanese water-color painting.

Mode. In music, division of eight diatonic tones of an octave into fixed intervals; arrangement of notes in a scale —major, minor, etc.

Monody. Composition for a single voice; originally applied to solos of early operas, oratorios, etc. (*ca.* 1600).

Montage (French, mounting, arranging, or putting together). Combination of several separate elements into a blended whole while retaining distinctive quality of each.

Mosaic. Technique of decorating walls, floors, and ceiling with tesserae, irregularly-shaped color pieces of glass, marble, tile, etc., embedded or inlaid in cement; ancient art form used by Romans, Early Christians, reaching perfection in 6th-century Byzantium.

Motet. Sacred polyphonic choral composition, usually without instrumental accompaniment; originally simply an accompanying part superimposed over the tenor, but having its own text; later applied to any elaborate polyphonic, contrapuntal vocal music.

Mudéjar. Style of Spanish architecture and decoration following Christian reconquest showing influence of Moors; since 1850 refers to folk art (wall decoration and wooden ceilings) of Andalusia, Aragon, and Castile.

Mullion. Slim, vertical bar dividing panes of a traceried window.

Muses. Daughters of Zeus and Mnemosyne identified with arts and science; Calliope, Clio, Erato, Euterpe, Melpomene, Polymnia, Terpsichore, Thalia, and Urania.

Nabis. Group of artists (Bonnard, Vuillard, Maurice Denis, Roussel, Vallotton, Maillol) organized by Paul Sérusier (1888); attempted to synthesize postimpressionist and symbolist ideas.

Nandaimon. Outer gate of temple area; South Great Gate in Japan.

Narthex. Porch in front of nave and aisles of medieval church; portico of ancient churches; one side or member of atrium surrounded by ambulatories.

Natya. Combination dance and drama of India.

Nave. Central portion of church leading from entrance to apse.

Negative space. Space between volumes.

Neumes. In medieval music dating from 8th century, an early system of symbols indicating pitch, placed above text; later appeared between two lines and were first step toward staff notation; developed from Greek accents.

Niello. Engraved, black design on metal.

Obelisk. Four-sided, tapering, upright pillar (stone, often granite) ending in pyramid; usually monolithic, non-representational.

Octastyle. Any building or portico having eight columns.

Octave. Interval measuring eight diatonic degrees.

Ogee. Classical molding with double curve; two S-shaped curves, convex curves meeting at point; popular in Georgian period.

Ogive. Arch or rib that crosses a Gothic arch diagonally; pointed arch.

Opera. Drama set to music which is predominant feature, consisting of arias, choruses, recitatives, orchestral accompaniment (occasionally dances); originated as art form toward end of 16th century in Italy.

Opus. A work; in music, compositions numbered in order of publication.

Oratorio. Lengthy dramatic composition, usually based on Biblical theme, set to music to be sung with orchestral accompaniment, without action, costumes, or scenery; arias, recitatives, trios, choruses, etc. included; Handel one of many famous composers of this form.

Orchestra. Group of instrumental performers; modern opera or symphony orchestras consist of from 60 to 116 performers.

Organum. Early attempts at harmony in music; voice part accompanying cantus firmus; melody in parallel motion; chords of fourths or fifths; diaphony.

Oriel. In English castles, projecting bay window at upper end of great hall.

Osiris. Egyptian god of the underworld, judge of the dead, often represented with wife Isis and brother Set, god of evil, in art of Egypt.

Overlapping planes. Series of partially visible surfaces placed in front of each other to create illusion of movement into depth of picture.

Overture. Introductory music; orchestral composition played before a cantata, opera, oratorio, suite, or independently (concert overture).

Pantomime. Play, drama, or other entertainment presented solely or almost entirely in dumb show, occasionally with instrumental accompaniment.

Pao-t'a. Single-storied pagoda, usually with cylindrical shaft.

Parapet. Low wall around or near the edge of a roof or elevated area.

Pastel. Drawing material made up as cylinder of ground color held together with gum and filled out with whiting; effect similar to water color in lightness of quality.

Pavilion. Small, ornamented building; part of a building (usually projecting) attached to main structure.

Pedestal. Base for column, statue, vase, etc.; simple shaft, block forms.

Pediment. Triangular upright front of roof of moderate pitch; triangular form made by sloping roof and horizontal cornice beneath it; used over doors and in furniture at head or tops of cabinets.

Pendant. Decoration that hangs down from arch or ceiling; part of structure in late Gothic architecture.

Pendentive. One of triangular pieces of vaulting springing from corners of rectangular or square ground, serving as part of base for cupola or dome; important in Byzantine architecture.

Pentatonic scale. Scale of five notes to the octave; fourth and seventh degrees being omitted in the major and second and sixth in the minor scales; used in traditional music of China, Japan, etc.

Peristyle. Continuous colonnade around sides of building, open court or cella of temple.

Perspective. Science of optics in which the illusion of three-dimensional space is created on a flat surface; use of overlapping planes receding toward a vanishing point on the horizon, creating illusion of depth by diminishing size of planes and by their convergence.

Pi hua. Chinese mural applied directly to the wall, similar to fresco.

Pilaster. Rectangular vertical support or pier projecting slightly from wall; treated architecturally as flattened column with base, shaft, and capital; also used in furniture.

P'ing chang. Group of narrow vertical Chinese scrolls designed to be hung together.

Plane: *Picture plane,* flat surface of canvas or paper; *static plane,* plane parallel to picture plane; *dynamic plane,* rotates or moves at angle to picture plane.

Plastic. Term used by contemporary writers and critics to refer to total organization and interrelationship of all elements (color, texture, line, space, planes, etc.) of canvas or work.

Plateresque. One of Spanish Renaissance styles, frequently used in Spanish America, characterized by lavish ornamentation applied to basically simple forms.

Plinth. Projecting base of column or building; square or octagonal block serving as base for statue.

Polyphony. Contrapuntal, many-voiced composition presenting several melodies simultaneously; counterpoint.

Polytonality. Use of two or more keys simultaneously; each superimposed melody, chord etc. defines a distinct or different tonality (key).

Portico. Covered colonnaded porch or gallery.

Predella. Small panels below central panels of altarpiece.

Propylon. Monumental gateway in front of main entrance to Egyptian temple or pylon.

Proscenium. Part of stage in front of curtain.

Pulpitum. Proscenium or front wall from ground to stage in ancient Roman theater; sacred song similar to anthem.

Pulvin. Pyramid-shaped member or ornament with reversed truncates in Byzantine arch and capital; also stilt-block.

Pulvinated. Convexly curved frieze.

Putti. Nude, cupidlike children used in painting, sculpture, and architectural decoration.

Pylon. One of decorated piers on either side of gate or door; one of two truncated pyramids, with gateway between, in Egyptian architecture.

Pyramid. Four-sided stone structure built on square plan; sides meet at apex; famed tomb of ancient Egypt.

Quadra. Plinth or lowest member of podium or pedestal; square frame surrounding bas-relief.

Quartet. Composition, usually in sonata form, written for four voices or instruments; group of four singers or instrumentalists.

Quatrefoil. Gothic form with four intersecting curves enclosed in circular shape; derived from four-leaf clover.

Quetzalcoatl. Aztec god of peace and

creation; originally worshiped as patron of arts and crafts by Toltecs; occasionally shown as white, bearded figure; associated with quetzal bird and feathered snake.

Quintet. Composition for five voices or instruments; group of five singers or instrumentalists.

Quoin. Cornerstone at angle of building.

Refectory table. Long, narrow dining table with heavy stretcher running lengthwise close to the floor; named after dining hall in monastery.

Reja. Wrought-iron or cast-metal grille or screen used in Spanish architecture to protect windows; often gilded when enclosing shrine, tomb, chapel, etc. in churches.

Repoussé. Decorative sheet metal work; patterns in relief hammered or pressed from reverse side.

Reredos. Decorated screen or partition wall behind altar of church.

Respond. Corbel or engaged pillar supporting arch or closing arcade or colonnade; pilaster supporting free column.

Rhythm. Organization or division of music into regular metrical portions; balanced movement; melodic accent and cadence; regular beats, time units (pulses) grouped into measures.

Rivaq. Covered, roofed arcade surrounding court of mosque.

Rondo. Vocal or instrumental composition with one prominent theme constantly reappearing in alternation with contrasting themes ("episodes").

Rosette. Stylized, floral-shaped disk ornament.

Round. Polyphonic vocal canon in unison for three or more parts.

Rustication. Architectural wall treatment; large freestone blocks with rough, rocklike or smooth surfaces and recessed joints; simulated in 18th-century furniture.

Rybalt. Czechoslovakian jongleur, minstrel, or troubadour of medieval period.

Sahn. Open court of mosque in Indian architecture.

Śākyamuni (Sanskrit). Name of Gautama Buddha (*ca.* 563-483 B.C.), founder of Buddhism.

Sarcophagus. Stone coffin or chest-shaped tomb; usually sculptured or decorated.

Satyr. Classical mythological sylvan deity or demigod noted for lascivious behavior; pictured with ears and tail of a horse or horned half-man, half-goat.

Scherzo. Prior to 1750 term applied to both vocal and instrumental compositions; thereafter, generally movement in symphony, sonata, etc. in quick triple time possessing trio; lively, animated music.

Seal. Design engraved or made so as to make impression upon soft substance such as clay or wax; appeared as early as 3rd millennium in cylinder seals of Sumer and stamp seals of Harappa; Dexamenos, from isle of Chios (5th century), great designer of seals.

Sensu. Brilliantly painted folding fan of Japan.

Sequence. Series or progression of similar chords or intervals; succession of repeated harmonic or melodic phrases; symmetrical chant of irregular meter put into verse and added to the *Alleluia;* also called *prose.*

Serpentine curve. Usually refers to furniture meaning waving or undulating surface; serpentine front of piece (commode) has convex center and concave ends.

Set (*Seth*). Oldest of Egyptian gods; god of evil; brother and enemy of Osiris; represented in art as human with animal head, pointed snout, and tall square ears.

Sfumato (Italian, "smoked"). Hazy,

misty effect in painting gained by blurring outlines and blending colors and shading; in music, very lightly.

Sgraffito. Incised decoration on walls, pottery, etc. produced by scratching through the surface layer to reveal dark or contrasting color beneath.

Sheraton. Late 18th-century style of furniture named for Thomas Sheraton (1750-1806), English cabinetmaker.

Shou chüan. Chinese scroll painting to be viewed (unrolled) slowly.

Sikhara. Turret on medieval Indian temple topped by *amalaka* (bulbous-shaped top).

Silk screen print (*serigraphy*). Latest print technique; design laid on stretched silk by stencil method; areas not stopped out printed by squeezing or squeegeeing (rubber handled tool) paint (special light oil paint resembling gouache) through openings in silk; each color goes on separately; one or more stencils or screens are used; popular, inexpensive print method.

Sinfonia. Orchestral composition; used by Bach and others as prelude; forerunner of overture. *See also* symphony.

Singerie. Rococo decoration of monkeys and other small animals; popular in murals.

Singspiel. German semidramatic opera popular in 18th century (Beethoven's *Fidelio*, Weber's *Freischutz*, others).

Siva. One of supreme deities of Hinduism; member of *Trimurti*; represented in art as many-armed human figure; represents power of destruction (and restoration).

Skald. Viking, Norse singers or reciters of eddas or sagas in Norway, Iceland, and Finland; these tales, retold for generations, formed basis of Wagner's *Nibelungen Ring*.

Skanda. Hindu six-armed god of war; son of Siva; shown riding on a peacock; also called *Kartikeya*.

Slip. In ceramics, watery clay used in coating, decorating (relief, sgraffito, etc.) clay.

Socle. Projecting foundation at foot of wall or pier; beneath base of column or statue; usually molded; not same as plinth or base proper.

Soffit. In architecture, underside of vault, arch, beam, cornice, etc.

Solar. Chamber or private room on upper floor.

Sonata. Instrumental composition, usually in three or four movements, contrasted in rhythm and mood but related in tonality, having unity of style; generally begins with slow introduction, allegro, then andante, adagio or largo, followed by scherzo or minuet and trio, and finale (rondo).

Sonata form. Refers to design of first movement of sonata; usually based on two themes in different keys, following plan: exposition, development, and recapitulation ending with coda; form applied to symphony, sonata, trio, string quartets, concerto, etc.

Spandrel. Space (usually triangular) between two arches and horizontal beam above them.

Sphinx. Mythical winged monster having lion's body and head and bust of a woman; Great Sphinx at Giza, Egypt, has man's head and body of lion; used in furniture decoration through many periods.

Spire. Pointed or tapering top of a tower; pyramidal roofs of Norman turrets early examples.

Spode ware. Famed porcelain produced at Stoke-on-Trent, Staffordshire, England by Josiah Spode (1754-1827).

Squinch. Diagonal arch, beam, or vault carried across the corners of a square or rectangular space to support circular structure (dome or spire).

Staff. Five horizontal, parellel lines, on or between which notes of music are written.

Stained glass. Brilliant pictorial or decorative composition made by joining pieces of colored glass with strips of lead and used for windows, panels, etc.; first stage in development traced to Celto-Germanic art of jewelry making in which precious stones were set between patterns of bronze and gold; Frankish enamels of Carolingian period added to technique, as did work of Saracens who fixed (or held) pieces of colored glass between stone or stucco plaques; by the end of the 9th century, first stained glass window had been developed in northern France and Germany; earliest known large windows made for Cathedral of Augsburg (*ca.* 1000); most famous examples at Chartres.

Stasimon. Choral ode performed by Greek chorus between two episodes of drama (tragedy).

Stele. Stone memorial; pillar or slab to mark grave or commemorate a site; usually inscribed or decorated in relief.

Strapwork. Decorative narrow band, fillet or panels based on interlaced strap-like design; used principally in Elizabethan and Jacobean periods.

Stretcher. In furniture, crosspieces or rungs connecting legs of chairs, tables, etc.

Stringcourse. In architecture, projecting horizontal band or molding along the wall of a building; usually a variation in design.

Stupa (Sanskrit). Shrine, formed like funeral mound (cylindrical or hemispherical), built to contain relics of a Buddha or Buddhist saint; usually surmounted by spire or umbrella.

Suiboku. Black and white Japanese painting or drawing.

Suisaiga. Japanese water color.

Suite. Series, cycle of instrumental pieces.

Sumi. Japanese ink; sticks of carbon and glue mixed with water used as painting or drawing medium.

Surrealism. French 20th-century movement in literature and art influenced by Freudian concepts; stressed creative potential of the subconscious and the importance of dreams, etc.

Swag. Festoon; decoration using draperies, garlands of flowers or fruit, ribbons, etc.

Symphony. Instrumental composition, in sonata form, for full orchestra; also instrumental movement in choral work.

Syncopation. Temporary shift or displacement of natural or regular metrical musical accent.

Tablature. Early form of music notation (by signs); important in designating pitch.

Taenia. Fillet or other projecting band at bottom of frieze, in Doric architecture, separating it from architrave.

Tanzaku. Small, decorative Japanese paintings on parchment, in margins or borders surrounding poetry (calligraphy).

T'ao T'ieh. Chinese "devil mask" used on sacrificial bronzes, etc.

T'ao Yung. Chinese pottery tomb figures.

Telamon. Carved male figure used as column to support entablature; also known as *atlante*.

Tempera. Painting medium tempered or carried by egg yolk (with or without albumen); gives matte finish; most popular medium until replaced by oil.

Temperament. In music, slight modification of intervals of pure scale; division of octave into twelve equal semi-tones; system of tuning.

Tempo. Literally from Italian meaning "time"; speed of rhythm.

Tenor. Male voice; range from C upon the second space in bass to G on second line in treble.

Teocalli. Aztec word for temple or "house of god."

Term. Tapering, quadrangular pillar, column, pedestal, or plinth with sculptured human bust or head at upper part;

used as accents in decorative furniture.

Terra cotta. Unglazed clay or earthenware used for statuettes, architectural decoration, vases, etc.; often light earthred in color.

Tetrastyle. Any building having a portico with four columns.

Thermae. Ancient structures popularly called *baths;* for warm spring bathing, but also presenting other forms of entertainment and relaxation.

Tholos. Beehive tomb; round building with dome.

Thoth. Egyptian god of wisdom and magic; inventor of numbers, measurer of time; scribe of gods; represented in art with head of an ibis.

Tien. Monumental hall; in painting, small dots of color or ink added to landscape for emphasis or added clarity.

Tierceron. Rib inserted in Gothic vault between transverse and diagonal ribs.

Toccata. Old form of composition for keyboard instruments similar to fantasia or capriccio; written to show off brilliant technique of performer; in modern works founded on treatment of single figure; characterized by free and rapid movement.

Tondo. Circular picture or sculptured medallion in the round.

Tonic. Keynote or first note of any scale.

Toran (Torana). Indian gateway of wood or stone having two upright pillars and one to three transverse lintels; carved entrance to Buddhist shrine.

Torchère. Delicate stand for holding lights (candelabra); often highly ornamented, with tripod base.

Torii. Gateway to Japanese Shinto temple; gracefully curved lines; post-and-lintel construction.

Totem pole. Carved and painted log placed before homes of several Northwest-American Indian tribes, primarily of Koluschan family.

Tracery. Decorative latticelike forms, with spaces for glass or openings, in head of Gothic windows; imitated in furniture, etc.

Transept. Cross-hall of cruciform church; commonly refers to arms of cross.

Transom. Horizontal division of window.

Transvesticism. In theater, playing the part of a character of the opposite sex; particularly used in periods when women were not permitted on stage.

Triforium. Gallery or wall passage of church between the arcade of nave and clerestory, or between gallery and clerestory; opens in arcades (often blind) toward nave.

Triglyph. Vertical grooved member in Doric frieze alternating with metopes.

Trio. Composition for three voices or three instruments; group of three performers; contrasting movement in minuet, scherzo, march, etc.

Triptych. Panel or altarpiece in three sections; later used for decorative mirrors.

Triskele (triskelion). Three-legged or three-branched figure; curved, radiating from center; three-armed cross.

Trumeau. Supporting central column of large doorway; in decoration, French overmantel treatment using mirror and painting, later used as detached mirror with commode, chest, etc.

Tsuitate. Japanese single-paneled landscape screen on two low transverse feet.

Turret. Small medieval ornamental tower attached to large structure; often contained circular staircase.

Tympanum. Recessed space, usually within a pediment or arch, often containing sculpture.

Uraeus. Serpent used as symbol of Egyptian royalty; seen on headdress and on either side of winged solar disc.

Vargueño. Spanish ornamented cabinet-desk with fall front.

Varuna. Hindu supreme cosmic diety; mythological god of reward and punishment; seen in art riding a *makara* (sea monster).

Vault. Arched masonry structure usually forming roof or ceiling.

Veneer. To overlay or decorate with finer layer of wood.

Virginals. Term originally used in 15th- or 16th-century England to refer to small rectangular harpsichord (spinet) placed on table for playing; later applied to all kinds of harpsichords; popular in 16th and 17th centuries.

Vishnu. Second god of Hindu *trimurti* (trinity including Brahma and Siva); Vaishnavas regard him as supreme deity; represented in the arts riding Garuda (half-bird, half-man), holding lotus in one of four hands, conch shell, mace, and disc of supreme power in others.

Volute. Spiral, scroll-shaped decoration; used on capital of Ionic (Corinthian, Composite) orders; Gothic form shows leaves curling inward.

Voussoir. Wedge-shaped block forming part of arch or vault.

Vyatka toys. Russian sculptured caricatures; known also as *dimtov* toys.

Water color. One of oldest known media; pigment (color) mixed with medium (gum arabic, egg white used in medieval period), that dissolves in water; can be transparent or nearly opaque; opaque water color is **gouache** that is mixed with zinc white.

Wayang Wong. Javanese dance-drama.

Wedgwood. Famed fine hard porcelain or pottery ware designed by Josiah Wedgwood (1730-95).

Wood cut. Relief print technique; design cut into wood, ink prints from uncut area; characterized by bold, contrasting blacks and whites.

Wood engraving. White line technique emphasizing tonal values; developed by Thomas Bewick (1753-1828) in England.

Xabardillo ("little crowd"). Group of Spanish strolling musicians; seen also in Mexico and southwestern United States.

Yama. Hindu mythological god of the underworld; represented in art as being green, having flaming eyes, wearing red clothes, and a crown, riding a buffalo, and holding a club and noose in his hands.

Yang. Male element in Chinese abstract art representing the sun and the positive aspects of life as contrasted with **yin**, female element of moon, darkness, and negative values.

Yin chang. Seal or mark of Chinese artist found on all paintings.

Yoko. Large, horizontal Japanese woodcut.

Zarzuela. Play performed to music in Spanish theater; forerunner of opera.

Zophorus. Classical frieze with relief sculptures of men and animals or both.

INDEX